SHOOTING HISTORY –
A PERSONAL JOURNEY

Jon Snow is one of the most highly regarded newsmen of our time, renowned for his integrity and independence of mind. The son of a public-school headmaster and future Anglican bishop, he taught for a year in Uganda, where he first met Idi Amin. He subsequently worked for Lord Longford's charity helping homeless teenagers, before becoming a newsman for ITN and Channel 4 News, reporting on savage battle-fronts from Iran and Afghanistan to Nicaragua and Angola. He spent five years as Washington Correspondent in America, and has interviewed many world leaders, including the Pope, Nelson Mandela and Mikhail Gorbachev.

SHOOTING HISTORY –
A PERSONAL JOURNEY

Shooting History –
A Personal Journey

by

Jon Snow

Magna Large Print Books
Long Preston, North Yorkshire,
BD23 4ND, England.

British Library Cataloguing in Publication Data.

Snow, Jon
    Shooting history – a personal journey.

    A catalogue record of this book is
    available from the British Library

    ISBN   0-7505-2439-1

First published in Great Britain in 2004 by HarperCollins Publishers

Copyright © Jon Snow 2004

Lines from 'On the Pulse of Morning' by Maya Angelou reproduced by permission of Time Warner Book Group UK

Cover illustration © Sam Taylor Wood by arrangement with D & V Management

The moral right of the author has been asserted

Published in Large Print 2006 by arrangement with HarperCollins Publishers

Magna Large Print is an imprint of Library Magna Books Ltd.

Printed and bound in Great Britain by
T.J. (International) Ltd., Cornwall, PL28 8RW

To Madeleine, Leila and Freya

CONTENTS

ILLUSTRATIONS

(Unless otherwise stated, photographs are from the author's collection)

General Tom, my twice-knighted grandfather, who hung above the mantel and seemed to have inspected every boiled egg I ever ate.

War wedding. My father and mother met and married in a matter of weeks.

My father's Hudson Terraplane Eight configured as a wartime fire-tender.

The damage caused by a Second World War bomb on the lawns of Charterhouse School; my father's one moment of 'action'.

A sunny Sussex childhood. Growing up in the aftermath of war.

No particular talent. Following childhood encounters with Harold Macmillan, my earliest ambition was to be a Tory MP.

My father with Macmillan at Ardingly. 'Do you know what a Prime Minister is?' he asked me.

'Are you married to the Queen?' I responded.

With Tom and Nick in the Terraplane; a happy contrast to the dining-table warfare.

The Queen visiting Ardingly. My mother had been to Harrods to buy a pair of Crown Derby cups and saucers from which the royal lips could sip their afternoon tea.

As a chorister at Winchester Cathedral in 1958.

My father, every inch a Bishop – eight feet tall in his mitre.

Back from Uganda. VSO had radicalised me, and one reason I wanted to become a journalist was in order to return there.

India in the summer of 1969, singing 'Hey Jude' in the Liverpool University close-part harmony Beatle band.

I was amongst several hundred anti-apartheid demonstrators who were arrested at the Springbok rugby match at Old Trafford in November 1969. (© *Popperfoto*)

Mass meeting of Liverpool students ahead of our sit-in. (*Special Collections and Archives, Sydney Jones Library, University of Liverpool, in P.2602/20*)

Pre-mobile-phone reporting for LBC in 1973, on a clunky old Motorola two-way radio.

An exchange with Ugandan dictator Idi Amin on the 1974 trip with Jim Callaghan to rescue Denis Hills.

Vietnamese boat people below decks on the refugee boat on which we found ourselves stranded in the South China Sea in 1976.

The shell of the Vietnamese refugee boat beached in Malaysia.

Interviewing the Somali President Siad Barre, a grumpy Moscow-educated ideologue running a classic Cold War Russian client state, in 1976.

With Mohinder Dhillon in Somalia. Mystified British viewers were treated to a travelogue in which an excitable white man jumped up and down talking about the threat to world peace.

Back to Uganda again in 1977, this time for ITN armed with Edward Heath's book.

Interviewing US President Jimmy Carter and Prime Minister Jim Callaghan outside Lancaster House in London, 1977.

Preparing to conduct the first ever English-language interview with a Pope, aboard John Paul II's plane in January 1979.

Standing outside Number Ten Downing Street on 4 May 1979, Mrs Thatcher's first day as

Prime Minister. (© *PA Photos*)

Afghanistan, 1980. With the Mujahidin in mountains above Herat in the immediate aftermath of the Soviet invasion.

Filming with Charlie Morgan at 'Desert One' in Iran in April 1980 amid the wreckage of Jimmy Carter's catastrophic attempt to rescue the American hostages.

The Iran–Iraq War in 1981. Wearing no body armour and no flak jacket, I was less than well prepared to survive the conflagration in which I was caught.

On the road to Suchitoto in El Salvador with Sebastian Rich and Don Warren in February 1981. (© *Sebastian Rich*)

Behind guerrilla lines with *'los muchachos'* in El Salvador, 1983. (© *Sebastian Rich*)

With President Reagan in the White House, February 1985.

I interviewed Iraq's Deputy Prime Minister Tariq Aziz several times in twenty-five years. (© *Sipa Press/Rex Features*)

The *Evening Standard* pokes fun at my naked arrest in Geneva in January 1991. (© *JAK/Evening Standard*)

It was the West's great fortune to find Mikhail Gorbachev in charge when it mattered most. (© *Sally Soames/The Sunday Times*)

Interviewing Nelson Mandela the day he became South Africa's first democratically elected President in 1994.

The *Mirror* took a dim view of our royal scoop. (© *The Daily Mirror*)

The full Monica. An exclusive sit-down with Ms Lewinsky in 1998, her first interview after the attempt to impeach President Clinton. (*Photograph by Chris Ridley © Channel 4*)

Return to Uganda in 1999, sitting at the back of the classroom in which I had taught thirty years earlier. (*Photograph by Neil Drabble*)

On the line in northern Ghana, exploring the Greenwich meridian in a classic 'Yendi smock' in 2000.

September 2001. The heart of the inferno at Ground Zero. (© *Joel Meyerowitz, 2004/Courtesy of Ariel Meyerowitz Gallery, New York*)

With cameraman Ken McCallum in Baghdad, November 2003.

Advertising Channel Four News, with trusty steed on Euston station.

ACKNOWLEDGEMENTS

I want to thank: Heli Sivunen for researching and checking my efforts; my agent Jonny Geller for provoking me to write a book at all and for helping me to arrive at what I wanted to write; my publisher Caroline Michel, who took the risk and believed in it; my friend and colleague Lindsey Hilsum for her wise comments on what I had written; my friends Helena Kennedy, Angelica Mitchell, Felicity Spector, Katie Razzall and my friend and PA Dierdre Dean for reading and reacting so constructively to the manuscript. Corinna Honan at the *Daily Telegraph* commissioned articles over the years and persuaded me that I might be able to write in a longer format.

Some of the key chapters were written in and around the Wellfleet homes of the wonderful Jocelyn Baltzell and her daughter Justina. Jocelyn's expertise as a literary critic was invaluable; very sadly she died from cancer while I was writing, and I miss her very much.

I also want to thank a few of those who enabled me to make this journey at all, above all my partner Madeleine Colvin and my editors – at LBC Marshall Stewart, at ITN Nigel Ryan, David Nicholas, Stewart Purvis, Richard Tate, and my foreign editor John Mahoney. I owe an enormous debt to the many crews I worked with, particularly the late Alan Downes, Don Warren, Mohinder Dhillon, Sebastian Rich, Malcolm Hicks and Ken McCallum. I'm grateful too to some of the journalists on the road who educated and inspired me – Michael White, Ed Boyle, Victoria Brittan, Philip Jacobson and Raymond Bonner. My editor at Channel Four News, Jim Gray, has been more understanding, tolerant and supportive than I deserve.

At HarperCollins Richard Johnson has been my instructive, patient, wise and most expert editor, and Robert Lacey's extraordinary skills as a copy editor reconnected my prose to the syntax and grammar of the English language. None of the above has any responsibility for any failings in the book; they are mine.

JON SNOW

May 2004

Prologue

The boat stood proud against the horizon, its curved bow and stern silhouetted on the skyline. We had been looking for it for a day and a night. As we drew near, what we had thought were ornate outcrops from the deck of the boat materialised into the bobbing heads and shoulders of a mass of human beings. The vessel was no more than forty feet long, but there were hundreds of people packed aboard it.

We had set out that morning in November 1978 from Trengganu on Malaysia's north-eastern coast aboard a fast local fishing launch. I was with my Swedish cameraman Claus Bratt and, somewhat unexpectedly, the books editor of the *Daily Mail*, Peter Lewis. Our quest was to encounter one of the myriad craft bearing refugees out of Vietnam across the South China Sea. These were the 'boat people' who in the previous few months, in their tens of thousands, had left the Vietnamese coast aboard almost anything that would float. The Vietnam War had ended three years earlier, but the flow of refugees was undiminished, orchestrated by traffickers and by the myth that America was waiting with open arms for any who fled.

The boat was well down in the water, with no obvious accommodation beyond a wheelhouse and two corrugated sheds at the back which were

19

clearly lavatories. I urged the fisherman who'd brought us to take us closer so that I could engage the captain in conversation. Eventually we came alongside, and Claus and I boarded the boat. At that precise moment our fisherman panicked, fearing that some of the Vietnamese might try to jump onto his vessel. He suddenly thrust his engines to full, pulled away from us, and sped off whence we'd come. I could see the *Daily Mail*'s books editor remonstrating furiously in the stern. Soon the fishing boat was but a speck in the distance.

There was almost no room to move on deck. We peered down into the cargo holds, and dozens of faces, young and old, boys, men and women, looked up expectantly. Many seemed to be very sick. Claus and I were led with difficulty towards the captain, who was at the wheel in the stern. I calculated that there were at least 350 people aboard a vessel that might have comfortably carried thirty. They had been at sea for the worst part of three weeks. The smell was overpowering; the dead body of an elderly woman wound in a sheet lay against the gunwale. The boat people seemed to assume that we were the advance guard of a welcoming party headed by the US Ambassador that would be waiting ashore with passports ready to usher them all to their new lives in California.

We'd been sent by my editor at ITN in London to find out how this huge exodus of people from Vietnam operated, and who was facilitating it. Until now, such boats had been seized the moment they made landfall in Malaysia; the boat people aboard would be rounded up and carted off to a kind of concentration camp run by the UN further up the coast on the island of Palau Badong. Consequently it had proved impossible to get to the root of how their journeying had come about.

The captain, a rotund ethnic Chinese, spoke excellent English and was candid about how much each person had paid – the equivalent of $2000 a head, extracted mainly from gold dental fillings and melted-down family heirlooms. He was more vague about how or where they were going to land in Malaysia; indeed, he thought he might even be off the coast of Indonesia. I asked him if anyone could swim; he thought not. There appeared to be no food on board, and the lavatories had become a foetid disaster zone, from which we tried to keep as far 'upship' as possible.

Towards nightfall we had our first glimpse of land. The captain decided to make a run for the shore. Within moments we were greeted by a hail of rocks and sticks, hurled by irate ethnic Malays who seemed to come from nowhere and swarmed out along the beach. The defenceless Vietnamese trapped on deck were being cut about their heads, and worse. Our boat turned broadside across the rollers, and threatened to capsize before finally making it through the surf and back out into the open sea.

We advised the captain to try further up the coast at first light, in the hope that any reception party would not yet be about. A ghastly night passed before we renewed our run at the beach. I suggested to the captain that he rev the engine to its maximum, and try to burn it out as the vessel beached. This way I hoped we could avoid being pushed back out to sea again. Claus had by now secured remarkable film of everything that had happened, an unprecedented record of the tribulations in the lives of fleeing Vietnamese boat people.

The noise of the screaming engine summoned a new batch of Malays down the beach, and another fusillade of projectiles. The engine blew, sure enough, but before the captain had succeeded in beaching the boat, which was now skewing dangerously in the surf. I grabbed a rope from the bow and leapt into the water, trying to lug the waterlogged hulk ashore. Gradually the sea itself seemed to bring it in.

Suddenly I was grabbed from behind and thrown beneath the water. Someone took hold of a hank of my then long hair and dragged me to the beach. I was spreadeagled on the sand while one man stamped on my arms and another beat me about the chest with a pole. Claus, still cradling the wreck of his camera, blood pouring down his face, was thrown down beside me. Malaysian soldiers stood idly beneath the palms at the top of the beach, watching the Malays assaulting the boat people. Nearly all the victims were ethnic Chinese. I learned later that the Malay/Chinese balance in Malaysia was fragile in the extreme, and that Malays would go to any lengths to prevent the expansion of the Chinese population.

After what seemed an age, the police came and arrested Claus and me. Snapping handcuffs on our bruised wrists, they threw us into the back of a caged pickup truck. At Trengganu's police station, the chief informed us that we were to be charged with aiding and abetting illegal immigration, an offence that carried a twenty-year jail sentence. We found ourselves in a disgusting fifteen-foot-square concrete cell with a steel door and a small barred window. The floor was awash with urine and faeces. In the gloom I counted eight others already inside. One of them turned out to be our battered captain, Lee Tych Tuong. Mr Tuong, it turned out, was a former printer who had never touched a boat in his life before. It had taken him and some of the other escapers eight months to build the vessel. He told us how they had become completely disorientated upon leaving Vietnamese waters, and how dysentery had claimed half a dozen lives during the voyage.

It was a good six hours into our ordeal before I heard the heaven-sent voice of the *Daily Mail* man in the passageway beyond the cell door. Peter Lewis had somehow not only tracked down our vessel, but had also managed to arrange the intervention of the First Secretary from the British High Commission in Kuala Lumpur. Our freedom came at the expense of most of the film we had shot. We were free to leave, so long as we boarded the next plane to London. It was a salutary introduction to the vagaries of investigative journalism.

I came of reporting age in the aftermath of the Vietnam War, one of the defining periods of post-Second World War history, when the Cold War warmed to major bloodshed. A quarter of a century later I would be reporting on the war on Iraq, one of the watersheds in the evolving new world disorder that in turn followed the end of the Cold War. Both conflicts were essentially American unilateralist pre-emptive responses to what Washington perceived as threats to US interests.

Like many of my generation, as a student I had protested against the war in Vietnam, and I felt frustrated never to have had the opportunity to report on a war in which many of my older colleagues had cut their teeth. To be dispatched as a reporter, at least to try to explore the war's legacy, even fully three years after its end, was some small recompense.

Our Malaysian adventure was set amid the prevailing certainty of global balances and security. Vietnam was now avowedly Communist, allied to the Eastern Bloc. Malaysia was emerging from the post-colonial era with its fledgling tiger economy, becoming an equally committed member of the Western capitalist bloc. It was possible to choose almost any place in the world and establish its position within the great Cold War tussle for control. In 1978 I was thirty years old, and my whole life had been set in the confident certainty that the ideological battle between left and right, between Communist and non-Communist, would prevail for all time. The world was relatively neatly divided. The idea that the Berlin Wall would ever come down, that Communism itself would ever fail, was simply inconceivable. We did not know that this order was about to suffer its first major violation, in the

24

form of a radical Islamic revolution in Iran. Western imperialism had all but decolonised Africa and Asia; now the main point of friction was whether the emerging post-colonial states would tilt towards Moscow or Washington.

So I was privileged to start my reporting career in Africa, and to observe a state like Somalia move from British and Italian influence to independence under first Soviet and then American patronage. Somalia was only one of a number of developing countries I watched drift into the chaotic status of 'failed state', wide open as a recruitment and training ground for al Qaida. The disengagement of the West from countries like it was matched by a corresponding failure by the Western media to remain committed to reporting them at all. Somalia's decline was mirrored by Angola, Sudan, Zaire, Uganda and others as we ceased to understand what was happening in them, and worse, ceased to care.

We in the West never expected to win the Cold War, or to lose it. When we did win, we were totally unprepared, and lost a huge opportunity to recast international institutions to fit the reality of a new world order dominated by one all-powerful superpower. Similarly, when Saudi militants attacked America on 11 September 2001, our response was militaristic and inadequate, and international solidarity with the United States degenerated very quickly into diplomatic warfare between much-needed allies. This book is the record of a personal journey that starts in the cosy years after the Second World War and treads the

25

key stepping stones since, to arrive at that great pre-emptive action that was cast as an endeavour to strike down a very immediate threat to our own survival, the war on Iraq.

Six months after that conflict began, I was at Amman airport in Jordan waiting for one of the rare flights into Baghdad. I found myself surrounded by pale British ex-servicemen trying to find ways into the country to take up jobs as bodyguards, and by heavy-set, unfit Americans who seemed never to have travelled outside Texas, carrying plastic bags filled with wads of hundred-dollar bills. The Americans were contractors on danger money coming in to fix the oil, water, gas and electricity infrastructure of a devastated country. It did not feel comfortable being among them, but they fitted well with my wider tale, one from which this reporter emerges at least as blemished as anyone he reports on.

ONE

Home Thoughts

'They're coming!' my elder brother Tom screamed. 'Run!' The wailing siren sounded close as he and my younger brother Nick fled out of the beechwood hollow. I was slow, wading through the leaves, my legs like lead weights. We had been playing on the edge of the school grounds in a towering section of the beechwoods called Fellows Gardens. Amongst the three of us, the identity of foe tended to settle on me. As they ran that day, my brothers were the friends. But there was a darker sense of an enemy beyond. Somehow the wailing siren seemed to signal the presence of a larger threat at hand. I burst into tears, stumbling to a halt, and found myself standing alone knee-deep in mud and leaves. Still the siren sounded. I suppose in retrospect it signalled only a fire, but then it sounded more eerie, more menacing.

I was born in 1947. My childhood was spent in the headmaster's house of Ardingly College, a minor public school set in the most green and rustic wastes of Sussex. Woven in and out of the sense of recent war and lurking threat were primroses, wood anemones, bluebells, and the sumptuous peace of countryside. From my bedroom window high up in the Victorian mass of red brick and scrubbed stone stairs I could see the lake, the woods, the rolling fields, and away in the distance, the long viaduct that bore the Brighton steam train to London and back. In the woods I, my brothers and the few other children that this isolated place could muster would play our own warfare.

My childhood swung between feelings of absolute safety and daunting vulnerability. The episode in the wood, when I was perhaps five, took place in 1952, when the war still cast a long shadow over our lives. The syrupy yellowy substance that passed for orange juice, in small blue screwtop bottles, still came courtesy of ration coupons. When I stood in the X-ray machine in Russell & Bromley's shoeshop in nearby Haywards Heath, where toxic rays revealed my dark feet wriggling inside green irradiated shoes, the ensuing purchase still attracted talk of shortages.

In the early fifties, the Germans were still the oft-mentioned core of enemy. The adult talk was of military service, of doodlebugs, of blackouts and loss. Hence the rumble of planes, the crack of the sound barrier, and that siren spoke with such clarity of present danger, and of the newer Russian threat and atomic war.

My father had not fought in the Second World War. Had he done so he would never have met my mother. This absence of service signalled early that he was different from other fathers. Too young for the First World War, he was too old to be called up for the Second. Besides, the fact that he was a cleric somehow seemed to seal the idea that he would not have been allowed to fight. His age – he was fifty when I was five – and his lack of experience in warfare were among the rare issues that rendered him slightly inadequate in my childhood. While others boasted of fathers who had bombed Dresden, I could only plead that mine had led the auxiliary fire brigade at Charterhouse School, where he had been chaplain. Of this he would talk endlessly. The responsibility had brought with it precious petrol coupons, as his eccentric open-topped Hudson Essex Terraplane Eight became the fire tender. On so many family outings in the self-same car he would recount how ladders were lashed to a makeshift superstructure, and he would roar around the privileged boarding school in search of bombs. And then, one blessed day, he found one. A bomb had fallen on the school's hallowed lawns. Even now I'm not clear what fire he may then have had to fight. But it became my father's moment of 'action'.

Freud might argue that my own subsequent exposure to all-too vivid conflict was some kind of attempt to make up for George Snow's absence of war. My father showed no inclination to fight, although his great height and booming voice gave him an intimidating, almost threatening presence. If only he had refused to join the armed services; but in our house in those days conscientious objectors were regarded as being as bad as the enemy themselves. His lack of a war record also represented a strange contrast to the military paraphernalia amongst which we grew up.

In our own childish warfare there was more

than a whiff of class. The few children of the teaching staff who lived near enough qualified for our war games. Oliver was one of these, a dependable friend who generally took my side against my two brothers, squaring up the numbers. But the children of the 'domestic staff' did not qualify for such sport. Susan lived across the road from Oliver, but she was the child of the school's Sergeant Major. Although enticing and blonde, she was to be kept at a distance, and so almost became a kind of foe – unspoken to, mysterious. Her father had charge of the school guns, of which there were many. I have vivid memories of boys strutting around in military uniforms in large numbers, and of invasions staged in the school quadrangles. They were a further signal of that persistent sense of the overhang and threat of war.

A remote rural English boarding school is at best a strange and intense environment in which to grow up. My father, as headmaster, was God. He was an enormous man, six feet seven in his socks, and at least sixteen stone. He wore baggy flannel suits in term time, and leather-patched tweed jackets in the evenings. In the holidays he embarrassed us all with huge scouting shorts and long, tasselled socks knitted by my mother. His hands were large and handsome, the skin cracked and tanned. He was old for as long as I can remember. To me he was strict, dependable, and at times remote. I was a very inadequate son of God. In the ever-present school community, I felt exposed and commented upon.

Many of the domestic staff who lived on the

school grounds seem to have been drawn from prisoner-of-war or internment camps. There were Poles, Italians, and others who appeared to have recently been released from mental hospitals. We knew them all by their first names. Among them was Jim, a kind man who was often to be found standing outside the kitchens having a smoke. One day, on one of my regular tricycle circuits of the school, Jim stopped me and asked if I'd like to come up to his room for some sweets. I was five or six. I left my tricycle and followed him up the dark staircase. Inside he sat me down and started to talk. Very soon he was undoing my brown corduroy shorts. I was worried that I'd never be able to do up the braces again – I couldn't handle the buttons on my own. Suddenly I had no clothes on. Jim undid his trousers, and produced something which to me seemed absolutely enormous. At that very moment from beyond the door a voice shouted, 'Jim! Jim! Come out here.'

'Quick!' said Jim. 'Under the bed!' He hoisted his trousers and left the room. I could hear raised voices. I recognised the voice of the other man – it was the school bursar, an ex-Wing Commander who often came to lunch at home. Home, three hundred yards away, suddenly seemed a very long way away indeed.

Jim returned, and peered at me under the bed. It seemed he'd been spotted abducting me. 'You've got to go,' he said.

'What about the sweets?' I asked.

'Next time,' he said.

'Will you help me with my braces?' I asked

31

anxiously. He did. I was never to see him again. My brother Tom told me some time later, when I cautiously asked, that Jim had been sacked. No one ever spoke to me about what happened. Yet I can't imagine that the bursar didn't tell my parents. The next time he came to lunch he didn't look me in the eye. I felt something bad had happened, but I didn't really know what.

Beyond the prison-camp feel of the domestic quarters there was one other place where there was evidence of war: Ardingly village, a long walk from the college. Most walks, most day care was in Nanny Rose's hands. She was a solid, dependable, working-class Kentish woman, with an irresistible laugh. We had two regular walks with her. The first would take us down past Collard's farm and the ageing foot-and-mouth warning signs on the gates, to the Avins Bridge Hotel, which straddled the little railway line that ran from Ardingly to our nearest town, Haywards Heath. This walk was always a treat, because Nanny would time it to coincide with the arrival of a train. The steam engine would let loose just under the bridge, and for an age our world would be enveloped in dense white cloud. After the train had gone we would wipe the sooty residue from our faces.

The second walk took us in the opposite direction, to the village. And there we would see them: men in invalid carriages, one with a hole where his ear had been, another with an open hole in his forehead. There were younger men too – men with white sticks and eye patches, back from the Korean war. There was a large war veterans' home in the village. Nanny said these crumpled humans were 'shell shocked'. They frightened me, and I wanted to know what had caused those holes, but Nanny's *Daily Sketch* seemed to have left her more comfortable talking about the royal family.

While hints of war lay around many corners, there was also the balmy, backlit sense of security that the harvest and the annual crop of Cox's orange pippins from the orchard yielded. The reaper binder tossed the corn, and men made stooks in the field beyond the herbaceous border. The wind caught the scent of the magnolia on the terrace wall, and bumblebees hovered around the delphiniums. My distant parents seemed at times to display more affection for plant life than for us, while in her own way Nanny loved us as if we had been her own. The contrasts of my childhood world mirrored those in the life of my family.

My father's lack of experience in the trenches was more than compensated for at the dining table by the exchange of verbal grenades with my older brother Tom from behind *The Times*. For as long as I can remember, Tom was on the war-path. He was a revolutionary almost as soon as he knew the meaning of the word, and his targets were my parents. Tom was to become a lifelong committed trade union official, representing some of the lowest-paid people in the country. From an early age he asserted that he intended to break with family tradition. For three centuries each eldest son had fathered a son, and each George had named that son Tom; each Tom had

33

followed suit with George. But this Tom was most assertively never going to call any son of his George.

The Toms and Georges from three hundred years dominated the walls not only of the dining room of our home, but the drawing room to boot. Most prominent of all the portraits was that of my grandfather, Lieutenant General Sir Thomas D'Oyly Snow KCB, KCMG, who hung scowling above the dining-room mantel. I never ate a boiled egg that he didn't seem to have inspected. He was a massive presence in the home, despite having died seven years before I was born. My father spoke of him with reverence and not a little fear. My brother Tom regarded him as a monster, 'one of so many in the ruling classes who had led their unsuspecting serfs to wholesale slaughter'.

From time to time our table warfare would be joined by my first cousin Peter – destined one day to lead many a sandpit war for both ITN and the BBC. Peter was ten years older than I, and in a better position to take Tom on. His father was a serving Brigadier, and Peter himself possessed more than a streak of the old General, our mutual grandfather, in his make-up. His main contribution to the table tensions was at critical moments to reach for, and upset, the overfull and highly unstable sugarbowl, scattering the stuff across the entire battlefield. Whereupon, of course, hostilities had to be suspended while Nanny was summoned to clear it all up.

Throughout the First World War General Tom, like so many of his time, had resisted mechanisation, believing in the value of the horse long after the tank had come to stay. I was perhaps six years old when my father recounted how his father had gone to Khartoum in 1885, after the failed attempt to break the siege in which General Gordon had been surrounded for ten months by the Mahdi. Tom had arrived too late to prevent Gordon's shooting on the steps of his residence, but soon enough to acquire a chunk of the step upon which he'd died and to cart it home. It was to languish in his home at 3 Kensington Gate in London until the Blitz struck the house in 1940 and the 'Gordon step' was rendered indistinguishable from the rest of the rubble.

As far as I could divine as a child, General Tom had been knighted twice, at least once for leading a retreat. Commanding the Fourth Division during the First World War, it seems his actions in sorting out the retreat from Mons in 1915 saved many lives. My brother Tom of course preferred to dwell on the lives the great man had caused to be lost, and of these there must indeed have been very many. General Tom was a large and austere man who ended his days in a hand-operated invalid carriage. His horse had been shot from beneath him in 1917, smashing his pelvis. He was probably one of the last British generals ever to ride a horse into battle.

Further round the dining-room walls from my grandfather the General hung the family black sheep. He was a yet earlier Tom, who had made a killing of a somewhat different kind from the South Sea Bubble in 1720. He had presided over

35

Snow's Bank, which stood on the street named after him to this day, Snow Hill on the edge of the City of London. Of this Tom little was said – so little indeed that at one point I thought he was such a black sheep that he was in fact black. Either it was a very dirty painting, or he appeared to be of an unusually dark complexion, with black curly hair.

There was no representation of my mother's family anywhere in the house. Like everything else about her, her forebears stayed obscurely in the background. The most interesting thing about her father, my maternal grandfather, Henry Way, was that he had been born in 1837 and sired her at the age of seventy-three. He was an estate agent in Newport, on the Isle of Wight. My mother was the last of nine children born to Henry's three wives, two of whom died in childbirth. Her eldest half-brother was fifty years older than she was.

Beneath the daunting images in the dining room, our family gathered for prayers at the start of every day. Adamson the butler, his wife the cook – always known as 'Addy' and 'Mrs Ad' – and Nanny Rose would join us three boys, my mother and the eternal conductor of this solemn moment, my father. We would stand in line in order of importance. Mrs Ad always saw to it that her husband came at the end of the line. She was a formidable woman who regarded herself and Nanny Rose as at least as good as those they served. Poor Mrs Box, who did the cleaning, and Mr Webster – 'Webby' – the gardener, didn't get a look-in. They were so far below stairs they never even got to glimpse the dining-room floor until it came to cleaning it or bringing in the logs.

'Our Father, which art in heaven…' intoned my father. This formal, ordered start to the day, which included the collect and a brief reading from the Bible, was part of the absolute security and order amid which I grew up. From the moment I could stand, I was in that line for prayers at eight in the morning, prompt. Then, while my mother and father and Tom took to the large oval dining table, my brother Nick and I, always referred to as 'the little ones' would go to the folding square table in the corner. My father would erect a home-made newspaper stand and settle to reading *The Times*. Tom would sneer at some upside-down headline that he'd caught from his vantage point, and the first salvoes would be exchanged. Sometimes, on a really good day, my mother would burst into tears, pleading with Tom to stop. 'Your father is right, Tom, he's not to be upset,' she would cry. Sometimes the fusillades would be so frightening that Nick and I would cry too, and then the proceedings would have to be halted as we were ushered from the room for making too much noise.

Happy days were those when some preacher or family friend had come to stay. This invariably stilled the warfare. Tom would be on his most charming behaviour. There was Aunt Rhoda, my father's sister, who'd married and then been immediately widowed by Alec Begg, a hugely rich New Zealander thirty years her senior whom she'd met on a cruise. She would talk of war, and how safe New Zealand would have been to live in had her husband not died. She was over six feet tall, thin as a birch sapling and mad as a March hare. She lived on her beloved Alec's money in a series of rambling hotels along the south coast. When she came to stay, we ragged her rotten.

My father had another sister, Mary. Confusingly she was called Sister Mary, and looked like a seriously overgrown penguin. At some stage the then Archbishop of Canterbury, Geoffrey Fisher, conferred an MA on her, allowing her to enjoy the title 'Church of England's top nun'. She must surely have been the tallest. Over six foot like her siblings, she visited only rarely, and then eternally adorned in her white head-dress and black habit. Deeply austere, she would talk of high-flown ecclesiastical matters with my father, and of little else to any of the rest of us.

Among the many preachers who came to stay were people like the Bishop of Bradford, Donald Coggan, one day to become Archbishop of Canterbury. Dad was an excellent Bishop-spotter. He always seemed to know who was on the up. This mattered because, as was often discussed at the table, my parents assumed that he would sooner or later be 'preferred' and elevated to some bishopric or deanery before his time as headmaster came to a close. Because Ardingly College was part of a religious foundation of schools, he was required to be both teacher and ordained churchman. Even as a child, the 'Church' felt to me like something of a war machine. The Church militant seemed to have an officer class – plenty of generals, with suitable quantities of gold braid – and my father was somehow, one day, bound to take his place in their ranks.

Among the big-shot visitors who came to stay were people of genuine humility. Standing out from all others was Father Trevor Huddleston, who was at the forefront of the anti-apartheid movement in South Africa. His Church seemed to be the total opposite to my father's, although of course it was the very same Anglican. Father Trevor wore a habit with a rope around the middle. His sandals were open, and I clearly remember his knobbly toes peering at me from beneath the dining-room table. My father was taken with his simplicity and holiness. I cannot imagine that he had a clue about Father Trevor's politics. Certainly he never raised with us the suffering of Africa or anywhere else. It was through Trevor Huddleston, sitting at his knee at the age of six, that I first learned about Africa, and about an unequal world very far from the one implied by Tom Snow's portrait above the mantel. 'One day, my boy, you must come to South Africa,' he said. 'You'd be amazed by the people, by the villages, the animals. You could come with me on my rounds.' I was to know Trevor on and off from my earliest childhood until his death in 1998.

These visits, when the outside world would come to call, were sadly all too rare. For the most part we were oblivious to what lay beyond the long trains that snaked across the viaduct in the far distance of our Ardingly world. If we did go to Haywards Heath we were barred from entering Woolworth's: 'You may catch something,' my mother would warn. Likewise the cinema – I didn't see a film until I was thirteen, a double bill of *Genevieve* and *Doctor in the House.*

My father listened to the BBC Home Service on the 'wireless' in his study, or to the BBC Third Programme in the drawing room. He was captivated by electronics. As a master at Eton College in the 1920s he had been the first member of staff to possess an electrically driven gramophone, and one of the earliest with a crystal wireless receiver. By the early 1950s, before the dawn of stereophonic reproduction, he had built a vast contraption out of light oak and plaster of Paris and set it in a corner of the drawing room. This was a state-of-the-art Voight mono loudspeaker. The sound came up from the belly of the beast, and was thrown up through an enormous plaster trumpet. It would then hit the canopy above and be splayed out into the centre of the room – theoretically, at least. I have no vivid memory of the sound, save that it was very loud, but the appearance was of a glorified ice-cream stand on Brighton pier.

We had no television. Indeed, until the coronation of the Queen in 1953, I had no idea that there was such a thing. Our neighbour in the adjoining part of the school had just purchased one. Derek Knight was a housemaster. He lived alone and chain-smoked Senior Service cigarettes, which stained his long fingers orange-brown and made his sitting room stink of tobacco. His entire existence seemed to centre on cigarettes. My mother had smoking in common with him, and had rather a soft spot for him. She did motherly things like darning his pullovers. One day he called us in to observe a new invention. An enormous walnut cabinet stood in the corner. It had a little window in the middle, with a couple of brown Bakelite knobs beneath it and a lot of wire hanging out of the back. This was my first sighting of a television set. I couldn't really make it out. After all, I had never seen a moving picture.

Shortly before this I had been taken on my first trip to London, to see the preparations for the coronation. I remember a hot, sunny May day. The roof of the Hudson was fully down. As we approached Buckingham Palace through throng-ing crowds we passed open dustcarts full of workmen throwing boiled sweets. I caught one. 'Don't eat that, Jonathan,' my mother chimed from the front seat. 'You don't know where it's been.'

In the smelly, uncomfortable safety of Derek Knight's sitting room, the thick brown woollen curtains were drawn against the summer sun. Ten or twelve of us craned at the little window to watch the great Coronation Day on 2 June 1953. The picture was a series of greys. It appeared to be snowing in London. From time to time I could detect a carriage, a white-gloved hand, and lots of men in ridiculous clothes. 'This will never catch on,' said my father of the walnut-facia'd contraption, and marched us out long before the service was over. The little window was certainly very small, and the picture indistinct, but to me it was still very intriguing.

Monarchy and the royal succession matched war as part of the background to my childhood world. The third fixed point was my parents'

41

marriage. Yet even here, war had played a role. In 1942, in addition to being the unpaid auxiliary fire chief and air raid marshal, my father was chaplain of Charterhouse School. This was an institution some notches higher up the league of English fee-paying schools than Ardingly, to which he was to move as headmaster in the year of my birth. In his role as a cleric he would go occasionally to the neighbouring YMCA, and it was in the canteen there that he encountered Joan Way, serving tea from a large urn. She was thirty, he was forty. In the extensive scrapbooks in which he recorded his life I can find no hint of a woman until that night. Indeed, my father, the indefatigable scoutmaster and housemaster, seems to have been far more interested in boys. That is not to say that he was a homosexual. More a self-obsessed man – he called his scrap albums 'Ego books' – he seems to have spent his holidays in the company of some of the boys he had taught. He and they built and maintained a narrow boat on the Grand Union Canal.

My mother's arrival in the 'Ego book' is sudden, and comes with their engagement. George, the seasoned bachelor, proposed within three weeks of meeting Joan, and married her six weeks later. 'That's how it was in those days,' my mother told me. 'We were so conscious that we might not even survive the war.' The engagement was so short that my father did not realise that my mother had no hair of her own. She had to tell him on the day he proposed to her that she had suffered an attack of *alopecia totalis* at the age of thirteen, after sitting her exams for the Royal

College of Music. Her hair had fallen out over three nights, and never came back. 'Your father was an absolute saint,' she would say. 'He asked for twenty-four hours to think about it after I told him, and he said he'd marry me anyway.' This defined her status thereafter: her life was dedicated to his every need. It was a status which defied the reality that she was a concert-grade pianist who had studied composition with Herbert Howells, one of the great influences on twentieth-century English classical music. She knew as much about music as my father did about the Bible.

For us, growing up with George and Joan, the lodestar was the war. Nothing was ever quite so good or quite so bad as it had been 'during the war'. Deeply conservative, they both worshipped order, an order in which everyone knew their place. Yet my father was not entirely conventional, for in addition to his love of the electronic he had a passion for fast American cars. Apart from this, in contrast to the absolutely dominant role America was to assume in my own life, George never went there, and he expressed little or no interest either in the place or its people. In his mind Britain still ruled the world.

The elevation from his 1920 Buick to the Hudson took place before I was born. The Hudson Essex Terraplane Eight was a rare beast indeed. Only six were ever made, and this one had been on the Hudson stand at the New York Motor show in 1931. Twenty-eight horsepower, she had a long bonnet and a very flat, almost unusable boot. My father had found and purchased the car through *Exchange & Mart*. In British terms, the Terraplane was like a cross between a Bentley and an MG. The dashboard looked like something from a makeshift cockpit: my father had installed an altimeter, a gradiometer and various other gadgets. The car was his greatest material joy. We would shop in it, pick up logs in it and go on holiday in it, squashed in the back, towing a vast caravan behind. My poor mother had to lash her wig down with tightly knotted headscarves.

One day in 1956 my father upped and sold the Hudson for £70 without warning. That was the moment that I discovered we were at war again. Our enemy this time was not Hitler, but someone called Nasser. It seemed funny to me how enemy leaders always seemed to end in '–er'. Ration books were back for petrol, and I was reduced to riding to school on the back of my mother's bike. My father regarded Anthony Eden, the Prime Minister who had precipitated the Suez crisis, as a 'good egg'. Many others thought he was un-hinged. Certainly we now know that he was on a cocktail of antidepressant and other drugs at the time. With his white hair, tall good looks and white moustache, Eden seemed very much out of the top drawer.

I was too young to grapple with the full story, but according to my father, 'This man Nasser, President of Egypt, has taken it upon himself to seize the Suez Canal, which we built, and will have to be dealt with.' Washington, for once, saw the adventure for what it was, and provided the pressure which forced the British, French and

Israelis to withdraw. The Anglo-French attempt to flash the flaccid tail of empire had failed. All I knew was that our world had retreated still further into the Sussex countryside. There was another consequence too, for Suez delivered a new Prime Minister.

From time to time on a Sunday evening I would go with my parents to 6.30 evensong in the school chapel. Sitting alone across the gangway, rather stooped, would be an old man in a tweed coat. One Sunday after Suez, my father introduced me to him. 'This is the Prime Minister, Jonathan,' he said.

I shook the man's hand and looked up into rather sad eyes and drooping eyebrows. 'Do you know what a Prime Minister is, young man?' Harold Macmillan asked me.

'Something to do with the Queen?' I suggested. 'Are you married to her?'

'Good Lord, no!' chortled Macmillan. 'One day you might like to be a politician. That's what I am.' With that he got into the waiting Humber and purred away to his huge country home, Birch Grove, just beyond Ardingly village. Little was I to know that Macmillan's wife Dorothy was probably at that very moment in bed with the scoundrel Tory MP Bob Boothby, with whom she maintained a torrid affair throughout her husband's premiership. Perhaps this strikingly sad man gained solace from the chapel services while she found hers between the sheets.

The only good politician in my father's house was a Tory politician. Labour never got a look-in. My father's Christian faith did not extend to embracing the birth of the welfare state. His faith *was* the Tory party at prayer: war, Conservatism and Anglicanism were the trinity upon which my father's philosophy was founded.

My mother never dissented from my father's view; if anything she was even more conservative. But my relationship with her was of an altogether different texture. I enjoyed her femininity, her Blue Grass scent, her pearls, tweed skirts and Jacqmar scarves. It was not until I was eight that her greatest burden, the loss of her hair, was shared with me. Consequently she was reserved, and never let me clamber about her or run my fingers through what I still thought of as her hair. It was not until after my father's death twenty years later that she discussed her loss of hair openly.

The piano was our thread of contact throughout my childhood. My mother was a wonderfully bold performer, in stark contrast to the retiring role she played within the family. Her long, slender, beautifully manicured fingers ranged powerfully across the keys as she played her beloved Brahms. She did not play often, and never without sheet music. I longed for her to extemporise and light upon some of the tunes I knew. She never did. Instead, from perhaps the age of four I began to pick up themes from her playing, and hummed or sang along with her. I was concerned that my brothers, who spent their time buried in my father's workshop soldering solenoids, might tease me for this, but gradually, by the age of about seven, I began to sing with more gusto. It was in this activity alone that my mother revealed her most demonstrative maternal delight. Her eternity ring would clink about on the ivories as I, who could only vaguely decipher the clusters of notes on the page, waited for the nod that would signal me to turn it.

'I say, Joan.' It was my father calling out from behind *The Times* one day at breakfast.

'Yes, darling?'

'There's a notice here about a voice trial at Winchester Cathedral to select new choristers. Shall we put the boy in for it?'

So began an intensive few weeks of arpeggios, harmonics and music theory. On the appointed day in April 1956 I turned up at Dumb Alley, a musty rehearsal room in the Winchester Cathedral Close where all the choir practices were held. Almost immediately I found myself standing next to the seated figure of the man who would be my choirmaster for the next five years, the aptly named Alwyn Surplice. After a rendition of the carol 'Oh Little Town of Bethlehem', I was in. I became a choral scholar at the Pilgrim's School in the cathedral close.

My father was visibly pleased with my achievement. 'You can have anything you want, under a pound,' he announced. This was an extravagant gesture for him, in response to my saving him some severe school fees for the next five years. It was well after five o'clock as we headed for the shops. 'You don't need to spend it now,' he said. But I wanted it right now, quick, before the shops closed at 5.30. Instant gratification, when we found the toyshop, came in the shape of a pale-blue Dinky Toy car transporter. It cost sixteen shillings and sixpence – no mean sum in those days.

Within three months I had arrived at Pilgrim's School as a very full-time boarder, my holidays truncated and term times extended by saints' days and high days, for which the sixteen members of the choir had to be present even when the other boys had gone home for vacations. The parting from Ardingly, treehouses, warfare with my brothers, music with my mother, was unutterably painful. At eight years old, I felt abandoned and inadequate. 'He can't do up his shoelaces, you know,' my father had called over his departing shoulder to my new headmaster. Yet within weeks I found myself becoming part of the medieval weft and weave of the cathedral. Snaking across the close two or three times a day, we sixteen choristers were with Trollope, and Trollope was with us. We had stepped into history and joined with the characters of Barchester: dry old Canon Lloyd, with long strands of oily black hair draped across his naked pate; fat, jolly Canon Money, who didn't seem to have any because his cassock was full of holes; and deliciously eccentric Dr Lamplugh, Bishop of Southampton, who still had a Christmas tree in the hallway of his house come July. These were the decaying generals of the Church militant, presided over by learned Dean Selwyn and the remote Bishop of Winchester, Bishop Williams. We choristers were in thrall to Alwyn Surplice, our organist and choirmaster, who smacked the backs of our hands with a ruler whenever he wanted better of us.

The fingers of Alwyn Surplice's right hand had

become closely clustered as a result of years of Morse-tapping and top-secret code-breaking at Bletchley Park during the war. This heroic condition was said to excuse the occasional duff notes in his organ playing. In reality, he played the organ like a demon. Practically all the staff at the school had been to the war. Principal amongst them was the dashing Rodney Blake, who was to run off to New Zealand with the piano teacher, deserting a wife with large ankles and two children, to the scandalised gossip of the cathedral close. Rodney taught me a love of the English language in general, and of the adjective in particular. He was a man full of mystery who had served on ships in the Atlantic, and his stories of derring-do had me ready for action any time.

I soon discovered that the entire cathedral was a kind of mausoleum to unbroken centuries of the direst conflict. Right in between the choir stalls where we sang lay the second proper King of England, William Rufus, with an arrow in his back. High on the side screens that led to the rood screen above the high altar were funny-coloured boxes in which the powdery remains of even earlier Kings lay, among them Canute and Ethelred the Unready. There was hardly a man interred in the building who had died peacefully in his bed.

On either side, all the way down the nave, the transepts were festooned with officers who had died from Afghanistan to Zanzibar. The two World Wars seemed to have taken half the population of Hampshire with them. Everywhere there were memorials incorporating guns, cannon, stone-cast flags, swords and worse. Every day we were amongst this stone-entrenched certainty of war. To crown it all, the great west window stood testament to the results of a cannonball fired by Oliver Cromwell from the hill overlooking the cathedral. Every piece of glass in it had been smashed and rescued. The result was a jumble that left a cat's head on a slice of human armour, a sword under the upside-down leg of a horse. Even the language of faith included words like 'defender', 'sword', 'shield', 'armies' and 'victory'.

Outside the cathedral, school in term time was a Dickensian nightmare: ghastly food, sour milk in small bottles, a potted sick-like substance called 'sandwich spread' on curling bread, regular beatings, cold showers and endless inspections of our fingernails. The headmaster, Humphrey Salway, was a former Guards officer with a fearsome capacity to inflict psychological and physical pain, the latter at the hand of a wooden 'butter pat'. This was a flat, spade-like object with a leather tassel attached. It had the facility to produce blue-black weals on your buttocks, laced with red slashes. We would stand in line in our shivering pyjamas outside the headmaster's study after being caught talking after lights-out in dormitory. The decision as to whether or not we would be beaten was entirely arbitrary. If we were, we would not be able to sit painlessly for a week or more. In a very rare act of theft, at thirteen years of age, I stole the butter pat on my last day at the school. I have often thought of old Salway, on the threshold of inflicting a sound beating, marauding around his study searching for the weapon and failing to find it. These days his motives would be questioned, but then he was a celebrated and feared figure in the cathedral close.

On 8 June 1958 I was summoned home from school to meet the Queen and Prince Philip. This was a huge event. The whole of the downstairs of the house had been decorated. The lavatory – euphemistically called 'the garden room' – where my father sat reading the traditionalist magazine *Time & Tide* for unreasonable quantities of time had been gutted and refitted against the possibility that one of Their Majesties would need a pee. My mother had made a special trip to Harrods in London to secure two Crown Derby cups and saucers from which the royal lips could sip tea.

The Queen and Prince Philip had opened Crawley New Town and Gatwick Airport in the morning, and were now descending upon Ardingly as part of the school's centenary. Suddenly my father and mother were not in their usual posts at the top of the social tree. The Queen's secretary, Sir Edward Ford, whom my father had taught at Eton, arrived early to see that all was in order. My father spoke of Harold Macmillan having played a part in securing the moment.

At 3 p.m. prompt, the biggest Rolls-Royce I'd ever seen steamed through the archway and onto the quadrangle in front of our house. My brothers and I stood at the top of the steps outside the front door. Our hands were shaken. The Queen was rather small, pleated, hatted and stiff. The

51

Duke of Edinburgh burbled, but I couldn't understand what he said. Then they were inside, and I began to think about the garden room. Even if not sitting there, the royal bottoms must by now be sitting on some of the cushions that I knew and loved so well.

Soon the Queen was gone, and I was on the train back to Winchester. Mr Salway treated me briefly like a conquering hero. At breakfast the next day I was allowed to sit next to his wife Lorna, a warm and affectionate woman who let me eat her fresh toast and marmalade instead of the usual soggy white bread and spread. But very soon normal sadistic services were resumed by her husband. This was, after all, term time.

Yet once the holidays dawned and the 'ordinary' boys went home it would be all smiles, and we sixteen who constituted the choir were never tyrannised or beaten. We were cast loose upon the town to spin out our tiny five-shilling budgets. We had absolute freedom in those days, and gained absolute sympathy too. We were spoilt rotten, people in both school and town taking pity upon us for our enforced separation from our families as we lingered on to service Christmas, Easter, Ascension and the rest. These days sowed a love of music and of the cathedral, and if not of religion, certainly of peace and contemplation in a great building. But they were also central to the destruction of our family lives. Holidays amounted to only four or five weeks a year for the five years of my time at Winchester. My father was so rarely encountered, I called him 'sir' by mistake.

From this familial wreckage emerged a confident, independent child of thirteen – primed for adolescence, or so I was indirectly told. For Humphrey Salway's parting shot was an obscure account of the 'facts of life'. These centred on the 'golden seed' which at some point I was going to wake up and find in my bed. Beyond rust spots inflicted by the mattress springs beneath, though I searched, I grew up minus 'golden seed'. Indeed, I left the choir school with my voice still unbroken.

The letter to my father from Number Ten Downing Street arrived at Ardingly just before I returned there from my last day at Pilgrim's: 'The Queen has been graciously pleased to appoint you Bishop Suffragan of Whitby.' The signature at the bottom read 'Harold Macmillan, Prime Minister'. The new Archbishop of York, in whose domain my father's territory lay, was to be his friend Donald Coggan. All my father's ducks were in a row, and the longed-for preferment had come on the very eve of his retirement from Ardingly. The Church, political, militant, ecclesiastical and old-boy network, had done its stuff, and we were all thrilled. We now had a new status in life, and after Ardingly a grand new home in darkest North Yorkshire.

The Old Rectory in South Kilvington, with its own little Saxon church in the garden, was as near paradise as the Brontës would have dared imagine. My new bedroom looked south and west over the garden. I was not to pass much time there, but I spent enough in that first summer to talk hungrily with the remarkable octogenarian who tended the garden. Joe Clarke had only ever left Kilvington once in his life, and that was to go to Egypt in the First World War to dig pit latrines for victory. Joe was conscripted into the First City of London Sanitary Corps. Wherever Allied man had to do his duty, Joe was there to facilitate the needs of the lower bowel. He served for five years. 'I tell you, master Jon, I had to give up on digging the waste to bury the dead, there was that many.' Joe, who had dug his way through Europe after Egypt, burying the war dead, now dug his way through the Old Rectory's rhododendrons. The carnage of the Great War was fifty years before, but Joe's memories were as vivid as if it were yesterday.

I wanted nothing more than to garden and learn with Joe, but I had a music exhibition to St Edward's, a minor fee-paying school in Oxford. The headmaster, Frank Fisher, was the son of yet another prelate, Geoffrey, Archbishop of Canterbury. He took pity on my father's high-born impecuniousness and secured me an ill-deserved cut in fees in the form of a choral exhibition. So on the one hand here was Joe giving me the side of war from the ranks, of which my family knew nothing, while through my father I was able to observe the insidious methods of the upper classes in securing hegemony in matters military, educational, ecclesiastical, even episcopal.

Three Bishops were 'done' on the day my father was consecrated in York Minster, and a grand affair it was. Eight feet tall in his mitre, my father was every inch a Bishop. The Whitby nuns had toiled through the nights to spin and embroider his voluminous cope. The silversmiths had beaten his pectoral cross and crosier out of some dead Bishop's leftover silverware. Fully adorned, my father was some spectacle; and the minster bounced with sound and colour.

It was as an innocent abroad that I arrived at St Edward's, a seriously Victorian environment. The first three weeks were spent mugging up for an initiation test, essentially a compendium of names and concepts that were peculiar to the school: 'chaggers' for changing rooms, 'beaks' for masters, 'boguls' for bicycles, and some ludicrous piece of ironwork on the chapel roof was 'the boot scraper'. Sixteen years after the Second World War, here was an institution still ordered around the ball and the gun. Games were everything, and when we weren't playing rugby, we were square-bashing in full uniform on the parade ground.

I didn't mind playing games, although my gangling form meant that my brain seemed to be too far from the extremity of my limbs. Messages as to when to kick the ball failed to connect adequately with the foot in question. In short, my hand–eye co-ordination was abominable. Watching games left me both physically and mentally cold. Yet the pseudo-military hierarchy of the place depended on hero-worshipping those who excelled in games. Because I failed to watch, or worse failed to concentrate when I was watching, I failed hopelessly at the hero-worshipping. When matches were being played I preferred to hide in the art room and paint, or strum on the piano in a practice room.

One day after a rugby match, still only fourteen years old, I returned to the day room, where perhaps twenty 'horseboxes' were arranged around the walls. The 'horsebox' was your own personal space – a small contained area with a seat, a desk, shelves, and somewhere to stick up pictures of Mummy, Daddy and the dog. On this particular day I made towards my horsebox, only to find that it was completely naked – the curtain, the photos, books, cushions, possessions, all gone. Suddenly I was jumped on from behind by half a dozen of the other horsebox-dwellers. Grabbed by the hair, I was shoved into the large wastebin in the corner. In the bin already were Mummy, Daddy and the dog, all ripped to shreds, while Quink ink and the Blanco used for greening our military webbing had been smeared on what remained of my precious possessions.

The bullying was institutionalised. The house-master, a shy, dysfunctional bachelor, lived next door to our day room, and must surely have heard all the noise. Sexual activity between the boys was also commonplace. Boys were talked about as sexual objects. Blond, blue-eyed new-comers – as I had been – were trouble from the outset, importuned by bigger boys for mutual masturbation. I remember how a prefect in the neighbouring boarding house, who was building a canoe in the basement, lured me down to see it. Before I realised it, he had his hand down my trousers, and demanded mine down his. Fagging, or acting as unpaid servant, was almost as exploitative as the sex. I fagged for a diminutive seventeen-year-old prefect who demanded that the insteps of his shoes be polished so they would glisten when he knelt for communion. It was a rocky and wretched introduction to adolescence, so far from Nanny and the backlit fields of stooks that I still dreamt of from childhood. Yet it also made me political, and made me yearn, if only subconsciously, for change, and later to campaign for it. Some of us went under. I remember one boy called Prythurch – I never knew his first name – who was teased mercilessly for his pink National Health spectacles. One term he simply never came back.

Academically, I was a failure. In a sense, the teaching mirrored the sport. If the school decided you were bright, you secured the best teachers, and were pushed. If you were deemed 'thick', you got either the rugby coaches who had to fulfil their teaching quota, or the straightforwardly unemployable. One of these was Stan Tackley. Stan was perhaps the most boring and uninterested teacher of Latin, English and French of his generation, and I had him for all three subjects. He taught with an elderly, flatulent golden Labrador at his feet.

My year with Stan and his dog Brandy delivered me bottom in Latin, bottom in English, and bottom in French. I was in the bottom fifth form, 5f; my brother Nick, two years my junior, was already ahead of me in 5b. Things were looking bad, and my father took me into his study when I returned home. 'Sonny,' he said, causing me to wonder if he used the word because he couldn't tell which of us was which, as we had been away so long, 'Sonny, your mother and I have decided you should leave St Edward's and become apprenticed at Dorman Long in Middlesbrough.'

'Crumbs,' I said. 'Me a steelworker?' Dorman Long had a vast series of steelworks on Teesside, and my father admired the heavy industry in his diocese, never having been exposed to it before. 'One more year, Dad,' I pleaded. When I returned to school, Stan was still teaching me some classes, but fewer of them.

In the afternoons, Stan was Major Tackley, and ran the Combined Cadet Force. The school would suddenly become a sea of khaki and air-force blue. Boys would run about brandishing bolt-action Lee Enfield guns. We were tutored in war. The staff's wartime exploits were the iconography of discourse at the dinner table. But no member of staff could hold a candle to the school's most famous old boys. These included Guy Gibson VC, who led the original 'Dam Busters' raids against German dams and was one of the greatest pilots of the Second World War, but died in action, and the legendary Group Captain Douglas Bader DSO, of 242 Squadron, RAF, who was very much alive, but literally legless. Bader was a living legend who had had both legs amputated when his fighter plane crashed during a stunt. He fought back to fly again in combat, wearing artificial pins.

Now, in the early 1960s, he would rock around the school grounds, stickless and unaided, a lesson to us all. He had no job there, he was just a professional old boy. Bader in many ways typified the politics of the school. If they were ever mentioned, the Labour Party, the burgeoning 'Ban the Bomb' anti-nuclear movement, socialism and, of course, Communism were the enemies of what we were about. It was a political culture that chimed with that of my parents.

My first memory of an ambition was indeed, at the age of fifteen, to be a Tory MP. Whether this aspiration derived from my early brush with Macmillan or from the school I don't know, but it was certainly there. My sense of the outside world depended almost exclusively on the *Daily Mail*. We were only allowed the radio on Sundays, when we would listen to *Forces' Favourites*, yet another reminder that all over the world there were British troops ranged against 'the enemy'. Otherwise we listened to Radio Luxembourg, the only pop station then in being. We had no access to television. So our knowledge of world events was narrow in the extreme.

I was fifteen at the time of the Cuban missile crisis. Bearded Castro, dictator of Cuba, and bald-headed Khrushchev, leader of the Soviet Union, were depicted as exceptionally unpleasant and dangerous men. Never more so than when the latter repeatedly banged his shoe on a desk at the UN General Assembly in New York in October 1960. By contrast the handsome and clean-shaven American President, John F Kennedy, couldn't put a foot wrong. And Harold Macmillan had by now been transmogrified into 'Super Mac'. The argument that Cuba might need Russia's nuclear missiles to guard against, or even stave off, another American invasion was simply never made. Russia wanted to put her missiles on Cuba to attack America, that was the only interpretation we were ever offered. This was the Cold War, the East–West standoff.

As the missile crisis deepened, we went through our nuclear protection exercises on an almost weekly basis – under our desk lids, heads in the brace position. It wasn't until much later that I began to learn about the abortive Bay of Pigs invasion in 1961, in which Kennedy had sent 1500 US-trained Cuban exiles to try to over-throw Castro. For a time the world was on the edge of the abyss of nuclear war, but I cannot pretend to have been aware of the true magnitude of it at the time.

By November 1963 the world had changed again. Adorned as a woman, I was strutting my stuff on the school stage. I was playing Eva in Jean Anouilh's comedy *Thieves' Carnival*. Of my performance, the *Oxford Times* wrote: 'the only giveaway is the too-masculine stride'. On the twenty-second of that month my mother and father drove down to watch the play. Act One passed without incident, but something happened during the interval. Somehow members of the audience found out that Jack Kennedy had been shot, and was dying in a Dallas clinic. The belly laughs of the first half of the performance were not repeated in the second. There was much whispering and talking low. People scurried away at the end. It was as if innocence itself had been shot. My parents were overwhelmed with gloom. 'Super Mac' and Jack had bonded like father and son. There had been a new optimism abroad, a new sense of Camelot and magic. And now this spirit was all but dead.

With Kennedy gone, the wheels started coming off Macmillan's wagon. The sixties began to swing. The *Daily Mail* revelled in telling us who was having whom, and where and how. Suddenly the where was Cliveden, and the who was the Minister for War, John Profumo. Profumo, who had had the misfortune to make love to a woman who was already sleeping with a Russian diplomat named Ivanov, a Soviet spy, was unhorsed for being economical with the truth about the matter in the House of Commons. We boys, reading this stuff, simply couldn't believe it. The entire British Establishment had its collective trousers round its ankles, and we were thrilled by it. One day I would encounter John Profumo myself, in a very different guise.

We, with our posh accents, sneered at the Yorkshire-accented Harold Wilson, who became Labour Prime Minister in 1964 with a wafer-thin majority. But he won us over the moment he set fire to his jacket pocket with his pipe. Few other outside events impinged upon our lives. And then, one bleak winter's day in January 1965, Winston Churchill died. Every living Field Marshal and more than sixty world leaders, led by former US President Dwight D. Eisenhower, attended the funeral in St Paul's Cathedral on 30 January. Classes were abandoned for the day, and we were allowed to cluster around the few black-and-white television sets near the school. The lying in state, the swarming crowds, the vast procession, the gun carriage and the service in St Paul's were all on an epic scale. Eisenhower, when

61

he spoke, made my backbone tingle.

I can presume to act as spokesman for millions of Americans who served with me and their British comrades during three years of war in this sector of the earth. To those men Winston Churchill was Britain... I, like all free men, pause to pay a personal tribute to the giant who now passes from among us... We say our sad goodbye to the leader to whom the entire body of free men owes so much ... and now, to you, Sir Winston – my old friend – farewell!

We weren't to know it, but this was almost certainly one of the last times that collective America ever looked up to a politician who was not an American. One much later exception might prove to be Nelson Mandela, who at the time of Churchill's death had already been in prison for treason for over two years, and still had twenty-four more to go.

Churchill's coffin was borne by barge to Waterloo. Hearing on the wireless that it had departed for its final resting place at Bladon in Oxfordshire, hundreds of boys from the school set forth, swarming across the playing fields, down across the swing bridge on the Oxford canal and across to the side of the railway line on the edge of Port Meadow. There, exposed to the full might of the mad January wind, we stood in our grey-flannel uniforms and waited, straw boaters in our hands. Bladon was only ten miles up the line, close to Blenheim Palace where Churchill had been born. And then we heard it, far down the stilled line.

Soon we saw the belching steam pumping into the brittle blue winter sky. Then the great Battle of Britain class locomotive was upon us. Irish Hussars flanked the catafalque. The sturdy, flag-draped coffin was clearly visible. We bowed our heads in genuine awe. As suddenly, it was gone. However brief, it was a passing of history that would inform my sense of Britain and America, and war, for the rest of my life.

America for me was still more than a decade away. That summer of 1966, at the age of eighteen, I went abroad for the first time with two friends from school. We bought a Bedford Dormobile for £50, converted it, and headed for Greece. Belgium, Germany, Austria and Yugoslavia yielded up an effortless tapestry of history and geography. More importantly, they generated a real thirst in me to go much further. It was that summer that confirmed in me the desire to spend a year in Africa or India, or some far-flung Pacific isle, to learn more about the world.

At the same time, having just left St Edward's with only one 'A' level – a C pass in English – I had to set about getting educated. That autumn I ended up at Scarborough Technical College, on the edge of my father's diocese. I was suddenly translated from dunce to intellectual. Fewer than twenty-five people out of the thousand at the college were taking 'A' levels at all; most were doing 'day release' courses in plumbing or bricklaying. Seven of us signed up to do law and economics at 'A' level. We had one lecturer, Bob Thomas, a wise and down-to-earth Welshman, and I learned more in a year with him than in five with the entire staff at St Edward's. He even saved me from a disastrous affair with a beguiling older member of the administrative staff. After I was spotted disappearing out of the grounds at lunchtimes in her car and coming back more than a little dishevelled, Bob sat me down and suggested that I had a long and successful life ahead of me, and that it might not be such a good idea to be caught *in flagrante* with a married woman on the Scarborough downs.

I left the Tech after only a year with two more 'A' levels, having done much to redress the ravages of private education on my confidence, ready to strike out into the world. My application to do Voluntary Service Overseas had been accepted. I was ready to go, but far less prepared than I knew.

TWO

Africa, Revolution and Despair

Two tumbledown corrugated huts at the side of the runway seemed to be the beginning and end of Entebbe Airport. The VC10 that had carried us via Rome and Tripoli appeared to be the only operational aircraft on the entire airfield. The terror that was to seize this place and inaugurate a new world of violence, in which the passenger became pawn, was still nearly a decade away.

It was September 1967. I had never been on an aircraft before, never been out of Europe, and only once out of England. I had felt compelled to shake my father's hand upon leaving home in Yorkshire, for I feared he might be dead before I returned. It was the only physical contact with him I can remember. He was still the Bishop, my mother still his ever-faithful retainer. I knew he would be impressed if I won selection for VSO. I knew too that it would offer me an escape from his world. In the build-up to my departure, Africa had seemed an exotic and distant place, Uganda even more so. But had committing myself to a year of Voluntary Service Overseas been such a sensible idea? Aboard the claustrophobic plane, on balance I was beginning to think not.

As the door of the aircraft opened, the wet heat and the brown-green smell summoned me from my seat. The sound of the engines had roused the few customs and immigration officials from their slumbers. Father Grimes, chain-smoking in black, nervous, very white, with thinning hair, waited on the other side of the sheds. His greeting was unmistakably Yorkshire: 'Welcome to Uganda! You've a long journey ahead of you, so let's be going.'

There were two of us VSOs, David James and me. David was what I would call successful public school, strong in the areas where I was weak – sporty and academically bright. It was important that we didn't fall out. Father Grimes was the head of the Catholic mission school where we were to teach for the year. The posting seemed more or less random, although we had been allowed to express a preference as to which continent we would be sent.

I had never known such soakingly wet heat. We got into Grimes's Volkswagen and set off. Lake Victoria shimmered invitingly, but the Father told us we could never swim either in it or in the river Nile that flowed from it. 'Not just the crocodiles,' he said, 'it's the snails. Bilharzia, rots yer liver.'

People were everywhere. There was nothing a bicycle could not carry. A husband pedalling, his wife sitting sidesaddle behind with one small child in her arms and a baby on her back, lengths of timber, sacks of corn, even a small coffin. I was overwhelmed by both the heat and the sights. The men were in cotton shirts, the women in elaborate and voluminous brightly printed dresses. In Kampala, the capital, Asian shops spewed their wares out onto the pavements, mopeds roared, cars tooted, dogs, goats, even cows, wandered aimlessly. On the outskirts of the city the low urban sprawl gave way to tall tropical rainforests. Then suddenly as we rounded a bend, armed men scattered across the road ahead, flagging us down.

'It's nothing,' hissed Grimes. 'Just the state of emergency.'

'State of emergency? No one said anything about that,' I hissed back.

As one of the armed men peered into our stationary car, Grimes added, 'It's King Freddy, you know, the Kabaka. He wants a comeback role. Obote, the President, wants it for himself. Freddy's gone off to the UK in a huff. Drinks a lot, you know.'

After only five years' independence from British rule, things in Uganda were already sounding shaky. Yet after the military men had waved us through, as we headed out across the Owen Falls, source of the Nile, and then the great hydro-electric dam, Uganda still looked at peace with itself. The waters beneath the road churned ferociously. Crested cranes stooped on the river banks, terns sat on the backs of cows taking their ease at the calmer water's edge. Once we were clear of the dam, jacaranda trees splashed unexpectedly potent blues along both sides of the road.

More than a hundred miles from Entebbe, and with the light fading, the tarmac gave way to the compressed red clay they called murum. In the dry season the road was hard as concrete, with a thick film of dust across it. In the wet season it became slithery mud. This night it was dry and spooky, the car's headlights picking out tall, dark organic forms on either side. Small animals darted back and forth across the murum, their eyes glinting in the lights.

'Only fifteen miles to Namasagali,' said Grimes. Those fifteen miles took nearly an hour to negotiate. And with each passing mile my heart sank further. It felt so very far from anywhere. I thought of home, of people and places I loved; for once I envied my brothers, and even missed my mother and father. I was not enjoying my entry into Africa. But although I was unaware of it at the time, this journey, and so much of the ensuing year, was to prepare me for far more harrowing and taxing trips through Africa in years to come. Not just prepare me, but radicalise and change me more than I could possibly imagine.

Kamuli College, on the banks of the Nile, was set in an old railhead at Namasagali, which had once been a trans-shipment point for cotton heading north. The engine sheds were now the school hall and the bookless library. The cotton warehouses had been broken up into classrooms. There was little light when we arrived at Grimes's house, which was where the station manager had lived. Inside, the four other *'muzungus'*, or European teachers, were waiting. Tom and Anne Welsh were a radical, committed Scots couple. Gus was a don't-care Scotsman on the wild side. The fourth was another priest, a warm and engaging Dutchman called Father Zonnerveldt. These, and the fourteen indigenous teachers I would meet in the morning, would be my isolated family for the next twelve months.

The house itself spoke volumes about what we were in for. A bare bulb dangled from the ceiling, the netted door frame opened onto a veranda where I could glimpse old boxes and cupboards scattered about. There was an ageing suitcase on a rickety table, with clothes tumbling out of it. Unrelated bits of furniture littered the living room, and through another door I could see the dining table, with ancient British consumer goods at one end: a discontinued line of Gale's honey, a jar of Marmite, and a Bible sticking out from under a box of Corn Flakes. This was going to be a challenge. I went to bed in Grimes's house that night feeling profoundly homesick and rather sorry for myself. I suspect David felt the same.

Feeling very white, the next morning we gathered around the flagpole for assembly. Grimes barked at the children. They were all crisply turned out, and seemed to know every word of the Ugandan national anthem, 'Oh Uganda, the Land of Freedom' 'Our Father, which art in heaven...' intoned Father Grimes. Suddenly the stark contrast with the dining room at Ardingly, General Tom, even Winchester Cathedral, sprang into my head. I was a world away, amongst the children of the still-poor elite in a country the General's cohorts had tried to run for more than half a century.

That night David and I moved into our new 'house'. It was more an outhouse, with a concrete floor, a living area, two bedrooms and a loo out at the back. There were beds but no sheets, mosquitoes but no nets. The night was a constant battle with insects and cockroaches seeking to share my bed.

We employed John Luwangula as our cook and houseboy. Dear John could not cook to save his life, and was well past being classified as any kind of a boy. But he was strong and confident, and a fast learner, and he attended to our every need for the equivalent of around £3 a week. My classes were large, one of forty souls, another of close on fifty. Many of the pupils were older than me, for as was often the case in Uganda, they had had to work for their school fees before they could take up a place. One morning while I had my back turned and was writing on the blackboard, someone made a rude noise. 'Who was that?' I asked.

'That black boy at the back,' answered Margaret from the front row.

'But you're all black,' I said, somewhat mystified.

'Ah, sir,' said Margaret, 'but some, sir, are much blacker than others. That boy comes from the north.'

The scales fell from my eyes. I, who had grown up in such charmed Anglo-Saxon circumstances, almost oblivious to black people, suddenly saw them as the rainbow coalition that they are: creamy cappuccino from the south-west of the country, blue-black Nilotic from the Upper West Nile region, nut-brown from the east. My new world was taking shape before my very eyes. The children at Kamuli College, precisely because they required money to attend the place, came from all over the country. The school reflected the tribal make-up of the entire nation, providing a living insight into the way the colonialists had arbitrarily decided the shape of the borders of Uganda.

Having at first wondered how on earth I could escape the place, within a few weeks I was trying to find out how I could stay longer. This was despite the remnants of empire and war that still percolated through every aspect of the teaching. The school followed the imperially imposed Oxford & Cambridge Examination Board's 'O' level curriculum. Thus I was saddled with teaching George Orwell's *Animal Farm*.

'What is Communism, sir?' asked one child.

'What's a carthorse, sir?' chimed another.

The fact was that neither Orwell's farm itself, nor the allegory it was intended to conjure, meant anything at all to my students. Trying both to teach the physical reality of an English farm to Africans and to interpret the book's ideological subtext was a challenge indeed.

Presumably I can thank the anachronistic imperial backbone instilled in me at school for the speed with which homesickness gave way to an enthusiasm for the whole adventure. Namasagali was beginning to get into my soul. The short evenings would find me down at the little dock on the Nile, where I would sit on the base of the rusting old crane watching the water go by bearing great chunks of papyrus. But it was not of Empire that I mused, despite the 'made in England' sign on the arm of the crane. It was of the half-naked children playing between the tracks that led to the dockside and their circumstances that I thought. They had no shoes or socks. These children from the village further up the river were too poor to attend school at all; some had distended bellies, some had evident eye diseases. Over the months I lived at Namasagali I became friendly with their families, taking John, our houseboy, with me to translate. It rapidly dawned on me that the students at Kamuli College, poor by my standards, were rich beyond the dreams of the villagers, whose lives ebbed and flowed with the seasons. There was poverty here that I'd never begun to imagine.

Two months into my stint at Namasagali I found myself at the wheel of the school minibus, slithering along the rain-soaked road heading out towards Kampala. I was taking six of the school's best boxers to a nationwide tournament.

Big Daddy, when I first saw him, was vast – huge in body, face, and personality. 'I'm the referee today,' he boomed as we neared the ring. Major General Idi Amin Dada was already head of the Ugandan army. My first encounter with a man who was to become synonymous with summary execution, massacre and wholesale deportation was relatively benign. In truth he seemed nicer than the then President, Milton Apollo Obote, who had ruled the country since independence. Amin was a former heavyweight champion of the Ugandan army, and it was clear that he loved boxing. He would dash across the ring after a bout and demonstrate, fortunately in only shadow terms, how it would have ended had he been one of the boxers rather than just the referee. He seemed to have a huge sense of humour, beaming at all times. He noticed me because, as he told me, 'I'm not used to meeting white men as tall as you. Your mother must have eaten much paw-paw.' Yet on the long journey through the night back to Namasagali, we all confessed to a lurking fear of the man. Too big and boisterous for comfort, we thought.

Father Grimes, despite his bantam appearance, loved boxing too, and his having that in common with Amin was later to spare the lives of many in the school. 'Amin was only a Sergeant Major in the First King's East African Rifles, you know,' Grimes told me. 'The British sent him to Sandhurst for four months and he came back virtually a General.'

The British, seeing the writing on the colonial walls, realised by 1962 that Uganda would have to join the queue of their colonised neighbours to become independent. In common with so many African armies, Uganda's had been left with few if any indigenous officers. A panicky last-minute course was put on in distant Surrey to convert Africans from the ranks straight to the higher echelons of the officer class. Almost overnight, one absurd, larger-than-life Sergeant Major was larded with ribbons and braid and elevated to a rank that no black man had enjoyed before him. Harmless enough in the boxing ring, perhaps, but what if such a man ever came to run the country? We would know the answer within three short years.

In the school holidays we met up with other British and American volunteers and set about seeing more of Uganda and the surrounding countries. We hitched or bussed to Nairobi, Mombasa and Dar es Salaam. We camped on beaches, wandered amongst the wildlife and watched the Masai tribespeople crossing mud roads ahead of us. They were intoxicating times in which it still felt utterly safe to be a foreigner in East Africa. It would have been inconceivable to imagine that within three decades this sweltering, peaceful place would become a battleground for al Qaida.

Among our group was Diana Villiers, whose father was running one of Harold Wilson's new-fangled economic power levers – the Industrial Reorganisation Corporation. As so often with the British top drawer, my father had taught her father at Eton. Diana, like me, was headed in due course for an encounter with the new world disorder, but on another continent. Our next meeting would find us both in very different circumstances, with her married to the man running America's Contra war against Nicaragua. But for now we were both at a point of transition, in Africa amid the passage to independence, and party to the massive afterburn of imperialism and colonisation. To me, surprisingly in 1968, it still felt comfortable.

'Mr Jon,' cried my houseboy, 'I'm going to get married.'

'My goodness, John,' I replied, 'I didn't even know you had a girlfriend.'

'Oh yes, sir, and I want you to be a best man at the ceremony.'

John's wife-to-be, Elizabeth, came all the way from Kamuli town, at the other end of the murum road; she had a large family, and looked gorgeous on the day. Generations of the bride and groom's families ran in and out of the open side walls of the church. Jesus wrestled with local tribal custom throughout the wedding ceremony. Long after I returned to England, I became a godfather to John and Elizabeth's first child by mail. But their marriage, the villagers, the school itself, were all for me a part of coming to terms with a world that a few months earlier I had not even dreamt existed.

Father Grimes ruled by missionary example and rod of iron, or rather of bamboo, which he wielded with great ferocity and regularity. I had upwards of 150 workbooks to mark each week. Hired to teach English, I ended up with both biology and technology added to my workload. In both subjects I would have to swot the night before to keep one step ahead of my pupils. I was constantly outsmarted by some of the brighter kids. Whatever happened to Noah Omolo, who wrote so lyrically and who, had he been tutored, could have made it into any top-flight Western university?

'I want to come with you when you go, sir,' he said to me once. 'I will be your servant, and look after you for the rest of your life, and your wife and children too.' Noah was to prove one of the very few Ugandans I would meet again.

Or Margaret Nsubaga: 'Dance with me when you leave, sir.' Adding, 'Come live with me in Uganda.'

Or Praxedes Namaganda, who came for a few weeks' teaching practice from Makerere University. We kissed on the banks of the Nile, but she was a good Catholic, and anyway the relationship was not to survive the unpredictabilities of the postal service.

On Saturday nights I had to organise the enormous disco in one of the former engine sheds, where I would dance rather too enjoyably with the older girls. On Sunday mornings I would set sail in the battered school bus for the twenty-seven-mile run to collect the Protestant padre – despite the Catholic mission status of the school, more than half the children were Protestants. Sometimes I wouldn't be able to find the man, who was frequently inebriated, and I'd return empty-handed to the engine shed, by now transformed from disco to matins, and have to take the service myself. 'Our father, which art in heaven...' 'Thank you, God,' I thought, 'for those dining-room prayers at Ardingly. Thank you, Jane Austen, for lying undisturbed in the nave of Winchester Cathedral while I intoned the *Te Deum*.' So 'to the manor born' was I that the kids asked me eventually not to bother with the padre, and to continue taking the services myself.

And so I became an inseparable part of this Nile-side community, talking liberation theology with the priests or Communism with Gus and the Welshes at night and working by day from 7.30 a.m. to 7.30 p.m., with an afternoon siesta. There were no newspapers. Early and late I would listen to the crackly BBC World Service fading in and out of the ether on our old valve-mains Marconi wireless. World events took on a new poignancy. I was beginning to set them in the context of my own new world. This was how, in April 1968, I heard the devastating news of the assassination of Martin Luther King, an event that was to impinge so forcibly on both my old and new worlds.

Fruit and flowers abounded naturally, as did sweet potatoes and every kind of banana. Wild dogs ran about, goats and chickens wandered aimlessly, and there was eternal talk of a leopard I never saw in the nearby forest. This was my isolated Utopia. My daily rations came from two identical Asian shops in Namasagali. Both were dusty and seemed to be collapsing under the weight of what they tried to sell – huge bags of rice and flour, small bags of smelly spices, batteries, spare bicycle tyres, elderly dry biscuits, cotton, and rusty tinned peas. Ugandan boys toiled for their Asian employers in the back of the shops. In earlier imperial days the British had brought many mainly Indian workers to East Africa to build the railways and staff the civil service; later they diversified into more entrepreneurial activities. The locals regarded Asian shopkeepers as exploitative. Even in remote Namasagali there was evidence of the low-level racial friction that Idi Amin would soon trade on for post-coup popularity.

Parting, when it came, was sore indeed. Each day towards the end of my time in Namasagali, as I walked from my little house to the classroom beneath the mango trees, looking out to the wide river beyond, I would think, 'I shall never come here again. This is almost the last time I shall tread this path.' On the final Sunday afternoon, putt-putting in the battered old school boat with its flat corrugated-iron roof along the Nile with a line draped over the stern – heaving in the massive Nile perch, enough for lunch tomorrow – I felt the tears of impending departure welling. No more tomorrows, I thought. On my final night I pledged to my students that I would return, little thinking I ever really could or would. In the event, I was indeed to be in Uganda again within a few years, although I wasn't to make it back to Kamuli College for three more decades.

I wrote to my parents of my last day at Namasagali, having gathered with the school to sing 'Oh Uganda' one more time around the flagpole:

Transport at the best of times is virtually non-existent. One or two taxis from Kamuli had heard that it was the end of term. 320 students waiting for transport at 7 a.m. By 9 a.m. a ramshackle forty-eight-seater bus and three 1950ish Peugeot estate car taxis deigned to appear. The bus managed to accommodate about ninety-five students with their boxes. With some of the other students heaving and shoving and with more than a little persuasion, it began to move. Needless to say, the starting mechanism had long since ceased to function, and it seems that it is an accepted part of one's fare to get out and push. The taxis, boxes piled dangerously high on the roofs, had their doors finally forced shut by gangs of students.

78

Inside there were at least fifteen visible bodies, with doubtless more underneath. The remaining students began to surge down the murum road, each trying to overtake the other in order to be the first to meet the returning bus or taxi. In this fashion several must have reached Kamuli on foot. My own departure was embarrassingly luxurious inside Grimes's Volkswagen with all our bags, a Ugandan drum, a spear, and a mere seven people filling the five available seats.

I left Uganda determined that whatever path my career took would bring me back there. I had not yet concluded that it would be journalism that would provide the means.

Liverpool University in the autumn of 1968 was a strange disjunction of active, potentially angry students, and a deeply conservative institution. My unremarkable 'A' level results, a C, a D and an E, in English, law and economics, had not tempted any university to offer me a place, despite my having penned many flamboyant application letters postmarked 'Uganda'. In the end, a chance meeting on a train between my father and the Dean of Liverpool's law school clinched an underhand entry to do legal studies, and delivered me within a week to Merseyside. Maybe there is a God in heaven, I thought.

Liverpool was a stark and sudden contrast to the remote banks of the Nile. By the time it reached this northern industrial city, the Mersey was as wide as the Nile at Namasagali. However, even without the African blight of Bilharzia, it

79

was far less inviting. The university was very much part of the city. It sat high on Brownlow Hill, nudging Paddy's Wigwam, the Catholic cathedral, at one end of Hope Street and within sight of the vast Victorian Anglican pile at the other. Unusually for a British university, some two thirds of the students lived at home, and the place had something of a nine-to-five feel about it.

In October 1968 we were 'seizing the time'. It was an era of revolution on the streets of Paris and London, and within more limited Liverpool confines I soon turned to revolt. There was a core of extremely active students. In my first few weeks I began to discover that my small pre-Uganda ambition to become a Conservative Member of Parliament had given way to a much larger one, to change the world altogether. It was a bit of a shock.

I won election to the Executive of the Students' Union as First Year Representative. Politically, Liverpool was a sea of red that was well beyond the wilting rouge of Old Labour. There were almost as many acronyms as students – IMG (International Marxists), IS (International Socialists), SLL (Socialist Labour League) and more. There were anarchists, Trotskyites, Maoists, British Communists and International Communists. I had little idea what most of them really stood for, save that they were hard-line and inflexible, and sold papers like *Big Flame* and *Socialist Worker*. The university was awash with issues that fought daily pitched battles with the sheer fun of simply being there. Where else in a year could you see the Who, the Animals, Georgie Fame, George Harrison, the Supremes and the Stones live in concert? The enormous entertainment budget of the Students' Union, combined with the very name 'Liverpool', home of the Beatles, had terrific pulling power. The raves were all staged in the capacious Mountford Hall. And there, amid the detritus of the Who's guitars, smashed the night before, we would gather in political solidarity and protest – protest that ranged over a whole gamut of disparate causes.

One of the most energised campaigns was in support of Biafra in the Nigerian civil war – an attempt by the country's most oil-rich region to break away from Nigeria altogether. We backed Biafra with a passion, even after we saw images of the Biafran leader Colonel Ojukwu's ostentatious white grand piano being hoisted from the dockside onto the ship that was transporting his possessions to some safe haven out of the country. Idealism overcame everything. Vietnam was in the air, and our protests were generally more pro-North Vietnamese than hysterically anti-American, although large numbers of us marched on the US embassy in Grosvenor Square. To my shame, my own personal journey of revolt had not yet evolved far enough for me to make the effort to travel down to the London demonstration, although my brother Tom did. Indeed my cousin Peter, already working for ITN, held a shouted dialogue across the street with him on the evening news as he disappeared off with Tariq Ali's breakaway group in a bid to storm the embassy itself.

81

It was around this time that I had my own first brush with broadcasting. BBC Radio Merseyside wanted a regular weekly half-hour of student news, and I was deputed by the Students' Union to provide it. I would cycle off to a shabby office at the back of Lewis's department store to talk about the week's events. Somebody at the station had already written my scripts, and while I did tinker with them, to say anything very radical seemed unnecessarily risky, particularly as I knew no one who ever listened to my broadcasts. Thus they were epic in their dullness, and certainly left me with no sense of romance about the career I would one day pursue.

In amongst the politics I got on with my law course, thrilling to cases that defined negligence like Rylands v. Fletcher, over who was to blame when a reservoir flooded a neighbouring mine; or Donoghue v. Stevens, over what duty of care a drinks company owed an innocent drinker who found a snail in his ginger-beer bottle. I learned much of public international law and nothing at all of tort, or personal property. Every one of my fellow law students wanted to join the legal profession. I thought I didn't, but that I might drift into becoming a barrister anyway.

I passed my first-year exams with flying colours in June 1969, and left the next day for the most extraordinary adventure by road to India. It was to take every day of the long vacation until the end of September. We who were to travel had to raise the money ourselves. One of my fund-raising stunts had been an attempt to break the world record for sitting on a lavatory. My bid was staged on a platform in the front hall of the Students' Union. Twenty-five hours I sat on the thing, with my trousers round my ankles, only to discover that the prudes at the *Guinness Book of Records* would not accept it. In truth I was never able to establish that it was a record anyway, but certainly no one else seemed to be fool enough to claim it. I raised £1200 from sponsors including Armitage Shanks, who made the thing, revealing an unexpected sense of humour. In the final hour students were allowed to buy eggs for 20p each, and reduce me to a ripe old mess.

Our passage to India was courtesy of Comex – the Commonwealth Expedition. This was a mad escapade run by an eccentric who we knew simply as Colonel Gregory. Gregory's dream was for every university in the land to send a busload of students on a cultural exchange to India, and for as many Indian universities as possible to do so in reverse. It was a brilliant and idealistic way of attempting to give new life to an institution – the British Commonwealth – that already had an elderly, even patronising air of imperial legacy and UK dominance.

I was to be one of our two drivers, so I had to train for and pass my bus driver's licence in between demonstrations and exams. We twenty-five souls aboard had to decide what our cultural offering should amount to. We suspected that many in India, if they had heard of Liverpool at all, would have done so because of the Beatles, so we lit upon the idea of a four-part close-harmony Beatle band with guitar and drums. In addition to driving, I was to supply the bass harmonies. I was

83

spared involvement in Sheridan's eighteenth-century play *The Rivals*, which the rest of the crew proposed to stage.

Somehow the Colonel had cajoled the manufacturers Bedford to supply all the shortened single-decker buses on some kind of subsidised lease-lend basis. When we gathered in Ostend for the first leg of the overland dash for India there were more than two dozen cream Bedford Duples lined up, one each for twenty-five universities, sporting the green-and-gold Comex livery. They looked like an advertiser's dream. But it was the last time they would. If they returned at all from their ten-thousand-mile odyssey they would have more than lost their sheen.

Once we were under way, countries I'd never expected to visit in my life fell before us like ninepins: Belgium and Luxembourg went without a stop. My whole sense of political geography was changing. Our first night, and first concert, was at a castle above Stuttgart. I found a Germany very far from the one I'd heard my parents talk about in childhood. It felt more prosperous than home, and more energised.

'Hey Jude, don't be afraid...' The close harmony worked beautifully, and the castle walls rang to the applause of the locals who'd turned out to hear us. *The Rivals* went less well, its complicated plot lines hanging heavy on the German night air. We slept en masse in a gymnasium. I had never slept in the company of so many women. But for our hippy appearance, the expedition had all the hallmarks of a travelling British holiday camp.

Crossing into Yugoslavia from Austria, we tasted

the only Communist regime of our journey. Tito was everywhere, or rather his bespectacled image was. The country felt surprisingly mellow, and beyond the somewhat monotone look of the traffic, gave little sign of being very different to the rest of Western Europe. On the wide road running south from Zagreb to Belgrade all twenty-five buses stopped on the hard shoulder to remember the members of an earlier Comex expedition whose bus had crashed at this spot. Seven or eight of them had died, and many more had been injured. It introduced a sombre note to our continuous fast driving and youthful over-taking.

That first glimpse of Yugoslavia was to stand me in good stead later in life, when the ethnic tensions beneath the surface burst into frenzied hatred and killing. In Belgrade, Tito himself turned out in the stadium for our concert. Tough, burly, beaming a warm welcome, he was clearly and massively in charge. I didn't get near him, but I did catch sight of his foot tapping as I belted out the bass line to 'All You Need is Love'.

It wasn't until we reached eastern Turkey that the buses began to pay the price for their large expanses of glass and glinting chrome – too much of a temptation for the locals, who extracted stones from the decaying roadway and hurled them with great accuracy at our passing cavalcade. We lost our back two windows, Cambridge lost all their glass down one side, Aberdeen lost their windscreen and East Anglia most of their windows on both sides. Crossing into Iran, the convoy had taken on a billowing aspect, with curtains and possessions blowing out of assorted openings. Somehow, without the benefit of mobile phone or internet, Colonel Gregory had lined up replacement glass to await our arrival in Tehran.

With nine years to go until the Iranian revolution, this was the time of some of the Shah's most ostentatious consumption. Persepolis was littered with the paraphernalia of his attempt to mark the supposed millennium of his phoney dynasty. Everywhere were the signs of Westernisation and Americana. The Shah's Tehran was more than ready for the Beatles, even the somewhat inadequate line-up we had on offer, and we played to packed houses in the basketball stadium.

We left Iran along the coast of the Caspian Sea. Gazing up at the hills overlooking the water, I spotted the telltale giant white golf balls of the early-warning station that the US maintained here against Russian missile tests in the Urals. I knew what they were from having seen a similar installation at Fylingdales, in the heart of my father's Yorkshire diocese. In a magical kind of way I was laying the superficial building blocks that would assist me later to track the evolving new world disharmony. Yet as we voyaged on towards Afghanistan I still had no idea of becoming a journalist, or of ever retracing my steps here.

The western Afghan town of Herat slumbered in the late-afternoon heat. Old men sat on their white-robed haunches, sipping tea at the roadside. Their hennaed beards and brown features stood out against the tea stalls beyond. Camels and mules fought for street space with ancient bicycles and the occasional highly decorated, heavily overladen truck. The main roads were the best we encountered east of the Bosphorus, for Afghanistan was the archetypal buffer state. They were so straight that they were only marred by frequent head-on collisions induced by sleep and mesmerisation. The international power play here was tense indeed. The United States had built the road from the Iranian border to Kandahar, the Russians had built the rest most of the way to the bottom of the Khyber Pass.

By now our caravan of suburban British buses had broken up into much smaller convoys, having become separated by punctures and breakdowns. Although our own bus was the nexus of our travelling lives, some of us had forged relations with people on other buses. By now the Aberdeen bus held a special attraction for me. I had fallen into easy conversation with one of their crew, Liz, but it was almost impossible to keep track of her; her wretched vehicle rarely coincided with ours. But trying to find her, and then unexpectedly encountering her, provided an extra frisson to an already incredible journey.

Kabul was the capital of the hippy kingdom. There were Western dropouts and druggies everywhere, some in an awful state. Others had simply merged into the scenery. The city was a mellow and tolerant place. What it lacked in tension, though, it made up for in mystery. Whatever the warlords were up to, it certainly didn't seem to be war. Opium appeared to be present more in the consumption than in the trade. This was a buffer state that, while operating at a barely tolerable level of existence, seemed to work nevertheless. It was hard to see why anyone would want to change it. Yet we were less than a decade from the Russian invasion that would herald the beginning of the end of the Soviet empire, and would sow the seeds of the Taliban and eventually of al Qaida. Sitting round our campfire near the British embassy on our third night in town, smoking marijuana and most definitely inhaling, we thought all was well with the world.

The Khyber Pass, on the other hand, had a distinct presence of the old world disorder: bandits. 'Passage only between dawn and dusk: military escort mandatory' read the notice at the bottom of the pass. We decided to divide our buses into convoys of five, with military vehicles between each. It took so long for us to wind up through the Khyber that dusk had turned to absolute darkness for the last stretch. From time to time we would stop while scouts up on the escarpments looked out for bandits. We could hear the Pakistani army and the bandits calling to one another across the valley.

It had taken us five weeks to reach Pakistan, where we travelled past the bustling arms and drug dealers of Peshawar on to Rawalpindi and the seething streets of Lahore, ending up pony trekking for a day in the Murray Hills to the north of the country.

India arrived gradually, its approach reflected in the evolution of the bread through our journey – upright Hovis in Britain, giving way to lower, rounder breads in France, flatter still by Turkey and Iran, until we reached the *chapatti* and the *nan* in India. She was to prove an inspiring climax.

This was one of the last periods in the drift to disorder when such an overland trip could be undertaken relatively safely. Our first stop was the sumptuous, and in those days peaceful, Kashmir. Land of mountains, lakes and wildflowers, and to this day one of the most beautiful places to which I have ever been. Thence to Nanithal, an old British hill station possessed of the most spectacular view of Everest. Sikh waiters served us tea and cucumber sandwiches on the lawn of the Nanithal Rowing Club.

By the time we reached Delhi we were fêted as if we *were* the Beatles. A hundred thousand people packed the main city arena that night to hear us in concert with local Indian musicians. We were mobbed, our hair pulled, our ears deafened by the screaming.

Our final destination, however, was not the Indian capital, but the University of Benares. Benares, the Hindu burial centre of the Ganges, was teeming with people. The funeral pyres burnt brightly on the banks, the mourners cascading into the water, boats bearing yet more pyres. Bodies were carried head-high for incineration. Unfortunately, by the time we reached it the University of Benares had been closed by the police after riots on the campus. It was an odd anticlimax to so spectacular an adventure. Three weeks later we had raced back across Asia and Europe to return to Liverpool for the first day of my second year.

In our absence, man had walked on the moon, Vietnam had suffered another massacre, and Nelson Mandela had passed his sixth year in jail on Robben Island. We were angry, stirred by injustice, shaken by other people's wars. We could afford to be: there was full employment in Britain then, we didn't lie awake at night wondering how we would earn a crust when we left university. However, our anger was but a bit-part player in the larger anger that still raged across campuses from the London School of Economics to the Sorbonne in Paris.

In some senses, in the autumn of 1969 we were actively in search of *the* issue with which to confront the authorities at Liverpool. Students at Warwick University had discovered secret files kept on the politically active; doubtless the same thing was happening at Liverpool. Nasty Nixon still had some years to go before his defenestration from the White House, and Vietnam simmered on, but that did not involve either the British or university authorities. Indeed Prime Minister Harold Wilson had wisely, and somewhat courageously, refused active British involvement on the American side.

It was Peter Hain, subsequently a Labour Cabinet Minister, who finally identified our cause. Nixon's Secretary of State, Henry Kissinger, had spent the previous months preaching 'change through economic engagement' with the South African apartheid regime. Wilson and others had gone soft on economic sanctions, and the apartheid state was consolidating its hold amid calls from Nelson Mandela's beleaguered

African National Congress (ANC) cohorts to black South Africans to burn their passbooks. British culpability and collusion with apartheid were clear, but what was Liverpool's connection?

Even in those days, the presence of the great Tate & Lyle sugar empire on the Liverpool dockyards was unmissable. Liverpool was effectively Tate & Lyle's British capital. The university had sizeable investments, and a goodly portion found its way to investments in South Africa, where Tate was still big. Hey presto! We had our cause. 'Disinvest from South Africa' became our clarion cry. The only bank on campus, Barclays, with its notorious presence in South Africa, became a target too. The sheer size of my overdraft rendered me embarrassingly unable to withdraw my funds to join the protest, but join I did, with my Barclays chequebook festering in my back pocket.

Liverpool at the time suffered from a kind of staff/student apartheid which meant there was no provision for resolving such issues through dialogue. The students had no representation on any of the university administrative or governing bodies, which meant that before we could demand disinvestment, we had to demand access to power and representation within the university itself.

These were heady days, when students of every political complexion and none would gather to plot and manoeuvre. One of the most active staff members was Robert Kilroy-Silk, a junior lecturer in the Politics Department, one day to become a Labour MP, later to host the BBC TV daytime sofa show *Kilroy*, later still to be sidelined from it for making allegedly racist comments about Arabs, and still later to rise again as an anti-Europe Member of the European Parliament. But in those days no one was more enthusiastic in his support of the students; no member of staff talked more earnestly of delivering revolution in their ranks. Kilroy was a rabid revolutionary.

In November 1969 Peter Hain, himself South African by birth, came north with his 'Stop the Seventy Tour' campaign. The South African Springboks rugby team were already in Britain, while a cricket tour was to take place in the summer. Hain's ultimately hugely successful campaign recognised that sport was very close to the heart of the apartheid regime. It was the public, competitive and white face of South Africa. We might not be able to spring Mandela from Robben Island, but we could at least stop his jailers from playing sport in our green and pleasant land. Hain's target was the Springboks' match at Old Trafford in Manchester.

'Come on, Jon, we need you over there today.' The call came from Dave Robertson, the Prince of Darkness, eternally turned out in black. He was the most articulate student operative on the left, the leader of the university Socialist Society, well to the left of anything I could have subscribed to. Nevertheless, I was flattered that he wanted me along for the ride to Manchester. Dave is now Professor of Politics at John Moore's University in Liverpool, but in those days he regarded me as 'a bloody public-school pinko liberal'. Several hundred of us hit the East Lancs highway bound for Old Trafford. Our job was to try to prevent that afternoon's match from taking place at all. I noticed some of our number carried less than discreet spades with them.

Old Trafford was set for war. There were police and demonstrators everywhere. Hain stood on a flatbed truck outside the ground together with other luminaries urging a peaceful protest. The men with the spades were already worming their way into the ground. It didn't take long for things to turn nasty. The police started trying to corral us into sectors further away from the gates, so that spectators could get in. The idea that someone had taken the decision to come and watch the match delineated them for us as out-and-out racists and supporters of apartheid, which in a discreet kind of a way I guess they were. Fights broke out. The police charged, and I felt a knee thrust hard into my groin. I thrust back, and within seconds I was pinned to the ground by three Mancunian cops and carted off in a paddy wagon to Old Trafford police station. 'Jonathan George Snow, you have been arrested and charged with assaulting a police officer.'

'Damn me,' I thought, 'that's my law career up the spout. No more barristering for me. Is this a criminal record I see before me?'

'Have you anything to say?'

'Not guilty, sir!'

It was six in the evening when I was taken down to the cells. The police wanted £10 bail for me, and I had no money to get back to Liverpool. I counted eleven others in my cell, and one bucket in the corner. There must have been ten cells, which meant maybe over a hundred arrested in this police station alone. Despite our numbers, I felt daunted by the charge hanging over me, and by the thought of what my father and the university authorities would say.

My turn for the solitary pay phone came at 4.30 a.m., by which time, having spent the night slumped on a concrete floor, I was in far from the best of spirits. In those days I lived in a flat on Liverpool's Mount Street next door to the poet Adrian Henri, a sweet place opposite the old College of Art where John Lennon had studied. My flatmate Simon Polito was a charming but completely apolitical character. He proved utterly dependable in a storm, however. He leapt out of bed in response to my plaintive call, summoned legal assistance in the inebriated student form of John Aspinall, later a judge, and hurtled down the East Lancs in his VW to our assistance. Simon fixed the bail and was not in the least judgemental, and John set to with how we would run the defence. I was remanded to appear before a stipendiary magistrate in a week's time.

The Liverpool law faculty had the decency to accept the basic tenet of English law, 'innocent until proved guilty'. My father hadn't found out. So for the moment I was in the clear, but it was a serious charge, and if found guilty I knew everything would change.

I decided to defend myself, and to go for the old chestnut of appealing to the magistrate's sense of social justice. In other words, to leave him in no doubt that we were of the same social class. I appeared with my shoulder-length hair neatly kempt, and my body in a suit borrowed from Simon, who fortunately was as tall as me.

PC Wilson was a small man for a policeman, perhaps five foot eight. I was six foot four.

'Officer, is it possible that your knee came into contact with my groin?' I asked straight off.

I had thought he would deny it, but no. 'Yes, sir, quite possible, in the act of perambulation, on the move, quite possible,' he said.

'Officer, could you please walk between the witness box and the dock?'

For a moment it looked as if the magistrate might refuse my request, but PC Wilson walked.

'Officer,' I asked, 'I wonder if we could estimate the height to which your knee rises in this act of perambulation?'

'Two foot I should say, sir.'

I addressed the magistrate. 'I think the court should know that my inside leg measures thirty-six inches. For twenty-four inches to collide with thirty-six inches would require a deliberate upward thrust. I would submit that it was I who was assaulted.'

I felt a pang of remorse for PC Wilson as the magistrate intoned, 'Case dismissed. You may leave the court.' I knew that if I'd been a working-class lad he'd have got me – after all, I most certainly had booted PC Wilson back. My legal career survived another day, but not for many more.

The university had been carrying on regardless in the meantime, refusing to discuss anything with its revolting students. The authorities were more concerned with the opening of the new Senate Block, an administrative preserve reserved for themselves. Princess Alexandra had been tapped to come and do the opening. Fired with renewed zeal by the Hain campaign, we had turned our attention to this event and to the impending arrival of the university Chancellor to officiate.

Robert Gascoyne-Cecil, fifth Marquess of Salisbury, had been Chancellor of Liverpool University since 1951. He was no friend to South Africa's black majority, and perhaps too much of a friend to Ian Smith's illegal seizure of power on behalf of the white minority in neighbouring Rhodesia. His speeches in the House of Lords were positively inflammatory. As the date for the Senate Block opening approached, hundreds of students gathered on a daily basis in Mountford Hall. The campus was alive with debate. Several thousand students marched to protest against the Chancellor continuing in office, particularly given that there were now some forty students from southern Africa on the university roll. Still the university refused to entertain even a meeting with the elected student body. So it was proposed that one of us be deputed to go to Lord Salisbury and tell him that his presence on campus could cause serious trouble during Princess Alexandra's visit. We also wrote to her to request a meeting when she came.

'You'd be the best to do it, Jon,' opined Richard Davies, who as President of the Students' Union might have been expected to talk to Salisbury. 'He'll understand you better, with yer public-school accent. Anyway, yer dad's a Bishop, that'll appeal to him.'

So it was that on the afternoon before the opening I found myself standing on a platform at Lime Street station in the best clothes I could muster, awaiting the London train. The Marquess stumbled out of his first-class carriage with a straggling retinue.

'My Lord,' I said, 'may I have a word?'

He was charm itself. 'Now, young man, who are you?'

Where now the rabid racist? In his place I had found a stooped old aristocrat. Could I bring myself to do it? It all came blurting out in one run: 'My Lord, my name is Jon Snow, and I've come to tell you on behalf of the Students' Union that if you venture onto the campus, your presence could ignite a riot.'

'Now,' he said, 'why don't you come and take tea with me at my hotel, and we can talk about it.' So the Marquess, his travelling staff and the long-haired boy from the Students' Union made their way in a curious-looking crocodile to the neighbouring Adelphi Hotel. There amongst the marble pillars we were served Earl Grey tea and cucumber sandwiches. We talked for what seemed like an age. I was afraid one of the other members of the student executive might be lurking somewhere, and would spot me so conspicuously supping with the devil.

'Very well,' said Lord Salisbury at the end of it all. 'I shall not come to the university. Indeed, I shall never come here again. I shall resign. I tell you frankly, Mr Snow, I've never much liked coming to Liverpool anyway. It's an awfully long way from home. I am relieved to think that when I board the London train in a few minutes' time, I shall never have to do it again.' And with that he and his retinue paid the bill and departed.

I walked back up Brownlow Hill towards the university, both depressed and elated. Depressed that I'd abused my roots, and been rude to one of those I'd been brought up to believe were my elders and betters. Elated because I'd scored a hole in one. Not just sent him home, but persuaded the old rogue to resign altogether – although I couldn't pretend it had been hard. Here writ large were the conflicting loyalties of my old and new worlds.

The university authorities were enraged. They only heard that the Chancellor had resigned through us. They knew it had been our doing. They had lost the one nob the place had been able to sport for all these years, and they felt reduced by his going. Thousands turned out to demonstrate when Princess Alexandra came the next day. She was grace incarnate, waving regally and smiling. We thought none the worse of her. We knew we had messed the entire event up already.

The Vice Chancellor continued to refuse to speak to us, the Registrar likewise. These days we'd probably discover that they were of the finest, but then they had fangs. 'Loathsome apartheid supporters', 'anti-democrats', 'fascists' – there was no limit to the abuse we were prepared to heap upon them. They in turn had marked us down. They would get their revenge soon enough. But now we were on a roll. Having got rid of the Chancellor, we prepared to force the rest of our demands upon the Vice Chancellor and his cohorts. 'Representation on university bodies', 'no secret files', 'a say in who the next Chancellor will be', and, more important than anything, 'disinvestment of all the university's holdings in South Africa' – and of course 'no victimisation of those who had pressed for these changes'.

The demands were carried over to the Vice Chancellor's office in the new Senate Block the day after Princess Alexandra had opened the building. They were dispatched by a mass meeting attended by more than two thousand students. The emissary returned, having been refused entry. I got up on the stage and bellowed, 'Occupy!' We all streamed out across the quad and stormed into the Senate building. The staff within were terrified, and fled. Suddenly, against all expectation and with no planning, we found ourselves in possession of the seat of the university's power. Fifteen hundred students had begun what in those days was termed a 'sit-in'.

The sense outside was that dangerous revolutionaries had seized the place. This was only exacerbated by the action of some of the more committed leftists in raising a red flag on the pole on the roof of the building. The truth below was more complex. The vast majority of the students had never been involved in direct action before. The formally ideological represented less than a hundred of our number.

'What the hell do we do now?' I asked the

President of the Union, Richard Davies.

'Keep meeting, keep talking, and organise,' he replied. So while he summoned the first of many mass meetings in the sumptuous new Senate meeting room, I set about organising the practicalities. The logistical problems were massive, from food to lavatories. Apart from anything else, we had to raise funds fast. Students came up with what cash they could, and the Liverpool Trades Union Council sent in more. Food runs were organised. Others started to devise an 'alternative university' that would run in parallel with our proper studies. The far left did their best to hijack the proceedings, but while Tariq Ali and Robin Blackburn from the LSE came up to lecture, there were simply too many occupiers for any single sect to prevail.

The occupation lasted several weeks. The numbers gradually dwindled to under a thousand, still sizeable in a university which in those days held seven thousand students. Negotiations with the authorities were sparse and unproductive. In the end the approaching Easter holidays called a halt to our small revolution. I was determined that we should leave the building exactly as we had found it, as to do so would rob the authorities of a propaganda coup that we had in some way defiled the place. An epic clean-up lasting two days and a night preceded our exit. In the end, a single cracked lavatory window was all the damage the authorities could find. As we filed out, we were all filmed and photographed.

Three days later ten of us, mostly elected officers of the Students' Union, were charged by the authorities with bringing the university into disrepute. Of Robert Kilroy-Silk, so voluble at the start, there was no sign. In the middle of the holidays a kangaroo court of seven professorial staff was summoned to 'try' us. Naturally there was no legal representation for any of us. The university's case was prepared and prosecuted by a local QC named Stannard. We looked in vain for anyone who would defend us, scouring the empty campus for witnesses, not least for Kilroy, but alas he must already have been 'tanning up' for his TV career.

Pete Creswell, a committed member of the Socialist Society, drew a water-pistol during the proceedings, and at least had the pleasure of seeing the kangaroos dive for cover. All ten of us were naturally found guilty of the charge of 'bringing the good name of the university into disrepute'. Creswell and an anarchist called Ian Williams were expelled, the rest of us were rusti-cated, or sent down, for one year or two. In my case it was for a year, on the grounds that my tireless efforts to sustain the fabric of the Senate building counted in my favour. The whole charade was so blatant a denial of natural justice, and the expulsion so large even in those rebellious days, that the national press picked up on it. Even the *Telegraph* led its front page with it.

Buoyed up, we decided to appeal. Suddenly the offers of legal help came forth. John Griffith, the celebrated Professor of Law at the LSE, came up at his own expense and slept on one of our floors. E. Rex Makin, a controversial local solicitor, nick-named 'Sexy Rexy', offered his help to me. Even

101

my dear father unexpectedly weighed in, writing a top-of-column letter to *The Times*, signed 'Bishop of Whitby'. It was somewhat undermined by his omission of the detail that he was the father of one of the students. Despite apparently sharing no common ground with any of our demands, he remained steadfastly supportive.

On the day of the appeal, the local unions called a one-day strike and demonstration on our behalf at the pier head. It had been called for 3 p.m., which we thought would be safely after the appeals had ended, so that we could join the protest. But Professor Griffith and Sexy Rexy entered so spirited a defence that it was five to three by the time the last four of us had presented our appeals.

'Never mind,' said Makin, 'I'll get you to the pier head. My car's round the back here.'

We had not bargained for a gold Rolls-Royce. 'We can't possibly travel in that load of capitalist trash,' said Ian Williams. 'I'm walking.'

'You'll miss the whole thing,' I said. 'It's a demo in aid of the Liverpool Ten. We can't leave them with just six of us.'

So we all piled in. As we neared the demonstration, the projectiles began to hit the Roller. Poor old Rexy: no fee, and damaged bodywork to boot.

The next day I left Liverpool with a very heavy heart. I did not know it then, but I was never to return to the university. My vast ambition, built on slender academic achievement, to secure a degree, and choices, and eventual return to Uganda, had crashed. I wasn't even a member of any political party. I had no ideology that might provide answers to what I perceived to be the unjust and archaic actions of a supposedly liberal seat of learning.

Things couldn't have looked worse. I felt that what I had done had come from my heart, had sprung from the African bush, from an innate sense of justice. At just twenty-two years old I felt very wronged, and very broken.

THREE

Of Drugs and Spooks

I did not see him at first, it was so dark. The seventh Earl of Longford sat in one of the little cubicles that lined the walls of the New Horizon Youth Centre in London's Soho. It was early May 1970, in a dingy room in which it was impossible to tell the staff from the young drug addicts who had dropped by. But even in a room full of odd people, Frank Longford stood out, with his erect rim of wiry hair around his famously bald, bright, but eccentric head.

Recovering from the ashes of my enforced Liverpool departure, I had sought another overseas volunteering experience, but no one would have me because of my student past. So I set about trying to do something like VSO inside Britain. I had heard through the grapevine that Lord Longford was looking for a new director for his drop-in centre for homeless teenagers in London's West End. The previous incumbent had suffered a nervous breakdown. His main qualification for the job, in Longford's eyes, seemed to have been that he had been thrown out of Hornsey College of Art following a riot. Longford had intended to run the centre himself following his resignation from Harold Wilson's Cabinet over the government's failure to raise the school leaving age to sixteen in 1967, but unfortunately his combination of age and eccentricity had rendered him the daily victim of robbery and battery at the hands of those he sought to aid.

'Lord Longford,' I said, 'it's me. I'm here about the job.'

'Ah, yes,' he said. 'I think your father must have taught me at Eton.' Even in this godforsaken place the old class connection chimed.

'Yes, that's probably true,' I said half-heartedly. Here was I, I teased myself, gone to the very barricades for the black majority in South Africa, and yet still apparently trying to secure a job in the scruffiest of day centres simply by dint of birth.

But it was as if old Longford could read my mind. 'Don't worry,' he said, 'I'm going to hire you anyway. Your predecessor was a success, so I'm going to appoint you. Your expulsion alone ensures you'll be a success here. You'll just have to see a couple of other members of the management committee first.' It was agreed that I would return in a week to meet them. I was off the scrapheap.

The two men were waiting in a nearby Soho coffee bar. Both wore trilby hats, large greatcoats and suede shoes. Sir Matthew Slattery, tall and bespectacled, was chairman of BOAC, forerunner of British Airways. He was rather direct, and I was afraid he'd find me wanting, but I survived his scrutiny. He clearly saw my expulsion from Liverpool as very much a disqualification, only ameliorated by my social class, which was probably the same as his.

He clearly didn't like my politics, and neither did the other man. Slattery didn't introduce his colleague, who seemed vaguely familiar, seriously dapper and precise. He proved to be John Profumo, the disgraced ex-Minister for War, now working out his redemption at a settlement in London's East End. 'Hello, Jon,' said Profumo. 'Do call me Jack.'

I felt an immediate affinity with him, for I too intended to purge my sins and work my redemptive passage. It was only seven years since Profumo's fall, but he manifested such humility, and yet such confidence. He was a considerable contrast from the wretched wreck that I had presumed a man who had suffered such public humiliation would have become. Lying to the House of Commons about an affair with a woman who had slept with a Russian spy may have shocked the nation, but it had also resulted in Profumo's coming to work for New Horizon. And work he did, ceaselessly, to get the funding and profile that the centre needed to survive. But the British Establishment had been so bruised, and was so far up its own class-consciousness, that to this day it has remained incapable of recognising the far more important role that he now occupied. Profumo seemed almost to have walked out of my 'A' level English text, Bernard Shaw's *Major Barbara*. Like the fictional arms dealer Andrew Undershaft before him, John Profumo, Minister for War, had determined to move from armaments to working with the poor.

Domestic Britain was still in transition from the unquestioning post-war, post-imperial order to something more multicultural, more egalitarian.

Slattery, Profumo, even Longford were all of the old order. The new was still formulating. It was going to be a struggle, and New Horizon wouldn't be a bad place from which to observe it. 'What I was to see was the harshest evidence of the consequences of upheaval and neglect.

The steps down to the underground station at Piccadilly Circus were wet, and stank of urine. Bodies slumped on the lower steps. The cubicles in the lavatories were littered with discarded needles. Blood was spattered on the dirty white wall-tiles. This was the epicentre of Britain's burgeoning heroin crisis, a stone's throw from St Anne's church in Soho, where New Horizon occupied the ground floor. We were open to anyone under twenty-one.

Hard drugs played a role in most of the problems we dealt with. The NHS drug clinics had just started dishing out legal heroin in an attempt to see off the Chinese Triad gangs that were taking hold around London's West End. The black market was rife, and we caught glimpses of it all the time in the day centre. Fifteen-year-olds would come in having injected Ajax scouring powder that had been sold as heroin. Teenagers already dependent upon the drug were cranking up barbiturates intravenously to blunt their withdrawal symptoms. The casualties were on a huge scale, too many for us to deal with. There was also nowhere for us to house them. What hostels there were wouldn't take anyone with a drug record, and without improving their living circumstances there wasn't much we could do about their habits.

In the first year Longford, Slattery and Profumo managed to raise enough money to expand and move the centre to Covent Garden. A caretaker's flat went with the place, and I was unwise enough to move into it. From the three staff I'd inherited, we grew to fifteen. We opened a hostel of our own in north London, together with an emergency night shelter.

In some senses I felt I was reconnecting with something that had lain beneath the surface of my time in Uganda: the consequence of great poverty. Forty per cent of the kids at New Horizon came from local authority care schemes. The word 'care' was a pretty gross misnomer. Many had passed through a dozen or more foster homes or institutions; almost none of them had any educational qualifications. The state had nurtured them for the refuse tip, or at least for jail, where I spent increasing amounts of time visiting our clients. Many of the other young people we saw had come from abusive or broken homes.

It was through working at the centre that I met Madeleine Colvin. She came in one afternoon, a stunning curly-haired lawyer in a summer dress who abandoned her white Fiat 500 at the door. She would come once a week to give voluntary legal advice. We started going out almost immediately, but it would be years before we settled into any kind of partnership.

Living 'above the shop' in the caretaker's flat became increasingly problematic. I well remember escaping with Madeleine one night, and driving off to a party in Oxford. At the party there was a particularly seductive-looking strawberry flan, and we all devoured it. Not long after, I began to feel queasy. Driving home along the M40 with five of us in my Mini, I began to hallucinate that the car was too big to fit beneath the bridges. The white lines became aggressive. Someone had spiked the flan with acid. I was tripping out. Only one of the five of us in the car had not eaten of the flan, and she took over and drove us home. Once Madeleine and I were back in the flat, the acid trip crowded in on us and we swigged orange juice to try to assuage it. But every time the Jacques Loussier disc on the record player stopped, we tripped out again. I supposed I had become party to the so-called 'drugs revolution'. The next morning I staggered down to the day centre and blearily took up my usual position with the register at the door. The room swam before my eyes as familiar figures swayed into view. Had I joined them? Was this the beginning of my end? It took me a few days to recover, and while the experience did not put me off cannabis, it made me very wary of anything stronger.

In a world with no experts, I soon became a 'drug expert'. I was even invited to appear on a television programme called *The Frost Debate* which involved David Frost debating the big issues of the day. On this occasion drugs were the issue, and I remember a heated argument with the great man. It was the first time I had ever appeared on television.

Some of the young people at New Horizon were virtually beyond hope. Jimmy King was just sixteen. He'd so mashed his veins that one day I found him unconscious on the loo, having been trying to fix barbiturates into the veins of his penis. Others had suffered gangrene and amputations. It was hell. But from it emerged Chris Pizzey, who gave me hope that it was all worthwhile. He was almost as far gone as Jimmy, but he had one glorious talent: he was an artist of considerable ability, a brilliant cartoonist. 'I have no sense of who my parents were,' he told me. 'I was in homes and fostered, and then I hit sixteen and no one would have me any more.'

I agreed to give him a home on the floor of my flat. There were many moments of failure, even a spell on remand in the secure young offenders' prison in Ashford. But after more than a year, Chris made it. We at the centre housed him and trained him; but perhaps more critically than anything, he fell in love. He never relapsed.

Kevin was another engaging boy, with tousled blond hair. My chequebook was too much temptation. He stole it with my bank cards, and ran up bills of thousands of pounds. He left my flat for jail.

As soon as one went, another would come calling. Graham was a drug-free male prostitute of sixteen, who looked about twelve. He sat on the chair in my office telling me, in floods of tears, of the abuse he suffered on the streets. He named MPs, a minister and a priest as being among his clients. I had no reason to doubt him, he identified them so clearly.

And then there were the young women. Jan was a regular, sixteen years old, addicted to heroin and barbiturates, and pregnant. The state could not cope with her, and she went to Holloway prison for a stretch. Then she came back to us. We got her housed in Hackney, but neither the council nor we could provide the support she desperately needed. She would come by the flat late at night, throwing milk bottles at the wall to get my attention. Eventually she was admitted to University College Hospital for the birth. I went to visit her, and for the first time in my knowledge of her young life she looked radiant, with the baby, who was miraculously unaddicted, in her arms.

But within a day or two my telephone rang at two in the morning. 'Ishhatt you, Jon?' The slurred voice was unmistakably Jan's.

'Where are you? Where's the baby?' I asked urgently. There was no answer. I ran down to my Mini and headed for Hackney. I had never been to the flat where she lived, but we kept her rent book, which had the address. I found the place in twenty minutes. It was in a tall block, the stairway stinking of urine. There was a human form slumped on the second-floor stairs. I could hear the baby crying when I was three floors below Jan's flat. I peered through the letterbox. No Jan, just the baby crying. I took a run at the door, and the lock gave. Inside, the baby was filthy, so I washed him. There was a tin of powdered milk, and I mixed a bit up with water. I think it was milk, anyway – I was pretty vague about what to do with babies. I fed him chaotically and

111

swaddled him in a blanket, then ran with him to the car, reflecting that I was now, almost certainly, officially a baby snatcher.

Wondering 'What the hell do I do now?', I headed for the only place I'd seen the baby really cared for, the UCH maternity ward where he had come into the world in the first place. Arriving at the night nurse's table, I pleaded for help.

'Sorry, but there really is only one way babies come in here,' she smiled, 'and I'm afraid this isn't it.'

'Where do I go, then?' I asked.

'Well, where did you find him?'

'Hackney.'

'Phone the emergency service for social services.'

So I did.

'Sorry,' said the voice. 'If the baby's no longer in Hackney, it's not our responsibility. If you're at UCH, you're in Camden. You'll have to phone them.'

By the time the emergency social worker in Camden finally agreed to meet me, it was six in the morning and the baby was in distress. I wondered what would become of him. Would he too go into care and grow up like his mother? Poor little mite – how badly we were serving him.

Jan was found dead of barbiturate poisoning three days later in a filthy squat in King's Cross. There were only two of us at her pauper's burial at the East Finchley cemetery, and I never discovered who the other person was. I cried as the scratched recording of 'Jerusalem' echoed in the empty chapel. I wasn't cut out for this, I reflected.

112

As I sat there, I felt that at least I'd had the privilege of meeting and knowing people at the far edge. I determined that if I did nothing else in life, I would try to keep my lifeline with New Horizon open for as long as I possibly could.

In retrospect, this was a critical moment in the evolving welfare state. The state was clumsily finding out that there were areas in which it was incapable of offering caring resource. The voluntary sector, places like New Horizon, was better at it. In the long run the state would start to provide us with significant funding to do the job ourselves. But that would take several decades. In the meantime our day centre was a very hard place to be.

However bad things got at New Horizon, the presence of Lord Longford guaranteed that there would always be bouts of light relief. From the beginning, he and I would have lunch about once a month. We were to go on doing so until he died at the age of ninety-five three decades later. Ostensibly the purpose of these lunches was to talk about New Horizon, but in reality we gossiped about current politics and about history. Though Longford was ribbed mercilessly in the media for his eccentricities, I learned a vast amount from him – about the rise of fascism in the thirties, about Ireland, about the war, about Catholicism, about the British Establishment and, more than anything, about politics and government. Here was a man who'd served as Minister for Germany under Clement Attlee in the 1940s, and Leader of the House of Lords in Harold Wilson's Cabinet in the 1960s. There was almost no one in public life he did not know. He was determined that I would go into politics.

Longford was also, perhaps inevitably, the inadvertent author of a cascade of bizarre events. One Sunday in the spring of 1972, Bobby Moore, the captain of England's winning 1966 World Cup football team, for some reason offered us a fund-raising charity match at West Ham's ground, Upton Park in East London. His team was going to play a celebrity side that included some Playboy bunny girls.

'Lord Longford,' I ventured, 'I don't think you should play.'

'Why ever not?' he retorted. 'I was pretty good at Oxford.'

'It isn't a question of how good you were, nor even the fact that you are in your mid-sixties. It's the fact that you are running an anti-pornography crusade, and the Playboy bunny girls are playing.'

'Oh dear,' he said, rather crestfallen.

Frank Longford was really pretty broad-minded, despite his reputation, and seemed to me to have been hijacked by some early neo-conservatives. He was insistent that he should attend the game, so on the day I picked him up from Charing Cross station and headed for Upton Park. Halfway there, Longford rolled up his trousers to reveal the hem of some elderly cream football knickerbockers.

'Oh my God! You *are* going to play!' I exclaimed.

'I may,' he said, somewhat sheepishly.

'Well,' I thought, 'he's a grown man, I've

warned him about both his age and the girls. What more can I do?'

At the ground, my worst fears were rapidly realised. The cotton-tailed bunnies did what they do, and 'Lord Porn', as he was by then tagged, was in their midst. The press had a field day. I don't remember much about who won, or indeed how much money we raised. But I can still see those blue-white legs adorned in half-mast grey socks, protruding from the cream 1920s football shorts flanked by bunny bottoms.

One day I was sitting in the day centre when the phone rang. 'Mr Snow?' asked a posh voice on the end of the line.

'Yes.'

'This is Squadron Leader David Checketts, Equerry to the Prince of Wales. His Royal Highness would like to invite you to meet him at Buckingham Palace. Would this be possible?'

Although bemused and instinctively suspicious of anything to do with the royal family, I was intrigued, and agreed. It is one of the strange and inexplicable things about evolving Britain that the royal family still has such pull.

At the appointed time, wearing rare jacket and tie, I set off down the Mall on my pushbike, my usual means of transport, then as now. Ushered through the great iron gates on the right-hand side of Buckingham Palace, I did as I was instructed and leant the bike against the end of the palace. The red-carpeted entrance was surprisingly dowdy and run-down. I was escorted upstairs to what I think was called the White

115

Morning Room. It was certainly white, and sun came pouring in through the windows. There were two others waiting to see Prince Charles with me; they too seemed to work in what we called the voluntary sector. A ludicrous butler wafted in with a silver salver of biscuits, tea and coffee. Suddenly the Squadron Leader arrived with his master. We all stood up. 'Good morning, sir,' was the order of the day, despite the fact that the Prince was virtually the same age as me. He was stiff, and even then fiddled with his index finger and the links on his cuffs. When he talked, he sounded like a forty-five-year-old.

'I need your advice,' he said. 'I want to do something productive with my life, and I gather that you three are engaged in the kind of projects I think might make a difference.' He'd been well briefed, and seemed to have an understanding of urban poverty. He'd obviously visited a number of projects. I suppose we were with him for a couple of hours. He was interested in setting up a foundation that would fund projects and people working in the poorer echelons of society. Prince Charles now says that that meeting was the moment of inception for the Prince's Trust, which to this day is one of the biggest and most successful welfare funding movements ever established in Britain. All this was long before Diana, scandal and absurdity.

For more than a year, one of the most regular visitors to New Horizon was nineteen-year-old Christine. Beautiful, with long straight blonde hair, she was partially sighted and very slightly built. She was intelligent, but had serious communication problems, and it required much patience to win her trust. I was one of the few people she did appear to want to talk to. As so often, she had come from a broken family and had experienced abuse in care. She suffered in many ways, but never took drugs. Even so, she was hard to accommodate and impossible to gain employment for.

One night the police called at my flat. Would I come up to St Pancras? The officers were worried about reports from a squat not far from the back of the station. The place could barely have been termed a house. The windows were missing, much of the roof had fallen in, but there were sheltered spaces within. The detritus and filth between what passed for the door and these spaces was unspeakable. In the gloom, there she was, a hunched pile covered in a coat and an old blanket. I burst into tears. Christine had died utterly alone, unloved and in complete animal squalor. I had known her for 10 per cent of her entire life. The policewoman with us led me out. We all felt completely defeated.

I had originally intended to stay at New Horizon for six months and then, having only been rusticated for a year, to return to Liverpool to complete my degree. I eventually stayed three years, and have no degree to this day. I was so frustrated by Christine's pointless death that I wrote a piece for the *Guardian*. 'Christine is Dead' was published on 8 June 1973, and it was my first piece of proper journalism. I was emotionally drained, exhausted, and most definitely better at writing about the work than doing it. This traumatic insight into the country in which I had grown up transformed my outlook on life, as Uganda had before. But I had to move on.

There were builders everywhere, carpenters putting up partitions, electricians laying cables. It was hard to find where my interview was supposed to take place. I was standing in the bowels of the building in Gough Square, off Fleet Street, where Britain's first commercial radio station, the London Broadcasting Company (LBC), was to start broadcasting in eight weeks' time. It's an incredible thought these days, but as late as 1973 there was no legal radio alternative to the BBC. Radio Luxembourg had beamed in from across the Channel for years, and there were a number of illicit 'pirate' stations like Radio Caroline with seasick operatives broadcasting from outside territorial waters, but otherwise there was only the Beeb. A year earlier, Prime Minister Ted Heath finally changed the law, breaking the BBC's monopoly and allowing the development of commercial radio. Now the race was on between LBC and Capital Radio as to who would be on air first. LBC was looking for a hundred or more journalists to run a twenty-four-hour news station.

I suspect that I secured an interview purely on the basis that Peter Snow, by now established as a correspondent at ITN, was my cousin. They were also looking for someone who had some sort of handle on social issues. Rather riskily, LBC was going to pioneer late-night 'phone-ins'.

Experience in America had revealed that a lot of people with serious problems phoned in, and any responsible programme would have to have someone available to deal with them. In the event I seemed to fit the bill, and was hired for a salary of £2650, double what I had been earning at New Horizon. Better still, I was veering towards a career in journalism. Maybe this would prove to be the route back to Uganda.

Two days before we went on air, the station had failed to appoint any newsreaders. Given that there was to be a news bulletin every half-hour, twenty-four hours a day, seven days a week, this was a bit of an omission. The managers had a problem. Very few people from the BBC had applied to work at LBC. Most BBC staff seemed to think that our commercial venture would be short-lived, and they preferred the safety of where they were. Hence a good number of Canadian and Australian voices had been hired, but very few Brits. The existing employees were all summoned for voice trials, and somehow I got the job. The welfare back-up for the phone-ins was abandoned, and I was scheduled to make my first broadcast on the first day of transmission.

Six a.m. on 8 October 1973 was an electric moment. The station hit the air running. At 10 a.m., with embarrassingly upper-class vowels, I delivered the news. 'Israeli tanks are heading for the Golan Heights...' We had come on air at a real instant of history, amid the Yom Kippur war, the last Middle East war in which it was possible to imagine that Israel's very existence was at stake.

The whole style of LBC was fresh, the journalism was keen, and we were constantly running rings round staid old Aunty. But it couldn't last, and within a few months of opening the station ran out of money. Advertisers were cautious about whether commercial radio would ever catch on. People had to be sacked, and the management went for the most expensive first. I survived, but the new editor Marshall Stewart, who'd been poached after successfully reinvigorating the BBC's *Today* programme, called me into his office. 'You can go on reading the news until you drop,' he said, 'but if you want to make a difference in life, you've got to get out onto the road.'

The road in 1974 was becoming increasingly cratered. The IRA had already started its bombing campaign on mainland Britain, and for what was almost my first reporting adventure I was sent to Northern Ireland. I arrived in Catholic West Belfast on 17 May 1974, during the Protestant workers' strike that was to bring the attempt to allow Northern Ireland to govern itself to an end. I was stunned by what I saw. I had had absolutely no prior sense of the scale of the deprivation and discrimination suffered by the Catholic population. But the poverty proved undiscriminating: the squalor and sense of hopelessness on the Catholic Falls Road were matched on the working-class Protestant streets around the Shankill Road. I'd never seen so many Union flags. Those who wished to remain British had a sense of Queen and country that I couldn't even begin to identify with. 'Pig' armoured cars careered around the streets, and groups of British squaddies patrolled with automatic rifles at the ready.

As the strike ended on 29 May, I remember standing outside the Harland & Wolff shipyard watching the exclusively Protestant workforce returning to their jobs. Not only had they destroyed a courageous attempt to share governing power between the two religions, but they passed through the factory gates as if nothing in their lives would ever have to change to accommodate the 40 per cent of the population who were not of their faith and not of their workforce. I could not believe that my own country had sustained and encouraged such a grossly unjust state of affairs.

I had always used a bicycle in London, and now my reporting life began to depend upon one. There were no mobile phones in those days, but we had clunky Motorola radios, which within five miles of the office could transmit a just-about viable signal. So when on 17 June 1974 an IRA bomb went off in the confines of the Houses of Parliament, while other reporters were clogged in the back-up of traffic caused by the emergency I was able to hurtle through on my bike, sometimes broadcasting as I pedalled. I could dash under the police tapes that closed off roads, and be in mid-broadcast by the time the police caught up with me. This meant that throughout this year of mainland bombings LBC was almost invariably first on the scene, and developed a kind of 'must-listen' quality that radio in the UK had never enjoyed before. The bomb in question had gone off against the thousand-year-old wall of Westminster Hall – you can see the scorch marks to this day; the stonework remains a discoloured pink. Eleven people had been injured in the blast.

The IRA clearly wasn't going to go away. Resolving how to reach an accommodation with people the state regarded as terrorists was to be another feature of the unfolding story. The low point of the IRA's wholesale killings of civilians came later that year, with the bombing of pubs in Guildford and Birmingham, in which twenty-six people were killed. The state responded by jailing the wrong people for both bombings.

Among all the bombings, two general elections were held in 1974, one in February followed by another in October. Amazingly, I found myself co-anchoring the second. Only one year in journalism, and I was already interviewing politicians from both front benches. It was an intense and 'on the job' introduction to journalism. Neither then nor at any time later did I ever receive a single day's training. I swotted up on the constituencies, the names and faces of the politicians, and the swings needed to take each seat. Harold Wilson's Labour Party scraped in in the first election, although they failed to win a majority of seats in the House of Commons until the second election, eight months later. There were suddenly people in government that I had worked with at New Horizon. David Ennals was Secretary of State for Health and Social Security: he and I had been trustees on the Campaign for the Single Homeless, a grouping that brought all the projects working with single homeless people under one umbrella and which survives to this day, renamed Homeless Link. My contacts were growing, and rather against my will I found myself creeping onto a lowly rung of the British Establishment.

In between those two elections I was dispatched to northern Portugal. Revolution had taken hold, a revolution that was going to have a huge effect in Africa. One of the seeds of the 'new world disorder' was being sown before my very eyes. Yet at that moment I could see no downside. Liberation it was, and heady was it to be there. I arrived on the morning of 5 April, hours after the fifty-year dictatorship of Salazar and his successor Caetano had been overthrown. All planes to Lisbon were full, but there was one seat left on a flight to the northern Portuguese town of Porto, so by mid-afternoon I found myself in the northern town of Braga. An industrialised concrete place, it proved to be an excellent vantage point from which to observe this most noisy and joyous of revolutions. I had hoped to grab a sandwich and then go looking for the revolution, but revolution was all around me. The streets were heaving with people; women pushed carnations into the barrels of soldiers' guns. At one moment there was an enormous explosion, and I said to my translator, 'Here comes the killing spree.'

'No,' he said, 'it's just a gas canister exploding in one of the celebration bonfires.'

A day and night of intoxicating freedom followed. The death of empire in Britain had never witnessed scenes like this – but then, despite empire, we had at least been spared dictatorship.

The overthrow of half a century of dictatorship in Portugal was completely bloodless. Which could not be said of what happened next in Portugal's colonies. Angry Portuguese settlers in Mozambique and Angola drove their tractors into ravines, smashed key capital equipment and ruined their factories and homes. Nevertheless, their return from the African colonies to their homeland would represent little short of a modern miracle – a small European state reabsorbing the equivalent of 10 per cent of its population without serious consequence. But while Portugal seeped back into being a comfortable corner of Europe, Angola and Mozambique erupted into two of the bleeding sores that would define Africa's emerging disorder in the 1980s and 1990s.

When I returned, Britain was in the throes of the build-up to the referendum on whether or not to remain a member of the European Community. In a sense a kind of revolution was taking place here too. The Tories under Ted Heath had taken Britain into Europe a couple of years earlier, and Labour had promised a vote as a means to resolve their own ambivalence and division on the issue. Many saw the referendum as a post-imperial struggle for the soul of Britain. Should we slide off into the transatlantic alliance and take up our position as Uncle Sam's fifty-first state, or embrace the heart of Europe and become part of the European continent? Truth to tell, I had decided to vote 'no' on the basis that I saw Europe as a rich man's club that was bound to end up screwing the Third World.

I was more involved than I pretended. My friend Ed Boyle, the political editor of LBC and one of the most gifted journalists I ever worked with, had agreed to put together some radio ads for the 'no' campaign. I guess he did it more to make trouble and to even out what he regarded as an unbalanced campaign than out of any very strong belief. He was a real original, mad as a hatter and the creator of brilliant, funny and informative journalism. His trouble was that he was too brilliant, too funny, too bright for his editors; he was therefore denied the profile and standing he richly deserved. Knowing that I was pretty strongly against EC membership at the time, he asked me to help out on the ads.

The fifty-first state argument held no sway for me. It was the love of Uganda and an awareness of how the North intersected with and affected the South that combined to convince me that Europe would thrive to the detriment of the emerging markets and nations of the South. I wanted out of this kind of a Europe with a passion. Michael Foot, at that time Secretary of State for Employment, was my comfortable leader in the cause, and the 'no' campaign enabled me to meet him for the first time, in what was to become a friendship that still endures. My uncomfortable leader was Enoch Powell, who was further right even than Michael was left, and against whom I had demonstrated at university. But he and Michael shared a love of Parliament and sovereignty, one of the causes which bound them both to the 'no' campaign.

The campaign itself was a complete shambles. We started with a substantial lead in the opinion polls, which we then proceeded to fritter away. Ed and I were so unpoliced that our radio ads only featured the 'no' views that reflected our own – references to the Third World and other ways of arranging a new Europe predominated. But the referendum itself, which took place on 6 June 1975, was nevertheless a defining moment in the emergence of post-imperial Britain. In voting to remain in Europe, which the British people did by a margin of two to one, many of us thought we had at least buried the Little Englander vote for all time – how wrong we proved to be.

Alas, we never actually embraced the Europe for which we had voted. Nor were we entirely to shake off our status as America's fifty-first state. We wanted to be for Europe, but not of it. And that condition dogs us to this day. My own position was to evolve gently from outright hostility then, to an ardent desire now to be much more a part of Europe than any British referendum has ever dared contemplate. But it has taken me three decades to travel so complex a journey.

It was only a month after the referendum, in July 1975, that my foreign news editor at LBC bellowed across the newsroom, 'Anyone ever been to Uganda?' One hand went up, and it was mine. 'We've got a free seat on Callaghan's plane,' he said. 'Get your bag and go.'

It seemed that the Foreign Secretary, Jim Callaghan, had been involved in some madcap dialogue with the by-now leader of Uganda Idi Amin over a white British lecturer, Denis Hills, who'd published unflattering references to the Ugandan dictator in a book called *The White Pumpkin*. Among other things, he'd called him a 'village tyrant'. Tyrant he had indeed become, aided and abetted by the British government. Amin had seized power in a military coup on 25 January 1971, while the democratically elected President Milton Obote was in Singapore attending a Commonwealth Prime Ministers' Conference. Obote's use of secret police and informers, and his intimidation and worse of his political opponents, had rendered him unpopular both inside and outside Uganda. Above all, Britain was concerned at the rise of 'African socialism', as espoused by Obote and by Tanzania's Julius Nyerere and Zambia's Kenneth Kaunda.

The arrival, albeit by military coup, of the seemingly more pliant, British-trained erstwhile Sergeant Major Idi Amin was greeted as something of a relief. Amin can perhaps be seen as an early volunteer for Western-supported 'regime change', with all its harrowing consequences. Within a year of the coup he'd appointed himself Field Marshal and 'President for Life', expelled sixty thousand Asians, and started killing his opponents. The Utopian Uganda of my late adolescence was fast evaporating. Amin soon took on more self-styled epithets, including 'Big Daddy' and 'Conqueror of the British Empire'.

Idi Amin was already renowned for humiliating the few whites still in Uganda. Denis Hills was languishing in Luzira prison, the notorious block in which Amin, and Obote before him, both kept and disposed of their opponents. Amin had had Hills sentenced to death for sedition, and had announced that unless the Queen apologised for his behaviour and Jim Callaghan came personally to rescue him, Hills would be summarily executed.

Looking back today, the idea that only three decades ago some African dictator could summon the Foreign Minister from one of the G8 nations to rescue a solitary eccentric from the hangman's noose beggars belief. Even then the trip had a distinct whiff of the absurd about it. Only a few months earlier Amin had had some of the remaining whites in Uganda carry him in a great sedan chair through the centre of Kampala.

The trip was inevitably to provoke in me a strong wave of nostalgia. On 10 July 1975 the RAF VC10 touched down at Entebbe, on an airfield looking only slightly more decayed than it had on my first landing. From the aircraft I could see that the grass was still long and unkempt, but that there were many more troops and guns about. The old terminal building had shed its last remnants of whitewash. The heavenly aroma of Africa wafted into the plane as the door opened. Here I was, back in my beloved Uganda, almost eight years to the day after I had left her. There really did seem to be some divine pattern to it all. Chance had delivered me 'home', even if only for a matter of hours.

There was no Amin at the airport. Instead we were hustled onto a bus at gunpoint by sweaty young soldiers and driven at speed to Kampala.

We passed the gorgeous bougainvillea and mown lawns of State House, where President Obote had lived during my time here. Our destination was Amin's official residence in the capital, the 'Command Post'.

By the time we reached the bustling suburbs of Kampala it was noon, the sun was high and the light outside was fierce to our unaccustomed English eyes. The Asian shops had become less tidy, less well-stocked African outlets. Amin's wholesale ejection of the Asians three years earlier had taken its commercial toll. The smell, the sweaty greenness, the puddles, the red-brown murum roads told me that this was unmistakably Africa, unmistakably Uganda. The jacarandas were in full blue bloom, bananas dangled in ripe bunches, everywhere was lusciously productive.

There were perhaps twenty journalists aboard our bus, not one of whom apart from me had ever set foot in the country before. Suddenly, as we neared the end of the road leading to the Command Post, I caught sight of a dishevelled white man being marched along by two guards. It was obviously Denis Hills. He was dressed in the fly-buttonless, stained remnant of the tropical suit he must have been taken to jail in. I told the bus driver I needed a pee and would walk from there. He stopped and let me out. I ran across to Hills and immediately started interviewing him, using the heavy reel-to-reel Uher tape recorder slung over my shoulder.

'How does it feel to be free, Mr Hills?' I asked.

'Better than being dead,' he replied, 'which I should have been at eight o'clock this morning if

129

Mr Callaghan hadn't come for me.' He seemed to have some teeth missing, but despite his run-down appearance was apparently in one piece.

'What's happening now?' I asked.

'I'm being taken to be handed over.'

Amin's Command Post was ostensibly a simple, square-built 1930s-style suburban house with spectacular views over Kampala. The white stucco walls sporting a green mould here and there were assaulted by vivid splashes of red, pink and purple bougainvillea. But when we got closer there was a distinct air of menace about the place, radio aerials protruding out of windows, wires hanging about, and sandbagged gun emplace-ments peering from the flat roof. Although there were guns everywhere, and paranoid figures look-ing at us suspiciously, there was no formal security cordon. I was able to approach cautiously and to enter, rejoining the other reporters. Callaghan and Amin were out on the lawn at the back. No sign yet of Hills, but Amin was already thanking the Foreign Secretary for coming, booming his words of satisfaction. I recorded the lot.

For almost the only time in my reporting life, my cousin Peter was one of the other corres-pondents on the trip, reporting for ITN. I took him to one side. 'Peter, I've got everything, inter-viewed Hills, done the lot.'

'But Hills hasn't appeared yet,' he said.

'Oh yes he has, and I've got his first interview as a free man. Trouble is, Callaghan's people want us straight back on the bus and off to Entebbe and the take-off. But I know where the international telephone exchange is here, and I could phone this stuff through to London and get a scoop on everyone else – including you.'

'Go on,' said Peter, 'take a risk. They may leave without you, but we won't be able even to phone until we get to the departure lounge at Entebbe, so you'll be at least an hour or even two ahead of anyone.'

I ran back out on to the road, flashed some pound notes and got a lift to the exchange half a mile away. This was the self-same building from which whilst on VSO I had been able to phone home. Somehow I managed to cajole them into giving me a line to London. I got everything fed from my Uher, using crude crocodile clips to connect the tape machine directly to the phone line. I also recorded a description of Hills's release. Twenty minutes later I was out on the street trying to get a taxi back to the Command Post, but no one dared go anywhere near the place, especially with a *muzungu*, a white man.

I decided the best solution was to head for Entebbe Airport directly in a service taxi, in the hope of reaching the plane before the bus did, or at least before take-off. So with a clutch of breast-feeding mothers, two goats, and at least five or six live chickens flapping about with tied feet, I set off in a battered old Peugeot 606 station wagon. The trouble was that our journey was constantly inter-rupted by the need to disgorge a mother, a goat, a chicken, or sometimes all three at once. Then another lot of human and animal cargo would board the taxi to inflict further stops on us.

As bits of Uganda flashed past, I considered the

131

place's weird predicament. Here was a country that Britain had had charge of until just over a decade before. Yet Uganda had been prepared in no way for independence. What cynicism could deliver a thuggish, paranoid Sergeant Major to lead its armed forces? The colonisers had believed in an imported white officer class until almost the day of handover. The country's institutions were remorselessly British in their make-up, and took no account of sophisticated local practice. Britain effectively prepared Uganda for failure. It's a telling insight into the British way of doing things, which was to be repeated in every corner of Africa that was ever pink.

After what seemed like hours we turned into the airport road. Proceeding in the opposite direction was our empty bus, returning to Kampala. I had nowhere near enough money to buy a ticket to London, I had no visa, the British High Commission had taken our passports upon landing, and I suddenly had visions of taking up Denis Hills's vacated death cell at Luzira prison. For sure, honest Jim Callaghan would not make a second rescue flight.

We swung round the high pampas grasses on to the airfield, and there was the plane, still on the ground. My cousin Peter was gesticulating wildly from halfway up the steps. 'Come on, we're going in seconds!' he shouted above the engine roar. Inside the cabin, there was Callaghan, in his tropical hat, looking red and impatient. Hills was separated off, crumpled up in a seat well back, and then came the journalists. They looked grim-faced and angry with me.

I asked Peter what the problem was. 'Bloody phones are down to Kampala,' he said. 'No one got to file a sodding thing. You've got yourself an epic.'

What a start, I thought. One year a journalist, and I've got a scoop of mythic proportions: 'British Foreign Secretary Saves White Man's Life in Africa!' I settled complacently into my seat. Our ten-hour flight, with a stop-off in phoneless Tripoli, should keep me well ahead of the game, I thought.

Fortunately the lines from Brize Norton, the Oxfordshire military air base where we landed, were working. 'Well?' I asked the foreign editor when my turn for the phonebox came and I got through.

'Well what?'

'My scoop.'

'What scoop?'

'Haven't you run my Denis Hills story?' I shouted.

'No.'

'Why ever not?'

'Yours was the only source. We knew UPI, AP and Reuters were all on the flight with you, so we waited for them, and when they failed to file we decided you'd got it wrong.'

'You idiot!' I screamed. 'I had the tape of Hills saying he was free, I had bloody Callaghan saying he was thankful, Amin booming away, what else did you want?'

'A second source, Jon. Now if you don't mind, I can see the first Reuters snap coming through, so I can let your stuff run.' With that he rang off.

'What's the trouble?' asked Peter as I came out of the phonebox.

'They didn't run it,' I said mournfully. 'They couldn't get a second source to confirm it.'

'Are they running it now?' he asked.

'Oh yes.'

'Well, don't worry, you've still got a beat.'

And sure enough, LBC and my report were used as the source for that afternoon's *Evening Standard* front page. It was an early tutorial in the ways of journalism.

It was a much bigger tutorial on the true condition of Great Britain. Amin, the jumped-up non-commissioned officer, had succeeded in humiliating the Foreign Secretary of his erstwhile imperial rulers. Britain was still finding her post-colonial feet, still unsure whether a Foreign Secretary should do this sort of thing. She had played an unwitting role in bringing Amin to power and keeping him there. The coup against Milton Obote had been seen as a benign and potentially beneficial development. The wholesale deportation of tens of thousands of people because of their Asian ethnicity was simply accepted. It might be argued that the office of the British Foreign Secretary seemed to have put more effort into saving one eccentric white man from execution than into preventing the abuse meted out to sixty thousand Ugandan Asians. Despite the furious immigration debate in Britain, those Asians were to prove Uganda's crippling loss and Britain's huge economic gain.

That autumn of 1975, imperial Britain's home-grown crisis was taking serious hold on both sides of the Irish Sea. On 3 October a Dutch businessman, Dr Tiede Herrema, was kidnapped by the IRA as he drove his Mercedes to work at Ferenka Ltd, the huge tyre factory in Limerick of which he was managing director. The kidnappers threatened to kill him unless Republican prisoners were released from jails in the Republic of Ireland. Ireland was in the throes of trying to leave her nineteenth-century backwardness and become a fully paid-up member of Europe, and the kidnap was a body blow, particularly as Ferenka's parent company was the hugely influential Dutch multinational Akzo.

For nearly three weeks no trace was found of the missing Dutchman. The kidnap made the Republic of Ireland appear a place of refuge for the hard men of Republicanism. Then on 21 October Herrema was located in a council house on the edge of Monasterevin in County Kildare, forty miles south-west of Dublin. He was being held by two IRA members, Eddie Gallagher and Marian Coyle. The discovery triggered an immediate siege. LBC dispatched me from London with almost no money and virtually no other resources.

The house stood at the back of a working-class, 1950s-built red-brick estate that gave onto farmland. From the far side of one of the fields it was possible to get a view of the back and side of the house. The Irish police, the Gardai, were everywhere, and the press were kept well back. Gallagher loosed off a couple of gunshots soon after I arrived, as if to support the police in their

135

endeavour to control the media.

LBC's appetite was voracious. At peak times they wanted a piece on the hour, every hour. Initially I was able to persuade the ITN correspondent and future bestselling novelist Gerald Seymour to let me use the back of his car as a base. The one motel in Monasterevin was already full, and was anyway too far from the siege house. Seymour was a star reporter, and I felt honoured to be allowed to use his car. That first night he slept in the front, I in the back. I remember his socks to this day. With the Irish mist hanging in the dawn light, I could just pick out the shapes of policemen wandering around the garden fence of the siege house. We were in for a long haul.

By midday, trucks had begun lugging caravans into position at the top of the field. A temporary press encampment was taking shape. Gerry Seymour upgraded himself to a four-berth mobile home, and I took over the whole of his car. At the vantage point we constructed a large brazier and filled it with peat briquettes. I must be one of the few reporters who has ever put in a charge for peat briquettes on his expenses claim form.

Although I spent more hours than most at the vantage point, there were times when I would retreat to the car to sleep. The problem was that the car was at least two hundred yards from the point from which you could see the house. So I went into town and bought a great length of bell wire, a buzzer, a bell-push and a battery. The buzzer was draped through the car window, while the bell-push lay near the brazier two hundred yards away. From time to time, once they'd checked I was asleep, one of the photographers down at the brazier would sound the buzzer just for the hell of seeing this half-naked hack falling out of a car pulling on his trousers in his haste to witness the end of it all.

There were very few real developments during the Herrema siege, but somehow it built up into a compelling twenty-four-hour news radio event. Eddie Gallagher, the IRA man whose hare-brained scheme the kidnapping had been, turned out to be in conflict with the IRA leadership. Indeed, this may well have been one of the early signals of division in the IRA between the political and the mayhem wings of the Army Council. Gallagher's girlfriend was not Marian Coyle, with whom he was now holed up in the siege house, but Rose Dugdale, who was later to marry Gallagher and bear him a child. Dr Dugdale was an English aristocrat and a graduate of the London School of Economics who was serving time for conspiracy to smuggle arms and explosives to Northern Ireland, and was one of the IRA convicts in return for whose freedom Herrema was being held hostage. She was also suspected of having seized a helicopter in 1974 and dropped two explosives-filled milk churns on a police barracks, where they failed to explode. Gallagher had been imprisoned after that episode, but had escaped four days after being sentenced. Technically, despite his stationary position in our sights, he was on the run.

It was not just the divisions within the IRA that the siege exposed. We also saw, writ large, a preparedness on the part of both Irish and British

137

governments to countenance an eventual deal with the Republicans. No one was prepared to go in with all guns blazing. But then, early one morning about a week into the siege, the Gardai grew impatient with Gallagher and decided to mount a surprise attack. I was at the vantage point. I buzzed the buzzer and a motley crew of my colleagues came running down the path from their encampment, led by the man from the *Sun*. Les Hinton was not only an excellent journalist, but good company. If I had been asked then to identify which of our band would one day become Rupert Murdoch's British supremo at News International, I'm not sure I'd have spotted him. It's an extraordinary journey from Monasterevin to the Murdoch summit in Wapping.

We were all flabbergasted by the crudity of the Garda assault. An old ladder was leant against the bathroom window at the back of the house, and a detective scaled it and tried to open the window. BANG! A terrific shot rang out, followed by a yelp, and the detective tumbled down the ladder. Gallagher had blown the man's index finger off.

The next day I received a hand-delivered note from the editor of ITN, Nigel Ryan. He had approached me earlier in the year about moving to television news, and I'd refused. This time his note said that if I accepted, the job as a reporter for ITN was mine. I decided to talk to my own editor when I returned home.

The siege dragged on for seventeen days. Eventually Herrema walked out unharmed, and Gallagher and Coyle gave themselves up. The brazier camaraderie came to a rapid end and we all went our separate ways. What we didn't know was that five of the twenty-five or so of us who had been the core of the siege-watchers had contracted a pretty grim lurgy that would strike a short time after we returned home.

Nigel Ryan was a highly regarded, patrician, Reuters-trained editor. He'd seen action in the Congo, but was also at ease in the British Establishment. I sat in his office on the second floor facing him. My editor at LBC had strongly advised me to cross to ITN while the going was good.

'So, which college did you go to?' Ryan asked.

'Ah,' I said. 'I wasn't at Oxbridge. I read law at Liverpool.'

He was rather startled, and I got the impression that if I did secure a place on the reporters' bench I'd be breaking with the Oxbridge norm. Fortunately he never asked me what degree I got, so I didn't have to cover up the rather serious matter of having been rusticated. To this day I often wonder whether he'd have employed me if he'd known. But the job was mine, and with three months' notice to LBC I would start in March 1976.

Two days later I woke up feeling utterly dreadful, listless and sick. I phoned a doctor friend to ask what he'd recommend for a 'pick-me-up'. 'Have a glass of sherry,' he advised. I did, and immediately vomited. Looking in the mirror, I saw that I was a noxious shade of bright yellow. I phoned my GP, and by the evening I had been admitted to Coppetts Wood isolation hospital in north London.

'Are you a homosexual?' The man in the white coat at my bedside wafted in and out of my consciousness. 'Have you had oral sex with another man?'

'Crumbs!' I thought. 'Is that the only way to get whatever I've got?'

'You've got Hepatitis A,' the doctor said through his facemask. 'It's highly contagious.'

'No, I'm not a homosexual,' I said eventually.

'Well, how did you get this?' he asked. 'Where have you been?'

'The Irish Republic – covering the Herrema siege,' I said. 'There was a cow trough with a tap in the field where we camped. I drank some of the water.'

'That's almost certainly it,' he said.

Soon it was confirmed that five of us had exactly the same complaint from the same source, and I'd had sexual relations with none of them. 'No alcohol for six months, and complete bed rest,' the doctor said, and left.

I was sharing a flat in Primrose Hill with Nick Browne, whom I had met at university. To this day, a truer friend I could not wish for. He had taken the route I'd been expected to and actually become a barrister. The day after I was admitted to hospital he came to my bedside with the mail. 'I couldn't help spotting this one,' he said.

'On Her Majesty's Service', it said in black print. 'Confidential, Personal' was typed in red. I pulled out the contents. No wonder Nick was looking curious. He knew exactly what it was, and so did I.

It read:

MINISTRY OF DEFENCE, Room 055,
Old War Office Buildings, Whitehall.
5 January 1976
Dear Mr Snow

1. I think it just possible that you might be able to assist me with some confidential work I have in hand. I therefore should be most grateful for an opportunity to have a talk.

2. If you are agreeable perhaps you would be kind enough to telephone me and we can discuss when it would be convenient for you to call. You should, incidentally, come to the side entrance of Old War Office Buildings in Whitehall Place and say you have an appointment in Room 055.

3. I will naturally reimburse you for any reasonable expenses. Please do not hesitate to take a taxi if you are pressed for time.

4. I should be grateful if you would treat this letter as confidential and not discuss it with anyone else; furthermore please bring the letter with you as a means of identification.

5. I very much regret that I cannot go into further explanations in a letter or on the telephone, but would naturally do so if we meet.

Yours sincerely,
D. Stilbury

Ten days later I was at the side entrance of Old War Office Buildings, a grey, uninviting building opposite Horse Guards Parade. I had called Stilbury and made an appointment. I figured that I should at least check the thing out. I mean, how often do you get an invitation to the epicentre of Britain's spy network?

I had decided to eschew the taxi in favour of my trusted bicycle. On my way I stopped off at the main concourse of Waterloo station to photocopy the letter. I was well aware that it was both my passport to, and my proof of approach from, Her Majesty's intelligence services. As I fed it into the plywood-boxed, freestanding photocopier in the middle of the station, the machine jammed. So paranoid was I that I had avoided photocopying the letter at LBC for fear that some stray copy would blow my cover. Now the even more public British Rail machine had the effrontery to jam. I tried again, and this time a copy spewed out onto the station floor.

As I had anticipated, the man at the Old War Office reception desk took the original letter from me, never to return it. A large woman in blue Civil Service rig sailed ahead of me along a labyrinth of corridors, up a few steps, down a few more. Grey stone, blue curtains, grey stone, blue curtains; everything was the same. She showed me into a bare and austere room. And there was Stilbury. He stood up from behind his desk, which was arranged across a corner. The only other pieces of furniture in the room were two low-slung modern tubular-framed armchairs in front of the desk. He pointed to one of them. He was tall, rather pale, public-school-looking, nondescript.

'Do sit down,' he said. I sat and was immediately reduced by the low-slung armchair to a height considerably below that of the now seated

Stilbury. I was already at a disadvantage. 'I'm Douglas Stilbury, and I work for SIS,' he said. I doubted that he was who he said he was, but I had no doubt he worked for whom he said he worked for. 'Do you know what SIS is?'

'Not exactly,' I replied.

'We are the Secret Intelligence Service, MI6. We are responsible for external, foreign intelligence.'

We started to talk. He had a considerable file on his desk which appeared to contain a very great deal about me. From women friends to politics, they had done their work.

'We'd like you to work with us,' he finally said.

'Full time?' I asked.

'Oh no, we'd like you to pursue your chosen career and do bits and pieces for us along the way.'

'What sort of thing?'

'Well,' he said, 'there could be someone we are interested in, a Communist, who is meeting people – we might want you to get to know them.'

'Sounds a bit domestic to me,' I said. 'But what really worries me, Mr Stilbury, is that I'm not sure you and I are on the same side.'

'Don't worry,' he said. 'We are accountable to the British Cabinet. As much to Mr Wedgwood Benn as we are to Mr Wilson.' Tony Benn was the Cabinet's unguided lefty at the time.

I think Stilbury could sense that I was thinking of saying no. 'No hasty decisions,' he said. 'We haven't talked pay. You would be paid direct into your bank account, no questions asked by the Inland Revenue, and the sum would be equivalent to your current basic salary, tax-free.' ITN was about to pay me around £6000 a year at the time, the equivalent of £20,000 these days. 'Now, if you want to know more about us, I suggest you read the report by Lord Justice Denning into the Profumo Affair. It gives the most coherent picture yet published.'

'This isn't for me,' I said. 'Any of my friends will tell you, I can't keep a secret. I'm about to become a television journalist. Rather a public job for such private activity, don't you think?'

'I'm not taking any answer from you this time,' he said. 'I want you to go away and think about it, then come back and tell me your decision.'

I stepped out into the sunlight, got on my bike and pedalled off down Whitehall, looking over my shoulder.

To this day, I have never read the Denning Report. Instead I bought a copy of the great MI6 Cold War double agent Kim Philby's book, *My Secret War*.

As I was still recovering from hepatitis, I decided on the spur of the moment to go skiing in the Spanish Pyrenees. I read Philby's book on the sun-splashed deck outside my hotel-room window in Formigal. It was clear from the book that to be a good spy – and I would have wanted to be a very good spy – you'd have to be a double agent of some kind, and that it would then completely consume your life and ultimately destroy you. I was pretty certain I'd never do it anyway, not least because Stilbury and his ilk seemed to represent the element of the British Establishment that I felt most uncomfortable with. And to be honest, I really wasn't sure they were on my side. I wanted change, meritocracy, progress. I suspected Stilbury didn't.

But how had this approach come about? MI6 clearly felt I was a good prospect – a chap with radical beginnings who had seen the error of his ways, and was moving up the Establishment – perfect! And how was it that I was being approached now, in mid-transition from LBC to ITN? Did ITN have some kind of 'controller' in its midst? In which case, how many of my new colleagues were up to it?

'How was Spain?' Stilbury asked. I had never told him I was going.

'I'm not going to work for you, Mr Stilbury,' I replied, pretty shaken by how much he knew about me and my movements.

Stilbury became brusque and unfriendly. 'Very well,' he said. 'I'm naturally disappointed. I think you are making a big mistake, but that's it then. You are never to contact us, and we shall never contact you again.'

For the last time, I left Old War Office Buildings by the side entrance and, rather frightened, beetled off on my bike, checking occasionally to see if anyone was following me.

FOUR

Tea with the Tyrant

Idi Amin is in a coma, a few weeks from death, in Saudi Arabia. It is August 2003, and alas his unconscious condition has come a quarter of a century too late to be of much use to Uganda. An international debate rages over whether his vast remains should be allowed to be shipped home to breathe their last. In the meantime he resides all plugged up in a Saudi clinic, as pampered in dying as he was in life. It is said he has ballooned from his presidential 250 pounds to the same number of kilos. How was this mass murderer allowed to remain unprosecuted in the poolside confines of a Saudi-government-owned villa in Jeddah for so long? To some tiny extent I suppose I had a hand in his survival, but I'll enter that admission later.

Saudi Arabia had granted Amin – a rare Haj-making African Muslim President – safety, along with two of his wives and twenty-four children, in 1979, after he was driven out of Uganda by force. He was allowed to spend his days 'fishing in the Red Sea, and playing his accordion, watching sports and CNN', according to one newspaper report. He was even permitted to plot an attempted return to Uganda through Zaire, in 1989.

When I joined ITN in the spring of 1976, Amin was at his worst. With the only ill-effect being a severe reduction of my alcohol intake, I had come through hepatitis in a matter of four weeks. It was within three months of my arrival at ITN, on 27 June, that Amin made his mark as a supporter of global terrorism. An Air France Airbus with more than 150 passengers and crew aboard, originating in Tel Aviv and bound for Paris, was hijacked after a stop in Athens. Two male members of the Popular Front for the Liberation of Palestine (PFLP), and a man and a woman from the extreme left-wing West German Baader-Meinhof gang, commandeered the plane eight minutes out of Athens, eventually forcing it to land, with just minutes of fuel left, at Entebbe Airport in Uganda. In London once again the newsroom cry went up: 'Anyone got any maps or photos of Entebbe Airport?' I had both, and started to piece together the scene from the studio. My blotchy slides of the old terminal where the hostages were herded made it onto that night's News at Ten.

Amin himself gave the orders for three more hijackers to be allowed to augment the four already in the old airport terminal. He deployed a force of Ugandan troops around the terminal buildings, and then proceeded to make a rousing speech on the runway in praise of the PFLP. To this day, this remains one of the few moments in history when a head of state has actively and publicly sought to endorse and assist an act of air piracy and terrorism. If the world ever needed a moment to draw the line internationally against a rogue state and its rogue President, this was it.

But none was drawn, and Amin was either gently isolated or passively tolerated for another three years of bloodletting tyranny.

The non-Israeli passengers held at Entebbe were released onto another Air France jet on the third day of the ordeal. It was left to Israel itself to spring a daring and effective raid to free the 105 remaining hostages. At 11.03 on the night of 4 July, four Israeli Hercules transport planes landed direct from Tel Aviv on Entebbe's tarmac. By 11.52 p.m. all the hostages were in the air, heading for the safety of Nairobi airport. Less than an hour after the first Israeli plane had touched down they had all gone, taking their three dead with them. The leader of the assault, Colonel Yoni Netenyahu (brother of the future Prime Minister), died in an exchange of fire with Ugandan forces. He was instantly projected into the Israeli pantheon of national heroes, while the assault itself consolidated Israel's reputation for invincibility wherever it was tested. Forty-five Ugandan soldiers died in the attack. There was one other notorious death, that of one of the Jewish hostages, seventy-five-year-old Dora Bloch. She had been taken to hospital in Kampala after a choking fit aboard the plane. On Amin's orders she was dragged from her hospital bed and murdered in a forest on the way to the airport.

We now know, thanks to British Foreign Office documents declassified in 2003, that Britain had a plan to invade Uganda in 1972 during the crisis over the Asian expulsion. But 'Operation Zeus', as it was code-named, was merely intended to save the seven thousand Britons still

148

resident in Uganda.

As a failing state – failing in no small measure due to the neglect of the former colonial power – Uganda was a forerunner, a challenge, even a potential test bed for what was to come. The whole of East Africa was to be destabilised by Amin's eccentricity and bloodlust, a destabilisation which may well have helped create the circumstances in which US embassies in Kenya and Tanzania were bombed by al Qaida nearly twenty years later. Yet Amin's support for such groups as the PFLP, and his constant denunciation of Britain and Israel, won him enough friends in the Organisation of African Unity and the UN to ensure that he was never completely cut off from international support. Gaddafi's Libya drip-fed him sufficient oil and money to stave off the complete disintegration of Uganda.

The Entebbe crisis and its aftermath drove Amin still madder. Public enemy number one in his eyes were the British press. In mid-July 1976 I was dispatched on my first foreign television news trip to get to grips with the East African disaster that was now Amin.

Standing on the banks of Lake Victoria just outside Kisumu, I looked north to the Kenya–Uganda crossing. Refugees were streaming out of Uganda with bundles of possessions on their heads. 'There's so little petrol in there,' reported a smartly dressed businessman, 'I've even seen the army pushing their own vehicles back to their bases.' Within a month of the Entebbe raid, landlocked Uganda was running out of supplies.

The economy was in ruins, and the country had run out of money to pay its bills. Any cash or food that materialised went straight to Amin's army.

The British High Commission in Kampala decided to close. This immediately sparked a wave of actions by Amin against the few remaining British citizens. One such was Graham Clegg, a thirty-eight-year-old British businessman married to a Ugandan. He and his wife Joyce had already escaped with their two children to a farm in northern Kenya. By the time I arrived Clegg had gone back into Uganda, and was now missing, together with another Briton, sixty-nine-year-old Jack Tulley, who'd been misguided enough to ask questions about what had happened to him. It was thought that Joyce might know more. Since foreign journalists were denied access to Uganda, and she was still in radio contact with people inside the country, she suddenly became a very important source.

The BBC's seasoned man in Nairobi was Brian Barron, and he worked with the legendary cameraman Mohamed Amin. Mo was to win every plaudit in the book for his work over the years, but he was to lose an arm in Ethiopia, and in 1996 his life in a hijacked airliner which crashed into the sea off the Comoros Islands. He, like Barron, was a charming if ruthless operator. My cameraman was the wonderful Mohinder Dhillon, a gentle, tall, de-turbanised Sikh. He was a brilliant but understated cameraman, who suffers from a very severe stammer.

These were the two teams that headed off in

their respective light aircraft from Nairobi's Wilson Airport in pursuit of Joyce Clegg and first-hand contact with one of the many of Amin's 'missing'. It was natural to take a light aircraft on such a trip. Wilson Airport had more air movements than even London's Heathrow. The distances were so great and the little grassy farm landing strips so plentiful that air travel was commonplace.

Mohinder's residual knowledge of Kenya was better than Mohamed's, so we had a good start on them. The flight was spectacular, low over the Great Rift Valley, skimming treetops, wildlife, all manner of terrain. The spume from vast waterfalls cascading into tropical ravines rose up from the escarpments. In my volunteer incarnation I had never flown in East Africa, and the sheer scale of what unfolded below us stole my breath.

We must have bumped down onto three or four landing strips before we finally located the right farm. Hearing on the radio that the BBC weren't far behind, we took off again and landed at a strip further away in order to confuse them. A local farmer was rustled up on the radio, and he arrived apparently from nowhere to give us a lift in his Land Rover.

Joyce, when we found her, was startled to see us. Her remote grassland farm was overgrown, and there was a rotting tractor to one side of the house. Two small children played around her ankles, and she was evidently pregnant with a third. Her radio contacts inside Uganda were mostly located towards the north of the country, and they described bloody visitations by Amin's henchmen. No one seemed to have any word of her husband, save that he had not reached their Ugandan home after crossing the border nine days earlier. Joyce broke down in tears as she described her own escape from Uganda with the children. She was terrified that not only was her husband dead, but that Jack Tulley had been killed as a consequence of merely asking after him. One part of me wanted to stay and help her, the other knew that we had an emotional and gripping account of the unseen tyrant rampaging around in the country beyond the blue mountains we could see from her front door.

We headed back to the nearest small town in our borrowed Land Rover, in the forlorn hope of trying to telephone a report to London of what Joyce Clegg had told us. We were just entering the town when Mohinder glimpsed Mohamed Amin in a vehicle ahead of us. 'Q-q-q-quick, J-J-Jon, into that t-t-t-tea s-st-tall!' he stammered. We dashed in and hid under one of the tables, as I desperately tried to explain to the Kenyan waitress that she should ignore us. Through the open door, we saw Mohamed race past in the wrong direction. It was a very rare moment of triumph in a dignified but desperate civil war that Mohinder and I waged with Brian's team over several years in East Africa. But this journalistic hunt sometimes obscured the importance of what was really going on. It is only now, with hindsight, that it is possible to see that those early post-colonial days in Africa had much to tell us about failing states and the 'First World's' contentment with simply letting them fail.

Uganda was a foretaste of Somalia, Rwanda, Angola, Sierra Leone, Liberia and so many more still to come.

On 25 July, a month after Entebbe, I received the final brush-off from Amin. 'I regret to inform you,' read the telex, 'efforts to obtain you an interview with His Excellency Life President Amin have not borne fruits stop. Signed J. Kihika, Director of Information.' So once again we turned up at Boskavic Air Taxis at Nairobi's Wilson Airport. We were to fly across Uganda to neighbouring Rwanda, to see what impact Amin's actions were having on Central Africa. As we flew low over Lake Victoria, the Ugandan fishermen stood in their boats below waving their shirts at us. The distant shores of Entebbe were shrouded in mist. We could only imagine what lurked beyond, and we did. Amin's regime had begun to assume an impregnability and order in its tyranny that far outstripped the reality of his buffoonish antics. He had free rein on Radio Uganda to make absurd remarks about the world's leaders and his personal capacity to defeat all corners. It was reminiscent of his jesting at the boxing matches I'd seen him officiate at nearly a decade earlier. In fact his position was much more vulnerable than his bluster admitted. But as the outside world was unable to see what was happening inside Uganda, the legend of Amin outstripped the larger-than-life figure he already was.

Flying over the Uganda–Rwanda border we could see the massive build-up of empty fuel tankers, food convoys and refugees clogging the area for miles around. Landing at Rwanda's capital, Kigali, we found the airport out of aviation fuel. We'd have hardly enough to get back. On the roads it was worse; there was no petrol at all. Amin had apparently seized thirty tanker loads, a week's supply for the whole of Rwanda. We loaded our equipment and trundled into town on an oxcart. The country was tranquil, and certainly gave no sense of the massacres of the past or the ghastly inter-ethnic bloodletting to come.

The central preoccupation in Rwanda was the Amin-inflicted shortages of everything. For Rwanda too was landlocked, depending extensively on supplies brought overland through Uganda from the Kenyan port of Mombasa. Amin had simply seized fuel and food bound for Rwanda to make good his own shortages. We were the only Western media in Rwanda at that moment. International interest was low. Yet the UN was present, as was the colonising power, Belgium. They knew that the economic crisis between Kenya, Uganda and Rwanda was threatening to tip over into war. Yet when Kenya's Foreign Minister asked for help on the floor of the United Nations in New York on 27 July 1976, neither Belgium nor the other post-colonial power, Britain, lifted a finger to help.

We landed back in Nairobi just in time to see the unexpected arrival of Amin's negotiating team, sent finally at the beginning of August to try to calm things down between Kenya and Uganda. They were due to meet the redoubtable eighty-seven-year-old Kenyan President Jomo Kenyatta. There was even a rumour that the

154

Field Marshal himself might be aboard the Ugandan plane. Even without Amin, the members of the Ugandan delegation were a heavy-set, ugly-looking lot in military fatigues. Not for the first time, my candour got the better of me as I scripted my piece for ITN's News at Ten. Mohinder and I were still shooting on film in those days, and I had to record a separate voice track and list instructions to the film editor as to how to stitch it all together when it finally reached London by plane.

After the news aired I received a telex of complaint from my editor, Nigel Ryan. 'YOUR DESCRIPTIONS OF THE UGANDAN TEAM TOO GRAPHIC STOP PLEASE STICK TO FACTS STOP RYAN STOP'. I looked again at my script: '...a rare chance to observe Amin's henchmen at close quarters ... led by Colonel Sabuni, and Captain Mohamed, two of Uganda's most evil men, with a long history of brutality behind them ... loathed by ordinary Ugandans ... the President is protected by such men who live in the knowledge that, should he be killed, their own chances of survival in the ensuing bloodbath would be minimal...' Pretty factual, I mused to myself.

The East African Correspondents' Association was a pretty select band in those days. Our main activity was to lounge around the edge of the pool of the Nairobi Intercontinental Hotel, where the Association was conveniently head-quartered. Actually I doubt that we had more than a postal address there. The dean of the

Association was the BBC's radio man John Osmond, whose importance transcended most of ours in that his reports were among the very few that could be received in Kenya itself. That alone made him a famous man. With his pale summer jacket and sunhat, he could have stepped straight out of Evelyn Waugh's *Scoop*, as I was to find out to my cost in Somalia the following year. The doyen of the journalists was the beautiful and radical Victoria Brittan, who was married to the Reuters bureau chief Peter Sharrock. For the rest, there were a few newspaper people like the *Daily Telegraph*'s indefatigable Bruce Loudon, the *New York Times*'s John Darnton, and agency men like UPI's Ray Whittaker.

Poor old Snow from ITN was seen as belonging to the more impecunious end of the market. Technically by now I had become ITN's East Africa correspondent, but my editors couldn't afford to post me there permanently. Consequently I'd always be turning up late and underbriefed. Victoria took me under her wing and ensured that I was up to speed, despite the fact that she worked perilously close to the luxurious confines of the BBC. What I lacked in local knowledge I tried to make up for in enthusiasm and preparedness to leap from the pool straight into Mohinder's wagon to head off in search of the story.

Having just got back from Rwanda, I was asleep poolside when Mohinder came running in. 'C-c-c-coup in S-S-S-Sudan,' he stammered. I donned my clothes and we rushed to the airport. There was an old East African Airways

DC3 trying to get out to Sudan with UN personnel on board, and Mohinder had blagged some seats on it, in return for agreeing to film the UN team going about their work.

Right up to the moment we entered Sudanese air space, we had no idea who would be in charge when we got there, or whether they would let us land. There was an outside possibility they might scramble their MIGs to see us off. Suddenly through the desert dust we saw the great divide in the Nile, and Khartoum spread below us. I'd never been there before, and I caught myself thinking about General Tom, my grandfather, and his perilous journey to try to relieve Gordon almost exactly a hundred years before. Here was I just three hours out of Nairobi; by the time he saw the same river he had been on the trek from Alexandria for three months.

Sudan was yet another African state in which the Cold War power struggle between Moscow and Washington was being played out. This time the coup had failed, and President Numeiri, who had played both East and West against the middle, had survived. The presidential plane bringing him back from a conference in Paris had landed early, avoiding the rebel Russian-made anti-aircraft gun intended to bring him down. By the time the rebels had realised what was going on he was already in the VIP lounge, about to be spirited into an unmarked civilian car which subsequently disappeared into the suburbs. Two days of fighting had ensued, in which both rebels and government forces suffered heavy losses.

The day after we landed, Mohinder and I were

taken to the old British-built presidential palace. Everywhere there were still symbols and signals of the former British presence. Numeiri had a soft spot for the Brits, which was why he'd agreed to see me. 'It's Gaddafi,' he complained. 'He couldn't get this country by negotiation' – there had long been talk of a Libyan–Sudanese union – 'so he came by force.' Then, in full military uniform, the Sudanese President marched us outside to look at the captured weapons with their Libyan markings. He told us six hundred people had been killed in the shoot-out during the attempted coup – more than in any battle in the country since Gordon's time.

Numeiri was a classic post-colonial operator. He was courted and extensively supplied by the Russians, and then as strongly by the Americans. Both superpowers saw Sudan's sheer size as a prize – it might one day yield oil – but also as a liability. They were alarmed at the thought of Africa's biggest country tying up with Libya, the continent's most prolific oil producer at the time. Added to which, Washington believed Gaddafi was clinically mad.

A couple of years later, when I visited the Libyan President in one of his colourful tents in the desert, I concluded that he was odd, but far from mad. It is little remarked upon today, but in his early days Gaddafi distributed the country's oil revenue in an extraordinarily egalitarian way, irrigating the land and developing towns and villages. Whilst devoted to Islam, he ran a secular state which had its own idiosyncratic form of village democracy, enshrined in his 'Green

Book'. In many ways, given the corruption of the Gulf oil producers, Libya stood out as a dangerous symbol of popular equality, even if its leader manifested a severe streak of eccentricity. Having led Libya for more than thirty years, from riches to the poverty now imposed by UN sanctions, he must be deploying something more than sheer terror still to be there.

Poor Sudan, courted so assiduously throughout the Cold War, was destined all too soon to be dropped like a stone by both superpowers. Famine, civil war and poverty were to engulf the country, leaving only Islam for succour. By the late 1990s Sudan would be a failing state, with Osama bin Laden in residence, and Bill Clinton loosing off a Cruise missile or two to detonate an entirely innocent German-owned aspirin factory as some kind of anti-terrorist warning shot.

Back in August 1979, Mohinder and I stumbled around Omdurman in insufferable heat. I had taken it into my head to try to retrace General Tom's footsteps. 'Gordon was shot somewhere around here,' I said to Mohinder, who was too generous to do anything other than feign interest. 'It could have been one of those steps over there.'

'Or th-th-those over th-th-ere,' he suggested less than helpfully. We had no idea. But what was clear was that the Sudanese people, with their long white *jallabiya,* ageing grey-flannel jackets and long windings around their heads, cannot have changed much in a hundred years.

'Is that you, Mr Snow?' I was sitting at my desk in London, and the voice on the other end of the phone was rough, slightly northern, and evidently a long way away.

'Yes, it's me.'

'It's Bob, Jon, Bob Astles. I'm in Kenya, fleeing for my life. I'm in trouble. I'm coming to London tomorrow. I need to meet you.' He rang off.

I'd only met Astles once, in the days of VSO a decade earlier. Then he'd been a rather scruffy newsreader on Africa's first national television service, Uganda Television. Now he was, by all accounts, Idi Amin's left-hand man. Whatever the President for Life wanted, be it whisky for his officers or taps for his bathroom, somehow Astles would come up with it. He also now ran some kind of national airline called Uganda Airways, which sent a weekly freight flight unmolested in and out of London's Stansted Airport. Such was Britain's tolerance of the Amin regime – no sanctions here, however many Asians he'd expelled or people he'd killed. Whether Bob Astles was into people-killing, I wasn't yet sure.

The next day the phone rang again. Astles was in a phonebox at Waterloo station. 'Could you come and meet me? I've no money to get any further,' he said rather pitifully.

Astles looked an absolute wreck when I found him opposite Platform 7. He was unshaven, his shirt was torn, his trousers and jacket were filthy. His greasy, black-flecked, grey nicotiney hair was unkempt. He didn't smell too good either.

'They're after me,' he said.

'Who's after you?'

'Those people round the President, coffee smugglers and the rest. They chased me out of

160

the country. I escaped with my life, I can't go back.' He ended his incoherent explanation for his shambolic appearance with droopy finality. 'I need money, Jon. You must help me, I've nothing beyond what I'm standing up in.'

'And that's not much,' I said, stating the obvious. I did not like Astles. I did not like his proximity to Amin. Yet something of the journalist in me told me he could be useful. Once he'd settled down from his ordeal, maybe he'd have a story to tell. At the moment he wanted no publicity, and I respected his wish. He wanted £200. I gave him the then enormous sum of a hundred, knowing I would never be able to get away with it on expenses. I didn't see Astles again in London. Once I tracked him to an address in Wimbledon, but then I lost him.

It was after Christmas 1976 that he called again. 'Bob here, Jon.' He sounded jolly and upbeat. 'I'm back in Kampala, bigger and better than ever. I told His Excellency of your kindness to me, and he's inviting you for an exclusive interview and to be his guest at the sixth anniversary celebrations of his coup on 25 January. Can you come?'

'Why yes, of course,' I said.

I soon found that I was to be part of a most bizarre gaggle of attendees at the festivities.

Mohinder and I decided we would drive to Uganda from Nairobi. I did not fancy joining the Uganda Airlines flight from Stansted. Nor did I like the idea of not having our own transport should a quick getaway be required. We set out across the Great Rift Valley in the late afternoon

161

of 24 January 1977, glimpsing the rim of pink around the edges of Lake Nakuru, where the flamingos packed the shores. We ground up the escarpments of the valley as night fell. It's at this point that drivers take their lives in their hands. Unlit trucks completely enveloped in exhaust smoke toiled ahead, without a rear light between them. As he drove, Mohinder talked of how his family had been brought by the British to East Africa to build the railways. It was only now that I learned that his father had been the manager of the cotton shipping station at Namasagali, and that Mohinder himself had grown up in the compound of what is now the school in which I had taught back in 1967. It was a stunning coincidence which only served to seal the bond between us. He was perhaps twenty years older than me, and had seen action in Aden and the Congo, and travelled across most of the African continent. He was very much my technical mentor, looking after the pictures while I tried to divine the political threads bound up in what we were seeing.

That night we stayed at the Kericho Tea Hotel in Kenya. Log fires burned in the bedroom fireplaces against the cold at the seven-thousand-foot altitude. Porridge greeted us for breakfast. Through the open dining-room window, the dew on the tea bushes was turning to steam in the morning sun. It was a pleasant contrast to the looming prospect of tea with the tyrant ahead of us. Western journalists had had little or no access to Uganda since Entebbe, and Mohinder and I were daunted by what we might find.

Approaching the border south of Mount

Eldoret I began to feel butterflies in my stomach. These are the moments when you think of home, of family and other log fires. But in the event we crossed without incident, and proceeded to our destination a few miles short of Kampala.

Cape Villas, on the shore of Lake Victoria, had clearly been recently and hurriedly completed. The presidential guest complex was a series of sumptuously appointed circular brick-built huts with brand new thatched roofs and bougainvillea in the gardens around them. Picturesque fishing boats were drawn up on the foreshore. It seemed about as far from mass murder as you could get. Then I remembered Archbishop Luum, Uganda's top cleric, murdered in a fake car-crash just up the road ten months earlier.

We'd been at our fancy abode for an hour when Bob Astles suddenly appeared. He was better dressed but no less nervous than when I'd seen him at Waterloo station. 'The Life President wants to see you now,' he announced. From under his arm he produced a grubby W.H. Smith paper bag with a book in it. I pulled it out: it was *The Joy of Sailing*, by the former British Prime Minister Edward Heath.

'What's all this about?' I asked Astles.

'It's your gift to the Life President. It's personally signed by Heath,' he replied.

I looked, and so it was: 'With best wishes, Edward Heath'. But someone had doctored it, adding the words 'To HE the Life President' above it.

'I told him you'd got him to sign it for him,' said Astles.

I wondered what on earth landlocked Amin would want with a book about ocean sailing – he'd sink any sailing boat just by boarding it. I was clearly going to be compromised. Still, I was probably compromised by being here at all.

On the eve of the coup anniversary, the Life President staged a welcoming cocktail party on the lawns outside Nile Mansions, the pre-coup five-star hotel in Kampala that was now reserved for his most loyal army officers. We were startled to find a considerable array of white men and women amongst the officers, Ministers and their wives. Some of them, like Peter Gamer, were opportunist businessmen who'd stayed on under Amin, turning a blind eye and making a fast buck while the country went to ruin. Gamer had lured a curious crew of Essex beef farmers out to Uganda to try to reboot the country's ailing farm stock. It seemed that they farmed near Stansted Airport, the centre of operations of Amin's personal airline, Uganda Airways. They'd sold Amin three thousand head of cattle, and travelled out with frozen buckets of semen to fertilise more. As neither Astles nor Gamer appeared to have any suitable farming contacts, they seemed simply to have looked in the Essex Yellow Pages under 'Beef Farmers'.

So here, fresh from their Uganda Airways flight were half a dozen unsuspecting men, led by the Chairman of the Essex Agricultural Society, sipping Amin's Pimm's in the heart of Africa's present darkness. Some of the Ugandans they mingled with had been identified by human rights groups as having been involved in disappearances and killings. Two officers implicated in Archbishop Luum's murder were there, as were two others who were later revealed to have abducted and murdered seventy-four-year-old Dora Bloch of the hijacked Entebbe passengers.

Suddenly the air was split by the moan of bagpipes. I looked up and saw two Scottish pipers in full fig marching towards me, and there, adorned in a vast kilt, with a white woman at his elbow, strode Big Daddy himself. Thinking Mohinder and I were the only journalists present, I was surprised to catch sight of Bill Lovelace, celebrated photographer with the *Daily Express*. He'd somehow got into the country illegally on a tourist visa. He didn't see Bob Astles creeping up on him as he snapped the Life President. 'Arrest that man!' Astles bellowed. Amin turned and gesticulated as poor old Lovelace was dragged away by his hair. The British guests didn't flinch for a moment. Now was not the moment to try to remonstrate with Astles; poor old Bill would have to languish until these proceedings were done.

I set about trying to find out who the woman on Amin's arm was. Gamer told me, 'She's an Africa expert, Judith, Countess of Listowel. She thinks Amin's been given a rough deal. She's here to help rehabilitate him. Not bad for seventy-three, is she?' As far as I could divine she was a Hungarian who had met and married an Irish peer at the London School of Economics in the 1920s and had been engaged in a kind of 'grand tour' ever since. Unlike her forebears', her tour had embraced East Africa, about which she had written extensively. How on earth Amin had inveigled her into coming here she refused to tell me. I suspected it was simply because he had paid for her trip.

The pipers too seemed to have come out of the Essex Yellow Pages. Alec McLathlan and Willie Cochrane were clearly more used to domestic weddings and funerals than to Amin's curious coup-related rituals. Certainly the Field Marshal cut an unusual dash with his skewed beret, his bilious red tartan sash, and his considerable knees knocking beneath his swirling kilt. Among the many delusions he suffered from was his claim to be 'the Last King of Scotland'. Hence the bizarre parade of all things Scots, from the pipes to the exotic tartans.

All over the lawns was evidence of the true extent of the part British business played in keeping this eccentric ruler in power. There was Captain Robert Critchley, who had managed the training of Amin's pilots. There was a banker, a farm machinery supplier, a food and wine retailer.

Suddenly Astles was at my shoulder. Amin wanted to see me. I was led to the far end of the lawn, where he was now sitting at a wooden desk. Astles signalled to me to present the Heath book. One of Amin's enormous hands grabbed it, the other grabbed me. We were long-lost friends. We talked of Namasagali, Father Grimes, boxing, anything but dead archbishops and killing. Was this journalism, I wondered, or fraternising with the enemy?

Amin was thrilled with the Heath book, and asked me to read out the inscription to him. Although I think he could read, he clearly couldn't

166

read Heath's handwriting. Close to, he positively rippled as he laughed, his flesh seeming to heave. But when I unwisely raised the matter of poor old Bill Lovelace, his eyes narrowed and he smouldered. 'Is he a friend of yours?'

'Are you going to do anything to him?'

'He's a spy,' said Amin.

'No,' I said, 'I know he's not a spy. He drinks too much.' Thankfully Amin thought this very funny.

A few minutes later Lovelace, looking frightened and beaten about, was dragged before us. I was left standing complicitly at Amin's side of the table as he lunged over, grabbed Bill's left ear and twisted it. 'I'm ordering my men to drive you to the Kenya border and to dump you there. What happens to you after that is not my business,' he said menacingly.

The celebrations the next day in Kampala's main soccer stadium passed off without incident. This time the Life President was in full military fatigues as he took the salute.

'Pssstt! Mr Muzira,' a voice whispered behind me, 'it's me, Noah Omolo.' It was hard to credit it, but here was my brightest pupil from Namasagali, still alive, and even reasonably prosperous looking, in full military uniform. He'd always called me 'muzira', the Lugandan for 'snow', even though few Ugandans knew what it was. 'Sir,' he whispered, 'things are desperate here, you have no idea how bad. I'm in charge of a couple of prisons, and they are full of teachers and doctors and people who know what's really going on here. I can't talk to you, but you must tell people how bad things are here. So much killing, so much blood, even my own family.' Pointing to the parade in front of Amin, he said, 'This isn't the story, this is show. Underneath there is nothing but fear.' With that he disappeared back into the rows of military standing around the stadium.

A day or two later, waiting at Cape Villas for my interview with Amin, I heard the shocking news on the BBC World Service that the Countess of Listowel and seventeen other British guests had disappeared in a thirty-seater plane in bad weather in the north of Uganda. In a trice, Astles was at the door. 'H.E. wants you now,' he barked.

'Has there been an air crash?' I asked.

'We don't know,' he snapped. 'Anyway, it's none of your bloody business.'

Amin was today decked out like a glorified Texan ranger, with a huge Stetson and his protruding pot covered in khaki. 'Come on,' he said, 'we are going to rescue them.' Mohinder and I were bundled into his convoy, which then sped to Entebbe. The old terminal was a shambles, covered in bullet holes – evidently untouched since the Israeli raid. Mangled military wreckage lay rusting around it. On the apron of the runway stood a small, gleaming Falcon executive jet.

'I shall fly you myself,' Amin announced.

'Please God not,' I prayed. My prayers were answered, as a ginger-haired Swiss pilot haled into view and clambered into the cockpit. The light drained from the plane as Amin wedged his way into the small cabin and sank into the seat next to mine. Very soon we took off, heading north with our hearts in our boots. Apart from

Mohinder and his nephew and sound man Paul, there was only the pilot and a burly air hostess at the back of the plane to keep us company. Amin almost immediately fell asleep. The Stetson slipped forward over his face and I was able to observe him undetected. I noticed that his holster was hanging down through the armrest of his seat, just a few inches from my left hand. There was a gun in it.

I started rashly to consider whether I should shoot him with his own pistol. As we gathered height I wondered what happens when you shoot a very fat man in the tight confines of a pressurised aircraft cabin. Does the bullet ricochet around inside his ghastly girth, or does it go right through it, and out through the fuselage, taking us with it? Then I wondered, is the gun loaded? Is he actually asleep? And what does the pilot do, what does the air hostess do? Presumably, if I succeeded, they would know it was in their best interests to fly the whole heap of him out of the country and deliver the carcass to the world beyond. Was all this some wretched test? Cowardice got the better of me, and I failed to finish him off. So there's my admission: Amin's poolside Jeddah life was partially down to me.

As for the Countess of Listowel and her fellow passengers, they were all rescued just before we reached them. Their twin-engined Otter had simply run out of fuel, and sat forlornly on a grassy area in the middle of Murchison Falls National Park. The Countess returned to Britain, and was to live on to the age of a hundred, dying in 2003. We returned to Entebbe having satisfied ourselves that her party was safe. We were all in one piece, our fuel had held up, Amin had not shot us, and I had not shot him.

On our last morning in our Cape Villas quarters I was awakened by a great clattering and raised voices on the foreshore of Lake Victoria beyond my window. Squinting through the shutters in the half light I saw Bob Astles, in a bloodsoaked shirt, coming up the beach, where a small boat had been pulled ashore. There were some equally bloodied African men with him. I roused Mohinder, and after they'd gone we went down to look at the boat. There was blood everywhere in the bottom, and a bloody-handled machete. Perhaps they'd had a run-in with a particularly large Nile perch. Mohinder could read my thoughts. 'H-h-h-h-um-m-m-an,' he said. Later in the morning, as he drove us to our interview with Amin, Astles said he'd had to 'sort out some coffee smugglers'. This was a euphemism, I suspected, for cutting up some political opponents. In my mind's eye I could see him back on Waterloo station again. As far as I know he may still be alive somewhere in South London. A strange, satanic yet engaging man who in another life might have had no more sinister duty than to explain the late arrival of the train from Penzance. There were – probably still are – men like Astles all over Africa, providing the most vital service to some of the most unpleasant people.

I grabbed my less than challenging interview with the Life President, and fled the country with great relief.

The radio operator in the Entebbe control tower refused to reveal who was actually in charge of the runway he was permitting us to land on. It was now April 1979, and from our little Cessna Mohinder and I could see troops and equipment dotted about the airfield. We had come from the Tanzanian capital, Dar es Salaam, where the assumption was that the Tanzanian army might be in charge of Uganda by now.

Throughout Amin's tyranny, Tanzania's President Julius Nyerere had granted safe haven to the deposed President Milton Obote, his fellow 'socialist'. For over five years Obote and Nyerere watched and waited for the chance to restore the old order. Their chance came in November 1978, when Amin rashly invaded western Tanzania. Nyerere's forces, together with a few Ugandan opposition groups, not only pushed Amin's army back into Uganda, but seized the chance to try to get rid of the dictator altogether. Now Tanzanian forces were closing in on Kampala from the west. Fortunately for us, they had captured the airfield. No one checked our passports, no one gave us permission to enter the country, but we did anyway. Outside the terminal, an officer allowed us to join a troop carrier. We sat rather exposed on the roof. As we trundled up the road to the capital, bedraggled remnants of Amin's army were running weaponless in the opposite direction with their hands in the air.

The city was in absolute chaos. Smashed-up military vehicles were strewn about the streets, fires burned, people stared at us vacantly. We were dropped off at the old Apollo Hotel, half of which seemed to have become a barracks. A knot of journalists loitered on the forecourt. The BBC was there in force, Brian Barron and Mohamed Amin giving every indication that they already owned the story. Indeed, as the only team to have managed to get in from Kenyan airspace they had opened a private bridgehead to Nairobi, which they exploited to the full, bringing in fresh food and drink and taking out shot film. Our poor old plane would have to go twice as far, to Dar, and even then there wasn't much there in the way of food and drink to be brought back.

I managed to get rooms, but as I was standing at the desk I felt a tap on my shoulder. It was one of the few women reporters in the city. 'Could I have a word?' she asked. 'It's desperately unsafe here. The soldiers are up to everything, there's a lot of rape and mayhem. Could I share your room?' I offered to share with Mohinder. 'That's not the point,' she said. 'I can't sleep alone, it's too dangerous.' We were to live and work together for three weeks, a sublime and, in my experience, rare collision of love and war. We were to part as friends, and never to see each other again. The room had no glass in the window, and the sheets were more holes than fabric. Every night was racked with gunfire and distant screams.

War brings you extraordinarily close to the people you work with. Your team become brothers and sisters, in an intense, almost familial conspiracy both to stay alive and to tell the story of what you have seen more graphically, more coherently, more speedily than anyone else. Sometimes the intensity spilt over into a kind of love, but not

172

often. It was a love born of shared danger, of living now, before it was too late. Curiously strong friendships also developed in the field. My closest were with my cameraman Alan Downes and sound man Don Warren. We would argue about Brahms and the Who, about our desert island discs, about Ted Dexter and Bobby Charlton. But when we got home we rarely saw each other socially. Then, when the whistle blew and we were once more in the field under fire, we were brothers again, just where we had left off. Today I'm the last one in the field: Alan died of a brain tumour, Don suffered a stroke.

The work in those three weeks was arduous and exhausting. We lived off *mattoke* (vegetable bananas) and sweet potatoes, and every day we would go to the front line to see how far the Tanzanians had pushed Amin's forces. They were already halfway down the Jinja road, twenty miles or more east of Kampala along the lakeside that led to the dam across the Nile, and eventually the border with Kenya. All along the road you could smell putrefying death. Look closely into the tropical undergrowth and the bloated body of a dead Ugandan soldier lay there.

One morning, instead of heading for the front line we ventured to Amin's Command Post. There had been terrible carnage here too. The stench entered our every pore. Underneath the complex was a kind of dank holding chamber where people had evidently been detained and tortured. There were manacles attached to the walls, and blood spattered about them. I thought of Noah Omolo, of Father Grimes, of all my students at Kamuli College. Had they survived? What unimaginable suffering had Amin's tyranny inflicted on them? Not for the first time on assignment, I began to cry openly.

Beneath the flowering bougainvillea, the lawns around the Command Post were feet deep in paperwork: pale blue files, orange files, buff-coloured files were strewn everywhere. Paper blew about all over the place. Amin's secret police kept exceptionally detailed and incriminating evidence of what they were up to. A few people poked about looking for information about missing relatives. The files were interspersed with dried pools of blood, old ammunition casings and worse. The testimony to Amin's brutality was everywhere; we simply didn't have the capacity to begin to chart it.

The building itself was in ruins. The top storey had gone, and much of the rest was badly scorched, as were many of the files. Someone had defecated in what had been Amin's presidential office. How had anyone maintained relations with this man? To what end? In whose interests? At the back of Amin's office were boxes of medals, supplied by some British outfit in London's St James's. Sumptuous silk ribbons were attached to silver circular representations of Amin in full uniform. They'd had a job squeezing him onto this dishonourable honour. I pocketed one, and have it to this day.

We returned to the hotel to find the BBC ostentatiously pigging out on steak and red wine. They had been able to beat us on shipments of film on a daily basis. Their exclusive Kenya link was so much better than ours to Dar. The front line had been moving so slowly that the BBC had stopped joining us on the dawn run to find out where it had got to. The sight of their breakfast marmalade, toast, eggs and bacon was too much for us as we wrestled with our bananas, so we continued to head out. One glorious day we drove down the Jinja road alone for mile upon mile. The front line had gone. We pounded on almost to the River Nile. There, suddenly, was the entire Tanzanian force, gathered for the final push across the dam and into Uganda's second city of Jinja. We teamed up with the only other cameraman there, Tony Avirgan of UPI. Within an hour of our arrival the entire convoy set off in pursuit of Amin, who was reportedly on the other side of the river.

The Owen Falls Dam is thrown across a rocky gorge at the source of the Nile as it courses out of Lake Victoria on its journey north. A vast race of water forces its way through the dam beneath the road that curves across its concrete crust. Amin must have been either in too much of a hurry or too ill-prepared to blow it up in his wake. We got stunning pictures of the huge armoured column on the dam top, and more as it fanned out to take Jinja.

At the very moment when Amin was about to be captured, a twin-jet Bell helicopter arrived to spirit him away from the centre of Jinja. It had Libyan markings, and within minutes it had lifted out of the trees ahead of us to take him to his eventual Saudi oblivion. It was all over. The fat man had flown, and we had the story exclusively. Uganda had been liberated, and us with it. We tore back along the Jinja road in time to see the BBC coming out of Kampala in their Mercedes, probably thinking we'd just had another boring run to the front line.

Nothing is ever as good as it seems. UPI's Tony Avirgan was technically allied to us and barred to the BBC, but somehow they managed to beg, borrow or buy his material. Fortunately our Dar aircraft connection held up for once, and on the one day that it mattered we beat the BBC and their wretched bacon and eggs. The episode brought particular pleasure to Mohinder, for not only had his childhood home been freed, but he'd scooped his old rival.

Eight long and bloody years of Amin's rule were over. From a superpower perspective, Uganda had no oil, no role in the Cold War, and so was not important. Amin could be left to fester, and to feast off the fruits of those British and other international interests which were prepared to go on tolerating him. Yet his tyranny laid the groundwork for years more of civil war in Uganda, and provided an incubator for the worst plague ever to visit our generation.

To my eternal shame, I did not return to Uganda in the time of AIDS, when life expectancy in the country fell from fifty-two to forty. I did not witness the inspirational coming in 1986 of Yoweri Museveni as one of the African continent's sparks of hope, the man who ended years of bloodshed and devoted his many years in power to daily campaigns to roll back HIV and

AIDS. He also pioneered a kind of one-party democracy that had far greater application in an African context than the Westminster model ever did.

It would be another twenty years before I would return, and only then did I reach Kamuli College at Namasagali and discover what had happened to the children I had taught three decades before.

Somalia did not have oil either, but it was of infinitely more strategic interest than Uganda ever was. At the height of the Cold War, control of the oil routes in and out of the Middle Eastern oilfields was a centrepiece of the foreign policy of both Washington and Moscow. On my first trip to Somalia, in 1976, I had been granted an interview with President Siad Barre. He was a post-tribal hard-line Communist, in his own words a 'scientific socialist'.

Mogadishu was a beautiful confusion of Arab, African and Italian influences nestling on the Indian Ocean. Our hotel, the Croce del Sud, could have fallen out of the pages of a Graham Greene novel. An oasis from the vertical sun beating down on the streets outside, the Croce sported a palm-shaded courtyard and rooms off open walkways. The cuisine was Arab/Italian; the service was so discreet it barely existed. From my window I could see the ocean lapping at the harbour breakwater. At the northern end of the sandy beach to the north of the capital stood the remnants of the American Colony Club. What it certainly did not stock in any form was Americans; there were none, a sure sign of Moscow's current upper hand here. But the beer still flowed, and it was a mellow place to hang out.

At the other end of town were two embassies of note. The Soviet outpost was a functional, dusty pile, festooned with aerials and listening devices, and heavily guarded. Our cameras were shooed away at their first appearance. Down a sidestreet, the British embassy, with a staff of four, was an altogether more accessible place. The Ambassador, Harry Brind, drove over in the embassy Range Rover to collect me after I had phoned for a briefing. He was the very best of British, committed, engaged, Arabic-speaking, and knew the country every whichway.

Half of Somalia, at the Red Sea end, had been a British colony; the rest the Italians ran until the Second World War, then Britain got to run the lot. The Ambassador explained the absurdly geometrical borders with Ethiopia, the straightest on earth: the Brits had merely wielded a ruler on the desert map and drawn a line dividing Somalia from Italian-ruled Ethiopia. Brind described an air of tyranny and Soviet permanence about the place. 'Terrible tribal tensions under the surface,' he told me. 'If Johnny Brezhnev ever gets out of here, the place will eventually go up, and not one of us will be safe.' Even then, Somalia was a powderkeg, and demanded all the skills of any colonial power, even the Soviets, to keep it under control. I looked at Brind's unguarded wooden embassy door and wondered how long it would protect him if his worst fears were ever realised. He was more prescient in his forecast than even he could have known.

For all its volatility, Somalia was a vital strategic asset in the evolving Cold War. Whoever controlled the country controlled the naval sea port of Berbera, and whoever controlled Berbera had a hold on the sea lanes leading to and from the Red Sea, with its vast array of oilfields upon which Western well-being depended.

Siad Barre sat in an austere office in a concrete-block building looking over the town. A grumpy, jowly man in a dark suit, he was a complete contrast to Idi Amin. I had the feeling that if he ordered the disposal of an opponent, it would be done within the hour, with ruthless efficiency. He was a Moscow-educated ideologue, running a classic Cold War Russian client state.

'I see you are allowing the Russian navy to base and bunker in Berbera,' I said in the course of my interview.

'There are no foreign warships there, and if there were, it would be none of your business,' he replied.

'Can we go and film there to see for ourselves?' I asked.

'Show Mr Snow out!' Barre shouted at an aide behind me. The interview ended uncomfortably, and we headed for Berbera.

Somalia was one of those countries where if you filmed a military spare tyre you'd be thrown in jail for espionage. So we had to film more or less anything else, in order to report about what we could not film. Thus Mohinder and I, spotting a spectacular herd of camels drinking at a rare stretch of river, would leap out of our vehicle and film as if it was our last. Our government-supplied minder must have been as mystified as our viewers, who were treated to a travelogue of a sleepy old country in which an excitable white man jumped up and down talking about the threat to world peace. With considerable subterfuge, and the deployment of gifts and raw dollars, we did manage to get a few glimpses of the funnels and superstructures of warships – enough at least to prove that the Russians were there.

Within six months they'd gone, and I was back in Mogadishu. The Russians had changed sides and embraced the emerging Ethiopian Marxist Derg, as the new administration in Addis was known, and were consolidating its power next door. Uncle Siad now had to adjust his rhetoric to fit with an American embrace. Who was bunkering in Berbera was now of rather less immediate import than who was fighting whom.

In the aftermath of the overthrow of Ethiopia's Emperor Haile Selassie in September 1974, Somalia had chosen the moment to sort out the British-imposed straight lines of the border between the two countries. The fact that the entire area was made up of the remorseless Ogaden Desert was of no consequence, beyond the fact that it gave the ensuing war its name. By the end of 1977 the straight lines had been well and truly bent. Somalia had captured 90 per cent of the Ogaden Desert, an area the powers in Mogadishu had felt belonged to them since long before colonial times.

Siad Barre had the witty idea of dressing up his invasion of Ethiopia as a war of liberation to be fought by the Western Somali Liberation Front

(WSLF). In reality the WSLF was a front for the Somali army. Even permission to go to the front had to be obtained from the Somali Ministry of Defence in Mogadishu. Barre believed that if the invaders were seen as a liberation force, the outcome would stand a better chance of international recognition than if Somalia simply annexed the Ogaden.

The usual gaggle from the East African Correspondents' Association, together with a visiting French crew, gathered in the tumble-down bar of the American Colony. This time the Associations' dean himself, John Osmond, was in attendance. Alas, Mohinder was not. Instead, because someone in the office had looked at the map and decided Italian-speakers would be useful, the Nocco brothers, Juliano and Massimo, ITN's crew in Rome, had been dispatched. The nearest they'd ever been to a developing country was probably Sicily, and they found Somalia rather too far from home. Juliano was a big chap who felt the heat badly, while his brother had the dashing looks and clothes of an Italian B-movie star.

At last permission to visit the front came and we set off in a great convoy into the desert, with Osmond very much in command. Despite his safari suit, I'm not sure that John, approaching sixty and a shade overweight, was cut out for desert travel. By nightfall only the considerable supply of BBC claret lowered his temperature. By the second night, with no sign of the WSLF, let alone the Somali army, Osmond had had enough. He stood on a small mound and declared the

181

adventure a disaster. Herding his supplies about him, he said he was going no further, and that everyone was free to join him. No one did. John humbly retreated to the stern vehicle, and we set off again through the night.

At dawn we came upon a small desert encampment; this was as far as our vehicles could go without the dust thrown up by their wheels disclosing our whereabouts to the enemy. We had to head onwards on foot. Our Somali guides had little or no idea how far we'd have to walk. We could hear the crump of heavy artillery, and the occasional jet, but we could see nothing but an increasingly steep hillside ahead. It was dry and very hot. About halfway through the day we came upon another outpost, where one of the sentries told us we had about another six hours' walk ahead of us.

Juliano was in trouble. Somehow he'd become bigger in the course of our struggle along the hillside track. His ankles had swollen up so much I thought he might have the dropsy, whatever that was. In any case, he wasn't going on, and we had to leave him in the shade with a sentry. Several others decided to stay with him. I felt churlish for not calling off our quest for the front line, but the competitive instinct prevailed.

The big problem now was that I had no cameraman; Massimo complained that he was only a sound man. It was clear I'd have to do it myself. We were armed with a CP16 film camera, heavy and complicated to the innocent eye. Mine was innocent indeed: I had never shot a moving picture in my life. There were now only two other cameramen with us. The BBC's man was concerned but unhelpful, but the Frenchman from the TV station TF1 did agree to give me tuition in Franglais as we marched.

'Keep ze lens wide, no zooms,' he said.

'How do I change the magazine?' I asked.

'Ce n'est pas possible pour toi,' he said.

I only had four hundred feet of film in the camera – about twelve minutes if I was lucky. The tutorial was suddenly interrupted by a great barrage of machine-gun fire, followed by wallops of artillery shells thudding into the hillside opposite us. We dived to the ground; there was no effective cover apart from the boulders that littered the scrubby hillside. Smoke from the explosions rose in the clear blue air. We were absurdly exposed. I began to think Osmond had been wiser than I had allowed; this was a crazy escapade. We were walking right into a battle about which no one in London would give a damn.

There was now a lot of movement about us. Dishevelled soldiers, some of them no more than fourteen or fifteen years old, began to appear from everywhere. Belts of machine-gun rounds drooped from their shoulders. Some were carrying weapons so heavy that they could hardly stand. I tried to film some of the scenes around me, but nothing I could see through the eyepiece suggested a front line. Eventually we learned that the real front was another half-mile or so further on. Our escorts decided that only cameramen could carry on, so the three of us advanced, crouching most of the way. Just over the crest we

183

came upon a labyrinth of trenches and an array of artillery pieces that must have been lugged there by human muscle. We jumped into the first available trench and almost immediately were overwhelmed by a series of devastating crashes and bangs. Smoke and smells erupted all around us. It felt like the sort of thing General Tom might have ordained, far removed from oil routes and the Cold War.

I tried to establish myself with the camera, keeping the lens wide as instructed, but every time someone opened fire I gave an involuntary jerk in response. My pictures would be all over the place. Somehow I had to grab a 'piece to camera' to prove I had ever been there. I found a ledge near the top of my trench, perched the camera, turned it on, ran back and gave a breathless account, trying to connect this chaotic scene with the unsuspecting viewer at home. We retreated fast under fire, amazingly in one piece. We found a dejected Juliano, still under his tree, and somehow carried or dragged him back to the convoy.

Back in the bar of the American Colony, with the Indian Ocean lapping about us, I tried to script my arid, overheated and obscenely dangerous journey to the front. It felt important. For all the remoteness of it, we had actually witnessed a Cold War flashpoint. Two sides, each armed by a superpower, had been slugging it out, fighting a proxy war to establish control of a vital chokepoint for oil. It was my first glimpse of the infernal combine of oil and war, the two heavy industries that in their own way fuelled both Russian and American

184

ambition. Yet the combatants had been child soldiers – this was the forerunner of so many African wars in which the ranks were almost exclusively filled by children under eighteen.

But I could not know this at the time, and dispatched my story as a slice of war with some good 'bang bang'. That was a commodity which in the aftermath of the Vietnam War was in thankfully short supply on television news. Alas, when my film reached London, the technicians thought the material so badly shot that they called an immediate trade union protest meeting to black it, rightly believing that it couldn't possibly have been shot by one of their members. Eventually my editors wrung a two-minute portion of my four-minute script out of them – all that risk and effort for two minutes of television news.

In all I was dispatched half a dozen times to Somalia in the late 1970s. Every time the strategic position seemed to shift, I'd be on a plane to Mogadishu. By 1978 Somalia had fifty thousand men in the Ogaden, together with tanks and planes. But the war had begun to turn in Ethiopia's favour.

In early 1978, dusty stuffed mongoose heads glowered down on us as we overnighted on the floor of the old British Club in the northern city of Hargeisa. This time we were to cross into Ethiopia, and right up to the front line in Jijiga and Dire Dawa. What we did not know was that Russia and Cuba had sent some 12,500 advisers, pilots and operational forces into Ethiopia in an effort to turn the tide. And turn it did. We had arrived in time to see the humiliation of Siad Barre.

The Somalis were now in full retreat, no longer even pretending to be the liberating forces of the WSLF. It was every man for himself; troops clung to anything that moved as trucks, tanks, ambulances, bulldozers and the rest clattered for the border. It was a signal of how little super-power force it can take to change the course of an African war.

The Horn of Africa was now the unreported cockpit of superpower engagement. America invested heavily in keeping Somalia pro-Western, matching Russian commitments in Ethiopia dollar for rouble. Sudan, to the north of both but bordering more of the Red Sea, was itself racked by a civil war which both superpowers gave every impression of being content to leave unfettered. The ingredients for another failed state were left to brew, to such an extent that one day Osama bin Laden himself would choose to make his base here.

Inevitably, I found myself dispatched to the Sudanese capital, Khartoum, to try to cover other aspects of the East–West power play in the Horn. Ethiopia only made sense to Moscow so long as she clung on to her Eritrean Red Sea coast. Eritrea had formerly been a nation in its own right, and had only been tacked onto Ethiopia following the upheavals of the Second World War. The Eritrean Liberation Front had long been fighting a secessionist war. Sudan was my only possible way in.

So here I was once more on 'General Tom's stomping ground. A new and opulent Hilton Hotel now overlooked the junction of the two Niles. My room looked over the pool. A gorgeous triangular brown-orange sail shaded the poolside bar, at which little stools sat beneath the water so that you could drink half-submerged at the bar. Beyond the shade of the sail, the temperature soared to 130°F. This time I had my most trusted crew with me, Alan Downes on camera, who had seen action in Vietnam, and my sound man Don Warren. We only had one night of comfort before we flew south to Kassala on the Eritrean border. Once across the border we had to sleep rough and trust to any conveyance that the Eritreans could provide. The Cubans were already in action overhead, piloting Ethiopian MIGs, screaming out of the midday sun.

Ten days' walking with guerrilla bands passed exceedingly slowly. We spent the time inventing imaginary outposts even more deprived of comforts than Eritrea. Our trek was to prepare us as a team for three or four years of forced marches everywhere from Nicaragua to Angola to Afghanistan. A rare Eritrean Red Crescent vehicle took us the last few miles to the ELF's desert headquarters. On a wall inside the commander's hut I was startled to see a huge poster of Fidel Castro.

'We were trained in Havana,' said Commander Aferwerke. 'He will not let us down.'

'His pilots are bombing you,' I said.

'It is his tactic,' he replied.

Throughout the thirty years' struggle, and even after the Russian-led intervention on the

Ethiopian side, the Eritreans had been Castroist Marxists to the very core. They organised their underground schools and hospitals along Cuban lines, and practised the military teachings of Fidel and Che. Latin America had no more ardent a revolutionary fan base than in Eritrea, yet now they were under punishing aerial and artillery bombardment courtesy of the very people they most revered.

We were to make two harrowing visits to Eritrea. During the second, in July 1978, we witnessed the bombing of the children's hospital at Mandefera, not far from the capital city of Asmara. Six-year-old Muna lost her hand; Ahmed, not much older, lost his leg below the knee. Doctors were running around in the wreckage as the Cuban-piloted MIGs dived and dived again, unleashing visible sticks of bombs as they swooped. Two dozen or more children died, many adults besides. I picked up a small boy who was bleeding profusely from the stomach. Someone told me his name was Meles. His eyes were still open. There was nothing I could do. He died in my arms.

We took our film back to London. It was a salutary account of Russian colonialism in action. When I got back to my desk, having voiced my account live in the studio, I found a note with a phone number on it, and the message 'Please ring Paul Getty.'

'Someone's having me on,' I thought. I dialled the number sheepishly. 'Is Mr Getty there?' I asked *sotto voce*, for fear my colleagues would overhear me making a complete idiot of myself.

'One moment.'

A few seconds later another voice came on the line. 'Hello, Mr Snow. This is Paul Getty. I've just watched your report on the news, and I want to help. Would it be possible for you to come and see me?'

'Of course I can,' I replied.

'Very well,' he said. 'Come for tea tomorrow at four o'clock – it's Christina Rossetti's House, Cheyne Walk, on the Chelsea Embankment.'

The iron gate screeched on its hinges. I pulled the old-fashioned doorbell and was ushered in by a manservant. The hall was an impenetrable jungle of furniture, books and pictures. There was only the narrowest path through it all. At the far end was Paul Getty, stooped, pale and out of condition, but charming. We sat beside a silver salver on the only two available chairs, and in the semi-darkness conjured the children's hospital in Mandefera.

'What can I do?' he asked.

'Well, I've talked with War on Want, who are the lead agency in Eritrea,' I said. 'They say more than anything they need a field hospital.'

'How much are they?' he asked, as if we could pop out and pick one up from Marks & Spencer's.

'£40,000,' I said, somewhat diffidently.

'I shall give two, then. Can you sort out how we do that?'

'Why, of course,' I replied. With that I drained the Earl Grey tea from my bone china cup, picked my way out through the furniture, and emerged to the sun glinting on the water of the Thames. Within six weeks two state-of-the-art field hospitals had been shipped to Eritrea from Paris via Port Sudan.

It would be another ten years before the Russians retreated from Ethiopia and Eritrea gained her rightful independence. In the same time Somalia's Siad Barre would be overthrown and the warlords would smash the country back to the Dark Ages. But for now we were still at the height of the Cold War. Only the extraordinary and spontaneous philanthropy of one man served to lift the gloom suspended over a region sporting all the hallmarks of perpetual war.

My next assignment would expose me to a quite unexpected force that was to play a pivotal and unlikely role in bringing the Cold War to an end.

FIVE

First Brick Out of the Wall

Was it white, or was it black? The colour was critical. The smoke appeared to be a greyish white, not as black as it had been on previous days. Maybe it is only in hindsight that the smoke presented an ill omen. I was at the beginning of a well-timed year-long assignment as ITN's Rome correspondent. There were perhaps a couple of thousand people in St Peter's Square on the long summer Saturday evening of 27 August 1978, watching that tiny chimney on the edge of the roof of the Sistine Chapel. Not many reporters expect ever to see it in their careers, but I did, even if at the moment of seeing I was uncertain that I had. Indeed, Vatican Radio, whose English service I had in my ear, reported, 'We can now say with total certainty that the smoke is either black or white.'

In fact, white it had been, and Albino Luciani, Archbishop of Venice, had just been elected Pope John Paul I in the secret conclave of Cardinals gathered inside the chapel. He was an outsider, but still an Italian. The big Cardinals, the barons of the Italian Catholic Church, Sin, Benelli, Baggio and Pignedoli, had knocked each other out. Luciani was an apparently simple character from the second tier of Italian candidates for

191

Pope. Had he failed to be elected, the Cardinals would have had to look for the first non-Italian Pope in 455 years. The foreigner who had looked most likely had been Brazil's Cardinal Aloisio Lorscheider. He was not only possessed of a brilliant mind, but he was loved and supported by the poor of Latin America. Lorscheider was seen as an active practitioner of 'liberation theology'. He sided with the poor against corporate and big government interests, preaching that a Catholic's obligation was to defend and fight for the oppressed. US government and clerical circles saw him as a dangerous radical. Intriguingly, Lorscheider's greatest advocate in the Italian Church was Albino Luciani. Indeed, in the ballot that gave Luciani the papacy, he is reliably reported to have cast his own vote for Lorscheider.

The Lorscheider–Luciani axis held its greatest threat to US interests in Central and Latin America, where the gulf between rich and poor was as bad as anywhere in the world. Lorscheider had already been trouble enough in his defence of the poor in Brazil, and the idea that his views and teachings might be extended elsewhere in America's backyard by his friend the new Pope was anathema even to the Godfearing Carter administration. John Paul I's audience with US Vice President Walter Mondale, which I was allowed to witness, was nevertheless friendly. That with the Argentinian Foreign Minister, General Videla, was positively frosty. Luciani hammered the man for being party to a military dictatorship that had systematically 'disappeared' its opponents.

David Yallop, in his book *In God's Name*, argues that Luciani, who named himself John Paul after his two predecessor Popes, Paul and John, was murdered. He points the finger at Mafiosi bankers with close involvements with the Vatican bank, who stood to lose much at the hand of the new Pope. I didn't go that far. Luciani's death after just thirty-three days as Pope had a seismic effect, and mystified many, but murder was further than we could take it. On the night of his death, 28 September 1978, I'd been back in London collecting my possessions for my year in Italy. I hared to the airport and persuaded an Alitalia captain to take me on the jumpseat of the first, already overfull, morning flight to Rome.

'Don't be ridiculous,' he said to me after I'd explained that I needed to get to Rome to report the death of the Pope, 'he's been dead for weeks, and buried too.'

'No, not that one,' I said, 'the next one. He's dead too now.'

One of the most mysterious aspects of Pope John Paul's death was the Vatican's refusal to allow an autopsy. He had had low blood pressure, and little evidence of heart trouble. There was also considerable confusion about who had found him, in what condition and how. One of my best contacts in the exceptionally political world of Vatican City was Father Vincent O'Keefe, who was head of the Jesuits in Rome. Vincent told me he'd met Luciani in the Vatican garden about sixteen days into his pontificate. 'It was a slow, warm summer evening,' he recounted. 'I saw him coming towards me in his white cassock. He was alone, and crying. When I asked him what was wrong, it all came pouring out. "They" – I presume the Curia – were putting endless pressure on him over everything from appointments to signing vast quantities of paperwork. Nothing he wanted done, could he get done. "They" hated his proposed changes and reforms. "They" hated his extraordinary communication with the people at large.'

It's easy to forget now that in the fledgling days of close-up television access to the Pope, Luciani graced his papal occasions with an infectious smile and a beguiling simplicity of message. He secured an immediate and passionate following which contrasted acutely with the dull dwindling days of Pope Paul VI before him. As journalists we feasted on the Catholic Church's discomfiture over his death, but no one was able to take the story further. He was dead, and so for the moment was the prospect of institutionalised 'liberation theology' fuelled from Rome itself.

There now followed some of the most extreme political manoeuvrings I've witnessed in any context. The forces of Catholic conservatism found common cause with temporal alarmists who feared trouble if any kind of Third World Pope were to be elected to follow Luciani. Enter two of America's most senior Cardinals, the Archbishops of Philadelphia and Chicago. Philadelphia's Cardinal John Joseph Kroll was a fluent Polish-speaker, had spent much of his childhood in Poland, and was well connected with the Polish Catholic hierarchy. Chicago's Cardinal John Patrick Cody hailed from the richest archdiocese in America. While the US Cardinals could only muster a voting bloc in any conclave of about 10 per cent, they had the contacts and could offer the inducements to encourage others. Most Pope-watchers had concluded that in the next conclave the Italian barons would knock each other out again, and that there was a good chance of getting a non-Italian Pope.

Kroll and Cody determined that this time they should not go in unprepared. Cody's Chicago constituency was predominantly Polish, with the most useful direct lines into an Iron Curtain country that any American institution had. Nowhere on earth was Catholicism more conservative than in Poland, and in no Iron Curtain country was so much of the population still wedded so strongly to their pre-Communist faith.

I talked to Kroll and Cody subsequently in Rome. They were the soft man and hard man of American Catholicism respectively. Kroll was charming, intellectual and persuasive. Cody was contrastingly arrogant, bloated and unpleasant. His assorted chins wobbled as he boasted of how he, Kroll and two or three other leading lights in American Catholicism had settled on the idea of a Polish Pope. He told me that originally they had pitched for the great Second World War anti-fascist, Warsaw's Cardinal Wyszynski. But at eighty years old, Wyszynski refused to run, telling them that they should push instead for the energetic and charismatic Karol Wojtyla, the much younger Cardinal from Krakow. Kroll knew Wojtyla well, and had even invited him to officiate at a big international function in Philadelphia in 1976.

Cody boasted of his role with the CIA. He said that the Agency had been actively involved in trying to see whether a Pope could be elected who was more sympathetic to American interests. Cody had discussed with them the impact an Eastern Bloc Pope might have on the East–West balance of power and the fostering of protest inside the Iron Curtain. Having changed horses to back Kroll's man from Krakow, he had additional reasons for wanting the right man to become Pope. He was under strong suspicion of corruption, and Luciani had reportedly intended to force his resignation from Chicago.

On 14 October 1978, thick black smoke belched almost ostentatiously from the little chimney on the first morning of the secret conclave of the Cardinals. No Pope had ever been elected on the first vote, and in the tradition of the moment the prelates were burning their ballot papers. The crowds in St Peter's Square were much larger than two months previously, as if they too recognised that history was in the making.

Two days and eight ballots later, there was no doubting the colour of the smoke: pure white. Within the hour Cardinal Pericle Felici was standing, arms outstretched on the balcony of the portico of St Peter's. I was standing below, with many thousands of people pressing in. *'Annuntio vobis gaudium magnum,'* he bellowed. *'Habemus Papam Carolum Wojtyla, qui sibi nomen imposuit Ioannem Paulum II!'*

'Goodness, a woman Pope!' an Italian next to me exclaimed. No one around me had ever heard

196

of him. It was a few moments before we realised he was a foreigner, and more, that he came from behind the Iron Curtain. The skiing Cardinal, the former footballer, the man who'd had a steady girlfriend before turning to the priesthood, the Polish Archbishop of Krakow, had become Pope John Paul II.

Kroll, Cody and the other American Cardinals summoned a press conference that evening. They were well pleased. We couldn't understand why they hadn't tried to secure an American Pope. What was all this excitement about electing a Pole? In reality, even they could not have known that they had just taken the first brick out of the Berlin Wall, the physical manifestation of the Iron Curtain that divided Communist East from capitalist West.

Kroll was jubilant: every one of the ten US votes had gone to his friend Wojtyla. Kroll served the new Pope closely for another decade. It would be another three years before US law finally caught up with Chicago's Cardinal. Cody was subpoenaed on suspicion of embezzling hundreds of thousands of dollars' worth of Church funds. He was suspected of having lavished $1 million on his lifelong friend Helen Wilson, paying her a secret salary over many years and buying her a home in Florida. Cody died before he could be tried; he spoke his last in the high-handed style in which he had lived: 'I forgive my enemies, but God will not.'

From the outset it was clear that this Pope was going to be quite unlike any other. He had a spellbinding presence, and could converse in up to twenty languages. His deep conservatism on everything from birth control to homosexuality did nothing to dampen the superstar treatment he was given every time he descended to St Peter's Square.

That Christmas my mother came out to Rome for the festivities. My seventy-four-year-old father had died of a stroke just before Christmas 1977. He had only retired a year earlier, after a decade as a Bishop, and my mother was feeling his loss badly. I hadn't bargained for the effect the Pope would have on her, thinking that she, who had questioned my getting involved with an albeit lapsed Catholic in Madeleine, was most unlikely to fall for this fellow. But at midnight mass on Christmas Eve in St Peter's, I caught this devout Anglican with a lifelong suspicion of 'Romans' standing on a chair at the back of the cathedral, craning to see, waving her prayer paper, noisily cheering the new Pontiff.

The voice on the plane's intercom was unmistakable: 'This is your Pope speaking. It is time for the Angelus.' It was 24 January 1979, and we were three hours out of Rome aboard a Vatican-chartered Jumbo jet, bound for Mexico on John Paul II's first great papal visit. Popes had not travelled extensively before, but this one intended to change all that. We bowed our heads at the back as, somewhere at the front, the Pope offered prayers and a few chants.

An hour or so later, the blue curtains sealing off the papal compartment opened and the Pope came into our cabin. We rushed him like elephants, tumbling over the seats, cameras, microphone poles and notebooks hurtling about like medieval weapons. He raised his hand and, in Italian, said, 'Don't worry, I shall come round to each of you in turn.' His Irish chaplain, Father John Magee, suggested we huddle into lingual groupings so that the Pope didn't have to change back and forth too often between languages.

Not only was I suddenly about to become the fourth television journalist ever to interview a Pope – there were three correspondents ahead of me – I was to be the first ever to have him speak in English. Close up, John Paul II was not tall, but even in his cassock he appeared strong, even muscular, handsome too in a Slavic kind of way. Though his head was slightly stooped in the low-ceilinged plane, he made firm eye contact. He seemed strangely heterosexual for such a monastic figure, a man who knew about women; I can't say why I felt it, but we correspondents all discussed it afterwards.

We were on 'double system' film, where the pictures came through the camera and the sound was recorded on another machine and then synchronised afterwards. I had to clap to provide a sound and vision synchronisation point. The Pope seemed quite unfazed when I commenced my interview with a sharp clap and an immediate 'Take one!... Holy Father, have you ever been to Britain? Will you be coming?'

'I'd like to come one day to England,' he replied. 'I have friends there. Are you a Catholic?'

'No, my father was an Anglican Bishop.'

He wasn't sure where to take that, so I asked about liberation theology and what message he would have for the poor of Mexico.

'I do not like a confusion of Church and state,' he said. 'The priests should stay in their ministries, the government should stay in theirs.'

My world exclusive was over. He put his hand on my head, blessed me, and moved on.

We were to refuel and overnight at Santo Domingo in the Dominican Republic. My team and I made straight for the TV station when we landed, processed the film and then toiled desperately to try to get the papal lips to move in time with what he was saying. But whatever 'double system' they were on, we were not. I'd already called London and enthused about our world exclusive English interview with the Pope, but it was a disaster: we could only use the bits where his head was bowed enough for the viewer not to be able to lip read. A five-minute encounter came down to two. I was in despair. I went out onto the balcony of the transmission tower, which looked over the Caribbean, and flung the spool with the sound on it into the deep. I was of course a complete idiot. Very soon, new video and digital technology would come along that could synchronise the whole thing at the flick of a button. The first ever English interview with a Pope is even now, I imagine, gathering barnacles off Santo Domingo.

Coming in low over Popocatepetl, with smog-shrouded Mexico City rolling out beneath us, we had no idea what awaited us, and nor did the rest of the world. The airport appeared to be under siege; there were tens and tens of thousands of people spilling out onto the apron. We stood at the foot of the Alitalia steps as the Pope came out of the plane, went down on his knees and kissed the tarmac. It was a sublime and unexpected moment that stole a million hearts and more.

John Paul II's week in Mexico brought record swathes of humanity onto the streets. On the seven-mile pilgrimage to the shrine of Our Lady of Guadeloupe, both sides of the road were lined twenty people deep all the way. I remember walking behind our media transport and looking into the eyes of Mexicans of every possible condition. Some cried as the Pope passed. Others tried to touch his vehicle, or us if they missed. We reckoned that ten million people saw him on that day alone. At the shrine a strangely Mayan Indian-looking figure loomed above the Pope, personifying the Virgin Mary, who was supposed to have appeared there in 1531. Her countenance confirmed my suspicion, deepened by later years spent in Central America, that the early Spanish Christians who colonised the region hijacked existing figures of belief and turned them into Christian saints, thereby greatly easing the import of Catholicism.

The Pope's appeal in fluent Spanish was simple, conservative, and about as far from liberation theology and the empowerment of the poor as it was possible to get. It was clear that he represented absolutely no threat either to the ruling Institutional Revolutionary Party in Mexico or to the United States and her Latin American sphere of influence beyond.

The colourful spectacle of the Pope's visit to Mexico took the world by storm. The vivid reds and golds, yellows and greens splashed live onto television screens in Europe and the Americas by the hour had an extraordinary effect. This charismatic man in white in his glass-topped vehicle, the 'Popemobile', introduced a whiff of the Second Coming into even the most materialistic atheist lives. The Communist authorities in the Eastern Bloc naturally ensured that the pictures never reached homes behind the Iron Curtain. But those authorities themselves saw them, particularly in the Pope's Soviet satellite homeland, and they did not like what they saw.

The Pope spared no effort in those early months to let it be known that he intended to go to Poland at the earliest possible opportunity. The Polish leader Edward Gierek made it equally clear that they didn't want him there yet, if at all. Soon after we got back from Mexico in February the Pope came to his window one Sunday morning and told the assembled crowds that he would definitely be going to Poland. In doing so he would become the first Pope ever to go behind the Iron Curtain. Gierek in turn washed his hands of the trip, saying the Catholic Church would have to organise it themselves, and that his government reserved the right to cancel it. The idea that in the colourless, repressed, locked-down Eastern Bloc country, millions of people would be allowed to rally, take mass and pay obeisance to something, someone other than the state, was unimaginable, but that was what appeared to be in prospect.

Come 2 June 1979, and Gierek had managed to

keep the crowds away from Warsaw's airport. There was little to be seen apart from the remorseless greys of the airport buildings. But as Alan Downes and I neared the capital, Vatican banners and Polish welcome signs began to unfurl from the tenement windows of the slab blocks that lined the road.

This was to prove a challenging journey in more senses than either the political or the religious. ITN had supplied us with the first electronic lightweight video ever deployed by a British television station abroad. Until now we had used film, having to bathe it in chemicals for several hours before editing. Now, theoretically, we had instant video. The trouble was that the so-called lightweight camera was twice as heavy as its film forebear. It also had difficulty balancing its light exposures against the strong Polish summer sun. But it was magically fast and seductive. It also meant that we could generate footage inside the Iron Curtain that was independent of the Polish television service. Formerly we had to use their chemical baths, and they could always confiscate or censor our material. As a consequence of all this, ITN had commissioned a special programme in addition to the nightly news reports.

It was only when we reached Warsaw's daunting grey Victory Square that we woke up to the sheer scale of what was happening. There, towering above the square, was not the hammer and sickle of Communism but the cross of Christianity. The Communists had restricted the attendance to a staggering three hundred thousand people. Furthermore, Polish television was covering the event live. It's perhaps hard now to comprehend what an extraordinary development this was. Here was a centrally controlled Communist society, an integral element of the Soviet Union's sphere of influence, in whose very capital (that had given its name to the very military pact designed to resist the threats of NATO) hundreds of thousands of people were being allowed to do something that millions more were being permitted to watch, that the state was neither authoring nor managing. In more than thirty years of Communist government, a Catholic mass had never been shown on Polish television.

Late that night, the Pope did what he did every one of the six nights he was in Poland. He returned to the dais from which the mass had been conducted, took up the microphone and held easy but explosive dialogue with the predominantly young people who turned out to hear him. The odd guitar would be produced and he'd sing somewhat tuneless folk songs with them. It had the feel of a rather wholesome Scout and Guide jamboree. He told jokes, which the Poles seemed to find very funny but which died when our guide tried to translate them into English.

Once out of Warsaw, the numbers who gathered to see the Pope exploded into the virtually uncountable. Despite unimaginable transport difficulties, a million or more Poles trudged in the rain to Czestochova to share in the papal mass there. What a place it was! Our Lady of Czestochova was a strange, dark creature with a tear which apparently sometimes sheds itself in literal form. In the grounds of the basilica, unbelievable arrays

204

of tack were on sale. Large versions of the seaside postcards that change their picture if you move your eye depicted Christ. There was a huge one showing him in his crown of thorns. As I passed it, the thing changed to show drops of blood from the thorns running down his face. There was a wristwatch which revealed Christ on the hour. It was a wondrously confusing experience, hard-line Communism outside the fence, and slushy Catholicism displaying capitalist verve selling its tattered wares inside.

I guess we were all weeping by the time we got to Nova Huta, the belching steelworks on the outskirts of the Pope's home town of Krakow. A million people turned out for his mass here, in the epicentre of his entire life's ministry. High above the factory, at Gniezno, a massive hillside arena had been prepared towards the Czecho-slovak border. Despite roadblocks set up by the Communist authorities for fifteen miles around, a stunning two million souls gathered here in the June heat for yet another mass. It was evident that some of them had walked for hundreds of miles. As the Pope's white-painted, Russian-built helicopter landed amongst them they cried openly, tears cascading down their faces, as if generations of oppression were being released at his coming.

'Our own Pope!' they cried, sinking to their knees. 'Our own Pope!' Even we cynical journal-ists, who questioned John Paul II's conservatism on so many social issues, could not escape the overpowering implications of what this genuine connection with hearts was achieving in minds across the Iron Curtain. I spotted a Czech flag, held high by a middle-aged man far to the left of the makeshift altar. The Pope didn't miss a trick. He read the man's banner out loud for the benefit of anyone who might have missed it: 'Holy father, don't forget about the children of Czechoslovakia.' It was one of the most hysteria-driven, emotional occasions I ever had to report. For good measure, the Pope addressed the people of the Soviet Union itself: 'We cannot forget these brothers of ours,' he said. 'I trust that they hear me.'

Things would never be quite the same again. I'm convinced that the very existence of the Polish Pope removed a critical brick from the foundations of the Berlin Wall on 3 June 1979, although the Wall would not fall for another decade.

John Paul's Rome-based presence was able to cast a supportive shadow over the fledgling workers' campaign 'Solidarity', which would eventually bring democracy to Poland, and which by the summer of 1980 was beginning to pressure the Polish authorities for change. By December that year Soviet forces were massing on Poland's eastern frontier, and Soviet warships stood off the coast. But the ailing Soviet leader Leonid Brezhnev bowed to international pressure not to strike militarily. Twenty-two years earlier he had been able to terrorise the reformist Czechoslovak leader Alexander Dubcek and send Soviet forces in to extinguish the 'Prague Spring'.

Five months after Russia's telling loss of nerve in Poland, in April 1981, shocking news came from

Rome. Pope John Paul II had been shot in an assassination attempt while blessing the crowds in St Peter's Square from his open-topped white Popemobile. He was hit in the intestines, and his right arm and left hand were also wounded. One bullet passed right through his body. Surgeons saved his life, Poland itself offering to send a surgical team to help and allowing wall-to-wall bulletins to be transmitted about the Pope's progress. Mehmet Agca, a twenty-three-year-old Turk, was arrested for the attempted murder. He appeared to be a politically motivated loner, but seemed too to have had contacts with Bulgaria, a hard-line Eastern Bloc country which would have been only too happy to see the end of the Pope.

John Paul II's incapacitation was a setback to change in Poland, but had he failed to recover, his death would almost have coincided with that of his old mentor, the anti-Nazi turned anti-Communist Cardinal Wyszynski of Warsaw, who was to die of old age only three months later. The loss of both would have robbed Solidarity of its protection. As it was, the economic and political crisis in Poland had projected General Wojciech Jaruzelski into the leadership, and full-scale martial law was only a few months behind. By now Solidarity's membership was reckoned to be around ten million, out of a labour force of eighteen million. A strange organism that combined trade unionism and Polish nationalism with a passionate belief in Catholicism, Solidarity had no parallel in any other Eastern Bloc country, but the seed of dissidence had been sown.

It was a year before the Pope was fit enough to

hit the road again. By then most phone and telex lines in and out of Poland had been cut, and he used endless transmissions on Vatican Radio in his attempts to break through. Sunday after Sunday he would come to his Rome window and use his midday appearance to plead for peace in Poland.

It was in the searing, dusty heat of the racecourse at Kuduna in northern Nigeria in February 1982 that I was next close enough to observe the Pope first hand.

'Hello, tall Englishman,' he said, rather endearingly.

'How's your recovery, Holy Father?' I asked.

'Very slow,' he said. 'I can't tell whether it's my injuries or the crisis in Poland that leaves me so depressed.' Yet physically he looked remarkably well, and his endurance was as striking as it had been the year before in Poland.

As well as Nigeria, we visited Benin, Gabon and deliciously obscure Equatorial Guinea. I wandered around its run-down capital of Bata in the hours before the Pope arrived. Yet another post-colonial African tyrant had had the place held down until recently. Priests, nuns and Church workers had been tortured and killed. The Catholic faith itself had been banned for a time. People were extremely subdued, even morose. The Pope's arrival in the main square transformed all that into a deafening roar and a furious waving of palms. Even here, as at every stop, a Solidarity banner would sprout, a Polish priest or businessman would appear, to mark the ever-present connection with events back home.

'Where there is discord, may we bring harmony. Where there is error, may we bring truth...' She was certainly not the Pope. But if he would prove responsible for removing the first brick from the Berlin Wall, Margaret Thatcher would certainly help to weaken a good bit of its mortar.

Less than a year after John Paul II had been consecrated Pope, Margaret Thatcher was standing on the steps of Number Ten Downing Street. It was 4 May 1979, and she had just been elected Britain's first woman Prime Minister. Somehow I had got myself wedged between the policeman and the railing to her right beside the door. I was craning over the policeman's shoulder, looking at the postage-stamp-sized note hidden in the palm of her hand, from which she was cribbing the words of St Francis of Assisi. '...and where there is despair, may we bring hope.' The prayer summed her up: she was certainly a woman of absolutes, even if they were to bring the opposite of harmony. Not for nothing was she quickly dubbed the Iron Lady, although it wasn't that difficult to administer the smack of firm government with her new Conservative majority of forty-three seats. Poor defeated Jim Callaghan had had to limp along on a Labour majority of one.

Indeed, in the closing days of the Callaghan administration I had been dispatched to try to hunt down his majority of one. Frank Maguire was a delightful but unpredictable publican from Fermanagh. An Independent Republican MP, he'd threatened to bring the government down before, but the mathematics never quite stacked up. On 27 March 1979, the day before a vote of confidence in the government, I was sent over to Northern Ireland to try to find him.

I had met Frank before, on a bizarre occasion that had started at London's Heathrow Airport. From 1970 cub reporters were sent to Northern Ireland to cover the 'troubles' on most weekends. Amazingly, the local Ulster Television shut down its news coverage at weekends, as if Northern Ireland's civil war would in some way pause for a couple of days before resuming on Mondays. Hence I got to know the Province, its politicians, tribes and conflicts intimately. It was an alluring and fascinating place that had very little in common with home. Life was lived on the edge here. Even the most 'loyal' Protestants were unlike any Brit I ever came across in England. The conflict had many of the attributes of an unhappy attempt to resolve the consequences of insensitive colonisation. Northern Ireland, above all else, was to prove the crucible in which the Iron Lady's mettle would be tested.

My Heathrow baptism with Frank Maguire and the politicians of Northern Ireland had occurred in 1976. I'd been signed up for the usual weekend tour of duty one Friday evening. 'I'm afraid Belfast Aldergrove has been closed due to fog, Mr Snow,' the British Airways check-in woman said. 'You'll have to wait over there.' Over there were the leader of the Ulster Unionists, Jim Molyneaux, the ultra-Loyalist Reverend Ian Paisley, the Catholic Social Democratic and Labour Party

(SDLP) leader Gerry Fitt, assorted other Protestant MPs, and the Republican Frank Maguire. It was a disparate crew. To one side was a pretty, well-dressed, unhappy-looking young woman.

'What's the problem?' I asked her.

'I'm due to be married tomorrow morning in Belfast, and British Airways are saying I won't make it,' she replied.

I went back to the check-in desk and said that it was of paramount importance that we reached Belfast by the morning. 'Can it be done?' I asked.

'Well,' the agent replied, 'you could fly to Glasgow, then catch the train to Stranraer, then take the boat to Larne, north of Belfast.' She looked at her timetable. 'Oh dear, I see the train isn't a proper connection.'

I went back to the MPs, explained the bride's plight, and told them that she and I were going to try it via Glasgow. Was anyone interested? They all were, so I herded ten MPs, a bride-to-be and her two large red cases onto the British Airways shuttle to Glasgow.

Halfway through the flight I asked to go forward to the cockpit to talk to the captain. He understood the situation immediately, and allowed me to use the radio to speak to Glasgow Airport. The train was scheduled to leave the Glasgow suburb of Paisley, five minutes by car from the airport, about fifteen minutes after we landed. If we missed it, we would miss the boat. I phoned the station and explained that I had ten MPs and a bride-to-be with me. I thought it might impress them that one of the party was Ian Paisley, so I dropped his name as well. 'Can you hold the train if we're late?' I pleaded. 'I promise we'll be there within a couple of minutes if we're not there on time.'

We didn't even circle the airport. The captain threw the 737 straight down on the runway, hit the airbrakes and the reverse thrust hard, and pulled us off on the first possible taxiway. Fortunately airport security was as nothing compared with today, and the authorities had arranged for three taxis to meet us right on the tarmac, at the bottom of the aircraft steps.

I got everyone off, and was in the process of loading them into the taxis when the bride exclaimed, 'My cases – where are the cases?' We'd disembarked so fast that the baggage handlers had yet to appear. The captain opened the cargo hatch and I jumped up into the hold, only to find the Reverend Paisley on my tail.

'What colour are they?' he panted.

'Red!' I shouted as I rummaged in the half-light. Suddenly there they were. I handed them to Paisley, and he in turn handed them down through the hatch. I was just in time to see the baggage handlers coming towards the plane, cursing. We were into the cabs and away. I reckoned we would make it with two minutes to spare.

As we approached Paisley station, I caught sight of the tail-lights of the train moving off. We abandoned the cabs and ran, but it had indeed left without us. The bride burst into tears on the platform, and the MPs started questioning my arrangements.

'What the hell's going on?' I asked the guard.

'It's still a minute to go before the Stranraer train's meant to leave, and it's already gone. These are all Members of Parliament, they've got to get back to their constituencies.'

'I'm sorry, mate,' he replied. 'When I told the driver he might have to hold the train for them, and that one of them was Reverend Paisley, he said he wasn't going to wait for *him* for all the tea in China.'

Ten sets of MPs' eyes and one tearful bride-to-be were looking hard in my direction. I ran out into the street. The posh cabs that had met us at the airport had gone. There were just three of the old-fashioned 'sit-up-and-beg'-style diesel taxis. I booked the lot for the seventy-mile odyssey, and we piled into them.

In my taxi, the bride-to-be insisted on sitting on one of the flap-down seats. Jim Molyneaux took the other. I sat in the middle of the back seat, flanked by Paisley on one side and Gerry Fitt on the other, the unlikely filling in a Protestant–Catholic political sandwich. We set off on our painfully slow progress across the Scottish lowlands to try to catch the boat. If we missed it there was no other crossing that would get us there before the following afternoon, and the bride-to-be knew it.

The windows of our old cab soon began to steam up as our quest for the boat became swamped by animated, jovial discourse. Fitt and Paisley, notorious political enemies, were getting on like a house on fire. Molyneaux seemed to be taking a fancy to me, while I in turn was trying to keep the bride afloat. In that strange, jolting encounter I learned more in an hour and a half than in twenty-five years of reporting Northern Ireland. These men had far more in common than they'd ever dare admit in public. Ian Paisley, whose vile anti-papist rhetoric provided so noisy a backdrop to the troubles, was charm itself, personable and seriously concerned about the future bride.

We reached the dockside in darkness. There was just enough light to see the last gangway being readied for departure. I leapt out of the cab and shouted at the man who was heaving it up. 'Twelve more to come,' I shouted. 'MPs and a bride.' The man released the gangway back onto the dockside and we were allowed to climb it.

Once aboard, Frank Maguire and I retreated to the bar. The boat was packed, and I was exhausted. We each had a double brandy and slumped onto one of the upholstered benches at the back. It was then that I began to get to know Mr Callaghan's majority of one. A Catholic and a passionate believer in a united Ireland, he was also a man of charm and humour. Our conversation would stand me in good stead, but it was brought to a sudden and noisy conclusion.

'Muster Snow!' boomed Ian Paisley, striding through the stunned bar. 'You've been supping the devil's buttermilk!' And so I had. At dawn we prepared to land at Larne. This time, Jim Molyneaux had ordered the transport. The bride was going to make it to her wedding. 'Where is it?' enquired Paisley, shaking her hand. 'I might like to come.'

'The Church of our Lady of...' She tailed off.

Paisley made it clear that he most certainly would *not* be coming. It was back to business as usual. We parted for another weekend of carnage and mayhem.

Frank Maguire's bar in Fermanagh was one of those classic stone-built street pubs with an old-fashioned Guinness sign at the door. Inside was a cosy cream-and-amber feel, and a long line of flat-capped Irish farming folk in decaying tweeds at the bar. A more improbable scene for the discreet but active support of the Republican campaign against the British government and the Unionists who wished to remain linked to it would have been hard to conceive.

Frank was not there, but his wife was. I'd been in a couple of times since my original encounter with Frank, and they both treated me like family. One of the advantages of appearing on the nightly news is that people who know you feel they meet you a lot more often than they really do.

This time, with a vote of confidence in Jim Callaghan's government being held that very afternoon in Parliament at Westminster, meeting Frank was more urgent than it had ever been. My team and I had flown over in a light aircraft and landed at the strip outside the town the night before, and we were still looking for Frank at nine o'clock in the morning.

Finally he appeared, apparently oblivious to the vital importance of his presence at Westminster. 'Don't be thinking I'm going to keep them going, Jon,' he said. 'Now that they have a report that tells them how they've been mistreating my people in those interrogation rooms, they've done nothing about it.' He was referring to the Bennett Report on the interrogation procedures of the RUC, published a week earlier, which had found evidence of the maltreatment of Republican suspects during interrogation. In truth poor old Callaghan had had his hands full. The British Ambassador to Holland, Richard Sykes, had been murdered by the IRA outside Amsterdam five days earlier.

'So you're not going to avail yourself of a seat on my plane then, Frank?' I said. 'Why not?'

He replied, 'I shall come and abstain in person.'

In the event both he and Gerry Fitt abstained over the non-implementation of the Bennett Report, and the Callaghan government fell. A general election was called, and Margaret Thatcher's day dawned.

Two years and a day after Mrs Thatcher stood on the steps of Downing Street praying for harmony, on 5 May 1981, Bobby Sands died in the most discordant political circumstances imaginable. Sands, who was in Long Kesh detention centre, better known as the Maze, for possessing a gun, had starved to death after a sixty-six-day hunger strike in protest at the Republican prisoners' conditions. Frank Maguire's Westminster seat, which had played so prominent a role in propelling Margaret Thatcher to power, had come into play once more.

Frank had died earlier that year, and Bobby

Sands stood from jail in the by-election to replace him as MP for Fermanagh. It was inconceivable that a convicted IRA terrorist serving time in prison could possibly win election to the 'mother of Parliaments,' and the British authorities did everything possible to try to prevent him. But in the end he won with a staggering 30,492 votes, 50 per cent of the total, defeating the prominent Unionist Harry West, who received 29,046 votes. Sands was too ill to take his parliamentary seat even if he'd been free to do so. He was a bare three weeks from death.

Long Kesh is a grim environment even in the sunshine. In the late-spring grey gloom it was daunting. The watchtowers regarded us from every quarter. Occasionally relatives of prisoners would appear with illicit photographs taken inside. Gaunt, unshaven men peered at the camera, wearing blankets and standing in front of walls smeared brown with human excrement. Republican prisoners were on a 'dirty protest' against being denied political prisoner status. Bobby Sands was the liaison prisoner in talks between the protesters and the British prison authorities. On 1 March 1981, at the age of twenty-five, he decided to go on a hunger strike in pursuit of their demands. No one thought either he or the nine other prisoners in their twenties who followed him would fast to the death. But gradually, to those of us who were interacting with the families on the ground, it became clear that they would. The pressure on Mrs Thatcher to give way was overwhelming. Other governments, newspaper editorials and protest marches on both sides of the Irish Sea and in America begged her to relent. She was unyielding, and at times seemed almost indifferent as to whether they lived or died. Her iron image took no hostages. Even Sands's election, which indicated that huge numbers of moderate Catholics supported him, left her unbowed. She rode out the deaths, but their consequence was to visit her some way into her second term.

By the time the IRA detonated a bomb in the Brighton hotel in which virtually the entire British Cabinet was sleeping during the Conservative Party Conference in October 1984, her iron status had already been confirmed in its full rustproofedness by the Falklands War. I shall return to that later. Suffice it to say that the complete demolition of the Grand Hotel, the deaths of five party stalwarts and the serious injury of two of her Ministers, but her own unscathed survival, only served to underscore the sense of Margaret Thatcher's indomitability.

In reality, the cost of the dead hunger strikers and the dangerously near miss of a terrorist takeout of the entire government chimed with the economic costs of having twenty-two thousand troops deployed in Northern Ireland, and the sheer expense of making good the damage inflicted by the IRA. The lady *was* for turning. Just over a year after the Brighton bomb she signed a document that must have been anathema to her. Although shrouded in language that respected Britain's right to be in Northern Ireland, the Anglo–Irish Agreement of 15 November 1985 was a treaty which, for the first time since partition, gave the Irish Republic significant rights in respect of the nationalist minority in the North. It was the point of no return.

Walking down the Falls Road in amongst the thousands of mourners behind Bobby Sands's coffin I found it hard even then to believe that anything would ever be the same again now that the state had allowed a man to die for political reasons. Nine more hunger striker deaths, the Brighton bomb and much else, ensured that change came. The very British Iron Lady laid the groundwork for a settlement that *de facto*, if not yet *de jure*, made a united Ireland one day inevitable.

Margaret Thatcher's iron image was in equally powerful play when it came to matters European. France's President François Mitterrand and Germany's Chancellor Helmut Kohl would try to humour her, charm her, even intimidate her. In the end, despite all the drama of endless refusals and nay-saying, she ultimately said yes to the second-most profound embrace of Europe ever made by any British Prime Minister, the signing of the Single European Act on 17 February 1986. It was a landmark moment from which all the European integration she preached against flowed. No united Ireland, no united Europe, yet in the end she took steps towards both. I suppose we found her iron in her presentation, but I suspect history will find her pragmatic in her execution.

Interviewing Mrs Thatcher was sometimes akin to an execution. It was in the course of the many European Summit circuses that I most frequently encountered her over the years. Dense, impenetrable meetings would wind on into the night, rarely resulting in anything definitive. At last she would emerge, and we, the press, would be taken to the British rooms with her. Someone would pour her a whisky and she would plonk down into an armchair. On such occasions she was almost seductive, crossing and uncrossing her legs, the subtle scream of her new-fangled Lycra tights cutting the night air.

'Well, Jon, how are you?' she would ask, not apparently wanting an answer, but delighting you that she remembered your name. 'I do find these European sessions perfectly frightful,' she would go on, then there would be some small talk, and then we would start. The moment the camera rolled, the iron would return to her demeanour. Some harmless question would issue from my lips, and she'd sit bolt upright. 'How can you ask such a stupid question?' she'd bellow.

'Damn me,' I'd think, 'have I said something silly? What a fool I am... I'm so sorry.' Then I'd pull myself together and remember, for an inadequate moment, that it was *I* who was supposed to be shaping the questions, and *she* who was supposed to be answering them. The interviews would always end up testosterone-strewn encounters, and great television in which she invariably came out on top.

Such moments gave us an insight into what it must have been like round the Cabinet table. A lot of mainly public-school-educated males suddenly confronted with matron. They had failed to wash between their toes, failed to brush their hair properly; how dare they now raise the matter of defence estimates or public spending? That's what it felt like at the time. How the men cried when they eventually kicked her out, and ultimately she, the Iron Lady, cried with them. No psycho-social study will ever do full justice to those years. It's hard to imagine that the Thatcher era could have happened without the extraordinary processes that went into shaping the British ruling elite. I can't think that the effect she had upon me was not shared by the other men who intersected with her in power – civil servants, ministers, journalists alike. Many of them had been through the public school system, deprived of female contact apart from matron. That system did not prepare you for the shock of a woman in absolute power.

Margaret Thatcher's effect on the opposition was little short of disastrous. Safe old Jim Callaghan made way for extremely unsafe and even older Michael Foot. Madeleine and I were later to become very friendly with Michael and his wife Jill Craigie, but even he would admit that he was never Prime Minister in waiting. Michael was one of our greatest intellectuals, writers and orators. He was far too honest and interesting ever to be Prime Minister.

'Mr President,' I shouted, 'you are live on British television.' Jimmy Carter spotted me and walked straight over to my camera. It was no matter of luck. I had become friendly with the then Prime Minister Jim Callaghan's chief of staff Tom McCaffrey. It was 1977: Mrs Thatcher was mere leader of the Conservative opposition at the time.

Carter was attending the G7 Economic Summit in London. Cameras only were allowed into the courtyard; I wormed in as a technician. Then I caught McCaffrey's eye and he told me he'd try to get Carter out while we were on air. Come 5.45 p.m., the news started with no sign of Carter. I did my piece, and handed back to the studio. Then, with two minutes to go to the end of the news, the editor decided to take a risk and cross back to me. At that very moment, over my shoulder, there was Carter coming out. My cameraman gesticulated wildly, I turned, and now here he was. It was almost certainly the first live British television news interview with an American President in history.

A strange, nice, Southern Baptist man, Carter seemed both honourable and dull. We overran our spontaneous live transmission with him by twelve minutes. In those days the engineers at the ITV regional control centres were supposed to throw the switches if the news went over its allotted time; all but one of them decided to stick with the interview. The one, Yorkshire Television, got flooded with complaints from viewers for cutting off the President of the United States in midstream. The smallest station, the Channel Island service, rang to complain that I had trashed their entire night's viewing, throwing every programme for the rest of the night out of kilter, and that it was never to happen again. My employers were thrilled; champagne was flowing when I returned to the newsroom.

Jimmy Carter was never going to dislodge even a crumb of mortar from the Berlin Wall. He espoused a decent, almost un-American devotion to human rights, which he rarely delivered on. He was hopelessly indecisive, and would soon be desperately and fatally undone by the unravelling of Iran. His successor, Ronald Reagan, would be the sledgehammer that would crack much more of the Wall.

And there was still Mikhail Gorbachev to come. It would be another decade before the Wall came down, a decade in which Central America, Afghanistan, Iran, Iraq and Russia herself would play pivotal roles in upsetting the Cold War order that had provided such relative certainty ever since the Second World War, and my own childhood.

The remorseless pitch of reporting assignments was to keep me on the road almost solidly from the mid-1970s to the late 1980s. Professionally, it was rewarding: I was well paid, and notched up plenty of awards. But at home it was disruptive. Madeleine continued with her legal career, and we were, in classic sixties terms, both together and untogether – at least until my improbable dispatch to work in the United States, which would change everything. But for the moment there was still some major reporting to do, not least on America's first brutal clash with radical Muslim militants.

SIX

Of Oil, Islam and Moscow

I suppose Dr Zubaydi will die. He gives the appearance of being about as close to Saddam Hussein as it is possible to be. Aquiline, with a full mop of distinguished white hair, he cuts the dash of an academic. Sipping tea in the unedifying confines of the restaurant in Baghdad's Al Rashid Hotel, Zubaydi talks of Shakespeare, his love of English, his respect for the British, and the infamy of war. We are talking on 28 January 2003, a few weeks before the Anglo-American war on Iraq.

'We have never had a relationship with the Americans, not a direct one,' he says. 'We have always seen America through British eyes. It's a strange way to relate to so dominant a power, particularly one that has now decided to finish us. I remember you reporting the Iran–Iraq war back in 1981. I was doing a PhD at the Shakespeare Centre, at Birmingham University.' Zubaydi reminds me of incidents and accounts that I had reported for News at Ten, and long since myself forgotten. He talks of Britain with an intimate fondness. I have to pinch myself to remember that the previous night RAF bombers were in action over his country's 'no fly zone,' and had taken out five communications centres. But from Zubaydi

224

there is neither malice nor hatred, just recollections of Birmingham and Britain.

Yet Zubaydi is almost certain to die. Technically he is Saddam's translator. In reality he is also a very close political aide. He is in the inner circle, at the table in so many of those dense grainy photographs of Saddam with his generals. White House briefings have talked of the need to take out 'between ten and seventy' people closest to Saddam. I suspect that Zubaydi is well inside the seventy.

Cultured, presentable, Westernised, Sadoon Zubaydi is not alone. There is Iraq's former Ambassador to Argentina, Ahmed Said, now gatekeeper to Deputy Prime Minister Tariq Aziz. A smart little man in his late sixties, he sits at a huge desk that groans with files that don't look as if they have been opened in twenty years. Another highly intelligent, Europeanised Iraqi, the Ambassador talks easily of the outside world and war.

I have been in Iraq for three days, and already I have penetrated a cadre of intellectuals who sit at the right and left hands of the 'Butcher of Baghdad'. At its head is Saddam's deputy, Tariq Aziz himself. It feels so very far from weapons of mass destruction, wholesale slaughter and torture that are the hallmarks of thirty years of Saddam's tyranny. Yet I know from the tangible shadows of terror that you encounter throughout Iraq that these things are there in all their enormity, and that these 'civilians' know it. Do they practise them themselves?

I am sitting in the engine room of the ruling

225

Ba'ath Party, six floors up in the vast, stone-built Cabinet offices, waiting to talk with Mr Aziz. I have sat waiting for Tariq Aziz before, not once, but twice. Indeed, my waitings for him span the extraordinary journey the world has made in twenty-five years – from a sense of predictable standoff to the potential chaos of unpredictable terrorist threat. I first waited during the Iran–Iraq war in 1981, on this very floor, in this very building; then in 1991 in Geneva, on the heels of a bizarre encounter between Aziz and US Secretary of State James Baker. Thus I had waited for him once in the freeze of Cold War, once in its warming aftermath, and now amid the torrid and uncertain fear of the post-9/11 world.

I find myself pondering, who is our enemy now? Once he was a Communist; now he is an Islamist. Once we knew the web, the connections that tracked from Latin America or Africa to Moscow. Once Saudi Arabia was our inscrutable oil-rich friend, now fifteen of her people have blitzed lower Manhattan. At least when I began in journalism it all had the easy simplicity of an American–Soviet fight. Now as I sit waiting on a floor frequented by Saddam Hussein himself, it feels so very much more complex, uncertain and dangerous. Even Tariq Aziz seems a bit-part player in a much bigger drama than whether Iraq has crateloads of anthrax or not. Presumably Aziz will die. Presumably this vast stone cathedral-like block of offices will be reduced to rubble. Somehow, sitting here, I do not feel Saddam himself will die.

Aziz is wearing the same old bottle-bottomed

glasses, and the same old khaki uniform. The pot belly is perhaps a little more pronounced, the hair perhaps whiter, the eyebrows still remarkably black. In truth, he seems almost unchanged by more than twenty years as the presentable face of Saddam Hussein. War, he seems to accept, is inevitable. 'They won't take me alive,' he declares. 'I will kill myself rather than be captured. In any case, we shall defeat them.' We talk a little after the interview. He seems to be preparing for the worst. His office is strangely anachronistic: no computers, not much paper either, and very elderly telephones. He and Iraq seem to be in a time warp.

In reality Tariq Aziz was to surrender to US forces less than three months later, on 24 April 2003, eventually to be joined in captivity by Saddam himself, to be held at Baghdad airport for alleged war crimes. Saddam's two sons, Uday and Qusay, were to suffer a more merciless end, dying after a long shootout with US Marines in the northern city of Mosul in July 2003.

One evening in that February before the war, on the recommendation of Dr Mudhafar Amin, the head of the Iraqi Interest section in London, I dined with three colleagues in Uday's disgusting Baghdad restaurant. It was one of the very worst culinary experiences of my working life. The food was filthy, but the taste enshrined in the decor was still worse. The place was packed, and we found ourselves at a table near the door. The clientele was prosperous-looking, somewhat overweight and, unusually for Iraq, almost all ostentatiously armed. Gold pistols

227

with pearl handles hung about their ample midriffs. Some of the diners were positively obese. Indeed in the course of the hour and a half that we were there, two chairs actually collapsed beneath the weight of their occupants. If this was the dynastic effluent from Saddam's regime, it did not appear fit enough to represent much of a threat to the rest of us.

The two weeks we spent moving about Iraq did not feel very threatening either. The approaching war was supposedly dependent on the discovery of an immediate threat posed by some nuclear, chemical or biological device. Every morning the UN weapons inspectors would set off on their quest. Sometimes we'd tail them to some remote farm, and find nothing. Other days we would head out on our own.

About sixty miles north of Baghdad we came upon the ziggurat at Samara, towering above the town. This extraordinary mud-built structure resembles an early helterskelter, save that you have to clamber *up* the curling pathway that winds around it. It was built for the priests, who would climb up it to get closer to their gods. Here was an eight-hundred-year-old symbol of Iraq's ancient roots. We decided that I should climb the ziggurat while the camera remained below, and would record some thoughts from the top using a radio microphone. Halfway up my lonesome trek I began to suffer waves of vertigo. Normally heights have little effect on me, but the three-foot-wide walkway round the ziggurat had no railing, the drop was sheer, and for some reason I could feel that slight magnetic draw to jump off. Gazing out across the Tigris river, I could see decaying ruins in every direction. In between my bouts of fear, I inevitably found myself conjuring a sense of nine thousand years of civilisation.

Funny old world, in which a two-hundred-year-old democracy feels emboldened to come and seize a country twenty-eight centuries older, whose own empire once extended to Spain. What do they know, I mused. In the teashops below there was not a whiff of hostility towards our unusual Western presence. At every level of Iraqi society we encountered nothing but charm and civility. Only in the ministries was there any sense of tension, and even then it tended to centre on whether we'd paid enough US dollars for our 'permissions'. The senior civil servants were competent and reasonable to deal with, although as the days leading to war ticked by they became more and more demanding of bribes.

Back on the road, as we drove another hundred miles north a telltale plume of fire and smoke announced that we'd reached the vast Kirkuk oilfield. In Kirkuk itself, an amazingly mixed town, we found large but mainly separate groupings of Arabs, Kurds and Turkmans. On the city's bridge, Kurdish traders catered to the needs of a heaving mass of Kurds who'd come down from the Kurdish-controlled region twenty-five miles to the north. In amongst them, buying anything from batteries to flip-flops, were groups of young, fresh-faced soldiers from Saddam's elite Republican Guard. They were genuinely excited to see us, and our camera. 'Photo me! Photo me!' they cried. And we did, arms about shoulders, posing in the spring sunshine with boys we would soon have to describe as 'the enemy'.

The next day, driving a hundred miles south of Baghdad to the Shia city of Karbala, we passed elderly anti-aircraft missiles ranged sporadically in arcs close to the road. The golden domes of the city's two mosques shimmered in the dusty morning sun. Arriving amid a dense and bustling series of streets, we stopped on one corner where scribes and Islamic lawyers wrote out all kinds of certificates, ranging from birth to death issues. People were easy with us, shopkeepers bought us tea and chatted. Our government minder, Mohamed, came to life. In Baghdad he had never revealed that he was himself Shiite. Now he told us his family was right here in Karbala, and how they had suffered at the hands of Saddam, the very man for whom he now worked policing our activities. Saddam himself came from the Sunni minority who had dominated the leadership of Iraq since well before even the British ruled here.

Mohamed pointed out that all the buildings in the centre of the city, clustered around the mosques, were new. He told us how Saddam had slaughtered tens of thousands of Shiites here in the uprising that followed the 1991 Gulf War. The Shiite majority, particularly here in the south, with its religious links with Iran, was always seen as a threat by Saddam and his secular but Sunni-dominated Ba'ath Party. Mohamed described how the Shiites had dared to challenge Saddam in 1991 because the American-led coalition that had overwhelmed Iraq after the invasion of Kuwait had encouraged them to believe that they would

230

intervene to protect them. Of course they didn't, and a hundred thousand Shiites were killed. The centre of Karbala was burned from end to end, hence the new brick structures in front of us.

It wasn't the first letdown the Iraqis had suffered at the hands of the West. The war between Iraq and Iran a decade earlier was seen by America as both a marvellous chance to get back at the Iranians for the consequences of their 1979 revolution, and a chance to keep both countries tied up in war by arming Iran too.

To be on the Iran–Iraq battlefront back in 1981 was to be in the very heart of hell. On either flank, artillery pieces lifting their barrels halfway to the sky belched great blasts of fire and smoke, followed by a delayed ear-splitting bang. The barrages lasted for hours, sometimes even days. From time to time something would come back, some rocket, shell or missile. One cold winter's morning I, Alan Downes, Don Warren and my faithful fixer Hamid were fleeing east along a highway out of the southern Iraqi town of Basra when there was a massive explosion right ahead of us. An armoured personnel carrier that had been moving in the opposite direction, towards the war front, was engulfed in flames. Horribly burnt men staggered from the wreckage. Not only were we in the sights of Iranian firepower, we were caught in the midst of that awful dilemma: to try to help the wounded, to film the disaster, or to flee. As so often, we attempted all three. The survivors of the blast were beyond help; the contents of our pathetic water bottles were no match for the fires that consumed their bodies. I can hear those men to this day.

Reviewing the footage recently, I saw a rather urgent, gangly white man in shirtsleeves speaking breathlessly to camera. He wears no body armour, no flak jacket, and appears less than well prepared for the appalling conflagration in which he is caught. The gangly man is me. We had gone to this First World War-like front completely untrained and ill-equipped; that is how it was. These days, just to visit Iraq demands a battlefield or hostile environment course. Our luggage is eternally weighed down with body protection, our rules of engagement are written down on five sides of A4 or more. How more of us did not die in the Iran–Iraq conflict I will never know.

The most bizarre aspect of that war was the ease with which we could cover both sides. In two days we could reach Tehran, then fly via Jordan to Basra, and attracting no particular interest find ourselves among the Iraqi positions opposite the very spot we'd vacated on the Iranian side just forty-eight hours earlier. To see the war from both fronts was to know that the conflict was completely pointless, wasteful and disastrous. Worse, being there was to see with my own eyes the cynical investment by both superpowers in the materials of war for both sides.

Iran had mountains of American hardware. Glistening brass-tubed shells stood in stacks of the ordered unspent and the disordered spent. The shell cases were so big you could imagine taking one home to serve as an umbrella stand. Standing outside Khoramshahr in Iran, watching

232

the loading, gorging and disgorging of the artillery pieces in clouds of smoke, conjured up the worst of First World War scenes. All too often the act of firing revealed the whereabouts of the battery and Iraq's response rained down on us. Death was commonplace, ghastly maiming and wounding more so. The majority of the men loading the guns were no more than boys, barely in their teens. I suppose that in that year of 1981 I must have spent in all some four or five months in this hell.

Once, from the Iranian side, I witnessed the carnage of a human wave close up. A murderous siren summoned all the boys from their tents; they poured up over the sandy ramparts, running at huge speed towards Iraqi lines. Wave upon wave of them, thousands of boys. The air was split with the terrible, slashing response of machine-gun bullets. So very many died; and after it the survivors began to dig new ramparts, perhaps two hundred yards further back or forward than the previous ones.

No more than two weeks later I had flown via Jordan again to the other side of the front line and the Iraqi forces. They were better trained, and less liable to send forward such suicidal waves. The Iraqis preferred to load and dispatch great trays of rocketry from their Russian-supplied 'Stalin's Organs' – hellish multiple rocket launchers that propelled twenty-five times the payload of a conventional artillery piece.

Despite being the supplier of the weapons, there was little active Russian interest in Iraq's fortunes, and none at all from America in Iran's misfortune. The Iranians were merely utilising the bloated arsenals Washington had assembled for the Shah. To this day I have never seen any other non-imperial nation display the sheer quantities of military possessions that Iran possessed. Lifting out of Mehrabad Airport in Tehran, you could look down upon rows and rows of militarily camouflaged Jumbo jets set in neat rows, troop carriers, transports and refuellers. Each one represented millions of dollars of capital cost – many barrels of pumped crude oil. For what kind of war had Washington ever conceived the Shah would need such an array?

America's only interest now was the defeat of what Washington regarded as Iran's inexplicable Islamic zeal. Any ally, any liaison, it seemed, was justifiable in such a cause. And as the marshy wastes and desert sands soaked up the blood, there were decreasing numbers of media personnel on hand to witness what was being done in Lincoln's name. It was so dangerous, so unreportably big, and so unchangingly active a war, that newsdesks stopped sending. Thus there was simply no pressure upon anyone to end it.

The Shatt Al-Arab waterway that divides Iran and Iraq and forms their geographical border is a particularly filthy stretch of water. It is both a sump for the oil industry on its banks and a route from Iraq's second city of Basra to the Persian Gulf. Throughout 1981 the Iran–Iraq war raged across its fast-flowing waters. Massive barrages of shells exploded above the international shipping still stranded in the waterway.

One night in April 1981 I received a telex from my editor, David Nicholas, at ITN in London telling me that a businessman had called saying that in the course of watching my report of an artillery exchange across the waterway he had glimpsed his missing ship. Peter Melia was the fleet manager for Silverline Shipping in London, and for six weeks he'd lost all contact with his brand new forty-thousand-ton bulk carrier, the *Al Tanin*. He'd asked the Iraqis, the Iranians and the British about it, and got nowhere. Now he'd suddenly seen it over my shoulder as I'd spoken into the camera beneath the shell fire. David Nicholas told me that Mr Melia wanted to appoint me the *Al Tanin*'s agent, giving me the power to try to rescue the fifty-seven souls stranded aboard the ship. I jumped at the chance. As well as anything else, it meant I'd be able to get into Basra dockyard, a place forbidden to journalists and crawling with war secrets.

The next morning, brandishing my telexed documentation, I entered Basra dockyard in search of anyone who might know anything about the *Al Tanin*. By midday I'd found a Norwegian tanker whose captain had been in discreet coded contact with the ship. I told him I wanted to get the British captain and his crew off. He laughed, but made a call to the ship. After a few minutes a soft but distinct British voice came on the line. It was the captain. It seemed that he had been in indirect contact with Peter Melia, but had had no way of talking to the combatants on either side to effect an escape. He told me there were three British wives, fifteen British officers and about forty Philippine ratings on board. They could generate power, but were low on food and water. He said he had sealed the cargo holds, and that they never went on deck. They were entering their seventh week of what he termed 'detention'. I told him I had an Iraqi commando friend, and that I would try to interest him in their plight. We agreed that we would speak again at the same time the next day.

Captain Ahmed, my commando friend, was completely disbelieving when I broached the matter with him later that day. 'No one there,' he said authoritatively. 'We watch everything, never see anyone.' Eventually, after much argument he said, 'Look, if there is anyone on there, and I don't think there is, then you and I will have to swim to the ship and see for ourselves. That is the only condition under which I will take this any further.' The ship was about half a mile out, in the middle of tidal water. The water, as I've mentioned, was disgusting. I agreed I'd try and swim there with him the next night.

When I got through to the captain again he was startled by the idea, but suggested I make the attempt at midnight, when the tide would be at its slackest. He said he would leave a long rope ladder over the port side, near the stern. Unfortunately, I failed to realise that maritime time is GMT, three hours adrift from Iraqi time. To make it worse, the code for hours and minutes was expressed in fruit and vegetables, and I messed up working out what banana past tomato meant in the first place.

That night Captain Ahmed turned up at the

decaying Basra Airport Hotel – three to a room plus cockroaches – which was a local media base for the war. He was armed with two frogmen's suits, a small rubber dinghy, some rope and a torch. I had never worn a wetsuit of any kind, nor swum in anything like the army flippers he provided. Outside he had trucks with men and ammunition aboard. We made our way to a point close to where I had been addressing the camera several days previously. The *Al Tanin* loomed in the moonlight. Robert Fisk, then of *The Times*, was with us; so were my cameraman Chris Squires and my sound man Nigel Thompson. Both of them thought I was barmy, and were having a good laugh about it. They were armed with a very early portable electronic video camera, which had a bit more of a chance of picking out what was going on in darkness than a film camera had, but they had made it more than clear that they were not coming with me. They promised to try to video the event from the banks. Fisk was more serious, but he had no idea how afraid I was.

Suddenly the men with us let fly a round of artillery fire across the waterway towards the Iranian front line. A noisy firefight unfolded, and Ahmed and I took to the water. It was obvious from the outset that the tide was very far from slack. Ahmed had me swim ahead of him, he towing the little rubber dinghy behind him. We'd started far enough above the *Al Tanin* to be swept down towards it by the tide, but I was worried that we would be washed past the ship and away to the Iranian side of the waterway – and we very nearly were. But Ahmed spotted the rope ladder and lunged for it, and I caught onto his leg. He tied the boat to the ladder, and with the greatest difficulty we heaved our way onto its first rungs.

A forty-thousand-ton bulk ore carrier is no rowing boat. The side of the thing must have been a hundred feet high. All the way up my knees bashed against the ironwork and my wetsuit ripped on the rivets. By the time I got to the top I was covered in a mixture of slime, oil and blood. In this condition we made it to the housing at the stern of the ship, found a door and descended the stairway. Five floors down we scared the living daylights out of the Filipino seamen, who were cowering from the shellfire in a dank and dark-ened hallway. We clambered down three more floors, and opened a door into the blindingly well-lit officers' mess. And there they were, men and women drinking canned beer.

'Mr Snow, I presume,' said the captain in a relaxed way. 'Thank you for coming.'

Ahmed could not believe his luck – here was his chance for heroism. 'Leave it all to me,' he said. 'I bring boats.'

'No you don't,' retorted the captain. 'All these people are coming off on my lifeboats. I can get them into two of our motorised launches.'

So it was agreed. The only problem was that as the gantries had not been greased in two months, the boats would make a dreadful noise as they descended fully laden from the derricks. 'Don't worry,' said Ahmed, 'we'll fire some guns.'

The next night, Ahmed, my crew, Fisk and the artillery boys took up our positions on the bank of the waterway. At the discreet flash of a torch, the derricks ground into action. The noise was infernal, and the artillery opened up immediately to drown it out. I heard a woman scream. After what seemed an interminable time, the boats puttered into view, fifty-seven pale faces turned towards us. Every one of them had made it, and I had played a minor role in securing their safety. We had a scoop, an incredible scoop. The next day, Fisk's piece dominated *The Times*'s front page.

The Basra hotel reception paged me on the Tannoy: 'Telephone call for Mr Esnow, telephone call for Mr Esnow.'

It was Robin Day on the line; he presented *The World at One* on BBC Radio in London. 'So you got the time wrong, you fool,' he barked.

'Yes, I'm afraid I did,' I said.

'So you could have messed the whole thing up and risked their lives into the bargain?'

'I suppose so.' There was almost no mention of the survivors. I went back to the warfront with my tail between my legs.

The episode does at least reveal yet again the extent to which the West had simply left Iran and Iraq to slog it out. There were over sixty international ships stranded in the waterway. The next day the Peruvian government contacted me, asking me to help get their people off another ship, two vessels away from the *Al Tanin*. I declined their invitation. The West wasn't bothered with war's outcome, for this was a war in which there could only be losers – the people of Iran and of Iraq – and it suited both superpowers just fine.

Islamic fervour would be dented in Iran; and secular bastardry at the hands of Saddam Hussein would run its course in Iraq. A million people from both sides died in the war, while both regimes survived to flourish for another day.

It was past its pre-Khomeini best, but the Intercontinental Hotel in Tehran was still a comfortable place to sleep. The kidney-shaped pool at the back had long since dried up, the fine selection of French wines in the bar with it. Indeed, I had been here when the waiters poured vintage after vintage into the street drains.

It was from here that I and a handful of others had witnessed the Islamic revolution in 1979 that finally deposed the already absent Shah. He had been a bulwark of the West's determination to hold the line against the Soviet Union's Communist empire, an empire that ran the full length of Iran's northern border. So obsessed was Washington with the vital listening posts along the Caspian Sea and the intelligence they gathered on Russia's missile testing in the nearby Ural Mountains that it lost sight of the Shah's reign of terror against his own people. I remember visiting Sanandaj in Iranian Kurdistan in those days, and seeing inside an Iranian Secret Service (SAVAK) torture chamber. There was blood on the walls, and a bucket in the corner with old and bloodied extracted toenails. The Kurds themselves were banned from speaking Kurdish, banned from wearing their distinctive baggy trousers, banned indeed from any of their rich cultural manifestations. SAVAK's terror was experienced right across Iran. The United States made little effort to pressure the Shah on human rights.

When the revolution came on 11 February 1979, I and my crew set off in search of the spy station on the Caspian Sea that I had driven past on that student adventure to India ten years earlier. All we had to do was to find those telltale golf-ball-like installations on the hills above the sea. But I couldn't remember exactly where, so in the midst of revolution there we were, speeding along the coastal road in search of golf balls. The atmosphere in the towns along the road was of emptiness rather than of heroic overthrow. Yet we knew that if we could find an early warning station, we would be able to depict Iran's strategic importance at the very crossroads of the Cold War with Russia.

In the chilly early afternoon we found one, nestling just below the cloudbase high on the hills overlooking the far eastern end of the Caspian. We drove up to the gates of the complex, the white spherical structures towering above us. The gates were open; a couple of youthful Revolutionary Guards mooned about inside. It was clear they had no idea what the place was. It was still humming.

My cameraman made to enter the first golf ball. 'Don't!' I screamed. 'It may be booby trapped!' It wasn't. It was here that America had been monitoring every Russian missile firing, every nuclear test for a quarter of a century. Huge computers poured screeds of paper covered in code and hieroglyphics onto the floor. The lights burned, and all the machinery seemed to be working. It had the feeling of a place very suddenly abandoned. This feeling was accentuated by what we found in the quarters of the Americans who had lived and worked here. Children's clothes still lay on unmade beds, food on kitchen tables. Whoever had left, had left in a hurry.

We had the feeling that whatever intelligence the US had been gaining by listening in on Russian detonations from here, they had gleaned almost nothing about the revolutionary inferno that had been brewing in the very country from which they were doing their listening. This pivotal spot in the East–West conflict had disintegrated in the face of their insensitivity. They had failed to notice, understand or engage with the Islamic-inspired forces that were seeking to redress the profound imbalances which America appeared so active and willing to perpetuate.

I remember wondering how this superpower, whose own constitution enshrined the rights of man, could become so active in supporting the tyranny that had deprived so many Iranians of precisely the rights America held dear for her own people. More recently I have wondered if I was witnessing the germination of seeds which would eventually render the horror and desperation of 9/11 possible. For the word 'Iran,' one could just as easily read 'Saudi'.

One morning in November 1979, sleeping in my Tehran hotel room, I was awakened by pounding on my door. It was Hamid, my locally hired driver and translator. 'They have taken the American embassy!' he cried.

'Who's taken it?'

'The students. They are shutting the roads, we need to get there.'

The US embassy was a low, hostile-looking building in the heart of town. Not an easy place to visit at the best of times, today in the dawn sun its dusty yellow brick walls were adorned with bedsheets covered in slogans. 'Crater is a Dag and a Dankey', screamed one. It took me some moments to work out that this meant '[President] Carter is a dog and a donkey'. At this point it was possible to wander around the outer area of the embassy compound with rather more freedom than before this clearly temporary student takeover.

Three hours earlier a horde of students had simply stormed past the sleeping sentries, invaded and occupied the building. There had been little or no resistance, and by the time I arrived the students still looked surprised to be in control of the place. Somebody was ripping up one of the bedsheets and producing makeshift white blindfolds for a cluster of diplomats who were being held in a reluctant group near the main door. Some already had blindfolds on. The atmosphere was noisy and slightly festive.

We weren't to know that this was to be our last glimpse of the fifty-two US hostages for more than a year. The blindfolds were to come to symbolise America's humiliation, and to inform America's view of Iran for more than a generation. This was indeed America's first 9/11 moment, a first headlong collision with Islamic fundamentalism. Despite being present at the taking of images that were to prove so iconic, we felt no particular sense of threat, nor could we be aware of these events' long-term consequence. Yet I believe that if America had managed to conceptualise and get inside what fuelled Iran's hatred and resentment, the course of subsequent history might have been very different.

On that November morning, Hamid and I agreed that the embassy siege would probably end as soon as it had begun, and that we should grab some shots before it did. Two or three students wanted to pose for the camera. They spoke English with flawless American accents. One told me casually, 'I did engineering at MIT.' Another said, 'I was at the University of Southern California. I got a doctorate in biochemistry.' Seizing the diplomatic compound of their former hosts seemed a bit of a wheeze to them. For me there was even a whiff of the Liverpool University sit-in about it. A couple of mullahs holding court on office chairs under a tree inside the perimeter walls were clearly taking it all rather more seriously.

What I did not recognise at the time was that this so-far chaotic but seemingly manageable event was to play a lead role in deposing an American President, and would set the United States upon a course that more than two decades later would find Iran catalogued in the very heartland of George W. Bush's Axis of Evil. Losing the Shah to a clerically-led Islamic revolution had been bad enough; losing an entire embassy and dozens of diplomats to student revolutionaries was quite simply unacceptable.

In these early stages of the siege it was easy to establish a dialogue with the students, to engage with them. But the humiliating impact of nightly television news shots of the bedsheets on the walls and the blindfolds on the diplomats' heads had an electrifying effect on domestic and political feelings in America. There was a sense of violation that was only to resurface again after 9/11, more than twenty years later. In what was an American election year, the political message was absolute. The diplomats became hostages. Dialogue was dead. 'Bring our boys and girls home, free the American hostages,' became the battle cry. The yellow ribbons were out, tied around the trees of middle America awaiting the day that the hostages would be free.

Sixty days on, as the United States became more bellicose and shrill, the students became more excited and determined. So many had lived and studied in America that they understood only too well the power of the TV news images. My good friend Ayatollah Beheshti, whom I came to know well in those days, had lived in both Germany and America. 'We were ourselves humiliated in America when we lived there,' he said. 'We were second-class citizens; they hated our faith and had no clue as to who we were. They wanted us to become good Americans. We wanted to become good Iranians.' Beheshti was to be killed by a bomb planted by radicals a couple of years later. Nevertheless he articulated the core dynamic between America and Iran. No one represented it more clearly than the Iranian Foreign Minister, Sadegh Ghotbzadeh. He'd spent twenty years as a student in the American Mid-West, and was fired by a sense of envy and resentment of the America he had left behind. He was not an impressive man, but he was engaging and remarkably open – too open for his own good. Despite the fact that he had held the hand of Ayatollah Khomeini throughout his triumph-ant return from exile in Paris to Tehran in 1978, he too was to be executed within a couple of years. His role as Foreign Minister rapidly became that of a clapped-out old student radical re-energised by the antics of a new generation of students.

In those early days I am convinced that America could have resolved the crisis. But with only a handful of diplomats on the ground, who'd had the good fortune to be outside the compound at the time of its seizing, and a history of so gravely misjudging what Iran was about, the chances were never good. Certainly no one could have been more surprised to find themselves regarded as a serious global threat than the students who now held the hostages. We watched their mood change from one of almost innocent pranksterism to arrogance fuelled by Islamic fervour.

Very soon after the hostage crisis dawned, all American journalists were sent packing from Iran. ITN would have sent me with them – after all, there were no British hostages, so they reasoned that there was no point wasting money on me staying – but they reckoned without ABC News in America. The hostage crisis had spawned a highly successful nightly programme out of

Washington, with the ringing title *Iran in Crisis, America Held Hostage*. It was hosted by Ted Koppel, and was eventually to become the late-night staple of American current affairs programming, *Nightline*.

'The Koppel Show', as its producers liked to call it, was entirely dependent upon major input from Tehran – guests, reporting and the rest. With no American journalists in Iran, this ratings-charged programme was going to suffer. So ABC asked ITN to second me to them. My editors agreed, and for the first months of the crisis I became a pseudo-American at the very epicentre of a nightly American drama. I'd never been to America, and had no idea how different the American television culture would prove to be. It wasn't just the language, it was that every single word I spoke had to be checked with the foreign desk in New York. Very often they would tell me that the facts I had reported were at variance with the US State Department's version, and would try to get me to change mine to conform with theirs. I kept telling them that unlike the State Department, I had the benefit of actually being on the ground in Tehran, but they were rarely persuaded.

From the first, New York would call me at some unearthly hour and demand inaccessible guests, or pictures, or reports, or all three. It was part of my job to ensure that ABC never found out quite how easy it was to secure such guests; after all, it affected what they paid me. The harder it appeared – and to them Iran was a vision of Dante's Inferno – the more they paid.

Amazingly, during the early days of the crisis Cyrus Vance, then US Secretary of State, said he wanted a live debate with his Iranian opposite number Sadegh Ghotbzadeh via the Indian Ocean satellite. Of course, I made out that it was very unlikely that Ghotbzadeh would agree, but I promised I would use all my good offices in an attempt to persuade him to turn out at what would be seven o'clock our time in the morning. An hour later I was knocking on Ghotbzadeh's door in the Foreign Ministry. In those days things were still extraordinarily informal.

'Sadegh,' I said upon entering, 'ABC want you live with Cy Vance tomorrow morning at seven.'

'Fantastic!' cried Ghotbzadeh. 'Isn't that great? Are you sure you don't want me any earlier?' Later, when we were talking privately about the crisis, he confided, 'I just can't believe that they are taking us seriously. Me, the serial academic failure over twenty years as a student in America!' The satellite exchange went ahead exactly as planned, with Vance embarrassingly grateful to Ghotbzadeh for agreeing to participate. Ghotbzadeh left the studio preening himself.

For many weeks of the early part of the hostage crisis, that is how it was. America was so fearful of what might have been unleashed that no serious attempt to engage the students was really made. Viewed from Tehran, the Carter administration in Washington seemed to be doing little more than agonising rather publicly about what to do. I believe that in this early miscalculation and inept assessment of what was really going on, the United States helped to lay the groundwork for a kind of fundamentalism that was to gain more confidence from American failures in Iran than from any other single development in the two decades that preceded 9/11. US fears were only consolidated by what happened six months into the hostage crisis.

On 25 April 1980 I was sitting by the telex machine off the lobby of the Intercontinental Hotel in Tehran, talking to London, when Hamid came panting in. 'Mr Jon, they have crashed in the desert,' he blurted.

'Who's crashed? Which desert, Hamid?'

Hamid had a brother who was serving in the Revolutionary Guards in a place called Yazd, about 370 miles from Tehran. The brother had reported that some kind of US hostage rescue mission had screwed up in the desert somewhere near him. It was clear as we emerged from the telex booth that no one else in the lobby of the Intercon knew anything about it. I got hold of my cameraman, the young and dapper Charles Morgan – now, believe it or not, managing director of classic Morgan Cars. 'Charlie,' I said, 'big fuck-up in the desert beyond Yazd. Yanks seem to have been trying to get to the hostages here, and have crashed. We've absolutely got to get there.'

'God,' he said. 'Bloody Yazd is hours and hours away, and there'll be Revolutionary Guard roadblocks everywhere.'

I said, 'Look, get the vehicle and get everything ready. I'll try to find out more.'

I got on to Ayatollah Beheshti's office. He knew

all about it. 'Helicopters,' he said, 'a dozen of them, burnt up during refuelling, plenty American dead.' He added that a busload of locals had been taken hostage for the duration of the inferno in case they got news out before the surviving US forces had been rescued.

Charlie and I decided we'd never get to the crash site in our own vehicle because of the security checks, but that if we could find the same bus the next night and simply take the commercial service across the desert, we just might make it. So we got to Zarand, an obscure and desperate place in the desert region well to the south-east of Tehran. We found the bus, bribed the driver with $250, crawled under a tarpaulin, and bucketed about at the back until we reached the crash site.

Emerging from the bus, bold as brass in the dawn sun, we were effusively greeted by Ayatollah Khalkhali, the Minister of Islamic Justice. He was apparently waiting for a VIP visit, and thought we were it. We did not disabuse him as he rushed about the site picking up bits of charred helicopter; at one moment he whirled the thighbone of a dead American above his turbaned head.

The footage was sensational, and so was the story. This was a much worse catastrophe than we had been told. Inspecting the tyre marks on the desert floor, it was clear that the refuelling C130 aeroplane had landed, and crashed into the last of a row of about ten American helicopters that had flown to this remote rendezvous point from carriers in the Gulf. While the plane was landing on the dusty surface, its central braking system had thrown the propellers into reverse, kicking up huge clouds of dust. This was no instrument landing; there had been nothing on the ground to work to. Human vision had been the determinant, and the pilots had simply been blinded. Not only had the refuelling craft exploded, but the fire had passed from chopper to chopper. Only the last three machines were left unscathed. Some of the dead were left behind. The uninjured, together with the horribly scalded and burned casualties, limped away in the surviving craft. It was a fatuous and disastrous mishap. By the time we reached Tehran, even Iranian TV was crying out for our footage. The pictorial proof of the American failure sent shockwaves around the world.

Together with the hostage seizure itself, this episode, which came to be known as 'Desert One', defined America's impotence. Washington's diplomatic, media and military engagement with Iran had been ill-informed, paranoid, unrealistic and a failure at every turn. I sometimes wondered at the time whether there were politically motivated elements within the US power structure who were actually interested in seeing Jimmy Carter and his team fail.

Whatever the immediate domestic consequences, for the hostages their humiliating detention was to last a total of 444 days. Carter was defeated at the polls, vanquished by Ronald Reagan's landslide victory, and it was Reagan who would take the credit for turning things around and winning the hostages their freedom when they were finally released in January 1981, a matter of hours into his presidency. The Carter team, who had actually done all the work, got no kudos at all. That much has been oft recorded. What has been less examined is the extent to which the episode informed Islamic fundamentalists of Western vulnerabilities, upon which they were to prey again and again. Charlie and I were one of only two Western news teams to make it to Desert One. We believed that the hostages could and should have been freed easily either by negotiation or by force within ten days of their capture.

I learned one more thing from it all. We had shot two four-hundred-foot cans of film, and on our way to Yazd it became clear that the Iranians did not want us to leave with it. But in three significant body searches they never found the cans. I had them compressing my genitals in my Y-fronts. Islamic sensibilities kept searching hands well away from so sensitive an area.

I had had to spend Christmas of 1979 in Tehran, since the Iranians had ordained that any Westerners leaving the country would not be allowed to return. So it was going to have to be plentiful supplies of Caspian Sea caviar and *blinis* instead of turkey. In the event I awoke to the news that the Soviet Union had invaded neighbouring Afghanistan. This was a huge and startling development for which neither I nor anyone else was prepared. The USSR had not attempted to seize any country since the 1940s. It had invaded its own satellite nations like Hungary or Czechoslovakia, but actually taking an altogether new state with military force was new.

Most news organisations were dashing for Pakistan's porous border at the other end of Afghanistan. I thought our best plan was to try to get up to north-eastern Iran, to Mashad. Maybe Afghan students and exiles there would be demonstrating. At least that would give us some pictures, I thought, and perhaps we could find an Afghan who would take us across the border illicitly.

On Boxing Day morning the streets of Mashad were alive with Afghan students chanting 'Death to the Russians', 'Go home Brezhnev'. As we milled around the demonstrators, a young Afghan student approached Hamid and started talking with him in Farsi. 'He can take you in,' Hamid translated. 'He can even get you across tonight. But it's too dangerous for Iranians, you would have to go on your own.' I was worried that we had no common language with the man. Then we discovered he spoke German, which Alan Downes, my cameraman on this occasion, had learned while doing his national service. So it was arranged that we would travel with Daud, who turned out to be studying dentistry in Mashad. I had also linked up with John Kifner from the *New York Times*, so with my sound man John Martin we were a team of four about to try to get into Afghanistan by a route no other Westerner had tried.

That night we drove for many hours, finally arriving at the border at four in the morning. We were shown into the house of a local Afghan mullah, who was surprisingly well awake. Hamid and our film editor, Fred Hickey, planned to stay here until our return in about a week. There was no formal sign of any border, and it was clear that people were crossing freely in and out of the country.

At the back of the house was a huge old Soviet-made army truck. It had apparently been liberated from the Afghan army some time earlier. This was to be our transport for the initial part of the journey towards the Afghan city of Herat. The hours ticked by with no sign of movement. Finally the mullah indicated that we could only move under cover of darkness. At one point in the day a young Afghan woman asked us to visit her house to look at a carpet on her loom. It was to all intents complete, and she wanted to sell it. For some reason I felt that to buy it would be taking advantage of her, and to my eternal regret I refused. It would have been a wonderful link with this remote and unvisited place, and I would have paid far more than she'd ever have got from any local.

As the sun began to sink and the colours faded we clambered into the truck, the Afghan dentist Daud in the passenger seat, we four Westerners with our few belongings on the open-topped back. Two days after the first Russian tank had rolled into Afghanistan from the north, we set off. We could see hills and tall mountains in the distance. Very soon the way ahead became deserted, dark and rocky, and the night began to turn extremely cold. The stars were out but there was no moon, so the truck was guided by its one surviving yellow headlamp. It was so cold on the back of the open truck, so unupholstered, that the four of us got into our sleeping bags and lay as close to each other as we possibly could for warmth. We travelled for all of twenty-four hours without seeing a soul, crossing hills and plains, the scenery spectacular, sporting purples, blues and yellows. Eventually we reached a deserted village and took shelter in one of the houses. We set a fire and tried to make ourselves comfortable. By day the temperature soared, but come the night it was back to below freezing.

'The camera is completely dead,' said Alan as I awoke the next morning.

'It's probably only frozen,' I said.

We re-energised the fire and started to cook the batteries. Amazingly, after ten minutes when we put them back into the camera it fired first go. That morning we saw our first sign of life. We had been batting along over the desert floor when a plane came out of the east. We abandoned the truck and threw ourselves to the ground. It never came near us, and we continued on our way. Our immediate destination was a Mujahidin camp high in the mountains above Herat.

When we got there, we found our hosts armed with everything bar the kitchen sink. The best of their weapons had been made before 1914. Bolt-action Lee Enfield rifles, that could have been captured from nineteenth-century engagement with British imperial forces, predominated. Those who had no gun carried pickaxes or shovels over their shoulders. In truth they were pitifully inadequately armed. With their red or white beards and turbans, these Afghans were an odd assortment of years and abilities. The real firepower seemed to belong to the teenagers.

Kifner, Alan and I were taken at dawn the next day to a rocky outcrop overlooking the main road from the northern border to Kandahar. Long Soviet convoys were still slowly snaking along the road below. From time to time a boy would dash out from cover and throw a Molotov cocktail into a passing vehicle, with spectacular results. Once I saw a child doused in petrol jumping onto an isolated tank and setting fire to himself close to the driver's hatch. The entire machine exploded in a ball of flame.

There was a frightening preparedness to die, a frightening fanaticism; I wondered even then what would happen if anyone ever managed to harness it and deploy it against us. As it was, Afghanistan was to become Russia's Vietnam, which suited the West fine. Over the next ten years America would arm, train, pay and encourage these very people to become a force of such ferocity that not only did the Soviets flee, taking Communism and the Berlin Wall with them, but the unprecedented Taliban government would come and provide active cover for Osama bin Laden and al Qaida to visit unimagined woe on the United States.

Hamid and Fred were in a depressed and desperate condition by the time we emerged from Afghanistan two weeks later than we had promised. They were worried sick that we had been killed, and had been about to give up when we appeared back at the mullah's house. Far from dead, we had survived to bring back a wonderful world exclusive account of the Soviet invasion at

Above: General Tom, my twice-knighted grandfather, who hung above the mantel and seemed to have inspected every boiled egg I ever ate.

Below: My father's Hudson Terraplane Eight configured as a wartime fire-tender.

Above: War wedding. My father and mother met and married in a matter of weeks.

The damage caused by a Second World War bomb on the lawns of Charterhouse School; my father's one moment of 'action'.

Below: A sunny Sussex childhood. Growing up in the aftermath of war.

Above: No particular talent. Following childhood encounters with Harold Macmillan, my earliest ambition was to be a Tory MP.

My father with Macmillan at Ardingly. 'Do you know what a Prime Minister is?' he asked me. 'Are you married to the Queen?' I responded.

Below: With Tom and Nick in the Terraplane; a happy contrast to the dining-table warfare.

Above: The Queen visiting Ardingly. My mother had been to Harrods to buy a pair of Crown Derby cups and saucers from which the royal lips could sip their afternoon tea.

Above right: As a chorister at Winchester Cathedral in 1958. We became part of the fabric of the building.

Right: My father, every inch a bishop — eight feet tall in his mitre. The Whitby nuns had toiled for many nights to embroider his robes.

Back from Uganda. VSO had radicalised me, and one reason I wanted to become a journalist was in order to return there.

India in the summer of 1969, singing 'Hey Jude' (third from right) in the Liverpool University close-part harmony Beatle band.

Left: Not me! But I was amongst several hundred anti-apartheid demonstrators who were arrested at the Springbok rugby match at Old Trafford in November 1969.

Below left: Mass meeting of Liverpool students ahead of our sit-in, me in the then inevitable Afghan coat.

Below: Pre-mobile-phone reporting for LBC in 1973, on a clunky old Motorola two-way radio.

An exchange with Ugandan dictator Idi Amin on the 1974 trip with Jim Callaghan to rescue Denis Hills.

Vietnamese boat people below decks on the refugee boat on which we found ourselves stranded in the South China Sea in 1976.

The shell of the Vietnamese refugee boat beached in Malaysia. We languished in a police cell, facing twenty years in prison for aiding and abetting illegal immigration.

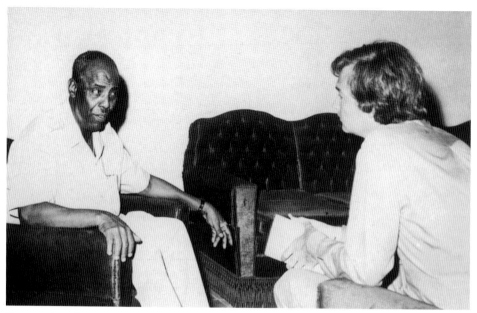

Interviewing the Somali President Siad Barre, a grumpy Moscow-educated ideologue running a classic Cold War Russian client state, in 1976.

With Mohinder Dhillon in Somalia. Mystified British viewers were treated to a travelogue in which an excitable white man jumped up and down talking about the threat to world peace.

Back to Uganda again in 1977, this time for ITN armed with Edward Heath's book. I wondered what on earth landlocked Amin would want with a book about ocean sailing. He'd sink any boat just by boarding it.

Interviewing US President Jimmy Carter and Prime Minister Jim Callaghan outside Lancaster House in London, 1977.

Preparing to conduct the first ever English-language interview with a Pope, in the confusion aboard John Paul II's plane in January 1979. It was to end in disaster.

Standing outside Number Ten Downing Street on 4 May 1979, Mrs Thatcher's first day as Prime Minister. She cribbed the prayer of St Francis from a postage-stamp-sized note hidden in the palm of her hand.

Afghanistan, 1980.
With the Mujahidin in mountains above Herat in the immediate aftermath of the Soviet Invasion.

Below left: Filming with Charlie Morgan at 'Desert One' in Iran in April 1980 amid the wrekage of Jimmy Carter's catastrophic attempt to rescue the American hostages — America's first 9/11.

Below: The Iran-Iraq War in 1981. Wearing no body armour and no flak jacket, I was less than well prepared to survive the conflagration in which I was caught.

Above: On the road to Suchitoto in El Salvador with Sebastian Rich and Don Warren in February 1981.

Below: Behind guerrilla lines with '*los muchachos*' in El Salvador, 1983.

With President Reagan in the White House, February 1985.
My interview with him was a complete failure.

Sitting at the right hand. . . I interviewed Iraq's Deputy Prime Minister Tariq Aziz several times in twenty-five years, but could never work out how much more than Saddam's presentable face he really was.

The *Evening Standard* pokes fun at my naked arrest in Geneva in January 1991 whilst waiting to interview Tariq Aziz yet again.

"Would you accept the apologies of the Swiss police again Mr Snow. It appears you did pay your parking fine!"

Left: It was the West's great fortune to find Mikhail Gorbachev in charge when it mattered most — an opportunity for global reordering which we ultimately wasted.

Below: A long way from anti-apartheid protest at Liverpool University. Interviewing Nelson Mandela the day he became South Africa's first democratically elected President in 1984.

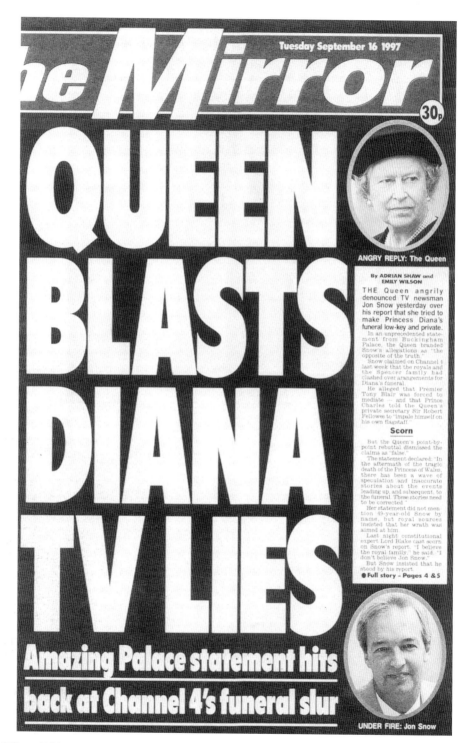

Tuesday September 16 1997

the *Mirror*

30p

QUEEN BLASTS DIANA TV LIES

Amazing Palace statement hits back at Channel 4's funeral slur

ANGRY REPLY: The Queen

By ADRIAN SHAW and EMILY WILSON

THE Queen angrily denounced TV newsman Jon Snow yesterday over his report that she tried to make Princess Diana's funeral low-key and private.

In an unprecedented statement from Buckingham Palace, the Queen branded Snow's allegations as "the opposite of the truth."

Snow claimed on Channel 4 last week that the royals and the Spencer family had clashed over arrangements for Diana's funeral.

He alleged that Premier Tony Blair was forced to mediate — and that Prince Charles told the Queen's private secretary Sir Robert Fellowes to "impale himself on his own flagstaff."

Scorn

But the Queen's point-by-point rebuttal dismissed the claims as "false."

The statement declared: "In the aftermath of the tragic death of the Princess of Wales, there has been a wave of speculation and inaccurate stories about the events leading up, and subsequent, to the funeral. These stories need to be corrected."

Her statement did not mention 49-year-old Snow by name, but royal sources insisted that her wrath was aimed at him.

Last night constitutional expert Lord Blake cast scorn on Snow's report. "I believe the royal family," he said. "I don't believe Jon Snow."

But Snow insisted that he stood by his report.

● Full story – Pages 4 & 5

UNDER FIRE: Jon Snow

The *Mirror* took a dim view of our royal scoop, in which Prince Charles suggested to the Queen's private secretary that he impale himself on his own flagstaff.

Left: The full Monica. An exclusive sit-down with Ms Lewinsky in 1988, her first interview after the attempt to impeach President Clinton.

Below: Return to Uganda in 1999, sitting at the back of the classroom in which I had taught thirty years earlier.

Bottom: On the line in northern Ghana, exploring the Greenwich meridian in a classic 'Yendi smock' in 2000.

Overleaf: September 2001. The heart of the inferno at Ground Zero. Some underestimated how much joy the attack brought to many poorer parts of the world.

With cameraman Ken McCallum in Baghdad, November 2003.

Advertising Channel Four News, with trusty steed on
Euston Station.

the western end of Afghanistan.

Three months later I returned to London. ABC had been shocked to discover that their seasoned Tehran correspondent had never actually set foot in the US of A, and generously decided to reward me with a Concorde flight to the America I had seen so often but never visited. I stayed for a week on the twentieth floor of the Essex House Hotel. I found New York hard to get to grips with. I knew no one, and no one seemed much interested in knowing me. It was a far cry from Iran, Iraq or Afghanistan. Yet so much death and destruction had been carried out in all three countries on behalf of the interests represented here.

I never believed I would ever come to live in America, or that there could still be so much more to learn about her actions overseas. For the time being there was still the Iranian hostage issue to be resolved. It was not until January 1981 that the hostages were freed, thanks to Algerian diplomatic intervention. I covered their release on a special midnight programme which I anchored from London.

The weekend before, I had had a tip from a telex operator at Coward Chance, a London law firm. She told me that she had seen transactions moving huge funds out of the United States and other countries to Algiers, where the hostage deal was being brokered. Altogether some $10 billion was in play, nearly all of it Iran's by rights anyway. Much of it had been purloined by the Shah and stashed in bank accounts across the world. Washington had frozen a few billion in

America at the time of the revolution.

I had met the American civil rights lawyer Leonard Boudin a year or two earlier at my friend Helena Kennedy's London flat. Helena had set up a radical set of barristers' chambers with Madeleine and others – the two of them had been pupils at the same time. While Helena specialised in crime and representing IRA operatives, Madeleine moved towards civil liberties and the then fledgling area of human rights law. Helena had held a party for Leonard, to which she'd invited me. When I discovered that he was representing the Bank of Iran in the money-for-hostages exchange, I had something of an inside track. He gave me much of the detail of the deal, and copies of some of the paperwork and exchanges.

Four hundred and forty-four days after they'd last been seen, fifty-two wan-looking hostages descended from an Algerian airliner at Algiers airport. Midway through their descent our satellite feed collapsed, and I had to extemporise for so long that I took to inventing the mysterious route by which the pictures were reaching us. I even went so far as to suggest that the signal had got lost somewhere in cloud over the Atlas mountains. It was pointed out to me later that it would hardly go south in order to come north. In the excitement of live late-night television, these things happen.

Despite the euphoria of getting the hostages back and the balletic timing that ensured that the new President, Ronald Reagan, experienced the release rather than the departing Jimmy Carter who'd suffered so much by it, and had been responsible for the negotiations, the night only served to accentuate the fact that this had been a very dark hour in America's history, one that Reagan and others were determined never to see repeated. Yet America's collision with militant Islam would return again and again, first in Beirut three years later, and then inside the United States itself on 9/11.

SEVEN

Uncle Sam's Backyard

The road might be mined; it was certainly deserted, and gave off an air of menace which was accentuated when we rounded a bend and encountered a heavily armed roadblock. It was February 1981, nearly a year on from the day that Archbishop Oscar Romero had been assassinated by a right-wing death squad whilst celebrating mass at the high altar of his own church in San Salvador.

The leftist guerrilla movement the Farabundo Marti para la Liberacion Nacional (FMLN) had just launched an abortive 'final assault' to liberate El Salvador from its military tyranny. El Salvador is a tiny, overpopulated country, no larger than Wales, squeezed between Guatemala, Honduras and Nicaragua, one of a string of banana republics slung between Mexico in the north and Panama in the south. Like its neighbours El Salvador was dominated by a small nexus of families whose senior members were the oligarchs who controlled every aspect of the country. The 'garchs' as we called them, had intertwined relations with US multinationals like United Fruit who ran great tracts of plantations across Central America, funnelling cheap produce north to the USA. The oligarchs controlled the armed forces, which the Americans armed, and which in turn subjugated the enslaved populations who toiled for US corporate greed and profit. That was how it had been for fifty years until now, in early 1981, when the people had finally begun to take up arms against their American-backed oppressors.

The assassination of so senior a cleric as Archbishop Romero was rare indeed, even in revolution-strewn Latin America. His murder had finally awakened outside interest in what was going on in El Salvador. There had been a fledgling Marxist revolutionary group, founded amongst radical Catholic students at the Jesuit University in San Salvador, since the early 1970s. The Catholic Church here was seen as entirely in tune with the brand of liberation theology embraced by those who had wanted Brazil's Cardinal Lorscheider to become Pope in 1978.

The country was now in the grip of a civil war in which the American-backed Salvadorean military were in league with the coffee-plantation owners against a rebel force of guerrillas who claimed support from the rural poor, backed by significant activism from within the Church. El Salvador had not enjoyed a civilian government since 1932; it had been in the grip of almost fifty years of uninterrupted military dictatorship.

When my foreign editor at ITN ordered me out there, I had no idea precisely where El Salvador was; indeed I did not even know whether it had a Pacific or an Atlantic coast. I had been 'on the road' virtually non-stop for five years since joining ITN, and my relationship with Madeleine had suffered as a result. We had finally begun to settle down at the very moment of my dispatch – the welcome and unwelcome escape from commitment and having to make decisions about marriage, houses and babies – an endemic condition in our industry. As so often I had boarded the plane full of emotions of regret and guilt, only to have them overwhelmed by the challenge of the new and unknown as I neared my destination.

I had been sent with my usual sound man, Don Warren, but this time my cameraman was Sebastian Rich – young, blond, macho, with his shirt open to his navel and a gold chain around his neck, Sebastian cut an incongruous dash. He had not been in a war zone before, but had shot beautiful feature films deploying filters and skills rarely seen in news reports. His images were to prove incredibly vivid and dramatic, and were part of what was to enable our trip to make such a powerful impact. I had one other invaluable asset, a notebook filled with extraordinary contacts and information provided by Dr Salvador Muncada. Muncada was part of a Nobel Prize-winning team of researchers at the Wellcome Foundation. But he had grown up in El Salvador and founded a guerrilla movement before fleeing for his life to London. He was FMLN's representative in Europe and is today a pillar of the British medical establishment. At this time however he was a wise and generous informant: our scoops were down to him.

We were picked up at San Salvador's airport by our fluent Spanish-speaking Italian fixer, Marcello Zanini. He was a wiry, Gaulois-smoking character, about my age, laid-back, cool, yet enthusiastic to pursue the story to the very ultimate. He immediately urged us to get straight out to see what was going on, and we chose almost at random to drive towards a town called Suchitoto, thirty miles to the north-west of the capital. This was a notorious flash-point for action between the guerrillas, '*los muchachos*', and the armed forces.

'You never know who controls any road at any moment,' Marcello said. 'This looks like National Guard. Be on best behaviour.'

'Where you going, gringo?' A helmeted National Guardsman at the roadblock was rattling the bayonet of his rifle from side to side of the front quarter-light of the car.

'Suchitoto,' Marcello replied.

'Bad things up there,' the Guardsman said. 'Fifteen of them dead in a truck last night. Take good care.'

We drove on apprehensively. There was not a soul about. The road was so unused that incongruous splashes of blue morning-glory trumpet flowers spread out from the gutter into the middle of the tarmac. The vegetation was thick, damp and green, and dangerously well engineered to hide guerrillas, death squads, or anyone else who might wish us ill. The last few miles into Suchitoto were eerie.

Finally we reached the low sprawl of single-storey plaster-walled houses on the outskirts. We could hear the funeral toll from the church bell long before we reached the main square. The church itself was yet another page from Graham Greene – white stucco walls, brilliant in the mid-morning sun, casting sharp purple shadows. The bell swung crazily out and back from the darkness of the belfry, the hammer clattering once with each swing.

Then we saw them, in a long line on wobbly trestles: fifteen coffins standing all along the front wall of the church. Each had a little open window at the head, through which the awful injuries of the people inside could be seen. Nearby, women wept. The scene was as picturesque and classically Latin American as it was shocking. We were immediately confronted with the first of a whole litany of images to which European television audiences had not been exposed before. When we found the bent, black-clad priest inside the church he invited us up to the deafening confines of the belfry for a better vantage point. A neat square with trees casting shade over shops and tea stalls lay below us. Beyond, orange, pink and brown pantiled roofs at conflicting angles spread in different directions.

'Those men down there,' the priest explained, indicating the row of coffins, 'they were coffee-plantation workers, peasants returning from the *finca* [ranch].' There was no doubt in his mind, nor in the minds of those who grieved, that the National Guard, perhaps the very ones who manned the roadblock through which we had passed, had massacred them. To the residents this was not unprecedented. Their small town was on the front line between government and guerrilla forces. In the two years before our arrival in the country Amnesty International estimated that forty thousand Salvadoreans had died in the civil war.

On the way back to San Salvador we were held up again. Long-haired young men, their faces masked in red kerchiefs, ran into the road brandishing automatic weapons. They were guerrillas from the FMLN, easy, talkative, and Marcello knew exactly what they wanted – war tax. They fund-raised for weapons by robbing unarmed users of the roads. We paid up.

San Salvador even at night was a city of acute contrasts. Spectacular fortified mansions alternated with ravines down which all manner of humanity tumbled in a chaotic disorder of shanty shacks. Naked children ran everywhere; blaring music was occasionally interrupted by the sharp report of a weapon being fired. In the centre of town Kentucky Fried Chicken vied with brightly-lit gambling halls. The Camino Real was regarded as the safest hotel in which to stay, so most of the small press corps would be found in the bar there of a night. We were divided between those who went out to find out what was going on, and those who sat in the bar to debrief those coming back so that they too could write about it.

On that first trip I was the only British television correspondent in the country. My greatest ally of the time was Ray Bonner of the *New York Times*, whose lone voice challenged America to wake up and look at what was being done in her name in her own backyard. Ray was a bright law graduate who'd moved on to the press. Intense, rugged and indefatigable, he was the best possible person to work with in such a place. We shared much the same view of the situation in El Salvador, which was that the military had made life so intolerable for the poor and the thinking classes that a coalition of intellectuals, student activists, trades unionists and priests had been forced into the bush to take up arms against them. The military had appealed to the United States for assistance, stoking Cold War tensions to whip up American fears of Communist insurgency, and now Washington found itself backing a military tyranny that was systematically killing its own people. Bonner's paper recalled him to New York in 1983 for telling the truth about a massacre at the far end of the country about which the US authorities had no small degree of knowledge. He left the *New York Times* shortly thereafter, and it was to take him ten years to win an apology and restoration of his job. Even in my own case, right-wing MPs raised questions at Westminster casting doubt on the impartiality of my journalism. It would get worse.

The Camino Real in 1981 was a fearful place. Most mornings we would awaken to find several bodies dumped in the car park, the latest victims of the death squads. Sometimes there were corpses in the underpass that led into town. Notes would be slipped under our doors with death lists upon which, from time to time, we would find our own names. One night, having done what I always did, which was to put a chair against the door so that I would hear it move if someone got in with a master key, I was awakened by a terrible shaking of the bed. I shouted out, 'You bastards!' But there was no one there; it was nothing worse than a mild earthquake.

By the second month of my first three-month stint in El Salvador it had become impossible to drive down the Littoral, the coast road, without finding human and economic carnage in your way. On one occasion the bodies of eight peasants were laid out on one side of the road, while their heads stood upright in the grass on the other. Sometimes the pictures were altogether too gruesome to transmit. There were the lava pits below the volcano outside San Salvador which had become the most notorious dumping ground for the death squads. Here the bodies were left on the unyielding black earth, to be devoured and pecked at by dogs and vultures. Upon arriving there we were greeted by a great flapping of wings as a hundred vultures rose as one, leaving the foetid mess of humanity lying about us. Perhaps a hundred or more bodies were there on the day we went. They ranged from fleshless skeletons to very recent fleshy leavings, on which perhaps an eye had been pecked out and a gunshot wound seeped from the chest. I felt physically sick, but Sebastian insisted I must do a report to camera in the fullest possible context of the bodies. 'Only then will they wake up to what is happening here,' he said. He was right: the shattered look of the reporter against the black backdrop peppered with bones and corpses was so shocking my editors were only just able to run it.

In the end, what shocked even more than the images was the complicity of the United States government. In his closing days as President, racked by Iran and the hostage crisis, decent, human-rights-espousing Jimmy Carter had given in to the hawks in the American Defense Department and allowed a staggering $160 million of emergency military aid, helicopters, artillery, guns, ammunition, training and US military advisers to go to the Salvadorean military.

I first met 'Major Bob' at the Sheraton Hotel in San Salvador in March 1981, in the very foyer where he'd had two American trade union advisers assassinated just a few months earlier. Roberto D'Aubuisson, a former National Guard intelligence officer in the El Salvadorean army, was a leading light of the country's right wing. He was small, sunglassed, forty-two years old, dapper and militaristic in his bearing. His shirts were always freshly ironed, and strangely blood-free for a man who had so much blood on his hands. 'All measures have to be taken to exterminate these Communists who threaten my country,' he told me. He was proud of his contacts with US intelligence, with the extreme political right, and with the military. Most of us who reported El Salvador had no doubt that he had at least given the order to assassinate Archbishop Romero, and may even have been present at the shooting that felled this much-loved priest on the steps of his own high altar with a bullet fired through his back that pierced his heart. D'Aubuisson had a network of death squads who represented the interests of the oligarchs who still controlled the military. The facts of his involvement were set out a decade later in a UN Truth Commission report. In the meantime he enjoyed unfettered movement in and out of the US-backed military high command, although denied access to the American embassy itself. Washington did nothing to bring about his arrest or to help take him out of circulation. In 1982 – within a year of Archbishop Romero's assassination – the US would even welcome his appointment as President of the country's new Constituent Assembly. Such was Washington's desire to see off the 'Communist threat'. In those months the death squads murdered a group of leading academics from the Jesuit university, four American nuns, countless teachers, doctors and students, and thousands of peasants. They also killed a number of journalists, and would later attempt to kill us.

In March 1981 Major Bob had gone even further with the Americans – the US embassy in San Salvador was sprayed with bullets in an attack that bore the hallmarks of right-wing terrorism directed by the Major. But despite issuing protests, the US authorities still did little to have the military they supported rein him in.

Washington had insisted that a civilian President ameliorate the more militaristic aspects of the junta's image, and Napoleon Duarte, a respected Christian Democrat, was chosen for the job. I visited him several times in his presidential office. 'I am powerless against D'Aubuisson,' he admitted in conversation. He went through the motions of having the most ostentatious killers arrested from within the National Guard, but could go no further. An engaging, comfortable man, with sagging, unhappy puppy-dog eyes, Duarte had suffered torture and exile himself. He had lost three fingers on his right hand, seemingly from a shooting accident rather than from his political enemies. The Americans hoped he'd give the military government a veneer of respectability.

In May 1981 I was back in my room at the Camino on another open-ended assignment.

'Mr Snow,' said a heavily-accented voice on the phone, 'I am Miguel from the Green Cross. We need your help, could I come up and see you?'

Normally it was inadvisable to allow anyone anywhere near your room, especially as we were now regularly on the death lists, but something in me believed him, so I told him to come on up. Miguel, who was from El Salvador's equivalent of the Red Cross, turned out to be genuine, and to have a harrowing tale of the human consequences of all the killing. 'Seven hundred and eighty orphans sixty kilometres from here, and we can't reach them unless the international press come with us to protect us,' he pleaded.

I managed to gather up Ray Bonner, the celebrated American photographer Susan Meiselas from the Magnum agency, the maverick reporter David Blundy of the *Sunday Times*, who was later to die in crossfire between government troops and left-wing rebels in 1989, and two other journalists. Our meagre convoy of three white-flag-fluttering civilian cars, with most of us adorned in white bulletproof flak jackets, set off at dawn the next day. In truth we were almost all that was left of the foreign correspondents – the rest had fled the continuous death threats.

As we were passing through the small town of San Lorenzo we suddenly came under fire. We scattered from our vehicles into any cover that would take us. Bullets seemed to be coming from every direction. The Green Cross vehicles, whose sanctity was akin to that of the Red Cross, took a couple of rounds. Then, as soon as it had started, the firing stopped. We debated furiously whether or not we should go on. The Green Cross workers were adamant that we must.

We crossed the Lempa River on a rickety wooden structure that had replaced the great steel suspension bridge that now lay broken-backed in the water, a testament to the rebels' ability to destroy the economic infrastructure of the country. Finally, way up in the most isolated spot, we found them camped out under trees, hundreds and hundreds of ill-dressed, hungry children. Bigger girls and boys cradled small babies. There was only a handful of adults in evidence. This was fiercely contested territory, yet these children appeared oblivious to the constant sound of gunfire in the middle distance. The army had visited the day before us, and had told the adults they wanted the children out of this camp, but would offer no assistance to move them. The children's families appeared either to have been killed or to have become separated from them during prolonged firefights. Some had fled over the border to Honduras. Their plight made brilliant television, but the huge question about how they were to survive remained. In the end we decided that some of us, including me and my team, would try to get back to San Salvador, three dangerous hours away, to raise the alarm. Ray and the others would stay to try to secure safe conduct.

Back in the capital, I was lucky to penetrate the great concrete blockhouse that was the US embassy. Acting Ambassador Frederic L. Chapin agreed to see me. I told him what we had witnessed. It seemed important that at least he knew we knew, and that we in turn knew that he knew. I told him flatly that if anything happened to the children while America, with all her military advisers and helicopters had stood idly by, the world would know. He didn't like my tone, and told me so. Officially there were still only about fifty US military advisers in El Salvador, but I suspected there were really many more in various guises.

Within two days we were back in the camp, reunited with Ray and his team and in time to see the children boarding UN trucks. We followed them down the treacherous road back to the capital and saw them settled into a makeshift camp under the supervision of the United Nations refugee agency, UNHCR, in the suburbs.

On the phone to London I was promising myself and Madeleine that I would soon be home, and that I'd never come back to El Salvador. But there was one key feature of this civil war that few had ever chronicled, and that was life behind rebel lines. The reporter's drug of wanting still more was eating away inside me. I broke my promise.

To penetrate the main guerrilla bases we needed to re-enter El Salvador by the porous, mountainous border with neighbouring Honduras, across which vital supplies flowed to the rebels. We flew to the Honduran capital Tegucigalpa, and then on with the French aid agency Médecins sans Frontières up to the border with El Salvador. The green landing strip was on a gradient at the top of a hill – you landed going uphill to slow the plane.

There was only a small fingernail of a moon as we set out from the village just inside Honduras. We – Sebastian, Marcello, Don and I – had waited six days for our guerrilla contact. Our escorts, seven of them, were evidently well used to picking their way along the rubble-strewn paths of the bumpy terrain that etches the border with El Salvador. The Honduran army was apparently camped out on the hillsides above us, and had been instructed to shoot anyone moving in this sensitive zone at such an hour. Even so, Sebastian asserted his right to stop endlessly and set up his tripod, load his filters and feast on the flowers, landscapes and weather patterns that defined the abiding beauty of Central America. The feature man in him exasperated the anxious newsman in me. But the film we were to make in the ensuing weeks was to be among the most beautiful and forceful I ever had anything to do with. We were both steadied in our exuberance by Don Warren, our much more seasoned sound man, who was more years our senior than he would willingly reveal. Once again we would spend the long arduous hours of walking and climbing by choosing desert island discs, or retreating to our old make-believe 'republic' in which things were even worse than this.

We had no idea how far we would have to walk, or for how long. Thankfully, our escorts carried much of our equipment. At three in the morning, as we came over the crest of yet another hill, we heard rushing water ahead. When we reached the Lempa itself, the river that forms the frontier with El Salvador, we could not see how on earth we were going to cross it. It was wide, and running at quite a pace. Wearied by hours of walking on city-soft feet, we slept for a while among the rocks at the water's edge.

We were awakened by our escorts, who were now gesticulating towards the far bank of the river, the darkness punctuated by torch-lights amongst the boulders. There was a clank of metal on stone, and then a splash. Ten minutes later a huge cylindrical zinc water-tank emerged out of the darkness, pushed by five men stripped to their underpants. Our clothes, the camera, and our escorts' weapons were wrapped in plastic and put inside. We moved upstream with the tank, and then, with all of us clinging to it, were swept by the current to the other bank.

We had arrived in what US Secretary of State Alexander Haig declared on 18 May 1981 to be the 'heart of Communist darkness'. Haig had published a 'White Paper' outlining what the fledgling Reagan administration perceived as the Communist threat posed by the left in Central America. Nicaragua's pro-American Somoza dictatorship had already fallen to the popular leftist Sandinista revolution in 1979. If El Salvador followed, there was no knowing what would happen. Haig's paper suggested that he could prove, from documents allegedly captured from Salvadorean guerrillas, that there was strategic and practical Cuban–Soviet involvement at work in Central America. It had the same hollow ring that Britain's 'dossier' on Iraq's supposed weapons of mass destruction was to have nearly a quarter of a century later.

ITN wanted me to penetrate the Salvadorean guerrilla lines – to 'put the record straight' that this was no war between rich and poor, but a concerted attempt by Russia to undermine and penetrate America's vital sphere of interest. 'Find those Russkies and Cubans,' my editor David Nicholas had telexed, only half jesting, from London. So here we were doing just that, on the prowl for Cubans and, less probably, for some very ill-at-ease Russians.

Soon after crossing the Lempa we found ourselves in a heavily populated village, the first of many we visited. We were to move through more than ninety miles of guerrilla-held territory in the northern Salvadorean province of Chala-tenango. We had expected armed camps bristling with weapons. That the civilian population so hugely outnumbered the rebels came as a shock.

The peasants, or *campesinos*, lived an arduous life which had hardly changed in three hundred years. Gathering and preparing their simple diet of maize and beans was time-consuming. Formerly they had travelled to work on distant coffee and sugar estates for around £8 a month. The war had cut their ties with the estates, lowering their incomes to below subsistence level. But the *campesinos* told us that in other ways their lives had actually improved. The guerrillas had trained many of them to defend their villages. Some told how before the civil war half a dozen

National Guard would arrive hunting a man who had criticised low wages on the local estate, or filed a complaint about dangerous machinery. If the soldiers found the man, the villagers said, they would beat him or even shoot him. If they couldn't find him, his wife or child would be taken instead. Francisco, who lived in the village of Pena Blanca, told me, 'Nowadays if the National Guard want any of us, they have to come with three hundred men. We hear them coming, and we evacuate the village for the day.'

While we were in Pena Blanca I nearly made a fatal error whilst preparing to defecate in the undergrowth. The village had a spectacular view over an escarpment, and I thought it might be rewarding to squat doing my business with a pleasing outlook. I headed down a track I'd not been along before, and for some reason spotted a small hole ahead of me. I suddenly realised that the entire track before me was a mantrap with a frail curtain of foliage draped across it. It had been set by the rebels to foil any invading army force, but they had omitted to tell me about it. I had very nearly fallen into a five-foot-square pit filled with vertical poisoned bamboo spikes. I was so shocked that nature's call stayed unheeded.

It was also in Pena Blanca that we shot a number of reels of film about daily peasant and guerrilla life. Sebastian would throw the little yellow film bobbins onto which the film was wound to the children to play with. Life was mellow here, wildflowers were plentiful, eight healthy-looking cows grazed nearby, and war seemed a long way away. Indeed, I remember thinking one lazy evening that although I'd once considered Uganda my Utopia, I could feel a creeping infidelity beginning to allow Central America to supplant that first love.

It was here that we encountered Sister Rosa, a Sacred Heart nun from New Jersey. 'I ran a hostel there for nineteen years for migrant Hispanic workers,' she told me. 'I've been in El Salvador now six years, but in January my parish priest was shot dead by troops, so I fled.' She had joined eleven other nuns and priests who now lived in the 'liberated zone'. She ran the school, teaching a class of some sixty children of all ages. Tattered school books were in evidence, but she'd run out of chalk and had little paper left either.

This was in stark contrast to the so-called 'British School' that I had visited just fifty miles away in San Salvador, thirty days earlier. Anyone who was anyone in El Salvador sent their children there. Ten of the thirty teachers were British, and they taught six hundred children aged from three to eighteen. Every morning streams of chauffeured Mercedes and Oldsmobiles, some with tinted bulletproof glass, would disgorge tidy children onto the carefully manicured lawns of the school grounds. It wouldn't take a Russian or a Cuban to intervene to exploit this yawning gap between rich and poor: El Salvador already had all the ingredients it needed for a full-blown home-grown civil war.

While we were with the rebels I copied down the serial numbers from a couple of automatic weapons carried by them. I wanted to see if Al

Haig was right, and they had come from illicit sales in Vietnam. In the event we were able to track them right back to America's own arms bazaar in Miami, Florida. Nor did we find the slightest sign of a Cuban or a Russian in a month behind the lines with pretty free movement. We were blessed with ponies to speed our way back to the Honduran border, but the nights were spent sleeping rough. So bad was it one night that my crew and I drew lots for a solitary old door that we found lying about. I got it, and as my reward a stray dog urinated on it and me the next morning. Our trekking was curtailed by a stroke of good timing. A lift was available on the same single-engined aid plane that had brought us up. The pilot took off using the downhill gradient.

We took the first commercial flight from the Honduran capital, Tegucigalpa, and apprehensively re-entered El Salvador legally. We had discovered that ABC had a small jet coming in from Washington. I had retained close 'post-Iran' links with the network, and ITN also enjoyed a commercial tie-up with them. We managed to coincide with the plane, so that it could carry our dangerous guerrilla footage out. As we approached the little plane, ABC's State Department correspondent Barry Dunsmore jumped out. It was rare to see an American television correspondent in El Salvador, so we were keen to assist him in any way we could. But Barry wasn't staying. He proceeded to do a report to camera with a confused-looking National Guardsman over his shoulder, then made to get back into the plane.

'You not staying, Barry?' I asked.

'I don't need to. I've just had a full read-out from State.'

'But what do they know?' I asked. 'Don't you need to see for yourself?'

'They know the lot, Jon, more than you'll ever know,' he said and, seizing our film, got back into his plane and whizzed off.

So American viewers that night were treated to a report that looked as if the correspondent was on the ground in El Salvador, and the content of which had come straight from the State Department in Washington. Our guerrilla-camp film was eventually to air on News at Ten to great acclaim, and to rather less appreciation on ABC in the States.

We left for the capital, San Salvador, fearful enough to wonder whether the authorities might find out about our month-long sojourn behind enemy lines. The next day the Camino's small band of correspondents was summoned to the Defence Ministry to meet Colonel Ochoa, a key anti-insurgent commander in the El Salvador army. Equipped with a batch of Bell Huey helicopters fresh from the US, Ochoa was leading a new offensive against the guerrillas in Chalatenango province, where we had just been. We were taken to the helipad to be whisked straight to the 'war front'. It was amazing to look down with such ease upon the dense terrain through which we had so recently trudged for so long.

Only when we landed did the eerie and horrifying reality dawn on us that we had been brought right back to Pena Blanca, the very village we had lived in until little over a week before. Rarely, if ever, does a journalist tread the very same terrain with each of the opposing sides in so short a space of time. Ochoa's forces had been through here with a vengeance. The eight cows were bloated carcasses, lying with their feet in the air. Of Sister Rosa, her sixty children and the entire population of the village there was not a sign. I was optimistic enough to believe that they had fled, for there was no evidence that they had been murdered here.

'A Western TV crew's been in here,' said Ochoa nonchalantly, picking up a telltale film bobbin. Our stomachs turned over. I caught Sebastian's eye. The macho man's face had drained of colour, and beads of sweat ran down the tanned skin revealed by his open shirt. Did they know it was us? Had they brought us here to torture and kill us?

The moment passed, and we walked on. Eventually we boarded the helicopters again and flew back to the capital, and that night we caught the plane for Miami. Things were getting a little close for comfort. The next two days saw our reports from both sides of the war zone go out back to back to eight million British viewers. There were more complaints from both Westminster and Washington that our reports were anti-American, and that in some way we had deliberately ignored the Cuban presence on the ground.

I could see the truck in the rear-view mirror. It was February 1982. I was back in El Salvador after a cleansing interval of three months. Despite the fact that we still chose to maintain separate homes in north London, mine in Kentish Town, hers in nearby Tufnell Park, Madeleine was by now pregnant with our first child. I'd promised I would only be away a few weeks. She was convinced she would give birth the next September as a single parent.

The truck behind us was carrying a large group of men in white shirts and straw hats. It was coming perilously close to our back bumper, and the dirt road ahead was narrowing. Finally we were forced to stop. The men jumped down and surrounded us, carrying guns. A Dutch television team had been murdered in a remote spot off the main road fifty miles east of the capital only the day before. But that morning President Duarte himself had led us all up here to prove how safe the area was. Now, having hung back to investigate further, we'd become victims of a similar ambush.

The men were jumpy as we responded to their orders to get out of the car with our hands in the air. I thought of home, and the people I loved, and of what a fool I'd been ever to come here. 'Madeleine was right,' I thought. 'She will give birth a single parent.' Several of the men began to ransack the car, throwing things about and smashing equipment. Marcello was brilliant, slowly, charmingly engaging a few of those who surrounded us. These appeared to be farming men, stallholders informally bound together in a death squad in order to protect themselves from the peasant-supported *'muchachos'*. After what seemed an age, Marcello was allowed to lower his left hand and extract a packet of Marlboros from his breast pocket. Twenty hands extended for a cigarette, and the determination to extinguish us appeared to pass.

By March 1982 there were hundreds of journalists in El Salvador, no longer chasing non-existent Cubans but in pursuit of democracy. Despite the scale of the killing by both sides, Washington had persuaded President Duarte to risk a parliamentary election. As well as Duarte's Christian Democratic Party there were five others running, the main contender being Roberto D'Aubuisson's Nationalist Republican Alliance (ARENA). Almost immediately it became clear that Major Bob, with his massive funding from fascist-leaning Latinos living in Florida, was going to sweep the board.

Once again I made my way through the fortifications at the US embassy in San Salvador. The Ambassador's role had been considerably uprated, almost to proconsul level. The new man, Thomas Pickering, a career diplomat later to become US Ambassador to Israel and then to the UN, received me in his office. He explained a subtle change in US policy. D'Aubuisson had originally been regarded by Washington as beyond political acceptability. But as he showed increasing signs of successfully buying the election, the US suggested he should no longer be judged on past performance but on future action. The guerrillas, Pickering emphasised, were not to be judged at all. They could participate in the election, or leave the country. Given the continued killings at the hand of D'Aubuisson's death squads, it did not seem a very equitable offer.

In the event D'Aubuisson all but stole the election, his ARENA party winning a majority of seats. Major Bob effectively became Speaker of the Constituent Assembly. Washington had to stumble on, working through Duarte as President.

That same March we flew south from Salvador for a week-long trip to Nicaragua. Arriving in the capital Managua, it was a shock to see the broken buildings that littered the streets. It was as if the earthquake that had all but destroyed the city in 1972 had happened yesterday. The then dictator Anastasio Somoza had diverted the relief funds to his own bank account. Now, ten years later, homeless families were still living in tents made of rigged-up sheets, and setting fires in the gaping holes that once were walls.

We'd travelled here to try to find out why so grindingly impoverished a state should apparently represent such a threat to the towering superpower to the north. The contrasts with El Salvador were sublime. There, I would enter my hotel room, check under the bed, in the bathroom, in the wardrobe, lest someone lay in wait to do me harm. On the streets you moved fast, and kept looking behind you. In the countryside we never travelled without a white flag, large TV signs on our vehicle, and full bulletproof flak jackets. Here in Nicaragua there was no sense of threat, there were no death lists, no killings. The revolutionary language could be tedious, the unquestioning enthusiasm could be wearying, but of threat there was none.

The part-Marxist, part-liberation-theology-driven Sandinista revolution of 1979 had deposed Somoza and replaced his junta with an eclectic Cabinet of rebels, priests and intellectuals. They took their name from the legendary Augusto César Sandino, who led peasant uprisings against US-backed oligarchs in the 1920s. What was indisputable was that the Sandinista revolution had provided Nicaraguans with both health care and education on a scale not seen before in Central America. Certainly there were Cuban doctors and teachers helping to improve infant mortality and literacy rates, but no soldiers. However, the incoming US administration of Ronald Reagan saw the Sandinistas in the same vein as it saw Castro's Cuba, as a dangerous and infectious Communist stain on Latin America. In Cold War terms, it regarded Nicaragua as yet another potential flashpoint for a Soviet challenge to America's domination of 'her hemisphere'.

In Nicaragua the revolutionaries had so enthusiastically embraced liberation theology that priests had actually entered the government as Ministers. Father Miguel D'Escoto was the delightfully round Foreign Minister, and I saw him often. American-educated, he was charming, avuncular and decidedly unversed in Marxist theory and rhetoric. Other members of the government, like the Ortega brothers, were less beguiling. President Daniel Ortega was later to be suspected of child abuse involving a member of his family, and the Interior Minister Tomas

Borghe was a serious hard-liner. But it was not these imperfections that made Ronald Reagan, from his first day in office, determined to effect 'regime change' at the barrel of a gun. It was Reagan's absolute conviction that the Sandinistas posed a direct threat to America and her interests throughout the region.

Sebastian, Don, Marcello and I had travelled north, through the blasted but beautiful city of Leon and out into the hills to the north of Esteli. One night in a remote village near the Honduran border I sat listening to the crackly reception of the BBC World Service. Snatches of a speech from President Reagan strayed in and out of audibility. But we could hear enough to learn that he was 'drawing a line in the sand' against the 'Communist threat'. In the verdant tropical vegetation around the village we couldn't see much evidence of either sand or Communism, but we knew full well what was intended.

So began the Contra war, a sordid, illegal, US-inspired export of weapons and violence to one of the poorest countries in the western hemisphere. The so-called Contras would be recruited by CIA agents and exiled Miami-based followers of Somoza from amongst the impoverished peasantry, and offered undreamt-of cash to fight the Sandinistas. Fifty thousand people were to be slaughtered in the fighting over the ensuing eight years. Any aspiration that the Sandinistas had of a peaceful, prosperous, egalitarian Nicaragua were to be blitzed. And after the US Congress refused aid to this CIA-backed conflict (of which more later), the Reagan administration was eventually found guilty of conducting illegal weapons trades with Iran in order to fund it – Iran, the very country that the Reaganites had so castigated Jimmy Carter for mishandling. Drugs, deceit and duplicity were all employed to keep this CIA-constructed, White House-inspired war alive.

By a cruel but brilliant coincidence, my old British VSO friend from Uganda, Diana Villiers, had married John Negroponte, at that time US Ambassador to Honduras. A former 'Kissinger boy', he'd worked in the ill-starred Cambodian 'engine room' during Henry Kissinger's fatal carpet-bombing strategy in South-East Asia. Negroponte, who later became George W. Bush's Ambassador to the United Nations, and sub-sequently to Iraq, was then effectively America's proconsul in Central America, leading the Contra war strategy from the front.

I called Diana, and she invited me to join her and her husband for lunch at the US embassy residence. She was, as ever, fully engaged in voluntary projects, bringing aid and succour to the suffering people of Honduras. I like to think she had no idea what sort of stuff was passing across her husband's desk when they were apart.

The breeze caught the crisp white linen tablecloth set on the terrace of the residence high above Tegucigalpa. A lovely spread of freshly baked rolls, Chardonnay and smoked salmon awaited. It was the most extraordinary collision of images – the sumptuous garden and its terrace table, set against the sprawling shanties of the Honduran capital below. Beyond the blue, distant mountains, Negroponte's war was beginning to reach full throttle. I was on my very best behaviour; he was such a nice man, and Diana remained the English rose I'd always known. We were all utterly charming to each other, I learned very little, and eventually departed wondering how anyone who was involved in what was being inflicted upon Nicaragua could sleep at night. It was a question I never dared to raise, for fear of losing so valuable a contact.

After several weeks in Central America I was on the verge of returning home to London and Madeleine, who was by now four months pregnant, when I was called by my foreign editor at ITN and told of a totally unexpected crisis further south, so serious that even my pressing compassionate grounds were not enough to prevent an immediate change of plan. I was to head straight for Chile, yet another country where the CIA knew a thing or two about 'regime change', having notoriously assisted in the overthrow and assassination of the democratically elected President Salvador Allende in 1973. The logical place for me to have gone would have been Argentina, but as the cause of my sudden move was the invasion of the Falkland Islands by the Argentine junta on 2 April 1982, it was felt that I should try to see what could be done from the nearest 'neutral' landfall in Chile.

It was a completely mad endeavour. Never having been to the country before, I was dispatched by air to Chile's southernmost town, Punta Arenas, two days after the Argentinians had seized the 'Malvinas', as they called the Falklands. Curiously, the islands had always held a certain mystique for me, and I had often thought I'd like to go there. Alan Downes was sent in from London as my cameraman.

So here we were, at the southern tip of General Pinochet's intolerant, US-backed dictatorship, watching the local battalion goose-stepping its way across the airport tarmac as they did every Friday. A smaller ceremony was under way in the town centre. Apart from being one of the most southerly towns in the world, I'd only ever heard of Punta Arenas as a haven for Nazi war criminals and a stopping-off point for Charles Darwin's voyage on the *Beagle*.

The somewhat uninspiring Hotel Cabo de Hornos was to become our home for the next three months. Our contacts with the outside world were sporadic at best, our dependence on the BBC World Service absolute. At first I'd imagined that Britain would simply organise some sort of evacuation of the Falkland Islanders. The UK had sent every conceivable message over the years that it did not intend to keep the islands, and now that the Argentinean invasion had taken place, it seemed that rehousing in the highlands of Scotland was perhaps the best the islanders could hope for.

I did not bargain on Mrs Thatcher, whose domestic political standing was at a low ebb. The history of Britain, Argentina, the Falklands and even a small part of Chile was about to be transformed. I confess to a sense of reluctant national pride as I sat in the main square outside our hotel listening to the news of the British fleet steaming off down the Solent headed for the South Atlantic. Even then I could not believe it would come to war.

There was now to be a long and tedious wait for a month until the ships, troops and planes reached the islands. The occasional ancient Vulcan bomber would fly the fifteen hours down the Atlantic to bomb the runway at Port Stanley and then lumber home again, but there was little for us to do. So Alan Downes, Don Warren and I set about trying to see whether we could reach the Falklands illicitly. We hired Jorge Freygang, a local pilot, for the duration. Although he had a beautiful, state-of-the-art turboprop Barron King Air propeller plane, what we really needed was an old flying boat. We were insane enough to believe that somehow we could fly in under the Argentine radar and land on Falkland Sound, the stretch of water between East and West Falkland.

We found a Catalina flying boat (built circa 1947) fighting fires in arid northern Chile. Its maximum cruising speed was 120 miles per hour, so it took more than a week to make the journey south to reach us. It was an absolutely gorgeous red beast, flown by an extremely ancient crew. It landed with complete grace on water, and took off again with equal ease. But now that it was here, we wondered what on earth we could do with it. We might have been in the right hemisphere, and nearer the story than practically any other journalist, but reporters were already 'embedded' with the British task force, and it was proving impossible to reach the islands. I reckoned that, for a rare moment in my reporting life, I was stuffed.

We devoted ourselves to putting the war in the context of the region, flying down the Beagle Channel between Chile and Argentina and explaining why the two countries hated each other, and why the war risked igniting trouble between them. We overnighted at Puerto Williams, the southernmost human habitation on the Americas. The population was made up of perhaps eight souls. A sweet place with a half a horse of a hotel, it sat at the bottom of a spectacular glacier; we could have been in Norway. There were moments when the reverse gurgle of the bathwater down the plughole was the only reminder that we were so very far from home.

Amid the boredom I managed to persuade ITN that we ought to do a report on the Antarctic Treaty and the implications that a war could have for the great white continent. So Jorge readied his plane for the four-hour dash across the open seas to King George Island and Chile's Marsh Base. We flew down the Beagle once more, glimpsing the grey outline of Ushuaia in Argentina over our left wingtip. Beyond the channel, we crossed the wild and uninhabited Cape Horn, and flew out into the wastes of the Antarctic Ocean. There was not a soul below, the waves were wild, and we all knew, gazing out of the plane's little oval windows, that if we were to go down it would be the end of us.

Gradually the occasional turquoise and white iceberg would loom into view, and then more, until finally, there was our landfall. The all-weather landing strip was already gusting with flurries of snow, the clouds were blackening, and Jorge warned us that we could be stuck there for more than our planned two days. It was not until we landed that he told us we were only the second commercial flight ever to land on the Antarctic – the first had stayed for only a few minutes – so we had an unexpectedly enthusiastic welcome from the Chileans who manned the research base.

We tidied our survival suits, put on our last layer of woollies and stepped out of the plane. It was an altogether brave new world that greeted us. At one end of the runway, close to where the plane had come to a stop, was a range of single-storey huts piled around with snow. We entered a modern but sterile environment. Denied a segment of the continent by the Antarctic Treaty, Chile had claimed one anyway, and set up a polar research base next to the Russians. Pregnant Chilean women were being flown down to the base to give birth so that the country could claim genuine citizens of the Antarctic to strengthen her territorial claim.

It was immediately clear that the Falklands conflict felt as far away from here as it did from London, and that it had zero implications for the Treaty. But we were not going to let the facts stand in the way of a magnificent story. During our weather-enforced stay in the succeeding days we filmed and experienced wonderful things. Great elephant seals slumbered while chin-strapped and emperor penguins stood about inscrutably on the snow and ice. The landscape changed every minute before our eyes.

One afternoon the weather lifted enough for the Chileans to take on the Russians at ice football. These two communities, whose countries had no diplomatic relations and whose regimes co-existed in conditions of strict hostility, enjoyed utter interdependence here on the ice. I found myself thinking of Ian Paisley and Gerry Fitt from Northern Ireland sharing laughter in that Glasgow taxi. Here Moscow and Santiago played football, shared a doctor and took turns in engineering air drops of vital supplies. This, I concluded, was the real world.

After a week we headed back out across the turbulent sea, across the unwelcoming Cape Horn and up into the relative safety of the Beagle Channel. This was the region where the hostility between Argentina and Chile was most apparent. Both countries claimed it, and they had even fought over it. The Pope had been asked to mediate. Spectacular scenery tumbled down to the water's edge on both sides, white above the waistline of glaciers and mountains, green nearer the water itself.

Finally we were home in Punta Arenas. That weekend we went to Jorge's house for a slap-up spread of Chile's best, cooked by his wife Suzanna. She and their three small children had already become our extended family in our long sojourn in the south.

Within a few days, on 1 May, the Falklands War finally began, and the Chilean navy began to boost its numbers in the port. One night there was a tap on my hotel-room door.

'My name is Captain Pablo Sanchez,' said the voice from beyond. 'I have news.'

'About what?'

'Matters about the war,' he replied.

I let him in, and Captain Sanchez rapidly established himself as a mostly dependable source. Chile had a sizeable naval centre at Punta Arenas; many of the ships were old British cast-offs, and many of the sailors had trained with the Royal Navy. The Pinochet dictatorship appeared to have been no impediment to these relations. Captain Sanchez, despite being somewhat creepy, appeared to be a spy with excellent access to communications with London, Port Stanley and Buenos Aires. As we had access to nothing other than the intermittent crackles from the BBC World Service, he was worth cultivating. His interest in US dollars was modest, never extravagant. He was perhaps in his early thirties, and looked like a rather moribund, bespectacled badger. His English was excellent.

Chile was discreetly keen to see Britain defeat Argentina, and so was our captain. The night after his tap on the door he took me to some sort of 'comms' centre to listen in on the radio traffic, most of which was in Spanish. It was beyond my taxi-driver Spanish, so I had taken our translator Carmen with me. She could hear unhappy Argentine soldiers using the radio circuit to call home. One man told his father he'd be home in two weeks. The soldiers would then be inter-rupted by their commanders demanding more supplies. Within a few days the verbal traffic ceased, and coded teletype messages in clusters of five letters started to come through. We also learned that Peruvian air force transport planes were bringing in military supplies for Argentina on the other side of Tierra del Fuego.

Sanchez told us, long before the news came out of London, that the British had attacked the key southern Argentine airfields of Rio Grande and Rio Gallegos, destroying the critically important Super Etendard fighter bombers with their payloads of deadly Exocet missiles. The curiosity of this war was not just that the old Empire was fighting so far from home, but that for perhaps the last time in history a war was being fought in which the participants were able to secure a total blackout of news. All information from the British side had to be reported through the Ministry of Defence in London. There were no independent sources at all.

We had bought up virtually the only Falkland Islander in Punta Arenas, a sweet, rather old-fashioned twenty-four-year-old fisherman called Monty Short. Monty scoured the local radio hams for anyone who might be able to get word from the islands. He may have seemed out of a different era, but he had, by Falklands standards, real 'get up and go'. Long before the war he'd got up and gone in search of, and had found, a Chilean wife. By the time of the invasion there were fewer than seven hundred women on the islands. He gave us a great sense of the Falklands capital, Port Stanley, and of the monotony and virtual unsustainability of the community there. It did not sound like a cause worth dying for.

At last, on a moonless night, the war finally came to Punta Arenas. Captain Sanchez was hammering at my door. 'Quick, Mr Jon, come quick!' he called urgently. 'Helicopter, yes, British helicopter ... crashed.'

We bundled into a taxi and headed out ten miles along the flat coastal lands in the direction of the little bothy in which Charles Darwin had hatched his *Origin of Species*. Suddenly, in the darkness, there it was, a dejected-looking Sea King helicopter, very much down on its knees. More a sandy crash landing than a crash, I would have said. The crew seemed to have been spirited away, but it was undoubtedly an RAF machine. Far from digging the thing out, a horde of Chilean labourers were trying to dig the thing in. There was the most literal and complete cover-up under way. By dawn the incident had never happened, and there was simply no sign of it. The bliss of totalitarian government – we never got a clue as to where the chopper had lifted off from, where it was going to, and why it had come down. It all fitted in with the legions of rumours in Punta Arenas in those days – stories of RAF VC10s at the airport, or of SAS men roaming Tierra del Fuego and inflicting heroic hits on the enemy. The only tangible clues I saw with my own eyes were two Canberra bombers at Punta Arenas airport. They were adorned in Chilean colours, but they appeared to be British manned. There were tales too from the other side of the coin. The British flagship, the aircraft carrier *Invincible*, had been hit, or even sunk, ran the ultimately untrue accounts.

In reality, the defining moment of the war was not the sinking of the *Invincible*, but the destruction of the Argentine cruiser *Belgrano* by the nuclear submarine HMS *Conqueror*. It happened on 4 May 1982, and every day thereafter we would fly with Jorge to the mouth of the Beagle Channel in the hope of seeing the survivors coming home. Four days after the sinking, we spotted the elderly, Second World War-vintage destroyer the *Hipolito Bouchard* coming slowly up the channel. She was a pitiful sight, with survivors from the *Belgrano* huddled on her decks, an escort ship on either side of her. These were the human remnants of a ship hundreds of whose crew had gone to the deeps. The *Hipolito Bouchard* had been escorting the *Belgrano* when she was hit. We flew as close as we dared, and filmed what we could. Then suddenly there was a shattering noise. The cockpit shook furiously, the avionics failed and our camera blew. I thought we were going down, but Jorge regained manual control and veered off up the Chilean side of the Beagle. Jorge reported over his shoulder that one of the escort ships had locked on with its missile guidance system and had blown all our electronics. In short, we had been electronically zapped. We hobbled back to land at Punta Arenas.

The next day, Jorge told us the plane could only be repaired at the Beechcraft works at Santiago airport, two thousand miles north. He would have to fly there as soon as possible. I offered to go with him, but he refused, saying that it might be hazardous, and that he preferred to do it alone. We waved him off, and later that day he called us to say he'd reached Santiago safely. The repairs took three days, and as the weekend beckoned I suggested that we would pay for Suzanna and the children to go up on a commercial flight to join him, and we would put them up in a Santiago hotel as a kind of thank-you for all they'd done for us. So it was agreed, and we drove the family to the airport and waved them off. It proved to be the last time we ever saw them.

On the Monday, the family took off with Jorge at the controls for the long journey south from Santiago. The children had plenty of toys to play with; it all sounded a bit of a treat for them. A few hours later, Jorge's hangar manager called me. 'Jon, very bad news,' he said. 'We have lost contact with Jorge's plane.'

We rushed to the airport and up the stairs into the control tower. A full emergency was under way. The air force, with whom Jorge enjoyed good relations, had been scrambled. The air-traffic controller relayed to us Jorge's last message: 'Mayday, Mayday, we have equipment failure, we are going down, the boat is at the door...' We knew from our Antarctic flight that the plane had an inflatable rescue craft and survival suits, though none small enough for a child. But just possibly, somehow, they might have survived a crash landing on water.

The Chilean air force established a search grid over the region in which they estimated the plane had come down. It was a desperately vast area. We readied our Catalina flying boat which, apart from its lumberingly slow speed, was a perfect search craft, donned our survival suits and set off. We flew at five hundred feet for thirteen hours a day for four days.

Chile is a long, thin country, nowhere more than a hundred miles wide, and with a three-thousand-mile coastline. We concentrated on the southern part of it. The far south is divided from the rest of Chile by an ice shelf; perhaps fifty souls live in an area the size of England. In four days we never saw a sign of life, never saw a boat, never had a single moment when our hopes rose. Jorge, Suzanna and their three children under the age of six were lost, presumed dead. I felt hugely responsible, ITN felt less so. We had hired a pilot and his plane to cover a war we never really saw, and they had died in that undertaking. I felt very much a central cause of their deaths.

The deaths of Jorge, Suzanna and their children went to the very heart of the obsessive nature of journalism. By any objective assessment the Falklands War was uncoverable from Chile. Yet we had been told to cover it. There was never any real prospect of reaching the islands from Punta Arenas, yet that was the motor force. This young family had died as a consequence of the war, through an unlikely and devastating catalogue of bad luck. Luck was supposed to be the one quality with which I was endowed. In reporting the Falklands War we were already in the age of satellite dishes and videotape. But the circumstances, even the cause, were out of a bygone age. It was this collision of capability and frustration – great potential for a scoop, coupled with the impossibility of delivering one – that created such a catastrophic opportunity for misjudgement.

So rich in its imagery and its environment, this Chilean adventure was a reporting failure. The Catalina was part of a fantasy, Jorge's enthusiasm knew no bounds, we constantly egged each other on to find a way to be part of an absurd conflict. In part I think his surviving extended family regarded it as simply a terrible accident. But I find myself thinking about him and them, and my culpability, to this day.

The Falklands War did perhaps achieve a kind of imperial closure that the Suez crisis had left raw and open. It may even have provided the moment of transition between lone colonial action and international peacekeeping that was to come. Although, as it soon became clear, the endeavour was very far from 'lone'. The division in the Reagan administration between the Reaganites who supplied Sidewinder missiles and fuel to ensure British victory, and those who worried about US–Latin American relations, was well known.

The involvement of General Pinochet's dictatorship in Britain's war effort was rather less explored. Pinochet's needs were grave: his country's economy was in tatters. Indeed, within six months I was to find myself in Chile's capital reporting riots against the General and the poverty he had spawned. The Santa Victoria *barrio* in Santiago was a desperate shanty suburb, where once again priests held the last line against tyranny. The ultimate experiment in the free market, launched by *'los Chicago boys'* – as Chileans dubbed Milton Friedman's Chicago economics team – had been brought low by the state of the world economy. Pinochet had tortured, exiled, jailed or killed his opponents, and the price was finally being paid in poverty and protest.

To this day it is uncertain what comfort Mrs Thatcher was able to bring the General after the Falklands War. When he came to call in Britain nearly two decades later, and found himself unexpectedly detained 'at Her Majesty's Pleasure' on 16 October 1998, Margaret Thatcher went out of her way to visit and support him. In retrospect, Pinochet's detention for war crimes seems to have been no more than a happy aberration and an official embarrassment. Britain's overall record with Pinochet was one of discreet but determined engagement. Although the idea of seeing him jailed for his offences against humanity gave pleasure to many, it remained only an idea, and few were surprised when he was eventually allowed to return home as a presentable, tweedy old boy.

In the spring of 1983, four years after the Sandinista revolution, two years after the murder of Archbishop Romero, the Pope declared his intention to travel to Central America. My daughter Leila was six months old, and as I boarded the papal jetliner in Rome, little did I guess how much her mere existence would affect the way I reported. For the first time I began to see the suffering of every child through my own.

If the overwhelmingly Catholic population of Nicaragua thought they'd receive succour and support from the Pope, they were in for a shock.

The Americans, with their grim record of regional misbehaviour, had nothing to fear from him. Less than six months after Reagan's foray into Central America with his personally orchestrated Contra war, Polish Pope John Paul II was on his knees kissing the tarmac at Managua airport. The entire Sandinista government lined up outside the terminal building, hoping for his political blessing. A huge portrait of the gaucho-hatted Augusto Sandino, flanked by Vatican and revolutionary flags, dominated the walls of the building. I was in a press pen, sweating in the midday sun, as the Pope came down the ministerial line towards us. Each Minister sank to his knees to kiss the papal ring. Then the Pope stopped at the Minister of Culture, Father Ernesto Cardinale. With the priest on his knees looking up, the Pope wagged his finger in his face. 'You've got to straighten out your position with the Church,' he said gruffly. Cardinale was little short of a Nicaraguan hero for the support he and others like him had provided in the guerrilla war which had preceded the revolution four years earlier. It was not a happy start for the Pope's visit, and things were to go from bad to worse.

That night the Pope said mass before a million people in Managua. Here he showed none of the sensitivity and passion that had bound him to his own Eastern Bloc compatriots. It is inconceivable that his Bishops had not told him that less than twenty-four hours earlier, in this very arena, they had conducted a funeral mass for seventeen of the latest victims of the Contra war. But the Pope chose never to mention them, even though the congregation appeared at least to want some papal acknowledgement of their suffering. The Nicaraguan Church hierarchy, its Cardinal and some of its senior clerics at the time were with the Pope. They regarded Cardinale and Father D'Escoto, the Foreign Minister, as members of a people's Church that identified too strongly with the poor. Some of the younger priests and one or two of the Bishops were with the Sandinistas.

Then, with the Pope at the high altar, the chanting began, muted at first and then developing into a roar. *'Queremos la paz, queremos la paz...* We want peace, we want peace.' With the old revolutionary Sandino as his backdrop, the Pope clung to the stem of his papal cross and presented it defiantly to the congregation. As the darkness of the night deepened, he went on the offensive. 'Find your peace with the Church,' he shouted. Then the relatives of the seventeen dead raised portraits of their loved ones. The disruption was clearly orchestrated by the Sandinistas, but seemed to strike a chord with many in the arena.

'Silencio! Silencio!' cried the Pope. But there was none. There was no common ground between the demonstrators and John Paul II.

'We want peace!' they called, one of their number now using a loudhailer.

'Obey your Bishops!' the Pope replied, endorsing Nicaragua's Cardinal, an outspoken critic of the revolution. And still they shouted.

'One minute of silence,' the Pope pleaded.

But it was not to be. 'Give us peace!' they continued crying out throughout the mass.

Some of the American press, in particular, reported that the Pope had been treated disgracefully by a tiny minority of protesters. But from our vantage point in the middle of the throng, the people's sentiments were against the Pope, who could so easily have made a nodding reference to their suffering. My lasting impression was that he saw no moral equivalence between the suffering of the Polish people at the hands of the Soviets, and the suffering of Central America at the hands of US-backed death squads. For him, liberation theology had to be stamped upon with the same ferocity as Communism.

The next morning we clambered back onto the plane and headed on to the next leg of the Pope's Central American tour. When we landed at the airport in Guatemala City, the marimbas clattered a fantastic welcome as John Paul II kissed yet another country's tarmac at the bottom of the aircraft steps. The stench of killing in Guatemala was as bad as in Nicaragua and El Salvador, but the American profile, and even that of the Church, were different.

Guatemala is a spellbindingly beautiful country, mountainous, green and strewn with wildflowers. The Mayan Indian population is much less diluted than anywhere else in the region. Generally in Central America the invading white Spanish conquistador blood predominates, with varying degrees of Mayan tinges. Here the guerrilla war was far more ruthless and more hard-line than elsewhere in the region, not least because of the unstated but active Guatemalan government policy of trying to obliterate some of the still-vibrant Mayan Indian-dominated areas.

The bands of *'muchachos'* were harder to find, although on my very first visit we found them on the airport road setting fire to a bus. Both sides deployed desperate tactics – the Guatemalan military were aided by the Israelis and the Americans; the guerrillas had been trained in East Germany. Once again this was a population historically subjugated by the big American multinationals, principally United Fruit. Hard-line pro-American military governments delivered what the big corporations demanded, cheap fruit and coffee courtesy of neo-slave labour. The victims were the Mayans in towns like Chichicastenango. There, as I stood in the market surrounded by women wearing gorgeous fabrics and windings around their heads and midriffs, it was hard to imagine what possible threat any of them posed. Along the nave of the church, the stations of the cross were intermingled with little piles of bones and mementoes. Pagan Mayan beliefs were interwoven with Christian.

Even before landing, the Pope had spoken out strongly against Guatemala's evangelical Protestant President, General Rios Montt. He was charged with condoning, and almost certainly orchestrating, the worst of the death-squad activity in Guatemala, which he claimed was 'God's work'. The Pope did not, and told him so. His robust performance on the side of Guatemala's poor sat at odds with his uncanny inability to do the same next door in Nicaragua.

Even before the Pope left the airport, the

traditional marimbas gave way to the unexpected and out-of-place tones of Dusty Springfield belting out 'You Don't Have to Say You Love Me'. The joke at the Pope's expense was almost certainly lost on him. He seemed at ease dealing with Rios Montt, although he refused to shake his hand. But his preparedness to go after Montt contrasted strongly with his failure to condemn the United States for fuelling so much of the killing in the rest of Central America.

As I watched the Pope blessing a million Guatemalans at a stadium in the capital, I found myself remembering my last visit here a year before, during an earlier Central American reporting swing. Driving north out of the capital, we had encountered a military roadblock. Troops had pulled a bus over onto the verge, and the passengers were spreadeagled along its side with their hands splayed above their heads. A man in military fatigues with a khaki beekeeper's hat that disguised his identity was picking out 'suspects'. We managed to film the moment secretly. It was clear that the man in the hat was an informer. The half-dozen or so 'suspects' were thrown into the back of an army truck. Our guide told us that they would almost certainly join the ever-lengthening list of the 'disappeared'.

There was an added poignancy to the violence in which two hundred thousand Guatemalans died in the early 1980s. The United States, three decades earlier, had carried out one of its first attempts at 'regime change' in Guatemala, over-throwing the democratically elected President

Jacobo Arbenz. The CIA coup in 1954 was only the second time the US had ever participated in such an action, and was followed by prolonged bouts of rule by pro-American military juntas. The first time had been in Iran in 1953.

It was against this background of encountering the darker consequences of American actions abroad that my reporting career was about to take a shocking and completely unexpected turn. I was to witness, from the very front row, the overture to a new world order and disorder in which the United States would be transformed into the lone superpower.

EIGHT

Potomac Fever

'CONGRATULATIONS STOP PROCEED WASH-INGTON IMMEDIATELY STOP PHONE EDI-TOR STOP'. It was August 1983, and Madeleine, our daughter Leila and I were on holiday in the French cottage that we and a group of friends had bought for £1000 ten years earlier. The mere delivery of the telegram to this remote spot in the Dordogne was shock enough; the postman never called. The four-hundred-year-old tumbledown house and barn were a mile up an unmade track through the woods, and few locals bothered to come along it. The place, set on the side of a valley of stunning beauty, was one of the factors that had kept Madeleine and me in the same ambit down the years.

The content of the cable threatened this delicate equilibrium. As a roving reporter with ITN, I had only put in for the job as the company's Wash-ington correspondent at the last moment, provoked by another reporter who told me he'd already got it, and who I regarded as next to useless. Madeleine had agreed that I should apply, on the basis that I wouldn't get it, but in the end it had been a run-off between Trevor McDonald and me. Trevor was regarded as 'a safe pair of hands'. I was regarded as a very unsafe pair of hands, but

307

likely to file more stories. So unsafe was I seen as being that a new job was created for a 'producer' who would keep his or her eye on my 'content'. My assignment was to be for two years renewable. Now Madeleine, as successful a lawyer as I was a journalist, Leila and I would have to move home across the Atlantic.

America, which had propped up so many indifferent or bad regimes across the world; America, overthrower of Mossadegh in Iran, Arbenz in Guatemala, Allende in Chile – now quite suddenly I was to live in its capital. The post-Second World War picture of America abroad was not a pretty one, and for me that was a picture that barely included Vietnam, Laos and Cambodia. You had to go back to the reconstruction of Japan or the Marshall Plan for European recovery in the late 1940s to find comfort in the idea of America abroad. As the plane touched down at Dulles Airport in the Virginia wastes beyond Washington, my thoughts were of mistrust for what America had done, of the death squads that flourished under the protection of US-backed military forces, of the dictators like Pinochet whom the Cold War had rendered 'best friends'. I would expose it all!

But within twenty-four hours of landing my mistrust began turning into an improbable and lifelong love affair with 'can-do' America. For me, the capital of can-do was my American-staffed office. Nestling in the ABC News bureau behind the Mayflower Hotel in downtown Washington, four minutes' walk from the White House, it was at the very heart of everything. Our studios in London felt like something out of the dark ages by comparison. Here there were live pictures streaming in from Congress, from the Oval Office, from right across the US and beyond. We had banks of record/replay machines, and three technicians did the work of twenty in London. There was no union demarcation; the office was about making television news, not about creating obstacles to making television news. Journalists had status; television was right inside the Establishment.

My very first day, 10 September 1983, I pitched up at the White House Secret Service office, in the old Executive Building next to the White House with my journalist's 'I' visa that would allow me to work in the United States. I was almost instantly rewarded with my security clearance and a White House press pass. At nine the next morning I was seated in the seventh row of the press room, fifty yards from the Oval Office, listening to Ronald Reagan's Press Secretary, Larry Speakes. My rights were the same as those of any American correspondent: complete access and a dizzying 'freedom of information' culture. I could wander in and out of the White House any time I chose, buttonhole an official, or wander into Speakes's outer office to make a request for information or an interview.

I had been a British-based journalist for more than a decade, and never put so much as a toe over the threshold of Number Ten Downing Street. Yet after just two days in Washington I was standing in the White House rose garden, less than ten yards from the President of the United States. In one leap I had been transported from the British gutter – where most journalists, whether tabloid or quality, were left to fester – to the American Establishment. The British political culture of the authorities telling us what they thought we should know was supplanted by the American culture of a journalist's inalienable 'right to know'. It was a heady and dangerously beguiling experience.

In reality, of course, it meant that journalists were so close to the centres of power that we were seduced by them: we rarely challenged them for fear of damaging our status, and we were frequently taken in by them. It took me some months to realise quite how quiescent the US press actually was. That quiescence would come home to haunt us all many years later, when most of the American press failed to question the false claims surrounding the reasons for the war on Iraq.

But for the time being, from the Pentagon across the Potomac River to the State Department in Foggy Bottom and on up to Capitol Hill, an access and ease were on offer that I had simply never experienced. Washington also turned out to be a beautiful city. The Lincoln, Washington, Jefferson, and Vietnam Memorials, the Mall, the east wing of the National Gallery, all contributed to my sense of wellbeing. Naturally, on those first autumn mornings on the newly constructed subway, I failed to notice that Washington was in reality a Southern apartheid town, in which white people lived in the centre and black people commuted in from the suburbs; that realisation would come later.

I thought I'd died and gone to heaven in those first days in Washington. At first I took up residence in the opulently appointed, brass bath-tapped, organic-mealed Tabard Inn on N Street, five blocks from the White House, but within a month or two I found a house on Macombe Street, in the sumptuous, leafy north-west triangle close to National Cathedral. The Mondales, America's former Vice Presidential family, lived across the street, and the great investigative journalist Seymour Hersh's home backed onto our garden.

The house was late-nineteenth-century, white wooden clapper-board with a pillared deck at the back. It was only available because no one else wanted to live in it. The Agence France Press bureau chief had lived in it before, and one night, while he was away, his wife had been assaulted and raped in the basement by an intruder. It was an immediate and shocking insight into Washington's residual violence: more people were murdered there in a year than in the entire United Kingdom. I called Madeleine in London and explained the situation, and amazingly she said she would not be spooked by it. She thought it unlikely that such a thing would happen twice in the same house. So I grabbed the tenancy. We were to live on a spacious scale and in a style to which we had never been accustomed, and never would be again.

Washington had a ridiculous power to impress upon you that it was the most powerful city in the most powerful country on earth, and you were now part of it. Riggs Bank, where I banked, took its ads one step further: 'The most powerful bank in the most powerful city in the most powerful nation on earth...' I was a naive abroad, for I had effectively never been to the United States. The unrewarding ABC trip to New York in 1980 and endless layovers in sleazy hotels in Miami, en route to Central America, were the only America I knew.

In my first week, I got lost crossing the Fourteenth Street bridge. I did not yet understand the grid system of the roads, and took the wrong turning as I came back into town. I ended up deep in the black district way beyond Capitol Hill. I was thankful for the company Volvo's central locking as I became aware of people in the streets giving this rare white visitation quizzical looks. It took me some weeks to discover why the leafy north-west triangle in which I'd chosen to live felt so odd: it was simply extremely white. I experienced early that uncanny American syndrome, the tasting of unimagined riches while ignoring some of the worst urban poverty anywhere in the developed world.

The President's hair seemed to be dyed. For a man in his mid-seventies, if it wasn't, it was most assuredly an unusually lustrous phenomenon; anyway, most of us assumed that it was. The debate about Ronald Reagan's hair was only one tiny element of a whole slew of stories and jokes about his intellect and his grasp on the events that were swirling around him. To that extent at least, Reagan gave off some of the aura of simple-mindedness that George W. Bush was later to convey in his early days in the White House. But whenever I saw Reagan, already two and a half years in office, in action he looked every inch a President. His B-movie-star career had prepared him well for the part. What none of us guessed at the time was his crucial future role in changing the world order. Indeed there were all too many events while I was in Washington that suggested that the world and America were continuing very much in their bad old ways together.

It was four in the morning on 23 October 1983, early in my Washington sojourn, when the phone rang. 'Massive bomb at the US Marine base in Lebanon, Jon, huge story!' My foreign editor Maggie Eales rang off, and within fifteen minutes I'd shaved, dressed and biked to the office down-town. Using my bicycle to get about in Washington was regarded as an even more eccentric activity than it had been in London.

The twelve-thousand-pound bomb detonated at the gates of the US military compound in Beirut killed 241 Marines, the worst ever wholesale slaughter of US servicemen in a single terrorist attack. It also shattered Washington's own sense of security. That night I cycled home past the main portico of the White House. Arc lights had been set up, and for the first time in history cranes were hoisting huge concrete barriers into position to guard against similar attacks in the US capital. The following morning, my cameraman and I spotted men on the roof of the White House, silhouetted in the morning sun, with the telltale outlines of anti-aircraft missile launchers on their shoulders.

Amid the wanton destruction of Lebanon's civil war, and the continuous instability around Israel's borders, people all over Washington had been warning about the dangers to the eight hundred Marines remaining in Beirut. Seventeen Americans, including the entire Beirut CIA station staff, had been wiped out by a truck bomb the previous May. Now a quarter of the entire US peacekeeping contingent had been massacred. America's fourteen-month trial peacekeeping presence in Lebanon had ended in a disaster of even greater magnitude than Jimmy Carter's failure at Desert One. It was America's second pre-9/11 major face-to-face encounter with the evolving world of Muslim militancy.

The finger of suspicion pointed at Iran and Syria. Four years after the US hostages were seized, America was still asking 'Why do they hate us so much?', and almost never answering her own question. I had been to Israel several times by now, and had been both intrigued and horrified by the experience. Intrigued by Israel itself, but even in 1983 horrified by the crude Israeli occupation of the Palestinian lands which was rapidly radicalising the immediate Arab populations. Americans saw Israel as they saw themselves: as pioneers, immigrants from other lands, blazing a trail towards the consolidation of a civilised land in the face of hostile indigenous peoples.

If Israel was 'public friend number one', Iran was 'public enemy number one'. The war with Iranian-backed militants was fought out on the streets of Lebanon. The Marine massacre was

314

laid at Tehran's door. Iranians had never forgiven the US for that first adventure in 'regime change' thirty years earlier, the overthrow of Prime Minister Mossadegh, and Washington's unrelenting backing for the pathetic yet ruthless Shah Pahlavi. That, in the aftermath of the Islamic revolution which finally overthrew the odious Pahlavi regime, America should be insensitive enough to admit the Shah into the United States for medical treatment in 1978 was one of a number of factors that had led to the seizure of the US embassy in Tehran by student hotheads.

The coup against Mossadegh in 1953, orchestrated by President Eisenhower through the CIA and by Prime Minister Winston Churchill through MI6, continues to this day to be a testament to the consequences of 'pre-emptive action'. This was America's first exercise in going into someone else's country to try to concoct a new order, without understanding the nature of the society to which they were doing it. Iran in 1953 was to prove a testbed for Guatemala in 1954, for Chile in 1972, and ultimately for Iraq in 2003. But it was one from which apparently no lessons were learned.

Within hours of the Beirut attack I was in the Oval Office listening to Ronald Reagan telling the American people, 'Our goal remains the same, we shall not withdraw from Lebanon.' Four months later, on 24 February 1984, America retreated ignominiously from Lebanon, and has never been back.

In the meantime, at five o'clock in the morning,

two days after the Beirut bomb, the phone by my bed at home in Washington rang again. Once more it was Maggie, on the foreign desk in London. She told me that America had just invaded the tiny Caribbean island of Grenada. The timing simply could not have been a coincidence; the British Foreign Secretary, Geoffrey Howe, was unusually explicit. He told Parliament in London: 'The invasion of Grenada was clearly designed to divert attention. You had disaster in Beirut; now triumph in Grenada.' Mrs Thatcher had been called in Downing Street by the White House to be told bluntly that the invasion of this British Commonwealth island was 'under way'; she was reportedly 'livid'. Even the Queen was said to be more than a trifle bothered.

Five months earlier, in May 1983, Reagan had appeared in the White House briefing room to unveil the latest hemispheric threat from the dark forces of the Soviet empire. Its epicentre, depicted in murky satellite photos, lay at Port Salinas on Grenada. Here an airport facility was being built by Cuba to 'bunker Russian Bear bombers'. This represented an immediate and pressing threat to the future wellbeing of the United States of America. Interspersed with convenient cloud cover were dark smudges in the photographs, which Reagan's intelligence experts told us were bunkers under construction to house the latest state-of-the-art MIGs. This was dastardly stuff, so I set off on the circuitous route to Grenada for a week-long stint to see for myself.

The sea lapped slothfully outside my beachside room at the Spice Island Inn. I had a clear view of St George's, the Grenadian capital, in the middle distance; cruise ships sat on the skyline. I was armed with Reagan's photographs of the airport, and primed for interviews with Maurice Bishop, the Prime Minister, and Bernard Coard, the Finance Minister.

In the government offices I found both paranoia and justified fear running high. 'They are going to attack us. They want to kill me,' Bernard Coard said to me of America's intentions. Bishop put it more moderately, but they both made it clear in their different ways that the pressure their fledgling government had been under for many months had begun to affect their judgement. Overt and covert threats from a country with a population of a quarter of a billion, against an island with a hundred thousand souls, doubtless felt pretty unpleasant, especially when the island was described as being at the 'cutting edge' of Soviet attempts to build a bridgehead for war in the hemisphere.

Bishop and Coard were both highly educated black West Indians, both thirty-nine years old, and had been to school together. Coard had been a PhD student at the University of Sussex, working on child psychology. When his book *How the West Indian Child is Made Educationally Subnormal in the British School System* was published in 1971, it was highly regarded and influential. A large, academic, bespectacled man, he appeared extremely bright, and displayed none of the sinister attributes of which he was later to be accused. The tall, bearded, slim and charismatic Maurice Bishop had studied political economy, also at the

317

University of Sussex, and been called to the English Bar. While Coard espoused an almost raw Marxist agenda, Bishop was more pragmatic, in favour of engagement with America and of an economic system that encouraged private investment.

Their New Jewel Movement had seized power in 1979, while the former Prime Minister and high-profile believer in unidentified flying objects Eric Gairy was out of the country. Gairy and his 'Mongoose Gang' of henchmen were widely believed to have rigged the elections. Britain endowed him with a knighthood anyway. Having displaced a corrupt Westminster-style system, Bishop's government instituted a Caribbean style of Marxism, with a Politburo and plenty of Communist rhetoric. But in no sense did Coard or Bishop or those around them see themselves as providing a bridgehead for a Soviet invasion of America. That, however, was the threat that Reagan said they posed.

After the coup, neither Britain nor America would give aid to Grenada. Bishop warned them that if they did not, he would have to go Coard's route and treat with Cuba. Castro was waiting, and willing. He supplied nurses, doctors, teachers and a technical advisory team to assess the island's needs. To reach Grenada from Europe in those days took two days' flying. Most small Caribbean islands reckoned tourism was their best option for economic development, and a ten-year-old World Bank survey had already indicated that a runway capable of handling inter-continental flights was necessary for Grenada to thrive. Antigua, a slightly smaller island about 350 miles away, had just built an even longer runway without complaint from the US or anyone else. The airport contract was first offered to US companies for tender, but was refused. Only then did Bishop agree to go ahead with Cuban construction.

Several hundred Cuban workers were on the airport complex when I visited it. Walking down the centre of the new runway, I took pictures in every direction. Why had President Reagan resorted to wonky satellite images when anyone with a Box Brownie camera could have come here and photographed to their heart's content? I could find no bunkers, or any evidence that they had been covered up. Even more extraordinary was the fact that at one end of the runway, behind the fuel storage tanks, lay an annexe to an American university located on the island, where seven hundred mainly American medical students slept in dormitories. Why hadn't Reagan phoned one of them and asked for a few photographs?

The President had also omitted to tell the American public that Britain and the European Community were deeply involved in the airport project. British technicians in short-sleeved white open-necked shirts moved around the developing air terminal. Britain's prime defence contractor Plessey had a £5 million contract, underwritten by the UK government, to install the air-traffic control systems. The company was furious at being accused of building a major facility for bunkering Russian Bear bombers, and denied it as 'fatuous in the extreme'. Finland was supplying the firefighting equipment, the trucks of which were powered by Rolls-Royce engines. Reagan's satellite photos described the simple huts where the construction workers lived as 'Cuban barracks'. There was no sign of any kind of weapon or uniform on the three occasions on which I turned up unannounced at the airport in my hired Mini Moke. Even the runway turned out to be a thousand feet shorter than Reagan had claimed.

Small though this little Caribbean cameo is, it's a neat insight into the kind of processes that would precede the 2003 invasion of Iraq, where weapons of mass destruction were said to be capable of use within forty-five minutes. That claim proved as false as Reagan's fanciful assertions about Grenada's readiness to serve as a Bear bomber base. Secretary of State Colin Powell would produce fuzzy images at the UN that were all too reminiscent of Reagan's cloudy shots of the Grenadian runway. Eventually, in 2004, Powell apologised for his fanciful presentation. Reagan never did.

Within a few months, as the tension and paranoia around Grenada mounted, Coard moved against Bishop, who was almost immediately executed. Coard and his fellow plotters were later found guilty of the murder, but had their death sentences commuted, and remain in jail on the island to this day.

Although I asked the Pentagon for accreditation to cover the American invasion of Grenada on 27 October 1983, in common with every other journalist I was denied. It was one of the very rare occasions on which America took not a single journalist into war with her. Ostensibly the aim of the invasion was to 'rescue' the American medical students from their annexe at the bottom of the runway. Five thousand US troops were sent on the mission. Instead of hitting the bunkers that didn't exist, they attacked the wrong building, a mental hospital, killing patients. Resistance was almost non-existent, but that did not prevent three US Black Hawk helicopters from crashing into each other while they assaulted another building which turned out to be completely empty. At the end of it all, after a couple of hours of 'fighting', sixty Cuban workers, twenty-four Grenadians and nineteen American troops lay dead. Most of the medical students complained that they didn't want to be 'rescued' at all.

The resonances with Iraq in 2003–04 are all too vivid. Here was an episode in which a small group of White House insiders had become so obsessed with their own prejudiced sense of what was happening – in this case a Communist takeover in the Caribbean and Central America – that they went to war with no international blessing and, despite trying to fix it, no legitimacy in law. Worse, once the act had taken place, Mrs Thatcher and other Western leaders simply decided to do no more about it. No lessons were learned and no methodology was developed that might kick in at a later date when American power was to become even more unchallengeable.

Even so, this great victory in the war against Communism was a diversion from Lebanon, and succeeded in briefly upsetting the placid old

British government into the bargain. And whatever we cynical correspondents may have thought, Ronald Reagan reckoned he had struck another home run for freedom. Standing once more in the White House rose garden he told us: 'If I had not attacked Grenada, Soviet bombers would soon be operating from the airstrip. I will continue to confront the Kremlin as a way of honouring our brave men lost in Beirut and Grenada.' As with George W. Bush twenty years later, neither the media nor the Democrats made much of an effort to challenge him.

The Reagan view of the world was very much a forerunner of George W's. Indeed, some of Bush's future lieutenants were already on deck for Ronald Reagan – John Negroponte at the State Department, John Poindexter at the White House, and Richard Perle at the Department of Defense. And Reagan was conjuring up the concepts of 'freedom' and 'evil' when the younger George was still roaming around Texas drinking too much and doing drugs. Two decades before our present enemies were consolidated into the 'axis of evil' by George W. Bush, Ronald Reagan had characterised the Soviet enemy as the 'Evil Empire'.

On 16 January 1984 the opening salvoes of the interminable US presidential election campaign were being loosed off in the snowy wastes of New England. The eight Democrat hopefuls were in debate. For the first time in many years, arms control and the depth of the Cold War freeze had become a serious domestic issue. Reagan, who was running for his second term, tried to reduce the tension by announcing an upgraded telephone 'hotline' between Washington and Moscow. Russia's Foreign Minister Andrei Gromyko flew to Stockholm to meet Reagan's Secretary of State, George Schultz. We all concluded that the Lebanon and Grenada rhetoric had got a bit out of hand. In reality, the right-wing adventurist exuberance of the Reagan administration happened to coincide with the atrophying of the Soviet leadership. They were already well aware that the Kremlin was in no position to hit back.

On 22 January the US military successfully test fired a missile at Vandenberg Air Force base in California, designed to intercept incoming Russian intercontinental ballistic missiles. It was a critical moment in the early development of the controversial Strategic Defense Initiative (SDI), or 'Star Wars' project. Washington was spending hundreds of millions of dollars in an attempt to establish an anti-missile shield in outer space that would seriously disorder the strategic balance between the superpowers. No one guessed that this was to prove a key weapon in the political armoury that within five years would bring the Soviet Union to its knees.

Relations between Moscow and Washington were now so bad, and US intelligence so poor, that America lagged behind Western Europe in learning on 9 February 1984 that the leader of the Soviet Union had suddenly died of kidney failure. Yuri Andropov proved to be a nearly dead man who for just fifteen months had filled an actually dead man's shoes. The former KGB chief had followed in Brezhnev's decayed footsteps, but had hardly lasted long enough for people in the West to learn how to pronounce his name. One more nearly dead man, Konstantin Chernenko, was to come before the arrival of the Soviet leader who really would inaugurate the new world order.

With the red flag slipped to half-mast on the 'Evil Empire's' secretive Mission on Sixteenth Street, just up from the White House, Ronald Reagan decided not to break his holiday on his ranch in California. Nor did the President deem it necessary to go to Moscow for the funeral of Andropov. Indeed, in the sixteen months since Brezhnev's funeral in November 1982 there had not been one meeting between any senior Russian and American figures.

Given that coverage from Moscow was so sparse and state-controlled, I was left to try to pick up the pieces in Washington. With the President out of town, and Secretary of State George Schultz reluctantly heading to Russia for the funeral, I had to fall back on talking with Schultz's predecessor, Henry Kissinger. Meeting Kissinger was always the same. You came into his office loaded with challenges and accusations stemming from his role in the illegal carpet bombing of Cambodia in the early 1970s, and much else, and left having achieved nothing.

In between, Kissinger would continue to be the ever-available 'expert' on international issues. He remained unfortunately undiminished and undented by whatever was said of him. Despite having arrived in America from Germany at the age of fifteen, almost fifty years of exposure to the English language had made his accent no more intelligible. On this occasion he proved his Cold War credentials by backing Reagan's decision not to go to Moscow, but he did think that it might also be a moment to talk peace.

There was, of course, another reason for the President's absence from Washington. The humiliating announcement that he was pulling American troops out of Lebanon had to be got out of the way. Then as now, an American foreign policy catastrophe in the Middle East was invariably followed by an ignominious plea to the United Nations to come in and help in its aftermath. Reagan's love of the UN was no greater than George W. Bush's later proved to be.

We were living the very year of Orwell's *Nineteen Eighty-Four*. The whole world was divided into good and evil – capitalist pro-American versus Communist pro-Soviet. Everything from Lebanon to Nicaragua was bludgeoned into this scenario. The direct dialogue with Moscow took place against a background of ever greater commitments of cash for Star Wars, and rhetoric riddled with the ostracism of everything the Soviet Union touched. An inevitable casualty was the Los Angeles Olympics that year, which Russia boycotted in response to America's boycott of the Moscow games four years earlier.

The Iran–Iraq war was still raging, American diplomats were killed in yet another Beirut bomb, but even these events, so rooted in the complex Middle East mix, were interpreted by Americans as evidence of Russia's dread hand. The Soviet client state was Syria, and more loosely Iraq and Libya were identified as being on the 'wrong' side. In fact the Cold War ensured that the West pitched up on the wrong side of almost every secular state in the Arab world. Oil ensured that we were on the 'right' side of totalitarian regimes from Saudi Arabia to Kuwait. Western sensibilities over human rights and democracy were suborned to the interests of the wider Cold War struggle.

In all this, Israel could do no wrong. As remains the case to this day, discussing the role Israel played in American politics was an ill-advised pursuit. Unlike many of the Senators and Congressmen with whom I had dealings, I had actually spent time in Israel and the Occupied Territories. I loved the country, the sense of living on the edge, the juxtapositions of Jewish and Muslim cultures: historic views from the Israeli-owned King David Hotel; balmy evenings at its East Jerusalem counterpart the Palestinian-run American Colony; wandering the dense streets and markets around the city walls; and contrasting nights in the discos and clubs of Tel Aviv. But none of us who worked there was blind to Israel's very real shortcomings: looming apartheid-style ethnic separation; the settlements; the illegal grabbing of still more Palestinian land. In Washington, Israel was an impenetrable blind spot. There was no creative discussion, and little representation of the true aspirations of the Palestinian people. Since the Middle East wars of 1967 and 1973 the Israeli containment of Palestinian anger and consequent violence had been both brutal and efficient. But as time would reveal, it was no answer.

Into all this obtruded the gathering pace of the 1984 US presidential elections. Foreign affairs slipped to an inside page, and my love affair with America took on an altogether more ferocious zeal. I had become two Washington correspondents: one aghast at America's roughshod riding over sensitivities from Chile to Angola; the other engrossed in what seemed to me on the surface a more democratic engagement with the people than I had ever witnessed before. The written constitution, the settlement between 'we the people', Congress and the presidency itself were in stark contrast to the British system, where there is no 'we the people', and we are the subjects of an unelected head of state. Only one part of our national legislature is elected, the others flowing either from appointment or bloodline.

My Washington crew and I had already made occasional sorties across to Iowa and up to New Hampshire, the initial feeding and testing grounds for the presidential elections. Reagan, despite his flaws and the passing of his seventy-third birthday, was the inevitable candidate for the Republican Party. So it was the identity of the Democrat who would oppose him that interested us most.

The undisputed frontrunner for the Democratic Party nomination, Jimmy Carter's former Vice President Walter Mondale, already had a huge press entourage, so we plumped for a relative unknown, the Senator from Colorado, Gary Hart. We had meandered round much of both states in Hart's ten-seater minibus weeks before. He had a kind of Kennedyesque strut about him. He talked about the environment, was compassionate about welfare, and moderate on defence. Yet he did not altogether convince us that he was quite the man he said he was. His name was really Hartpence – he'd changed it in 1961 – and his age was really forty-seven, not the forty-six he claimed in the campaign.

Following a primary caucus in Iowa was seductive. This farming state of wide, flat fields interspersed with old red Dutch barns added to my sense of the breadth of America. All the candidates for the Democrat nomination visited the state to prove their farming credentials by cradling a piglet or sitting on a bale of straw. The caucus we attended was held in a public library in the town of Ames. Large round tables had been arranged around the room, each with a dozen chairs and the name of a candidate on a scrap of paper in the middle. Gradually people arrived and headed for the table of their favoured candidate. There were perhaps a couple of hundred participants.

One or two of the candidates wandered through to try to win people across to their tables. The first American to orbit the earth in space, the now Senator John Glenn, tough on defence and as conservative as Reagan himself on many issues, was doing none too well. I saw Gary Hart ease his way over to the Glenn table and 'steal' four voters for his own. You needed ten votes to go through to the next stage of the process that would eventually end up at the Democrat Convention in San Francisco that would make the final choice of the party's nominee to run against Reagan. What was remarkable was that voters who had formerly supported the hawkish Glenn had defected not to the nearest candidate ideologically, but to a liberal on the opposite side of the spectrum. Maybe our man Hart had something, we thought. Walter Mondale used the Democrat machine to hoover up Iowa, but Hart came in a surprising, and many thought flukish, second.

It was snowing in New Hampshire a week later when Gary Hart stole the show altogether. This time it was not a caucus but a test of voters' desires through the ballot box. Hart romped home, and the press minivan following him became a plane, then a bigger plane, and finally several jetliners. Gary Hart had 'the big mo', the momentum towards victory. An American presidential dream had been born. Alas, it was to prove only a dream. Gary Hart's candidacy eventually foundered over a number of issues, but was finally destroyed when he was photographed on a boat called *Monkey Business* with a woman who was not his wife. Nevertheless, he'd provided us with a telling insight into the fabric of American politics.

If my affection for the system was to take a battering, it was not from the casualty of monkey business, but from the role money played in securing the nomination. Candidate after candidate put himself in hock to moneyed interests, from food retailers and oil prospectors to trades unionists.

Flying south to Atlanta, Georgia, and squeezing into the back of the Ebenezer Baptist church, scene of the great Martin Luther King's sermons, we saw another remarkable feature of this election – a black candidate. The power of the black vote inside the Democrat Party is significant; the problem was that Jesse Jackson was a controversial figure. He claimed to have cradled King's head as he lay dying from the assassin's bullet – something the King family questioned. Their support, and that of others in the black community, would be given to Mondale. Even so, Jackson tapped many poorer black hearts, and his record of having helped rescue Americans held prisoner or hostage anywhere from Cuba to the Middle East rendered him strong enough to make it through to the Democrat Convention that August with 85 per cent of the black vote.

It was in the South that I began to value the strength of my Washington team. My video editor Dave Sampi was black, and had grown up in the South, in Louisiana. My cameraman Ed Castner was a liberal Democrat from Pittsburgh. Balance was restored by my efficient Reaganite producer, Christine Kelleher. When Jesse Jackson proclaimed of the Southern black population, 'Hands that once picked cotton can now pick a President,' Dave Sampi responded, 'He's talking about me.' The eclectic political mix of the team led to richly informative debate during our long hours on the electoral trail.

The campaign that summer provided an amazing if superficial insight into the real America. We dashed from the smokestacks of Pennsylvania to the cattle ranches of Texas; from the riches of Hollywood to the poverty of Harlem. There were incidents aplenty. One morning in Colorado, Mondale had his pilot take us down below the rim of the Grand Canyon in his Boeing 727, a scary but unforgettable experience. On another occasion we noticed one of the engines on Hart's campaign plane belching flames as we landed at Chicago's O'Hare Airport.

Arriving for their Convention in San Francisco in August 1984, in what by American standards was the rather small Muscone Convention Center, the Democrats had a vast mountain to climb. Ronald Reagan was still looking pretty unassailable. But from the outset this was to prove one of the most exciting political fiestas I have ever attended. Breathtakingly beautiful, ethnically diverse, San Francisco was the scene of a rekindling of hope amongst Democrats that Reagan could after all be beaten. The curtain was raised by the best President America never had, the Governor of New York, Mario Cuomo. His 'I am an immigrant' speech gripped us by the throat, bound us to the wheel of American history at home and drowned her more squalid foreign adventures. It was lyrical, heartrending oratory of the very highest order. Cuomo had us weeping, laughing and eventually praising his vision of a caring, compassionate America, in which all shared in the nation's vast fortune. The standing ovation simply would not subside, as down-trodden Democrats found their voices and hearts uplifted at last.

Jesse Jackson deployed equal passion, and if

anything, more pragmatism. In the course of the campaign he had referred to Jews, a key Democrat constituency, as 'Hymies', and to New York as 'Hymietown'. Jackson had much repair work to do, and he did it: 'If I have offended,' he said, 'blame my head, but not my heart.' And they did.

Then there was the unexpected and galvanising moment when Walter Mondale revealed his Vice Presidential running mate, the Congresswoman for Queens district in New York, Geraldine Ferraro. It felt, on the floor of the Muscone Center, like a moment of emancipation, even liberation – the first woman ever to run for so high an office in America. Even the somewhat dull, and politically European, Mondale was lit up.

We returned to Washington, where our enthusiasm was soon hosed down by Reagan and the Republicans. The economy was going their way, world events were going their way, the nation felt comfortable with the old actor. By the time of the Republican Convention a month later in Dallas he had become, at seventy-four, the oldest man ever to hold the presidency and the oldest man to bid for it again.

You step from the plane at Dallas Airport into an air-conditioned, tinted-glass terminal hall; from the terminal hall into a tinted-glass, air-conditioned taxi; from the taxi into the tinted-glass, air-conditioned Hyatt Hotel. Dallas was even cold. But if you braved it into the Texas summer sun, it was a baking 108°.

Inside the air-conditioned convention centre, the stage was set for a coronation. This Republican Convention was emphatically not a place for serious debates on the floor. The Democrat fight and oratory of 1984 may prove to be the last time any American political party goes into a convention without having pre-planned the exact outcome. Historically the business of choosing a candidate allowed serious debate at the convention. But as San Francisco demonstrated, the live transmission of such debate on television seemed to give voters the impression that there were splits in the party, rather than that it was a sign of healthy democracy in operation. Television was deemed to be God, so henceforth politicians would convert their gatherings from debating houses to predictable showcases for their policies and their people. There was no greater showcase than the Republicans' multi-million-dollar film of Ronald and Nancy Reagan amid backlit, schmaltzy scenes of private and political joy with which their convention opened. Here was the first actor to become President, the 'great communicator' to his admirers, but accused by his enemies of falling asleep in Cabinet and of doing less than a full day's work as President of the most powerful nation on earth.

The following morning the evangelical chorus of the Christian right made their entrance at a prayer breakfast, with the Reverends Jerry Falwell and Pat Robertson strutting their eerie fundamentalist stuff. In Dallas that August they were already highly influential in the political wings of the Republican Party. Two decades later George W. Bush was to see such influences at centre stage.

Reagan emerged from the convention still

further buoyed in the polls. Not for nothing was he known as the Teflon President: no bad news ever stuck. Relaxing on his Californian ranch after the convention during a breakdown in arms talks with the Russians, we asked him what he was doing about it. Reagan looked utterly stumped, so his wife Nancy whispered audibly to him, 'We're doing everything we can.' And he, like a Dalek, repeated just that: 'We are doing everything we can.' It may have been an early sign of the Alzheimer's that would blight his retirement, but the American public did not care. Nor did they when he was jokily testing the microphone before his weekly radio address to the nation: 'My fellow Americans, I'm pleased to tell you today that I've signed legislation that will outlaw Russia forever. We begin bombing in five minutes,' he said, live on air.

As the contest between Mondale and Reagan unfolded, the only chink the Democrat could find in the President's armour was the tension in East–West relations. Eventually he goaded Reagan – who had never met a Russian above the rank of Ambassador – into a singularly unproductive meeting with the old Cold Warhorse, Soviet Foreign Minister Andrei Gromyko. America's psychological, emotional and military build-up continued unabated. In November Reagan romped home, sweeping all but two states in the Union.

US television news mimicked the priorities of the voters, and it was therefore rare to see a foreign news development anywhere near the top of the headlines. But on 16 December 1984 Mikhail Gorbachev, a hitherto obscure Soviet Agriculture Minister, came calling on Britain's Prime Minister Margaret Thatcher, a meeting which created more than a few ripples across the pond. America was transfixed: here was a Russian who laughed, and who charmed and beguiled all those who encountered him. The Iron Lady had as yet developed no rust spots. Her anti-Communist, anti-Soviet armour was at its most burnished. But when she and Gorbachev came out to meet the press after their encounter at Chequers, it was clear that it had been love at first sight. 'This is a man I can do business with,' she announced. The television pictures beamed into our office in Washington revealed an open-faced, straight-talking man, considerably younger than the typical member of the Soviet Politburo.

It was a refreshing moment, but Gorbachev was still only the Minister of Agriculture, and this had been his very first visit to Europe. Indeed, he had only once before ventured out of the USSR, and then surprisingly to Canada to attend a farm show – although the real reason for the trip had been to re-engage with the dynamic Alexander Yakovlev, who'd been exiled to Ottawa as Soviet Ambassador after being caught hatching progressive ideas for change.

We still had one more dead man to get through. Seventy-three-year-old Konstantin Chernenko had taken over as Soviet leader in February 1984, despite his doctor's warning that he was too ill to serve. He was still just alive.

Three days after the Gorbachev–Thatcher love

fest, the US Defense Secretary Caspar Weinberger took the rare step of summoning me and a few other non-American correspondents to a briefing at the Pentagon. He was a great anglophile – so much so that he was later to accept a knighthood from the Queen. 'The Star Wars programme will go ahead,' he announced, and then proceeded to outline the potential for superpower war in space. Washington was turning the screw on the ailing Chernenko. Yet Weinberger never used expressions like 'beating the Russians', or 'winning the Cold War'. Even though we were less than five years from its end, and someone somewhere must have noted the signs, no one ever spoke of what we would do if the West won the Cold War. Washington was laying no plans in the event of victory over the 'Evil Empire'.

For the time being, America's massive military build-up continued. Indeed, in the course of the election campaign I did a computer run of Congressional districts and arms production facilities, and found that there was not a constituency in the entire United States that did not benefit from some small or larger segment of the arms boom. The investment in winning the Cold War by now knew no bounds; preparations for winning the peace were contrastingly non-existent.

Two days before Christmas 1984, Margaret Thatcher came calling. The weather at Andrews Air Force Base was filthy. After a twenty-one-hour flight from Hong Kong she was forced to eschew the helicopter in favour of a long, wet drive to Camp David in Maryland. My cameraman and I trailed along behind, only to be dumped unceremoniously at the heavily policed outskirts of the rustic presidential compound. The Reaganites had been alarmed by the way Britain had been bowled over by Gorbachev. Worse, they were seriously concerned that Mrs Thatcher did not seem to share Reagan's enthusiasm for the Star Wars enterprise.

During a break in the talks, Reagan's spokesman Larry Speakes came out to brief us. The usual on-the-record guff about how Mrs Thatcher had congratulated the President on his stunning electoral victory, and how in tune they were on everything, was somewhat undermined by what Speakes told me off the record. It appeared that Thatcher had had a brief but seriously angry exchange with Reagan over Star Wars. 'It won't work,' Speakes reported her as saying. 'I know, I'm a chemist.' We had to scratch our heads a bit at this. Then we recalled that before she became a lawyer, Mrs Thatcher had indeed secured a third-class honours degree in chemistry at Oxford. She clearly regarded that as ample authority for her opinions on the mechanics of Star Wars.

Actually, Mrs Thatcher's more deep-seated concerns centred on Reagan's belief that such an anti-missile shield could render nuclear weapons obsolete altogether, and warrant getting rid of all of them. She and most of those about her were advocates of MAD – Mutually Assured Destruction – which they argued had kept the Cold War peace for a generation.

Being based in Washington meant that I was able, from time to time, to dip south into Central and

337

Latin America.

There was still a whiff of romance about in Managua, Nicaragua, despite Reagan's Contra war. In November 1984 we were out in the heart of the city watching the more radical world leaders from as far afield as Mozambique and Angola, who had assembled to celebrate the inauguration of Daniel Ortega as the country's first elected President. The Sandinistas had prevailed in what was judged to be a fair election, giving the lie to any idea that the Contras enjoyed popular support. Neil Kinnock, the new leader of Britain's Labour Party, was there with John Reid, his bag carrier, himself one day to be translated into a pugnacious Cabinet Minister. But the romance was centred upon just one of their number, the surprisingly slight figure of Fidel Castro, President of Cuba.

We were at last far from the realms of Potomac Fever, a malady that afflicted the reporting patient with a fear that if he or she left Washington, Ronald Reagan would invade another country while they were out of town. I'd been sent to Nicaragua simply to link up with Kinnock and try to find out more about him. When he'd been in Washington a year before, I'd talked to him briefly after he had described US Secretary of State George Schultz as 'out of his pram' following a row about US support for Central American death squads. Managua provided a more intimate chance to get to know him well.

Either I was getting old or political leaders were getting younger, for in Kinnock it appeared that here at last was a relatively normal man who seemed to be from my generation, and to think in the way that my generation thought. One night he mentioned that Castro had agreed to see him, and asked if my film crew and I would like to come along. The meeting was set for ten the next night. Nearly five hours after the appointed hour we were still waiting for the great man. Kinnock, rather endearingly, was at least as excited about meeting him as we were. 'How long do you think it is appropriate for the leader of Her Majesty's Opposition to wait for the President of Cuba?' he asked me, half-joking.

'Hours and hours,' I said enthusiastically.

It was 3 a.m. before Castro finally appeared. His beard was more scraggy than in photographs, but nevertheless he had huge charisma. It was evident that the Cuban leader peaked at about 3.30 a.m. He was in boisterous mood. 'They tell me you may become the next Prime Minister of England,' he said to Kinnock. 'Normally I have good relations with you politicians when you are not in government, but as soon as you are, I never see you again.' Banter about beards and baldness followed, with Castro declaring that he saved eighty hours a year by not shaving.

More seriously, he identified a truism. Few Western governments have ever thought it worth an open disagreement with the United States over Cuba. America's obsession with this outpost of Communism ninety miles off Florida has known no bounds. Blockades, assassination attempts, invasion have all borne witness to Uncle Sam's fixation. The wounds of the Cuban missile crisis three decades ago remained raw and open more than ten years after the Cold War had ended. Injured American pride and the extremists among the Cuban emigrant population in south Florida have ensured that Castro has never been brought down by 'engagement'. Britain, like most other Western states, has had the minimum possible involvement with Havana, trading a few London buses in exchange for grapefruit, and nothing more.

I asked Castro about cigars.

'I have had to give them up – doctor's orders,' he said ruefully.

'Didn't the Americans once try to kill you with one?' I asked.

'Oh, they try anything. They tried to plant an explosive cigar; they thought it would set my beard on fire.' He was vitriolic when it came to the US-backed Contra war, and much else. But as so often, it was not what he said, but who was saying it.

The snow lay six inches deep on the ten thousand chairs set out on Capitol Hill for Ronald Reagan's second presidential inauguration. Dawn on 21 January 1985 revealed a complete Washington whiteout. The wind-chill factor was minus 23° Fahrenheit. It was so cold that I had to don a pair of Madeleine's tights under the rest of my clothes before I set out for the open-air inauguration. In a strangely physical way the weather seemed to mark a new nadir in the Cold War freeze itself. The ceremony was shunted indoors while we un-successfully attempted hatless reports to camera outside, but the rhetoric remained the same.

Three days later, the public launch of a secret payload from Cape Canaveral announced the militarisation of space. Aboard the Space Shuttle for the first time was an astronaut who was not answerable to NASA, but to the US Defense Department. The Shuttle's payload was entirely military, and included a geosynchronous satellite to monitor the eastern part of the USSR. In short, some of the earliest ingredients for Star Wars were on their way to outer space. The practicalities were beginning to catch up with the rhetoric. Throughout the voyage there was an eerie silence both from Mission Control in Houston and from the spacecraft itself.

Mrs Thatcher was on her way back to Washington again in February 1985, leaving the British miners' strike behind her. It was about this time that I was asked to sign an appeal to be run in national newspapers on behalf of a hardship fund for miners' families. In my Washington outpost I had little idea how divisive and bitter the strike had become, and how political. Publicly to endorse the appeal was perhaps morally right, but journalistically extremely unwise. When I did, the balloon went up. My editor, David Nicholas, who had always had great faith in me, warned me on the phone from London that my job was on the line, and that he was considering bringing me back to Britain immediately. My conspiracy-seeking mind immediately concluded that Mrs Thatcher must have nobbled him. He let me hang out to dry for a day or two before dispatching a deputy who informed me that I could no longer expect to become political editor in London when my Washington stint ended. Instead, the current diplomatic editor, Michael Brunson, an altogether safer pair of hands, would get the job, and I would be demoted to his. I suppose I was disappointed, but in retrospect I don't think I'd have survived as political editor. And the diplomatic job, when I returned home at the end of 1986, was to provide a grandstand position from which to view the collapse of the old Cold War order.

In those days, when there was to be a Summit between Reagan and another leader, a journalist from that leader's country would be permitted to interview the President. On the occasion of Margaret Thatcher's visit in February 1985 the opportunity fell to me. My film crew and I were allocated a room in the East Wing of the White House, and set up with three cameras, lights, and a large canvas sheet stretched over the floor to protect the rugs. At last, after years of covering America's misdoings abroad, and Reagan's in particular, full of the bile caused by what I had seen in Grenada and Central America, here was my great chance.

Reagan came in smiling, and immediately tripped over on the canvas floor covering. 'God darn it!' he cried. 'You'd think I'd been in enough movies not to do that!' We were immediately disarmed; he was at his most charming and avuncular. Reagan was brilliant at making you feel that to attack him would be hitting a defenceless old man when he was down. For me, the interview was a complete failure.

When she arrived the next day, Margaret Thatcher attracted precisely the same kind of gushing enthusiasm from the Reagan administration that Tony Blair was to secure from both Bill Clinton and George W. Bush. America could not get enough of her – she was Winston Churchill in drag. The 'special relationship' seemed alive and well. Perhaps not that well, because her iron will was still opposed to Reagan's obsession with Star Wars, an issue over which she had not the slightest effect. Indeed, like Tony Blair two decades later, there is little evidence that she ever succeeded in influencing US policy in any way. Her one notable victory, two years before, had been to win the supply of US-built Sidewinder missiles and jet fuel during the Falklands War. In that she defeated another of the most formidable women of the time, the US Ambassador to the UN Jeane Kirkpatrick, who in common with many in the American Establishment felt that maintaining relations with Latin America was more important than doing so with the dwindling power of Britain.

As I peered down into the Congressional chamber, the excitement amongst the massively male-dominated membership of both the Senate and the Congress was palpable. The red necks craned, the pork bellies pressed, to get a glimpse of Mrs Thatcher as she entered to deliver her formal address. It seems they did not need the inculcation of the British public-school system to fall beneath her spell. Matron was on spectacular form, and she had them fawning in the aisles. Even if she held back on Star Wars, she let the unfortunate decaying Russian leadership have it with both barrels. In terms of rhetoric she could match the old cowboy in the White House shot for shot.

The one blind spot that was evident on this trip was Ireland. Here was a woman who had narrowly escaped death at the hands of the IRA addressing a group of politicians some of whom actively supported the organisations that were bankrolling the bombers. That aside, she went down a storm. The Reagan–Thatcher love-in in the Oval Office later was pure saccharin; the public display of affection, not for the last time, masked a private failure of influence. Reagan was going America's way, and Britain could come along if she wanted. And Mrs Thatcher wanted.

So did Saudi Arabia's King Fahd, who had preceded Mrs Thatcher at the White House a week before. He had looked like a waxwork, sallow with illness. He was another 'best friend' in the war against Communism. The hard drinking, womanising and money-squandering that went on among some Saudis residing in America were never publicly contrasted with the austere religious regime at home. The Saudis were 'on our side', and the possibility that there might be darker anti-American, anti-royal forces at work there was undiscussed. Saudi Arabia had oil, and that was what mattered.

By early 1985, America's deployment of multi-headed MX missiles and the continued development work on the Star Wars was creating such furore in Europe, and such fear in Moscow, that talks on disarmament were held in Geneva. On 8 March I was in the Oval Office shouting questions at Reagan's chief arms negotiator, Max Kampelman. Two days later, after thirteen months as leader, Konstantin Chernenko died, the third Russian leader to do so in just over two years. As I walked out from my office across Sixteenth Street, the flag on the Kremlin's grim old embassy outpost was already at half-mast. It was an intriguing contrast to one year before, when it had been left to British intelligence to reveal Andropov's death to the world. The Soviet Union was changing.

Quite how much it was changing came as a shock. We might have heard of Mikhail Gorbachev, even hoped he might one day become Soviet leader, but the Politburo's decision to skip two decades and appoint him as Chernenko's successor was positively revolutionary. Gorbachev was only fifty-four; Chernenko had been seventy-three. The open face, the all-seeing eyes, the wine stain on the forehead – we were excited by this man. Suddenly the Russian leader was twenty years younger than his American counterpart, and it showed.

We did not see Gorbachev's call, in his very first speech as Soviet leader, for a freeze on arms deployments as a clue as to what was to come. We had no sense that the Cold War was inexorably moving towards its end; it seemed rather that the Soviet Union had simply devised a new and more civilised way of doing things.

The police encampment on Massachusetts

Avenue, almost opposite the British embassy, had become more or less permanent. The process of protest outside the South African embassy had been honed to a fine art. It might have been 1985, but America had only just woken up to the existence and evil of apartheid. While the Sharpville massacre of 1960 had assaulted British sensibilities, South Africa's apartheid excesses had attracted almost no interest in the US mass media. Only now had black America in particular begun to flex its muscles on behalf of the black majority in South Africa.

We were kept back behind a police cordon as we observed the enactment of what had become a daily ritual. Today it was ex-President Jimmy Carter's daughter Amy whom I watched as she stepped off the road and onto South African diplomatic territory beyond the kerb. At once she was politely and gently arrested, handcuffed and escorted into a police wagon. Yesterday it had been Senator Ted Kennedy; tomorrow it would be Martin Luther King's daughter.

South Africa had been racked with riot and protest against the apartheid system for months. American television was at last taking notice, and transmitting searing images of racial oppression. It might be happening in a distant land of which Americans knew little, but the nightly images chimed with scenes from their own Deep South that were still all too fresh in their collective memory. I found it curious that a society with such a significant black population had known and cared so little about South Africa for so long. Britain, where the Afro-Caribbean population was relatively small, had a far greater awareness of the scandal of apartheid. But now, when British viewers had become almost inured to the violence of apartheid, Americans were suddenly and profoundly shocked by the 'discovery' of such evil.

A union-led boycott of US companies doing business in South Africa was announced, and black workers in America began to demand disinvestment. Coca-Cola, Ford, General Motors, all sorts of household US corporate names were beginning to feel the pressure. New York City banned all South African goods and services. Philadelphia removed $90 million of pension funds from companies investing in South African stocks. MIT and Harvard disinvested their funds from South Africa. Suddenly there was a clout being exercised that Britain had never been able, or never wanted, to wield. It was to be a determining force in bringing down the apartheid regime.

The former Liverpool student sent down in 1970 for his activities in the same cause began to feel rather comfortable observing the unfolding daily drama on Massachusetts Avenue. The police dared not take the high-powered protesters to court, for fear that the demonstrations would grow still larger. As soon as Amy Carter entered the police wagon by one door, she was released through another.

Nelson Mandela's twenty-three-year-long and continuing incarceration was hardly known of in America, so that when South Africa's apartheid President P.W. Botha offered him freedom in

347

return for eschewing the armed struggle and political activity in January 1985, it caused no stir when Mandela turned him down. We had no sense that the apartheid regime was near its end; we thought it would take between twenty and fifty years for that to come about.

Ronald Reagan, like Margaret Thatcher, had no interest in pressuring the South African government. They were both sympathetic to the view that Mandela was a 'terrorist'; both articulated their policy towards changing the apartheid regime as one of 'engagement'; both regarded the government in Pretoria as a strategic Cold War asset. Indeed, in August 1985 I actually heard a speech in which Reagan seemed to have convinced himself that P.W. Botha was a 'reformist President' whose government had 'eliminated the segregation we once had in our own country'. Two days later I asked Larry Speakes whether Reagan really thought racial segregation had been eliminated in South Africa. Speakes replied graciously, 'Not totally, no.'

Reagan's sense of 'engagement' embraced more than a quiet tolerance of apartheid. His administration favoured a number of dubious leaders from the developing world. Jonas Savimbi, leader of the rebel National Union for the Total Independence of Angola (UNITA) movement, was one such. A charismatic but misguided tribalist, Savimbi was to ensure that the devastating civil war already gripping Angola would continue for the worst part of two decades. I was in the press huddle in the West Wing one morning when Savimbi was swept into the White House in full uniform, fêted like a President. It almost seemed he was the old man's favourite African son. Sitting in the Oval Office, Reagan welcomed Savimbi and talked of him 'winning a victory that electrifies the world and brings great sympathy and assistance from other nations to those struggling for freedom'. This was a sentiment that the President did not advance on behalf of Nelson Mandela or the twenty-five million black people suffering oppression at the hands of the apartheid regime. The neo-conservatives loved Savimbi, and it was American cash and arms that lay at the root of his costly and long-term survival. Angola, richer in oil and minerals than almost any other country in Africa, was an enticing prize. The neo-cons were banking on the egotistical tribalist Savimbi to deliver it to them. Savimbi failed, but was not finally to succumb, to an Angolan government army bullet, until February 2002.

It was in mid-March 1985 that we journalists who trekked in and out of the White House and the State Department began to pick up evidence that the CIA was stepping up its activities in Afghanistan. The neo-conservatives in the Reagan administration had long argued that the best way to hit the Soviet Union in practical terms was to suck it into a Vietnam-War-style quagmire. Where better to do it than in Afghanistan? In the early stages of the Soviet occupation, Reagan was too taken up with his mythic 'war against Communism' in Central America to do much about Afghanistan. Congress was persistently causing him difficulties over his Central American adventures, partly because they were within their own hemisphere and were easily comprehended. But with Afghanistan, about which hardly anyone on Capitol Hill knew much, Reagan found he was pushing at an open door.

I never got into a cab in Washington without asking the driver where he came from. One of the ways you could get an early warning about which of the world's troublespots was brewing up was by keeping tabs on the origins of the city's taxi drivers. In 1985, Afghan cabbies were in the ascendant. It was through one of them, a PhD student at George Washington University, that my attention was drawn to the American change of tack on Afghanistan.

Through contacts in the Pentagon and in several Senators' offices on Capitol Hill, I began to assemble a picture of what was happening in this far-flung battlefield that I had last rattled across in that cold winter of 1979. In the immediate aftermath of the Soviet invasion that I had witnessed on the road north of Herat, the CIA had stepped up its co-ordination of weapons supplies to the Afghan Mujahidin. Within a year, the crazy old bolt-action First World War Lee Enfield rifles had given way to Soviet-style weapons paid for by America and supplied by Egypt, China, Israel and Iran. The funding came partly from America's own back pocket and partly from the Saudis. The key link on the ground was a man named Mian Mohamed Afzal, who was the director of military operations in Pakistan. He visited the White House in December 1982 as a member of the team that escorted Pakistan's military dictator, General Zia ul-Haq.

By the middle of 1985, Soviet military targets in Afghanistan were being lined up on US satellites and the information fed straight to the increasingly high-tech equipment now in the hands of the Mujahidin. Congressional investigations later revealed that sixty-five thousand tons of US military supplies reached the guerrillas that year: anti-tank missiles, state-of-the-art shoulder-launched stinger missiles, long-range sniper rifles. At the same time swarms of CIA and Pentagon operatives were streaming into the Pakistani Inter-Services Intelligence (ISI) headquarters in Rawalpindi to help plan the Mujahidin strikes.

The Afghan genie was out of the bottle. At the time we had no idea how far things had gone. We were never told that the ISI had been enabled by CIA funding to trawl the world for radical Muslim volunteers to join the war against the Soviets. Nor did we know that the smiling figure of General Zia was funding hundreds of new *madrassahs* or religious schools along his Afghan border. And we certainly had never heard of Osama bin Laden, who even then was involved with the CIA/ISI operation, making his family millions of US dollars and bringing some four thousand Saudi volunteers into the war theatre that very year.

In this wondrous open society with its Freedom of Information Act, and our privileged access to the comings and goings in Washington, we knew nothing of the seeds of utter disorder that were being so professionally sown to try to destroy the Soviets and win the Cold War. The Russians were

351

certainly hated by the Afghans for their violent subjugation of the country, but of the alternative that was being brewed up by Washington in those days we had only the taxi drivers' words. Regrettably, I for one never believed a tenth of what they told me.

In the autumn of 1985 Democratic Senator William Proxmire sat behind his huge desk in his office on Capitol Hill. His obsession, besides the strange weaves to which he seemed to have subjected his whitening hair, was not Afghanistan, but America's massive arms build-up. Things were coming to a head with the building of the MX intercontinental ballistic missile. Whatever it was doing to world peace, it was most certainly putting a spurt into the already overheating American economy. Thirty-eight thousand new jobs had been created overnight, in manufacturing hubs stretching from Utah and California in the west to Florida and Massachusetts in the east. Subcontracts were flowing to eighteen other states. 'Who,' Senator Proxmire asked me as I sat down to interview him, 'is ever going to vote against this lot?'

It was Proxmire who that year uncovered the scandal of the inflated US defence bills: the $600 lavatory seat; the $3 spanner that turned up in a defence contract at $427; and the ten cent bolt that cost $1000 in another. The arms manufacturers had the Congress by the balls. In an age long before scandals like Enron undermined American confidence in corporate governance, we learned that the former managing director of

General Electric's electric boat division, Takis Veliotis, had been involved in massive overcharging for submarine contracts. The accountants eventually discovered that company plane flights to the chairman's farm, country club fees for directors, even kennelling charges for a director's dog, were all effectively being paid for by the Pentagon. As America stepped up its pressure on the Kremlin with the Star Wars, MX missile and Trident submarine programmes, Reagan's budget deficit ballooned while the pockets of his cronies in the arms manufacturing business bulged. Congress poked about with a lot of noise, but to little effect. The pressure on the Kremlin was beginning to show, and that was the only thing that mattered.

Gorbachev struck on 20 November 1985, the very day Reagan left Washington for yet another vacation on his ranch in California. With an American Congressional delegation already on the ground in Moscow, the Soviet leader went against all precedent, suddenly announcing a freeze of Russia's deployment of her arsenal of massive SS20 intercontinental missiles. Washington was stunned. Reagan was riding about in cowboy boots on his ranch as besuited Gorbachev was unilaterally responding to the demands of Europe's increasingly vociferous peace movement.

We were hurriedly summoned to the White House briefing room, where there were perhaps ten of us in attendance as the old boy's voice was piped in from California. The body language, indeed the actual lack of a Reagan body to respond to Gorbachev's unexpected move, was rapidly becoming seriously awkward. It was evident that after years of having it all his own way with a dying Kremlin leadership, the 'great communicator' had suffered a turning of the tables. The sight of Britain praising Russia's move only served to worsen matters.

The White House tried to tell us that it was a bluff, that the SS20 had anyway been replaced by a more dangerous SS24. But Gorbachev was very quickly becoming a challenge, and for the first time the Americans started to talk of the need for a coherent disarmament agenda. Already there was plenty of talk that Reagan and Gorbachev would have to meet. Life in Washington was beginning to take a fantastic turn.

NINE

Talking with the Enemy

The stench of tear gas, the nausea, and my streaming, scorched eyes came courtesy of an unconventional welcome in Spain. It was May 1985. I was midway through my stint as Washington correspondent for ITN, and had not been in Europe for two years. The mood was angry; Ronald Reagan was far more hated than I had imagined. We were on a rare foreign foray with him, timed to coincide with the fortieth anniversary of VE-Day. Ten years after the death of General Franco and the birth of Spanish democracy, President Reagan was being accommodated in the old dictator's palace.

Tens of thousands of demonstrators surged up and down Madrid's boulevards, the worst of the confrontations occurring right outside the American embassy. Cold War considerations had led America and other NATO allies to turn a blind eye to Franco's dictatorship in the interests of securing strategic air bases on Spanish soil. The people on the streets wanted them out. 'Why do they hate us so much?' one of Larry Speakes's aides asked me. That same question that would echo nearly two decades later, when George W. Bush was strutting his stuff from the White House to the streets of London. Both men were seen by huge swathes of ordinary Europeans as warmongers. Reagan's arms build-up was scaring the pants off more than just the Kremlin.

Reagan's visit to Spain came hard on the heels of a humiliating defeat in his own Congress, where he had failed to win approval for aid for his Contra war in Nicaragua. The Spanish, with their historic links to Central America, loathed everything Reagan had done in that region. The dashing Felipe Gonzales, Spain's young socialist Prime Minister, spared no effort in telling Reagan of their disgust to his face.

As he pounded around Europe, from Strasbourg to Lisbon, Reagan's rhetoric of hatred and distrust towards the Russians was winning him no more new friends than did his bile-strewn views on 'dangerous' revolutionary movements in his own hemisphere. To add insult to injury, while he was in Portugal the US Senate, which his own party controlled, had moved to refuse his defence budget increases. Things were coming to a head.

Back in Washington I and other correspondents were summoned by Anatoly Dobrynin to the Russian embassy. Dobrynin was a tall, distinguished figure whose professional life had spanned the entirety of the Cold War; he'd been Ambassador in Washington ever since the Cuban missile crisis. I had never been to the embassy before. It was a dim, underdecorated building that brooded on the sidewalk along from the glitzy Hilton Hotel, two blocks from my office.

'The General Secretary and the President are to meet in Geneva in November,' Dobrynin announced without emotion. I hared back to the office with the news.

There was no celebration down the street at the White House. The announcement was over-shadowed by yet another of a succession of hostage crises, this time, on 20 June 1985, in Lebanon. A TWA plane with over a hundred US citizens aboard had been hijacked by Amal Shiites from their stronghold in southern Lebanon, who were seeking the release of hundreds of their people held prisoner by the Israelis. All the ingredients of perennial Middle Eastern-generated American pain were present: Lebanon, Islamic fundamental-ism, Iranian and Syrian complicity, and Israeli intransigence. The image of the all-American Captain Testrake leaning out of his cockpit win-dow with a pistol at his head came to symbolise US impotence in the region. Reporting the crisis from the United States simply served to under-score to me how remote Americans felt from the chaos in the Middle East, and how oblivious they were to the way people in the region felt about them. While the pictures poured in from the edge of Beirut airport, our concentration was focused on the Oval Office in Washington.

Six years into the Reagan presidency, here were the same scenes, the same atmosphere, the same sense of crisis and helplessness that had be-devilled Jimmy Carter during the Iranian hostage crisis. Here were Caspar Weinberger from Defense, Bill Casey from the CIA, Robert 'Bud' McFarlane from National Security, hurrying in and out of the Oval Office, the President being rushed back from Camp David by helicopter. Late at night, a few blocks from the White House, I stood on the sidewalk in Foggy Bottom looking up at the State Department lights burning on the seventh floor. These were the offices of the hostage task force, where agents were listening in on all four of the frequencies that the hijackers were using from aboard the plane to negotiate with Beirut airport's control tower.

'We want those hostages out now, and without preconditions.' The words of Reagan's spokesman, Larry Speakes, were tough and uncompromising. But behind the scenes, Vice President George Bush was heading a team that was looking for any way out of the crisis. Through Ambassador Dobrynin, the Russians had been called in to pressure the Syrians to help. Bush's team even began to lean on the Israelis, who were the real power in southern Lebanon, and who held the prisoners whose release the hijackers were demanding. At one point Bush demanded that seven other assorted American hostages held in Lebanon be included in the negotiations. US warships moved to within sight of the Lebanese coast, and there was talk of US special forces already on the ground in Lebanon awaiting orders to strike.

Two days into the crisis I'd gone home to Macombe Street on a sweaty Washington summer's evening to host a rare dinner party for some of the people we owed meals to. There were our neighbours who had a Chagall in the hall and a sumptuous, beckoning pool into which they seldom invited us. Washington without a pool is

Washington without life, and we had no pool. My great New York lawyer friend Leonard Boudin and his wife Jean were in town, and the Middle East expert Milton Viorst and his feminist writer wife Judy had come over from their home two streets away. The social life in Washington generally was like that of a company town, save that in the case of Washington the company was government. If you were in a position that was linked to the company – lobbyist, lawyer, politician, journalist – you could be party to the social life. The only other route in was to be somebody's spouse. Madeleine was an independent woman suddenly required to be a spouse, and neither of us liked it. She went further: she hated it. Visa requirements denied her a job commensurate with her standing as a successful lawyer in Britain. Now pregnant with our second daughter, Freya, she had decided to give birth back in London. She would have much preferred me to go too, but ruthless ambition and an obsession with the story got the better of me, and I decided to stay. That night, however, with perhaps a dozen people on the deck overlooking the lawn beyond our impressive white-pillared veranda, Madeleine cooked a sensational meal, the wine flowed, and Leila gambolled around our feet.

At about midnight my American producer summoned me to hurry back to Foggy Bottom. I found the State Department ringed by police, fire engines and ambulances. At the height of the hostage stand-off, a man with a gun had broken into the seventh-floor hostage task force's offices, and had shot a woman who worked there, within a hundred feet of Secretary of State George Schultz's office. Marines were deployed for fear of terrorism, but as so often, the incident proved to be domestic. America's tangle with the gun had managed to infiltrate even this international crisis.

By now Ronald Reagan was beginning to look as feeble as Jimmy Carter on the issue of terrorism. The return of the flag-draped coffin of the one American to die in the crisis, a US Navy diver, Robert Stethem, who had been among the passengers on the hijacked plane, did the President no favours. His body was followed into Andrews Air Force Base by those of six US Marines killed in El Salvador. The media was depicting a weakening President. People in America were angry; it was precisely to stop this sort of thing that they had elected Reagan, not once but twice.

Finally, three weeks after it had begun, it was over. Although the White House denied it, there was a straight swap of hundreds of Shiite prisoners held by Israel for the American hostages held by Shiite Amal. The Red Cross, Israel and Syria had all played a part. The extra seven hostages demanded by Reagan were not freed, and the US had to make the humiliating announcement that it would not attack Lebanon in retaliation. It was a low point in the second Reagan administration and in America's sense of its own power, and a sharp reminder to the White House that none of the failings that had led to the Iranian hostage crisis six years earlier had been addressed. US policy in the region continued to be viewed through the prism of Israel's interests; there was no dialogue with Tehran; and there was no understanding of Arab aspirations in the region. It was in this hour that the fledgling hawks who would one day become so influential in George W. Bush's presidency learned their lessons. It was in this hour that the Pearls, Wolfowitzes, Rumsfelds and Negropontes determined their determination that never again would America be held to ransom. The neo-conservative axis, forged in South-East Asia during the Vietnam War and honed in Central America, would have to wait another decade and a half before it could deploy the 'pre-emptive' action that its members believed would prevent such international lawlessness.

On 13 June 1985, into this Washington maelstrom descended the charismatic Rajiv Gandhi, the former airline pilot suddenly transmogrified into Prime Minister of all India in the wake of his mother Indira's assassination seven months before. The lawn at the back of the White House had been transformed into something out of the last days of the Raj. Turbans, ceremonial swords and saris swirled in the summer heat as Gandhi and his Italian wife Sonia, who in 2004 would herself win but reject the premiership of India, were fêted with the full honours of a state visit. Rajiv was fresh from a similar visit to Russia where he'd picked up $1 billion of aid, or as Reagan's people liked to put it, 'Communist aid'.

Thus the visit was not without tension. India had proved a past master of playing one superpower off against the other ever since the demise of the British Empire. Its first post-colonial Prime Minister, Jawaharlal Nehru, had insisted on equal ties with Moscow and Washington. Nehru's daughter Indira Gandhi had followed suit. And now here was Rajiv, Nehru's grandson, Indira's son. Indian correspondents vied with each other to bounce the story home to their seven hundred million viewers on early satellite dishes spread out beyond the White House railings. Prominent amongst the assembled dignitaries sat Russia's Ambassador Dobrynin, in a straw hat.

As I was to discover later in his visit, Rajiv Gandhi was one of those rare people who made full eye contact with you as you spoke to him. This was perhaps a result of his having come to the media glare later in life, for he made none of the standard moves to avoid real engagement with the journalists who questioned him. I had interviewed him ahead of the visit, and had found him engaging and accessible. For all that he was later accused of involvement in shady arms deals, I confess I liked him.

Now the erstwhile pilot was grasping the hand of the former B-movie actor. Yet beyond the *bonhomie* that thinly disguised the mutual suspicion between them lay a new shared concern: nuclear Pakistan. India had already developed a nuclear bomb; now the Pakistanis had too. America had long refused to sell Pakistan the much desired F16 fighter bombers and other military equipment, but with the Russian invasion of Afghanistan, newly nuclear Pakistan had become Washington's friend and bulwark in the region.

We scrunched into the Oval Office for the 'press opportunity', our microphone poles hitting the chandeliers, the ludicrous woolly-dog-like microphone shields sticking out ahead of us. Beyond the heaving hack pack, Rajiv Gandhi sat across from Ronald Reagan, begging him to look more closely at Pakistan and its involvement in the war over the border in Afghanistan. Rajiv had a catalogue of evidence that the Pakistani secret service was effectively fighting the Mujahidin war against the Soviet army, and that that force might itself become impossible to contain. Little did we know how far-sighted he was to prove to be. For not only would Pakistan's radical Islamic war in Afghanistan come to haunt America, so too would Islamabad's preparedness to export Pakistan's nuclear know-how, not least to North Korea. We now know that the 'father of Pakistan's nuclear bomb', Abdul Qadeer Khan, was already selling the technology and capacity to the most unscrupulous purchasers anywhere.

It was easy in Washington to become detached from the realities of nuclear war. For some months I had been asking the Pentagon to allow me to visit America's hush-hush nuclear front line. Finally, in early May 1985, the permission to do so came through.

The blast doors of the Consolidated Space Command Center were claimed to be able to withstand a direct nuclear strike. They weighed a hundred tons apiece. We were the first foreign news team ever to penetrate these vast mountain vaults in Colorado Springs. Yet the purpose of this facility was not to guard against rogue nuclear states like Pakistan or North Korea: the secondary clock on the wall in the Commander's office was set to Moscow time. Outside in the Cheyenne Mountains, the only signs of the place's existence were the satellite-tracking dishes. Inside this James Bondian bunker, everything that moved in space was tracked. Today it was the jerry-built Russian orbiting space lab Mir with which the white-coated scientists were fixated.

This blue-lit command centre was the cornerstone of America's military effort in space. Already it was boasted that US satellites could read a car numberplate in Moscow's Red Square. Within a few hours it began to become obvious why we'd been allowed in. This was supposedly the control centre for the Star Wars project. Every military manoeuvre by Shuttle or satellite in space was ordained and controlled from here. The bunker for training military astronauts was here too. Yet the place had a musty sense of age and gradual disintegration about it; the red Bakelite hotline in the corner was not working.

Perhaps we were pawns in the American wish to frighten Moscow amid the torrid pace of the build-up to the great Strategic Defense Initiative, the Star Wars shield that would intercept every hostile missile Moscow could ever fire. What the Americans would have preferred us not to notice as we left the cavernous complex was the construction of an entirely new secret facility on the flat grasslands beneath the mountain range. Here we could see vast tunnel-borers and stone-carting trucks of a scale that rendered a human the size of a wheelnut. We passed at speed, our cameras confined to their cases, but not so fast that we could not see the triple rows of razor wire, the surveillance cameras and the armed watchposts that scanned every movement.

The next day we flew on to California, to the amazing sprawl of the Lawrence Livermore Laboratories. If the Cheyenne Mountain complex had been about the tracking and execution of military activity in space, Livermore was the father and mother of America's entire nuclear arsenal on earth. Sprawling across the floor of the desert, the epicentre of the place was an unending tunnel of a shed in which the 'nova laser', the world's most powerful, was housed. Here one beam was divided through tubes the length of football pitches, then refracted through angled mirrors and brought together again in a spherical chamber – all in one billionth of a second. We were told that this produced the power of a hundred Shuttle launches, or the equivalent of two hundred times that generated by all the power stations in the United States. The purpose of the beam was to zap incoming Russian intercontinental ballistic missiles. What was going on now was an experiment to introduce small nuclear explosions into the equation, to hurtle the laser beam yet faster. Amid the glug-glug of a fish pool in a neighbouring lab, other scientists were working on particle-beam accelerators, generating electrons to provide still stronger lasers. The next big step would be to reduce the size of the apparatus needed to generate such remorseless power.

While we were there the staff were still celebrating the achievement of unleashing a laser beam from Hawaii and bouncing it off the hull of a Shuttle deep in space. It was clear that no expense was being spared. 'It will be fifteen to twenty years before this stuff is usable in space,' the laser-programme director told me. The next phase of the SDI programme, 'Son of Star Wars', is coming to fruition just now; Washington's request to deploy facilities at Britain's Fylingdales came in 2003, exactly eighteen years after that Livermore prediction. The development of 'Star Wars' seemed to brook no interference from earthly developments like the disintegration and implosion of the Soviet Union.

Polyps in the colon had never made it into a lead story before, but now they did with a vengeance. Suddenly on 13 July 1985, in the midst of the instability in the Middle East, the massive build-up in the arms race and the tension between India and Pakistan, Ronald Reagan was carted off to hospital with serious trouble in his bottom. We all scurried out to the Walter Reid Naval Hospital on the outskirts of Washington. Here was ashen-faced First Lady Nancy Reagan, for a rare instant tearfully dropping her guard as surgeons talked more intimately of the President's lower bowel than any scientist had spoken of anything at Livermore. Bowel cancer was suddenly all the rage.

For three hours, George Bush Senior became President while Ronald Reagan went under the knife. For the following seven days the White

House moved to the seventy-four-year-old's hospital bed. Finally he came to the window to grace our cameras with a classic Hollywood thumbs up and a wide grin from the now restored Nancy. Reagan's return to the Oval Office coincided with a visit from the Chinese leader Li Xiannian. He was one of the last of the Chinese leadership who had been with Mao on the Long March fifty years before. To prove it, the old man still had a bullet lodged in his left leg from some skirmish on the route. Poor Reagan looked seriously old himself, his blue suit hanging off him like a sack. Thankfully China was one Communist country with which America had not picked a fight during the Reagan years, and the visit passed off without incident.

Reagan's hospital confinement also coincided with the continued awakening of America to the evil of apartheid. August 1985 saw the US Congress finally flexing its muscles against South Africa. Reagan's first post-operation Cabinet meeting was dominated by the question of what to do now, after four and a half years of 'constructive engagement' with Pretoria. Eventually he and the Congress argued furiously over some particularly mild sanctions, the first America had ever contemplated, which included a ban on dealings in Krugerrands on US territory. It was a start, but none of us saw it having much impact. With the matter still unresolved, Reagan flew off for his summer break.

We did the same, Madeleine, me and three-year-old Leila driving north in the company

Volvo for ten hours, up the New Jersey Turnpike and beyond, to Cape Cod. During our four-week vacation we would spend a little time on the island of Nantucket, and more in Wellfleet on the Cape itself. Nantucket was enjoying its last summer before the fateful decision to open its little airport to jets from New York's La Guardia Airport. Until now, ferries had been the only method of getting to the island, with just a few light aircraft for the very wealthy. As a result, time in this haven of myths and centre of the old whaling industry had stood still. There were perhaps a dozen taxis. The pace was slow, the cobbled streets of Nantucket town painful under the sandalled foot. Here we could cycle and swim and talk politics. But alas, the island was living on borrowed time. Soon the jets would come, the roads would fill with huge four-wheel-drive monsters, and the countryside would sprout vast white mansions. A place that had seemed in touch with original Pilgrim America died in the two or three years we became acquainted with it.

And so we defected permanently to Cape Cod. Ever since we ceased to live in Washington we have returned every summer to this white-clapperboard remnant of old New England. The town of Wellfleet is towards the northern tip of the lobster-claw-like spit of land that curves into the North Atlantic off Boston. It is here that we still muster in a summer rental with friends from both sides of the Atlantic. Amongst them that summer of 1985 were Leonard and Jean Boudin. I had first met Leonard in London, and later in Tehran where he was representing the Bank of

Iran in its battle to wrest its frozen assets from Jimmy Carter's control. He was in his late sixties, a seasoned civil liberties lawyer who had come to fame in the McCarthyite witch-hunting period. Charlie Chaplin, Paul Robeson and many others had been helped by him. In the Reagan period he took the White House to the Supreme Court to challenge the administration's right to restrict the freedom of Americans to travel to Cuba. He was a rare, ageless friend with whom I could talk about anything under the sun, yet he was also a slice of living American history. The issues concerning which he had attended the Supreme Court stretched from labour laws in the 1950s to racial and political discrimination in the 1980s. He had also legally represented just about every country on earth that did not have diplomatic relations with America – among them her then principal enemies Angola, Cuba and Iran.

Jean Boudin was an accomplished poet. Together they were a dynamic, beautiful pair, an out-of-the-ordinary liberal Jewish couple whose Sunday-brunch table in New York entertained an eclectic and fame-drenched array of literary, journalistic and diplomatic friends. They were the parents of Michael, a Federal Appeals Court judge in Boston, and Kathy, who was serving twenty years to life in Bedford Hills jail in upstate New York for terrorism. Kathy's notoriety added a *frisson* of danger to the brunch table. She had long been underground when I first visited the Boudins' home at St Luke's Place in the heart of Greenwich Village. She was one of the 'Weather-men', a group of radical activists three of whom blew themselves up in a townhouse nearby while trying to make a bomb in March 1970. Kathy had only just survived, and had disappeared to elude the FBI for another decade. She'd finally been rounded up in 1981 after the disastrous attempted robbery of a security van. Given that the Weathermen were supposed to be fighting for equal rights for black people, it was ironic that the victims of their crazy escapade were a black policeman and security guard who died in the shootout. Kathy was driving the getaway car. In his remaining years Leonard had fought with every fibre of his being to get her sentence reduced, but he died in 1990 still grievously perplexed by the political extremism that had driven his daughter, and with her still in prison.

Throughout my time in America I seized every possible moment to visit the Boudins and stay a few nights. I became a kind of son to them, as my friend Helena Kennedy became a kind of transatlantic daughter. It was through the Boudins that I learned most about how the USA really worked. Through Leonard I met Senators, Congressmen and Supreme Court Justices. His exceptional personality and legal skills meant that the arrest of his daughter for so heinous a crime cost him few of his high-placed friends.

To some extent the Boudins, and Jean's remarkable brother-in-law, the great campaigning Washington journalist I.F. Stone, were the thread that kept my love affair with America alive. Despite El Salvador, Nicaragua, Grenada, Chile and Iran, there was a purity of purpose in what the 'Founding Fathers' had set out to build that I continued to find deeply attractive. I was indeed lucky to know Izzy Stone and his wife Esther, who was Jean Boudin's sister. Many were the evenings when we would meet them in the grim Chinese restaurant that was Izzy's favourite near their home close to Connecticut Avenue. Since 1953 his political journal *I.F. Stone's Weekly* had used the government's own sources against it to searing effect. Izzy had a massive intellect, and I felt very small in his presence. When I knew him, in his seventies, he was teaching himself classical Greek in order to write a new bio-graphical assessment of Socrates. He was short, wiry and slightly shrivelled, with thick-lensed wire-framed glasses, and was still as sharp as a tack. He was the finest and most passionate investigative reporter I ever met, and was a constant and generous source of brilliant stories, ideas and insights. The most powerful voice of the Vietnam era, he brought a perspective to bear that remains potent even now, more than a decade after his death.

Ronald Reagan returned from his 1985 summer holiday to a welcoming party of staff and Ambassadors on the White House lawn. Amongst them was the distinctive white-robed figure of the Saudi Ambassador, Prince Bandar. America's relationship with her principal oil supplier was complex, and was rendered the more so by her relationship with Israel. Prince Bandar held court in the vast Saudi ambassadorial pile on New Hampshire Avenue, a stone's throw from the White House. Still in his mid-thirties, Bandar was the Prince of Washington, and of all he surveyed. Washington gulped from his Saudi trough; the excesses of his hospitality were legendary. I did not see him often – we non-American hacks were riff-raff in his book. But he had a soft spot for England, having been educated at the Royal Air Force college at Cranwell, and though he speaks pure American, there's a part of him that still answers to the English public school. Most of my time in Washington, Bandar was to be found in the Pentagon or on Capitol Hill trying to do defence deals. He it was who allegedly fixed up illicit Saudi funding for Reagan's Contra war; he it was who became the pivot in the vast Saudi element to the war in Afghanistan against the Soviets. And it was out of this relationship that Osama bin Laden eventually sprang, outraged at the stationing of 'infidel' American airmen on Saudi soil.

What Bandar could not secure, in the face of the Israeli lobby in Washington, was a massive contract that would transform the entire military profile of the Kingdom. Reagan encouraged him to go to the British, and Mrs Thatcher was able to pull off one of the largest arms deals of all time, although it was shrouded in secrecy. Even America's leaky top table would not disclose the true value of what became known as the Al Yam-ama defence deal. Included in it were seventy-two Tornado fighter aircraft, endless airbase infrastructure, and much more; the eventual value was somewhere between $30 and $50 billion. It was described to me subsequently by a top Foreign Office mandarin as the most corrupt

British contract in modern history.

A few months earlier, in July 1985, unknown to us, Bandar had jetted off to Austria, interrupting a rare Thatcher holiday in Salzburg to initial the deal. When it came to secrecy about the contract and the fabulous backhanders that flowed from it, the Saudis met their match in Britain. No one was ever prosecuted, but numerous well-placed people and their relatives profited from assorted back-pocketry. All we could be sure of in Washington at the time was that there was an odour, some of it no doubt fuelled by envy, but most of it coming from the chat amongst politicians and officials about who had benefited from the usual Saudi practices. Endless pro-Israeli Congressmen would try to point us this way or that, but we were never able to identify the actual value of the deal, or of the associated bribes, or the proximity of the recipients to key British politicians in power at the time.

1985, six years into the Soviet occupation, marked the approach of the high-water mark of America's orchestration of the war in Afghanistan. As with the Contra war, open, accessible political America was somehow able to spend many millions of dollars on causes its electorate knew nothing of, and which stood every chance of rebounding horribly against it. We knew the CIA was the lead agency in Afghanistan, but the fact that in this period some thirty-five thousand Muslim radicals from forty-three countries across the Islamic world were funded, trained and armed by Saudi and US agencies was far from well

373

known. In all, it is estimated by UN officials that a hundred thousand foreign Muslim fighters were exposed to warfare in Afghanistan between 1982 and the war's end in 1992. While Washington may have been comfortable with the Afghan *jihad* against Russia, there was no guarantee the tables would not turn, and the same fanatical force be visited upon the United States. Those of us who had lived through the Iranian revolution knew full well what pent-up hatred and resentment there was for the West. Not many of us would have advocated the idea of going out to recruit those who felt that hatred, and even pay them to experience war against the infidel.

In any case, the Russians were feeling the heat. Eduard Shevardnadze made his maiden UN appearance as Soviet Foreign Minister in New York in late September 1985. Shevardnadze's shock of white hair and open, professorial count-enance were in stark contrast to the gloomy, dark old features of Andrei Gromyko, his long-serving predecessor. There was already no doubting that Shevardnadze and Gorbachev were as one in wanting to bring about a change in the super-power relationship.

To be inside the UN cordon off Second Avenue is to be in a little piece of America that is forever United Nations territory. I interviewed 'Shev' as we used to call him, on his second day in New York. He was hanging around waiting for us, and I dutifully took my place behind the *Wall Street Journal* and ahead of CBS Television. Despite the fact that we were working through an interpreter,

Shevardnadze's language, about peace and force reduction, was quite different from anything that had gone before.

The backdrop to the UN deliberations was an unprecedented spate of top-level defections from Moscow, including the alleged number five in the KGB, Vitaly Yurchenko, and the opening of the trial of John Walker, a low-level, toupéed Soviet asset in the CIA who'd only spied for the money. There had also been yet another test firing of an MX missile as part of the orchestrated build-up to the StarWars deployment. Couple all that with the burgeoning Afghan disaster, and it must have been no fun being either Shevardnadze or Gorbachev a few months into a new Soviet administration. For them, the Geneva Summit planned for November 1985 could not come soon enough.

The Americans and their NATO partners devoted immense resources to trying to win the Cold War, yet in all my reporting of this period I never encountered a single official who could map out what would happen if the West should ever win it. Indeed, the only speculation was about what would happen if they lost the Cold War – a possibility never seriously entertained since the Cuban missile crisis more than twenty years before.

At the same time the balletic build-up to Geneva continued apace. It was only slowed slightly by the departure of the aforementioned Vitaly Yurchenko through the lavatory window of a celebrated Georgetown restaurant. Yurchenko had allegedly been in the hands of the CIA for three months, and had been 'singing like a bird'.

The news of his 're-defection' sent us all bolting for the new Soviet embassy up the hill towards National Cathedral. The Russians had done their stuff, got their man, and were now parading him in prime news time at one of the most bizarre news conferences I've ever attended. These guys were learning something at last. Here was the most senior Russian to defect in fifty years, suddenly back in Russian hands. But there was something odd about it all. I became particularly intrigued when a Russian journalist sitting next to me asked Yurchenko a provocative question in English about his motives.

Yurchenko answered emotionally, also in English, ending by saying that the CIA had offered him $1 million to stay in the West. It was hard to make head or tail of his story, save that he claimed he'd been kidnapped while visiting the Vatican museum in Rome, and had been in a Virginia safe house until he gave his minder the slip in the Georgetown restaurant.

The next day I was in my office when the Russian news agency TASS reported that Yurchenko had landed safely in Moscow. But that wasn't the wire story that most intrigued me. Another, datelined Toronto, reported that a Russian woman had plunged to her death from the twenty-seventh floor of a city apartment block. It seems that Svetlana Dedkova, married to a Russian working in the Soviet trade mission there, had been Yurchenko's lover. The CIA immediately leaked the fact that Yurchenko had pleaded to be allowed to call her from his safe house the previous Tuesday. In some way their love pact had fallen apart. He 'de-defected', and she committed suicide. It was a distraction from the Summit build-up, and a sad everyday story of spying folk. I found myself thinking, 'Thank goodness I turned Stilbury down all those years ago at MI6.'

There was one more diversion, of an altogether non East–West nature. With six days to go before everyone headed for Geneva, Washington was subjected to a visit from the Prince and Princess of Wales. Charles and Diana, still looking like a royal couple, took the staid old capital by storm. They were there to open a vast exhibition at the National Gallery called 'Treasure Houses of Britain'. The combination of it and them seized every front page, and fulfilled every imaginable American-held stereotype of Britain. Prince, Princess, palaces, pomp and absurdity. Into this mix stepped a President who was himself occasionally prone to fantasy, and his wife Nancy; the tableau was complete. Reagan was so often accused of muddling Hollywood fiction with fact that this time he must have been completely confused as the two merged seamlessly together, requiring neither effort nor input from himself. The two most famous couples in the world triggered a thousand exclusive camera shutters, and Reagan must have gone to bed wondering which B movie he'd just starred in.

The start of the most important journey in the world on 16 November 1985 was mundane. My crew and I sat at Andrews Air Force Base outside Washington in the press's chartered Pan Am Jumbo, awaiting the arrival of the Reagans'

helicopter from the White House. The circumstances were far less dramatic than the moment.
The presidential couple made the transfer to the
vast and gleaming Air Force One, and we were
away down the runway. As I reported that night,
'No American President before him has spent so
much on the arms race; no President before him
has attended a Summit in a position of such
military strength; and few American Presidents
have expressed such forcible dislike for the Soviet
systems.' The excitement amongst Washington's
po-faced press corps was palpable, as was the
clash of egos aboard the press plane. The big
beasts of the network on-screen jungle, ABC's
Sam Donaldson, CBS's Bill Plant and NBC's
Tom Brokaw, were already vying for air suprem-
acy. Indeed Sam Donaldson was so big a beast
that *Playboy* magazine sent Ron Reagan, the
President's ballet-dancing son, to follow him to
Geneva and write about it.

Halfway through the flight a White House
official came to the back of the plane to give us a
briefing. 'Reagan will be Reagan,' he said when
we pressed him over the agenda. It's hard now to
describe how bad relations between the superpowers had become. There was a real sense of
worldwide anxiety, now balanced by huge expectations of the US President's forthcoming
meeting with a man who had only been the
Russian leader for half a year.

Upon landing in Geneva we were herded into
the Intercontinental Hotel, close to the UN
compound on the airport side of the city. Reagan
was spirited off by motorcade to a princely stone

house on the edge of Lake Geneva that belonged to some branch of the Aga Khan's family. There now set in a total news blackout, dictated it seems by the Americans; the entire Summit was going to be fiercely controlled, with extremely limited access.

By sheer good fortune, my name was among those drawn for the very first 'pool' of twenty reporters who were to be allowed to witness the first exchange on behalf of the several thousand media folk holed up at the Intercontinental. Gorbachev's convoy of curtained Zils snaked into Geneva from the airport under cover of darkness later that night. I was standing on a cold corner on the lakeside street beneath the Beau Rivage hotel. It was impossible to tell which of the shiny, low, box-like black limousines he was in. There was a spooky tension in the air. The two superpower bosses were in town, but they were a city's breadth apart, and would not meet until ten the next morning.

19 November 1985 dawned damp and grey, the lake barely visible. The trucks that were to take us into the hallowed presences called at 8 a.m. The loud Sam Donaldson was the louder for the greyness and tension of the day. To hear him, you would think it was just another ordinary day. For the rest of us, we were conscious that we were about to set eyes upon the leader of the 'Evil Empire', see the breaking of the ice of six and a half years of non-superpower communication, and discover whether the West really could 'do business' with Mikhail Gorbachev.

We were swept between tall hedges and along

the curved drive to Reagan's château, and held beyond the gravel at the foot of the steps where the first encounter between the two leaders would take place. The Summit planners had decided who hosted whom first not on the basis of whose nuclear throw weight was heaviest, but on the simpler basis of which superpower's leader had done it last, six and a half years earlier. Reagan's Chief of Staff, Donald T. Regan, told us later that the President had spent the final hours before this first meeting with Gorbachev worrying not about the hordes of nuclear warheads ranged against him, but about whether or not he should wear his overcoat for it.

Spot on ten o'clock, the Zils slid along the gravel, looking like a Brooklyn funeral cortège. They halted at the foot of the stone steps that descended from the front door of the château. Gorbachev, coated, scarfed, hatted, bounded out energetically. Reagan, hatless, coatless, and noticeably twenty years older than the Russian, came uncertainly down the steps; I remember fearing he might trip. The American President looked vulnerable in the cold as they shook hands and lingered for the cameras. We were stunned by how animated the Russian was in contrast to the old actor's rather stiff performance.

Within minutes we were all inside the château. In this overdressed rococo palace the two men were wrapped in huge matching chintzy armchairs facing each other. Gorbachev was smaller, more compact than his pictures had suggested. The wine stain on his forehead was a positively handsome blemish. His eyes were bright, and seemed to engage with each of us. He looked more interested in us than in the old boy sitting rather too bolt-upright in the chair opposite him. I was no more than ten feet from Gorbachev, maybe fifteen from Reagan, and found myself thinking, 'Someone's actually paying me to be here.' I'd have given my eye teeth, and so would any other journalist. The small salon was an absolute scrum, the press's behaviour, as ever, way below the level the historic moment demanded – but we needed our pictures and our answers.

'How does it feel?' A ludicrous question, given that the two men had met for the first time only a few minutes earlier. 'How's it going?' fared no better. Needless to say, Sam Donaldson stole the show with, 'Mr General Secretary, Andrei Gromyko says of you, you have a nice smile, but iron teeth.'

Gorbachev replied, quick as a flash, 'It hasn't been confirmed, but as of now, I'm still using my own teeth.' It was hugely effective, absurd, irrelevant and funny, despite being slowed by having to travel through his interpreter.

At the end of that first day nothing of substance had been agreed, but the pictures, and the impact of the world's greatest enemies being together, were spellbinding. By common consent Gorbachev had seized round one of the encounter, running rings around the 'great communicator'.

In many ways that day characterised the entire Summit. Little actually happened, although that would have been hard to admit to our viewers and readers around the world. What did happen was that the two leaders had met and smiled, and agreed that an arms control process should be accelerated and that they should meet again. Equally important, all the human processes of encounter had now rendered it harder for Reagan and his cohorts to go on 'Evil Empiring' their enemy. The worm had turned, but we hadn't a clue by how much. What we were sure of was that Gorbachev was already proving a highly unusual and beguiling Soviet leader. Viewed from Lake Geneva, it seemed that the Soviet Union was here to stay, but possibly with a more humane face and a cleaned-up act.

When we stopped off in Brussels, where Reagan was to brief NATO on the Summit, we found him being hailed as some kind of conquering hero. This was even more evident when we touched down back home in Washington, and in an unprecedented move he took his presidential helicopter right onto the lawn in front of the rotunda on Capitol Hill. The politicians surged towards him, simply wanting to touch the hand that had shaken Gorbachev's. It was a surreal moment to be amongst these legislators who for so long had voted so much money towards the military annihilation of the USSR, and who now so urgently wanted to share in the international euphoria that had greeted the outbreak of peace.

Even as the hands were stretching out to the President, dastardly activities were still going on at the White House. Reagan's National Security Adviser, Bud McFarlane, was already back in his office in the West Wing, putting the finishing touches to a scarcely believable plot to sell Hawk missiles to Iran via Israel, in return for the release of Western hostages held in Lebanon. The plan went hopelessly wrong, not least because they turned out to be the wrong sort of Hawk missile, and the crates in which they were delivered were, to the fury of the Iranians, labelled in Hebrew. But the affair was a tiny insight into the lengths America was prepared to go to to supply both sides in the continuing Iran–Iraq war. Until now we had thought that the US was only discreetly arming Saddam; now it seemed the Ayatollahs were getting armaments too. McFarlane resigned a few days later, less for trying to do the deal than for letting people know about it, and about too much else besides. In his departure we hacks lost one of our best sources in the White House.

That Christmas of 1985, as we reflected on the great superpower breakthrough, someone detonated a nuclear bomb in the sea off South Africa. To be more precise, someone had done it on 22 September, but no one had believed the trusty old Vela satellite that for fifteen years had tracked some forty-one nuclear tests by assorted parties across the world. Exhaustive cross checking by the CIA had revealed that Israel and South Africa had detonated this particular device together. Had it not been for the diligence of a black pressure group and one black Congressman on Capitol Hill, we would never have learned that the nuclear club had just been expanded to include its first member from below the equator. Not for the first time, and not for the last, America's blind eye was dangerously turned to

Israel's transgression. At the very moment that the superpowers looked like taming the most threatening arms race of all, new players were coming onto the block. It appeared that the Israelis had introduced another.

My mother, with my brothers and their partners, came for Christmas. Far from being the excluded third party of childhood in the family, I was suddenly the kingpin, and I made the most of it. It was my last encounter with my mother before she started her descent into Alzheimer's. No one knows how to do Christmas like the Americans do Christmas. God provides the weather, frequently white and crisp and cold. Mammon provides the shops and malls heaving with every seasonal fantasy you could conjure. Georgetown DC and Alexandria, Virginia, became fairylit visions of every Christmas past.

Madeleine, now back in London, was too pregnant to fly. It was strange to be back in the pre-adult bosom of my family. With nine months to go on my contract in Washington, my office had become my family, principal amongst them my video editor, Dave Sampi. We made an incongruous pair, the black sharecropper's son from Louisiana and the son of the very white Bishop of Whitby.

On 28 January 1986, Dave and I were standing in front of the racks that carried the transmission feeds into and out of our Washington studio. We were watching the monitor at head height. It was around noon American time, 5 p.m. London time. Live pictures were streaming in from four of five cameras trained on the Space Shuttle

Challenger, which was about to launch at Cape Canaveral. This was, like any other launch, the victim of small technical delays. It was only distinguished by its crew, which included a young woman who had come to be regarded as the first 'ordinary American' ever to be given the chance to travel into space. Christa McAuliffe, the mother of two children aged six and nine, had been chosen from eleven thousand applicants to be the first teacher in space. Her parents were given pride of place at the launch complex, the TV cameras occasionally cutting to them as the pre-launch smoke and steam belched from beneath the *Challenger*.

Moments after lift-off, something possessed me to say to Dave, 'I have a bad feeling about this. I think it's going to crash.' A few seconds later the white vapour trail in the sky divided, one strand leaping forward, one curling back. 'We have a problem, Houston...' someone intoned across the ether, and then, after an age, the same voice concluded with the word 'malfunction'.

The effect on America was devastating – so public a disaster whilst reaching for that final frontier. Not for nothing, it seemed, was the shuttle christened *Challenger*. The country was convulsed with grief; in those pre 9/11 days the Shuttle disaster, in which the entire crew of seven died, somehow touched every American, appealing in a raw and unexpected way to the very core of who they were. Those white separating plumes were broadcast again and again. And as with the waving hands high in the World Trade Center beseeching for rescue, here were little parachutes of hope we could glimpse on our screens – but they were no ejection capsule, merely paramedics being air-dropped into the rescue zone off Florida. In the great lexicon of television news moments, beginning perhaps with Kennedy's assassination, traversing later through the death of Princess Diana and 9/11, the Shuttle disaster was another image that triggered a kind of international hysteria.

It was now that we learned not only what role the thirst for the ultimate played in American life, but the extraordinary capacity of the old B-movie star of a President to connect with it. A few days after the crash I was dispatched to the coffinless memorial service at the Johnson Space Center in Houston. A makeshift arena had been constructed on the lawn. The wives of the six dead astronauts, and the husband of the seventh, were gathered in the front row.

Christa McAuliffe's parents preferred to stay home in New Hampshire. It was their loss that had so personalised this American tragedy.

Reagan had somehow understood his role, the need to coax the national grief into some final moment of outpouring. When he arrived he went to each astronaut's spouse in turn, stopped, and held each head close to his chest. The camera caught the line of five waiting widows, their heads up, their eyes welling, lips pursed, and the band played on. It might have degenerated into Coca-Cola kitsch, but somehow it did not. In that moment my own harboured resentment of Reagan's culpability in tearing so many families apart in Central America gave way to a reluctant admiration that he could carry this off.

Ideological, passionately anti-Communist, Reagan demonstrated there in Houston a sensitivity that is seldom possessed by ideologues on the right. Indeed, Reagan's ideology was less demonstrated from within himself than by the band of brothers he chose to gather about him – Perle, Rumsfeld, Cheney, Poindexter. We weren't to know it, but we would meet them again in another time, and with a less sensitive, less dextrous, less charming, but no less destructive President.

You could not be a correspondent in Washington in the mid-1980s and not be conscious of the name Nathan Sharansky. Locked up in a Soviet jail for nine years, he was the standard-bearer for Russia's Jewish refuseniks. His wife Avital, who had fled Russia to lobby on his behalf, was a familiar figure on Capitol Hill. Sharansky had been translator for the equally beleaguered Andrei Sakharov, the father of the Russian atom bomb-turned refusenik, then languishing in internal Soviet exile. On 11 February 1986, with no warning, Sharansky was hauled out of his Soviet cell and bundled onto a flight to Israel. In that moment we knew that Mikhail Gorbachev had proved a man of his word. If there were to be one human totem to Gorbachev's trustworthiness, it would be Sharansky – the man who because of his outspoken criticism of the Kremlin it would be hardest for any Russian leader to free; yet for precisely the same reason, the man American legislators most needed to be freed.

Sharansky was not alone; twenty-five other refuseniks were allowed out with him. Gorbachev had taken a symbolic step towards confidence-building that promised well for missile reductions to come.

The following month one of the greatest living pianists, Vladimir Horowitz, was permitted to return to the land of his birth for the first time in decades. Just before he took off for Moscow, I visited him in his Manhattan apartment close to Central Park. The traffic was backed up below as a massive mobile crane dangled Horowitz's treasured grand piano, having heaved it from his open window on the tenth floor. Fortunately I was to find he had another. I rang the bell, and the door was answered by the formidable Mrs Horowitz. She was very much Horowitz's manager, in every sense of the word – she managed him from dawn to dusk. Although eighty-three, he had an amazingly childlike simplicity about him. She shouted at him as if he were a naughty boy. 'Vladimir,' she called from the kitchen in her strong Slavic tones, 'are you going to play for Mr Snow?' This was a rather important question, as unless he played we'd never get a report on the air, and his publicist had warned he might well not. But Vladimir was being a good boy, despite the loss of his second-best grand through the still-open bedroom window.

I did a short interview, with him giving his answers in his guttural tones, and then he played Paderewski wondrously expressively, his fingers moving up and down the keyboard with incredible agility. At the climax he paused, played the final chord, paused again, and stuck his tongue out at the camera. It stole the show on that night's News at Ten.

The runway was familiar, but I had never actually landed on it. Now, on 20 February 1986, I was touching down with Ronald Reagan on the very Cuban-built airstrip whose construction he had used as a pretext for his invasion of Grenada. The Caribbean island was at its most seductive, verdant, slow and sunny. Reagan had chosen to visit one of the few small corners of his foreign policy where his actions had matched his rhetoric. Not everyone in Grenada was particularly thrilled about their 'liberation', and a small protest had gathered in downtown St George's. But for the rest, with the import, courtesy of the US Air Force, of a number of other toadying Caribbean leaders, the moment was a great celebration two and a half years after the invasion.

In truth many of us regarded Reagan as a shambling failure overseas. The Contra war in Nicaragua was proving both controversial and unsuccessful. His policies were in serious trouble from Libya to the Philippines. And on the bigger stage, the arms control talks with the Soviets were stalled in Geneva. Worse, a whole slew of Russian diplomats at the UN were expelled as spies. Throughout the early months of 1986 we were writing Reagan off as a misguided and ill-informed failure in foreign policy.

There were some chinks of light though. As I witnessed the Irish Premier Garret Fitzgerald's welcome in the West Wing, he seemed almost too charming, too intellectual, to have survived any country's political system, let alone Ireland's. Yet here he was, with the ink on Mrs Thatcher's signature on the very first Anglo–Irish Accord still drying in his pocket. It was hard for us, standing there in the White House, to imagine the fiercely Unionist Protestant Conservative Margaret Thatcher as the mother of a deal which, for the first time since 1916, recognised the Irish Republic's right to a say, however small, in the governance of Northern Ireland. That it was so was owed in part to Fitzgerald's guile, and in part to Reagan's American money – $50 million over the next five years to cement the deal.

Reagan was so old that it was felt he should be sent by the long, slow route to Japan for the impending G7 Summit of Industrialised Nations. It would therefore take us all of five days to get to Tokyo with him. On 30 April we White House correspondents and our crews mustered at Andrews Air Force Base for the long trek west.

Sadly, this was to prove one of my last assignments as ITN's Washington correspondent. I had done three years in America. Madeleine had already gone home to have our second baby, and had restarted her legal career. Freya was born a few months before the end of my tenure, and though I badly wanted to stay in America, there was no choice but to return to London. At the time I could imagine living and working in the United States for the rest of my life. Fortunately my family spared me that fantasy, but as I sat on the tarmac at Andrews, waiting for Reagan, I pondered how much I was going to miss being in the eye of the storm – because that is always where Reagan was.

Our journey to Japan was to be an extraordinary stopping odyssey. We headed first for California, for Reagan to do an appalling glitzy fundraiser for the Republican Party. We steamed around Los Angeles in a vast phalanx of presidential limousines, buses and police motorcycle outriders. Everywhere we went the freeways jammed, the helicopters hovered and people came out with their flags. The secret service was eternally fearful of a domestic assassin. One night in LA and we were back at the airport, lifting off towards Hawaii.

Honolulu was one of those rare stops where there was no news, merely the presidential death watch. News organisations lived in fear of letting the President travel anywhere unaccompanied. Then, as now, the terrorist threat was ever-present. The press hotel gazed temptingly over the beach, and the President's safety was soon forgotten as we bounded about in the heavy surf. Next we were off to the utter tropical safety of Bali, which at that time was perceived to be about as far from the threat of international terrorism as it was possible to fly. Today, too painfully, we have learned a different story. On the first of our three mornings in Bali, the seventy-five-year-old Reagan tipped out onto the empty beach below my hotel window in his swimming trunks to play ball with his security detail. He appeared in remarkably good shape. We left Bali with Reagan telling us at the airport that he was going to use the Tokyo Summit to 'find common ground with the allies for an attack on terrorism'. *Plus ça change!*

We lifted out of Indonesian airspace in shimmering heat, and landed in darkness at Tokyo. The scale of the security on the ground was exceptional, even by presidential standards. In the centre of the city, police and secret servicemen ran alongside Reagan's car, and a mile-wide *cordon sanitaire* had been thrown around his hotel. I'd never been to Japan before, and first impressions were hugely disorienting. That night I went out into the garish fluorescent-lit streets around the hotel. There wasn't a word anywhere in English, and when it came to the metro, it was utterly confusing. The whole experience was both mysterious and beguiling. Somehow I made it back to the hotel and relaxed with a massage which seemed to involve someone walking about on my back.

The Summit took place inside the armed camp that the city centre had become. All the world's key leaders and their teams were compressed into this densely urban square mile. Japan faded into the distance. What suddenly loomed very large was Chernobyl. Some time on the opening day of the Summit, in the Soviet nuclear power station eighty miles north of Kiev, reactor number four blew its stack. News of the devastating explosion and the ensuing atomic cloud that swept out over north-western Europe engulfed the media village. Whatever the diplomatic warming between the superpowers, Chernobyl seemed to testify to the physical decay and disintegration of Soviet industrial infrastructure. The Summit agenda was hurriedly reordered to address the disaster and the nuclear fallout. I was worried that Madeleine and the girls might be affected, but when I called them in London they sounded as remote from it all as I felt in Tokyo.

In amongst the talk of nuclear fallout and Middle East-based terrorism was the political love fest that continued between Ronnie and Maggie. So smitten was Ronald Reagan that he compared the relationship to Roosevelt's friendship with Churchill. How Mrs Thatcher purred; and not for the first time or the last, a US President waxed lyrical about the most important friendship in the world – we would hear it again from George W. Bush of Tony Blair in the aftermath of the war on Iraq.

We left Japan with all seven leaders pleading with Mikhail Gorbachev for more information about the Chernobyl disaster. Reagan flew over the North Pole, touching down in Alaska for refuelling before crossing continental America and landing back at Andrews Air Force Base. The dialogue with Moscow had become frenzied. The US had arrested a top KGB man named Zakharov; the Russians had responded by lifting an American journalist in Moscow called Nicholas Daniloff. Reagan had the Soviet Foreign Minister Eduard Shevardnadze into the Oval Office to tell him there would be no swap, and no more talking until the Russians yielded up Daniloff. And that's where matters stood as I packed up the house in Washington in time for one more family summer in Cape Cod before we returned to London.

Mercifully denied the domestic political job at ITN by my support for striking miners' families the year before, I took up my position as ITN's diplomatic editor. It would mean continuing to cover foreign affairs, and continuing to travel. I had never thought of myself as particularly diplomatic, but it was a brilliant moment to land the job. I was thrown straight into the maelstrom that East–West relations had become. Within a few weeks of my starting, on 30 September 1986, the loudly rejected Daniloff swap went ahead, and Reagan announced that there would be another Summit with Gorbachev in less than a fortnight's time. This time it was destination Iceland.

TEN

The Whole Lot Comes Down

The Hofdi House in Reykjavik looked as if it might have fallen from an early pilgrim vessel off Cape Cod. It was of white clapboard and looked far too small to host a tea party, far less a super-power Summit. And that perhaps was its beauty.

Reagan flew in to Iceland a day early, having had only a few days to prepare for the Summit. He needed 'downtime', both to adjust to the four-hour time difference and to read his brief. So we all snouted about outside the Hofdi House. It was surprisingly accessible, despite standing alone on the city's waterfront. It didn't take long to assess the place, and I stole the chance to run up to the geysers on the edge of town and bask in the steamy absurdity of sitting in the boiling water, gazing across the bay at the chilly arena for our coming days.

Beyond the simplicity of two men meeting on the wooden steps of the Hofdi House on the brittle, cold morning of Saturday, 11 October 1986 – with the world's destiny in their hands – there was nothing particularly auspicious about the day. The first moments of this Reagan–Gorbachev Summit featured fewer limousines, fewer flashing blue lights, fewer guns, than their meeting in Geneva had. It was a day of modest expectations and occasional comings and goings of suited officials through the white wooden doors at the top of the steps.

The second and final day of the meeting was altogether different. We stood in the arctic wind on flatbed trucks two hundred yards from the front door of the Hofdi House. Human rights, intermediate nuclear weapons, intercontinental ballistic weapons – we knew what they were talking about, and we knew they would not be talking at all if there wasn't a chance of at least a minor breakthrough.

It was all supposed to end at noon. But noon came and went, and they didn't. It was long after two o'clock in the afternoon when a rather haggard Reagan appeared, and walked straight to his limo without comment; Gorbachev followed soon after. Reagan's hard-line adviser, Assistant Secretary of Defense for International Security Policy Richard Perle, came over and told us the two men would meet again after three o'clock, and would then go home. They did indeed meet again after three, but they didn't go home. Something was going on, and the rumours were flying that whatever it was, it was very big indeed.

Our spies at Iceland's Keflavik air base told us that Air Force One had been readied once, and was being fired up a second time for take-off. But the white wooden doors of the Hofdi House stayed unyieldingly shut as darkness fell; the excitement was palpable. Seven hours after their planned departure time, both Reagan and Gorbachev came out of the house looking like death. They parted perfunctorily, and drove off in different directions. The Summit had collapsed in failure, at least that's what it looked and sounded like. And in a sense it had; there was nothing immediate to show for it.

In order to get access to the presidential camp I had flown to Iceland via Washington, and I was now returning on the presidential press plane to the US capital to try to find out more. What I learned was that Gorbachev and Reagan, in their eleven hours of face-to-face talking, had been unbelievably candid with one another, and that each had raised the possibility of a world without nuclear weapons. I learned too that Reagan, while agreeing a ten-year moratorium on setting up his Star Wars system, had rejected Gorbachev's request that he restrict tests to inside the laboratory. And Gorbachev had refused to detach other arms issues from that of the Star Wars programme.

Back at the White House, Reagan now started referring to SDI as a 'peace shield', and responsibility for the killing off of the longed-for Washington Summit was laid squarely at Gorbachev's door. Yet as I looked around the White House briefing room, it was very clear that there was something different going on. Reagan's chief arms negotiator, Max Kampelman, who I knew slightly, seemed close to tears. Emotions were running high, and it was evident that whatever had transpired inside the Hofdi House had come very close to a truly sensational move towards world peace. With the benefit of hindsight, we now know that Gorbachev had already determined that the global arms race had to end, that Moscow could afford to throw no more money at it.

In that moment we should have been able to piece together the reality that Russia under Gorbachev had no stomach for a 'hot war' with the United States, and that indeed we were on the very brink of the end of the East–West stalemate. At the same time, both sides continued to talk of arms control programmes extending over ten years.

On an autumnal October morning in 1986, Sir Geoffrey Howe was tucking into a full cooked breakfast. We, the diplomatic correspondents, sat at his circular dining table, devouring our eggs, bacon and fried bread. Sir Geoffrey was in the middle of his six-year stint as Britain's Foreign Secretary. Once a month, without fail, he would ensure that we diplomatic correspondents got together with him for breakfast to rake through the state of the world. He was candid, informed and perceptive. The fact that he regarded the press as so important an element of his work may well have been one of the reasons he survived the challenge of being Mrs Thatcher's foreign policy man on earth for so long.

As if to obliterate any hint that superpower relations were seriously on the mend, that morning the United States had announced another round of tit-for-tat diplomatic expulsions. In Russia the American embassy was sacking 260 locally hired employees suspected of espionage, and Moscow itself was expelling five US diplomats on similar grounds. Alas, even Sir Geoffrey did not spot the ending of the bigger picture that hindsight now reveals.

On the road, I found myself staring yet deeper into what still appeared to be the Cold War abyss in Vienna and Stockholm, where further international disarmament talks were supposed to be taking place. The Hofdi House high moment seemed to have come apart. Russia's Foreign Minister Shevardnadze and his US opposite number George Schultz did meet again, but found no common ground. The occasions provided me with an opportunity to wander around two spectacularly beautiful cities under their white blankets of snow. Once again I found myself standing on a street corner and musing, 'Someone's actually paying me to be here!'

A few days after the Stockholm talks, in late November, I was off to Washington with Mrs Thatcher. The Prime Minister was doubly fired up as she boarded her ageing official VC10. She was incensed that Reagan had been trying to 'sell the shop' at Reykjavik. She was convinced he'd been offering to give too much away, and needed his backbone stiffened. But she was also in full cry about the burgeoning Iran–Contra scandal.

Margaret Thatcher had few qualms about Reagan's illegal war in Central America, but she was enraged to find that he'd been funding it by selling arms to Iran. Britain had lost tens of millions of pounds in potential sales of spare parts to the Iranians to keep their British-made Challenger tanks going, because she had respected the UN arms embargo which Reagan had been secretly and systematically flouting.

Intriguingly, I find amongst my notes for the trip a Gallup poll taken in Britain that week. To the question 'Is the United States as great a threat to world peace as the Soviet Union?', 63 per cent of Britons answered yes. Twenty-six per cent said no. And this was 1986, not 2003.

Two seminal events closed this year of turbulent connection between the superpowers. On 18 December the Americans detonated their twenty-fourth nuclear test since Moscow's voluntary ban had been announced sixteen months earlier. The following day, Mikhail Gorbachev announced the release from distant internal exile of Andrei Sakharov. Sakharov was the ultimate emblem of dissent in the Soviet Union, and Gorbachev could have released no one more important. In freeing 'the father of Russia's hydrogen bomb', but now the country's greatest critic of human rights violations and dictatorship, he had met the demand of every Western leader and every person of consequence with whom he had ever had dealings beyond his own frontiers. He also freed a second leading dissident, the noisy, committed Christian poet Irina Tatushinskaya.

I flew to Moscow to be with Yelena Bonner, Sakharov's brilliant, chain-smoking and remorselessly campaigning wife, as she waited for the train from Gorky to pull into the station in Moscow. In the past I had spent many an hour in their tiny Moscow flat, recording interviews with both of them. I had been there first soon after Sakharov won the Nobel Peace Prize way back in 1975. The vast majority of people spilling on and off the station platforms had no idea what was going on, or even who Sakharov was. By definition, he was far more famous beyond Russia than within. And suddenly, there he was, his pale bald head and wan face bobbing along in a sea of photographers, cameramen, fur-hatted KGB absurdities and well-wishers. The very presence of the Western press suggested profound advances in Gorbachev's oft-preached policy of *glasnost*, or opening. Rigidly controlled from the centre, absolutely censored, for seventy years Russia had known nothing of free debate. Gorbachev was trying to loosen the reins so that the Communist Party might free itself up and function better. All his reforms were intended to bring about a modern state run by a modern party; he never envisaged the rapid demolition of both the state and the party.

What a way to end the year. Once again we had that sense that we'd experienced outside the Hofdi House in Reykjavik, that something was happening, even if we couldn't very clearly define what it was.

The wind scudded around our feet in the salt-swept gardens of the Governor of Bermuda's looming grey residence on the tip of the island. I had flown in with Geoffrey Howe for his talks with George Schultz. It was 6 January 1987, and the plan was simply to review the new detente that had broken out between Washington and Moscow, and what it presaged for divided Europe. There was something about this rocky imperial outcrop that made it feel as if the old empire was being left behind by the sheer pace of events in the rest of the world. Retainers bustled about in the wind, and the Governor's dog was running amok in the gorse.

Schultz's helicopter landing left Howe's substantial head of grey white hair looking considerably tousled in comparison with the American's well-greased pate. They hurried into the house, and we were left to explore the rest of the island, a strange pink place that thinks it's more British than it is, and is more American than it knows. Oddly, the key issue that had brought about these talks was the perennial threat of a trade war between Europe and America. However good the special relationship, trade always loomed as a potential spoiler, as proved to be the case when at the height of the Iraq War in 2003 the US imposed massive tariffs on all steel imports, causing Europe to threaten a boycott of Florida orange juice in return.

Unbeknown to either man, matters were moving fast. Irrespective of their shadow boxing on trade, the war in Afghanistan was entering a decisive phase which would signal yet another stepping stone towards the ending of the Cold War. Within a week of the Bermuda squalls, Afghanistan's President Najibullah in Kabul was announcing a timetable for the withdrawal of a hundred thousand Soviet troops. Getting Moscow's army out of Afghanistan had been a central pillar of Western ambitions, and here it suddenly seemed to be on a plate.

In less than two years Gorbachev had freed key refuseniks, inaugurated a programme of *glasnost* and *perestroika* (reform), enthusiastically entered arms control negotiations and announced a pull-out from Afghanistan. Yet even in 1987, Western rhetoric had yet to catch up with the reality in the Kremlin.

Outside the Soviet Union, Western Europe, apart from the Thatcher hard-line economic revolution, appeared to be unchanging. Certainly there was no sense whatever that the continent was about to experience a seismic alteration, of an extent never before achieved outside war.

The windows in the Christian Democrat (CDU) party headquarters in Bonn were lit from top to bottom. From this glass and metal structure that looked like any other big, boring office block, the party had delivered another election victory for Helmut Kohl, who himself looked something of a big, boring block. There was nothing inspiring about him, nothing exciting, and certainly nothing that suggested that within three short years he would vastly increase the size of the Germany over which he presided. I must have interviewed Kohl three or four times, and each time I was rewarded with nothing beyond a laundry list of platitudes. As seemed so often to be the case, his opponent, the social democrat leader Johannes Rau, was engaging, humorous and personable, but at that moment unelectable.

Further afield, matters in the Middle East were going from bad to worse. Terry Waite, the Archbishop of Canterbury's troubleshooter who was in the region trying to free British and American hostages, had himself now been taken hostage in Lebanon. The Iran–Iraq war was still raging ten years on. Add to all this the fact that on 4 February 1987 the United States detonated yet another nuclear test, and the world was feeling far from peaceful.

Gorbachev, however, was by now on a roll. He summoned a vast Peace Forum to Moscow, studded with all sorts of stellar Western household names including Hollywood actor Gregory Peck, pop star Kris Kristofferson and my own literary hero Graham Greene. He also released another 150 political prisoners. Then, on 26 February, the Soviets detonated their own nuclear device, the first such test since their self-imposed moratorium had started eighteen months earlier. For one awful moment, wandering about the Foreign Office off King Charles Street in London, I wondered whether we'd got it all wrong. Was the Western world's love affair with Gorbachev, of which I was most assuredly a tiny and inconsequential part, over? Two days later Gorbachev was out again on the steps of the Kremlin, offering to clear Europe of all medium-range nuclear weapons. That would mean effectively removing the option of nuclear attack from either side on the continent. America simply wasn't ready for such a move. Star Wars and its deployment were still the priority.

Within a month I was in a snowblown Red Square preparing for the Iron Lady's first visit behind what still remained the Iron Curtain. Margaret Thatcher was awaited with keen anticipation in the Kremlin, partly out of anthropological fascination, and partly because she was seen as a clue to the real mood of Ronald Reagan. In retrospect, it's doubtful she carried much in the way of hard proposals from the old boy, and certainly there was no talk yet of another Gorbachev–Reagan Summit.

The Kremlin itself had previously been an almost impenetrable zone for journalists, but two days before Mrs Thatcher arrived, a gaggle of British hacks was ushered into the sumptuous gardens amid the onion domes of the churches within the Kremlin walls. Eventually, having passed across the wooden inlay of the spacious floors of St George's Hall, we were led into the General Secretary's office. I was to be granted a few minutes' interview with Gorbachev. I'd only ever been able to shout questions at him from the media crowd, but now I got to sit opposite him, if only briefly. I was both nervous and excited. His desk was laden with assorted telephones, one of which was red: the hotline to Reagan? or the nuclear button?, I wondered. There was a lot of green baize about, and much dreary furnishing.

But there was nothing dreary about Gorbachev when he strode in. The wine stain on his forehead, airbrushed out in Soviet presidential photographs, and so prominent in Western images of him, in the flesh simply added to his aura. He seemed seriously interested in meeting us. Almost as if unused to interviews, he looked me absolutely straight in the eye, and gave every sense that he understood everything I said, though his interpreter insisted that he did not know a word of English.

We talked of Reagan first. 'He's a staunch

conservative,' Gorbachev said, 'but coming from that background it's far easier for him to move towards us and meet us halfway. I'm as far left as he is right, and neither of those positions is as far right or left as you think they are.' And of Mrs Thatcher: 'Very strong personality, very strong politician. And in spite of us arguing at every meeting, we respect each other's position.' Just as I was turning to leave, he sat me down again and put his hand on my arm. 'Mr Snieg,' he said, 'the nuclear arms race should never be taken into space. It is difficult enough to limit the nuclear arms race on earth.' So that was it, I thought. Reagan had got under his skin with his Star Wars shield, and Gorbachev had looked over the abyss and been horrified at what he'd seen.

Perhaps inevitably, Mrs Thatcher was wearing strident blue when she appeared at the top of the steps of the VC10 at Moscow's Sheremetyevo Airport. Her route had involved interesting diversions to Paris and Bonn to consult her political allies – France's President François Mitterrand and the man who was, to her annoyance, still Chancellor Helmut Kohl. She'd been persuaded to make the detour by Mitterrand, who had been concerned to warn her that French and British nuclear weapons had nothing to do with Soviet–American negotiations. Kohl's concern was the Berlin Wall. He was the man who had to live next door to the empire of the Russian bear, and the consequences of its post-Second World War acquisitions and behaviour. He certainly didn't want Margaret Thatcher doing any negotiating on his behalf. Their relations were anyway

406

marvellously brittle. Geoffrey Howe, still Foreign Secretary, once told me how Mrs Thatcher, who rarely took a holiday, found herself, with her husband Denis, on a five-day break in a small town in Austria. By some ghastly mischance, the Kohls were at a hotel nearby. She decided she'd best nip trouble in the bud, and sent word to the Chancellor suggesting a casual meeting. He replied that he could not possibly find time to see her, being too tied up with work commitments. That afternoon, she and Denis took a stroll, and there, three streets from their own hotel, was the substantial figure of Kohl sitting happily with his wife Hannelore and a solitary security guard in the sun outside a café, devouring a vast cream bun.

Nevertheless, Thatcher survived her stopover in Bonn, and here she was, if a little late, in the epicentre of the 'Evil Empire'. The hearse-like Russian Zils sped down the centre of the wide, pungent and smog-ridden boulevard that leads from the airport into Moscow. The drab grey tenements raced by on either side. Physically Moscow looked as forbidding as ever, yet the changes beyond the dank exteriors had already been more profound than the British seemed to realise.

Britain's Moscow embassy seemed not to have entirely caught up with the pace of *glasnost*. Before leaving Downing Street, Mrs Thatcher had sent word that she wanted on this trip to test the Soviets to the very limits, to see just how far they really were reforming. Thus she demanded to be allowed unfettered access to Soviet television to talk to the Russian people; she demanded to be allowed to meet the Sakharovs, the Hebrew teacher Yosif Begun and other prominent refuseniks; and finally she wanted to be able to 'go walkabout' wherever she chose. All this in addition to the hours of straight talking that she expected with the Soviet leader.

As she arrived that night, the embassy was in a tizz over Begun's noisy public boast that he'd be seeing the British Prime Minister for breakfast. Diplomats feared that pre-publicity might lead to the whole thing being called off. In reality the Soviets had already discounted the damage such a meeting might cause, and decided to live with it.

With Mrs Thatcher safely arrived we went in search of supper, or the indigestible overboiled cabbage that passed as supper in a steamy Russian eating house. Thence to the Rossia, the world's biggest and most rapidly deteriorating hotel, just off Red Square. This was a wondrous 3200-bed testament to Russia's Stalinist heyday. Yet in a strange and deprived way, it was clean – kept so by the *babushka* stationed on each floor. They seemed in part to be on parade to keep the prostitutes at bay, in part to keep an eye on the guests, and in part to provide tiny stale biscuity breakfasts. The Rossia was built around four deep concrete quadrangles, and it was easy to lose any sense of location. If you were very lucky, from your window you glimpsed the onion dome of the neighbouring church, or even the walls of the Kremlin itself. And of course you were in the heart of everything – the Party headquarters were nearby, and the barren GUM, supposedly the best department store in the Soviet Union, although rather better for bottled gherkins than for tights.

The next morning the Thatcher cavalcade headed for the glorious monastery town of Zagorsk, an hour out of Moscow. The place was a feast of gold domes even in the smog-laden skies, providing a stark contrast to the grey approaches. Cavernous baritone intonations echoed out of the open doors of the churches. For an oppressed religion, the Orthodox Church had not done a bad job of surviving here in Zagorsk. The music was heavenly, and I could see in her face that Mrs Thatcher was having to re-evaluate her take on Mother Russia. The faces in the congregation were Brueghelesque, medieval, candle-illuminated figures in old scarves and huge coats against the cold. Set against what we knew of the suffering of religious activists, the visit was emotional. As the priests sang, Thatcher raised her head towards the startling gold-leaf mosaics in the vaulted ceiling, and I dared to think she might shed a tear. I did, she didn't. In truth, her people were more interested in the spellbinding photo-opportunities. It is certainly no surprise that today under Putin, more than a decade and a half after the death of Communism, the Orthodox Church has once again seized all the national dominance it enjoyed under the Tsars.

At a nearby housing estate Mrs Thatcher was mobbed by inquisitive tenants. She was mobbed again on Moscow's only posh shopping street, the dowdy Arbat. That night she went to the Bolshoi

Ballet for *Swan Lake*. I was lucky to get a press pool place, and stood amongst the red velvet seats as she, Denis, Mikhail Gorbachev and his wife Raisa bowed from the Tsar's box. Bizarre it was, and one sensed again that something was on the move. Margaret Thatcher had none of Nancy Reagan's problems with Raisa Gorbachev. She recognised her for what she was, an academic and an achiever. Nancy resented her for her intellect and her lack of interest in Hollywood. By now Mrs Thatcher must have been wondering how soon she'd get to see the real 'evil' in the empire; she must have worried that Russia was fast becoming a dangerously beguiling place under Gorbachev.

She was of course, perhaps unwittingly, Reagan's Joan the Baptist, sent before the President to test the waters. But at this point the arms negotiations were so stalled in Geneva that another US–USSR Summit seemed off the cards. In all Mrs Thatcher had seven hours of talks with Gorbachev, confirming that they really could do business with each other. That night he fêted her in the great St George's Hall deep inside the Kremlin. The high gloss on the marquetry of the wooden floors shimmered beneath the flaming candelabra. The great gold doors opened at either end of the huge room, allowing a choreographed advance by both Russian leader and British premier, who met in the middle amid an orchestral crescendo. It was completely over the top, but compelling. Somehow, pointing missiles at each other was beginning to feel more than a little superfluous.

The final day in Moscow was a gorgeous and

embarrassing muddle for Mrs Thatcher. She wanted to entertain the Sakharovs to lunch rather more than they wished to be entertained. Never ones to use a car if a bus would do, the couple waited on the street corner for the embassy car that would pick them up. The car was late – leaving them trying to get into the wrong vehicle. When the right one did turn up, the driver failed to recognise them – no *glaznosist* he – and drove on. So in the end the father of the Russian bomb and winner of the Nobel Peace Prize got into the back of ITN's battered old Lada, and we drove together to the embassy. Mrs Thatcher got her wish, becoming the first Western leader ever to meet him. Afterwards he told us that she'd tried to side with him against Gorbachev, questioning how real the reforms were and whether they were going fast enough. Sakharov, however, had sided aggressively with Gorbachev, leaving us with the firm impression that the arch dissident and the Soviet leader were very much aboard the same movement; that seemed to leave Mrs Thatcher in a somewhat lonely and obscure place.

As she flew back via Georgia, there were many at home who suspected the entire trip, at least for her, had merely been an international curtain-raising exercise for a British general election to come. Within a couple of weeks she had indeed triggered the poll for 11 June.

I was tasked with following the Labour leader Neil Kinnock in his forlorn quest to prevent Mrs Thatcher from winning a historic third term in Downing Street. Before the formal campaigning

411

got going, I went down to Blackwood, the Kinnocks' home base in his Islwyn constituency in south Wales. It seemed important to meet his family and set him in the context of where he had come from. So before reaching Blackwood I stopped off in Aberdare to visit most of his surviving family. His mother and father were both long dead, and it was Neil's eternal sadness that they didn't live to see their son challenge for the highest office in the land.

Aunty Sadie, his mother's sister, waited on the scrubbed stone doorstep of her neat home in the heart of Aberdare. She had gathered eight of Neil's close friends and relatives into the tiny front room. We crammed the camera in, and recorded an emotional account of an only child of working-class background who after becoming 'the first Kinnock in a thousand years to go to university' had made his way through the trade union movement and education to the very top of the Labour Party.

When we reached damp, underloved, grey Blackwood we found the Kinnock home, a small two-up, two-down terraced house fronting straight onto the street. There were no Kinnocks at home; instead, from somewhere round the back emerged a faithful local party stalwart, Gwynne Evans. He was open-faced, enthusiastic and trusting. 'Come on in,' he said. 'I'll show you round.' There was very little to see – a few family photos and simple furnishings. Gwynne suggested that while we waited we go down to neighbouring Tredegar to see Aunty Dor. She was the nearest person to Neil's mother, and had known him since his

412

childhood. She had never seen a television camera before, and was stylishly shocked by the scale of our invasion of her home. She talked ninety to the dozen, filling in the gaps in Neil's very normal, very Welsh upbringing.

Finally, towards nightfall Neil and the vivacious Glenys, his wife and student sweetheart, bounded into the Blackwood house and we sat down for a long interview. As we talked it was clear that beyond the extrovert and gregarious exterior lay a very emotional man. About an hour into our session, when I raised the fact that neither of his parents was around to share in the moment, he started crying, tears streaming down his face. It took a walk and at least half an hour for us all to recover. I never for one moment thought that Neil Kinnock could win, but he seemed a more than decent man, who believed passionately in doing better for his fellow human beings, and who seemed alarmingly normal.

The Labour campaign itself was youthful, small, exuberant and highly mobile. It was clear that if only in terms of flexibility and zest, Kinnock was going to give Thatcher a run for her money. In that 1987 campaign we could detect the seeds of the methodology that was to deliver Labour victory a decade later. For here on the 'battle bus' was a young, moustachioed Peter Mandelson, and frequently in one corner the formidable political editor of the *Today* newspaper and sometime *Mirror* man, Alastair Campbell.

Kinnock managed to give the impression that he was setting the agenda for the campaign, suddenly pitching up in Manchester to give his daily news conference, instead of doing the predictable thing and counterbalancing Mrs Thatcher in central London. Hence it began to appear that she was having a problem keeping up with him. His Mandelson-managed events were far more televisual than hers. She was looking like a leader who had taken the electorate for granted.

It all came to a climax six days before the vote as Kinnock, on a Welsh pool table, potted the Thatcherite blue ball with his first shot. This was the dawning of what came to be known as 'wobbly Thursday', the day on which Mrs Thatcher reportedly confessed her doubts about winning to her party chairman, Norman Tebbit. Conservative Central Office filed a formal complaint with my editor that we were giving Kinnock too kind a run. In truth it was hard to do otherwise, because the choreography of his campaign was so keenly focused on playing well for television, and the Tories simply had not yet cottoned on.

Unsurprisingly, 'wobbly Thursday' evaporated into yet another enormous win for the Conservatives, who beat Labour by 376 to 229 seats, but Kinnock lived to fight another day for locating the party's electoral bedrock and coming back a little from it.

If there was *glasnost* in the north in Mother Russia, there were the seeds of opening in the south too, not least among those movements like the ANC in South Africa for which the Soviets had provided support.

On 9 July the tropical sun beat down on a Senegalese beach across the water from the Île de

Gorée. A group of Africans mingled with white men dressed in light slacks, open-necked white shirts and Panama hats. So far the thawing of the Cold War and the edging towards East–West detente had been reported as an event largely rooted in and affecting the developed world. Here in Senegal, the North–South dimension was just beginning to stir. To this day, I do not really know how I managed to be present. In the aftermath of the British general election, my newsdesk had little interest in the outside world.

As the group moved up through the narrow streets of the town I could hear someone playing Bach on a piano through an upstairs window. The heat bounced off the pink plastered walls below, vines tangled at the doorways. Beloved Africa, that scent, that beat, and yet today somehow French and classical too. We were wandering through the very marshalling yard of West African slavery, where hundreds of thousands of men, women and children had been sifted and sorted for the transatlantic voyage to America. We were as near New York as it is possible to be in Africa.

There was one woman on the beach: Danielle Mitterrand, wife of the French President. The Africans were members of the African National Congress, waging physical and psychological war, to apparently little effect, against the Western-backed apartheid regime in Pretoria. The whites were predominantly South African businessmen, but included in their number the radical Afrikaner cleric and activist Beyers Naude. Apart from me there were almost no other journalists. It was Madame Mitterrand's Foundation that had brought the two groups together for this unprecedented encounter. It could never have happened in those days within South Africa – the whites would have been arrested for fraternising with the enemy; the blacks would have been locked up for being there at all.

The white South Africans numbered about thirty, and they had come north at considerable risk to themselves and their businesses at home. There were fewer ANC people, and they had come from all over the world. Thabo Mbeki had flown in from Stockholm, the Pahad brothers, Aziz and Essop, from London; others had come from Addis, Lusaka and Dar es Salaam. The white team was led by Frederick Van Zyl Slabbert, former leader of the South African opposition and every inch the white settler, abetted by the writer Alex Boraine, a handsome and engaging intellectual. But the critical figure appeared to be the exiled Afrikaans poet Breyten Breytenbach. He had flown in from Paris, and it was he who seemed to have engaged Madame Mitterrand's interest together with significant funding from her Paris-based human rights charity France Libertés. She chaired the proceedings in a wonderfully aloof French way.

We were all holed up in the same hotel, and for four exhilarating days we bonded and mixed as equals as we talked about the possibility of a future liberated South Africa. It was heady stuff, yet I don't think any of us present saw change happening inside a decade, and many still thought it would only come about after a protracted and bloody war. We talked, ate and drank late into the nights, and breakfasted together in the mornings. Even then Thabo Mbeki had the air of a leader; Aziz Pahad was to become South African Deputy Foreign Minister; and the man I bonded best with, his brother Essop, was to become Minister in Thabo's office when he became President. Before then there would be pastas in Soho and animated encounters whenever any of them passed through London. But for now we were wrestling with the distant prospect of a new, free South Africa.

It was here in Senegal that we first heard the debate surrounding 'truth' and 'justice'. Alex Boraine, one day to join Archbishop Desmond Tutu as co-chair of South Africa's Truth and Reconciliation Commission, outlined how justice might have to be sacrificed in order to win truth. Thabo was at this stage wedded to the idea of putting the apartheid leaders on trial in a Nuremberg-style court. What we witnessed in our Dakar hotel was the birth of a process that did not jail or execute, but through amnesty and dialogue was to try to reach back to the full truth of what had happened. It was a proposal that was, in one way or another, to inform many peace processes in the future. Needless to say, my desk in London found all this very boring and unproductive, and I was lucky even to file three short reports.

On the full Air France Airbus to Paris I found myself unexpectedly upgraded to first class. The seat next to me was already occupied by a sleeping woman beneath a blanket, from which her dark-red-varnished toenails peeped out. Soon after takeoff the woman unwound herself from

417

her covers and revealed herself to be Danielle Mitterrand. I wanted so much to engage her in my haphazard French, but she was never to know. Shortly afterwards a screen was wrapped around her, she got into her nightie, and slept the whole of the rest of the way. I was left with only the occasional glimpse of her toenails for company.

Little did I know on that flight home in what good stead those few days in Senegal would stand me. Nor did I begin to understand how the thawing of the Cold War would manifest itself south of the equator.

And there was another arena showing signs of change at last. After seven years of mounting Iraqi and Iranian death tolls, detente between the two superpowers delivered joint action in that region. Washington and Moscow started to provide naval escorts for oil tankers in the Gulf. America wanted a peace deal, having lost thirty-seven men in an Iraqi missile attack on 17 May, 1987 on the USS *Stark*, a frigate on patrol there. Both sides were worried about the gathering strength of the Iranians, and the possibility that they just might manage to capture Basra and trigger the establishment of a fundamentalist Shia regime in southern Iraq. How that fear has informed our times. Hence, at last the Peruvian UN Secretary General Javier Perez de Cuellar flew to Baghdad and Tehran to negotiate.

As for Europe, if there was about to be change, there was no sign of it in the West German capital

418

of Bonn on 7 September 1987 as I stood outside Chancellor Kohl's office waiting for the arrival of Erich Honecker, President of East Germany. We were celebrating the fact that the two Germanys had come so far that it was possible for the leader of the one to visit the leader of the other.

The ceremonial band at the gate intoned as yet no death knell for East Germany. Nor did the British Prime Minister when I accompanied her on a photogenic visit to the German front line later that month. Mrs Thatcher peered through her binoculars at the East German border guard who was peering at her through his. We were in the heart of Berlin, just along from the misnomer of a gate that was the concrete-walled Brandenburg. 'Mr Gorbachev, tear down this Wall'; the words of Ronald Reagan had echoed at this place only a few months earlier. It felt like a forlorn call. Mrs Thatcher did not need to add much to it, because the real superpower ballet had entered the next phase without her intervention. So long as things were going badly between Moscow and Washington, she could always hope to play the part of honest broker. But a December 1987 date for another Reagan–Gorbachev Summit had just been agreed, and the arms reduction arm-twisting was under way in Geneva and elsewhere.

As the Prime Minister surveyed the Wall, we journalists enjoyed the romance of crossing and recrossing it through Checkpoint Charlie. Mrs Thatcher's worry now was not so much the Wall as her fear that in the enthusiastic dash for the Summit, nuclear disarmament in Europe might get out of hand, leaving Western Europe exposed to attack. Once again, she seemed to be slightly cool on it all; caution was her watchword.

On the final night of her visit we decided to stay in the newly opened Grand Hotel in East Berlin. Checkpoint Charlie was as eerie and unpredictable as ever, the brusque US guards dependably humourless. The East Germans kept us an hour, checking our camera equipment. Then we were once more back amongst the shops selling little but pickled gherkins, the bread queues, and the shapeless grey-clad men and women moving along gloomy streets.

The Grand Hotel was very grand indeed. It was a cross between a Louis XIV palace and a bordello. There was a lot of marble, a lot of brass about the bathrooms, and very big beds. Its opulence provided a weird disjunction with the fading utilitarian basics of the surrounding streets. Yet it also seemed to be an optimistic pointer to the East Germany to come, a whiff of confidence in the most successful state in the Soviet empire – although that was a distinctly relative term.

When we crossed back into the West, the barrier had a ruthless air of permanence. Even amid the rich abundance of colour in the turning autumn leaves, the Wall stood daunting, unchanging, alien and slightly repulsive.

Just a few weeks before the Washington Summit, scheduled to take place in December, peace was beginning to break out in yet another East–West theatre in the 'South' – Central America. While he was treating with Communists in Moscow, even Ronald Reagan found it hard to go on prosecuting a war to 'draw a line in the sand against Communism' in Nicaragua.

Flying in to Managua at the beginning of November was both an uplifting and a depressing experience. Uplifting because even at the airport there was a noticeable sense of ease and relaxation amongst all the people I encountered. Depressing because Nicaragua itself had gone horribly downhill. Where under the Sandinistas literacy had reached 80 per cent, it was now on the slide towards 50 per cent; universal healthcare had crumbled, taking most of the tangible benefits of the Sandinista revolution with it. American money and seeping corruption within their ranks had defeated the Sandinistas at the polls, and they had been replaced by a compliant right-of-centre pro-Washington party.

The offering of an amnesty by the new Nicaraguan government to the American-backed Contra rebels had provoked great resentment amongst the relatives of dead Sandinista soldiers, so there were grieving mothers outside many government buildings. At the border with Honduras I watched as isolated, frightened-looking returning Contra fighters strained their eyes towards us, looking for loved ones from whom they'd been separated for more than four years.

Suddenly I realised how much the people on both sides were victims of a much bigger power play, way beyond their control. Still at the northern border, I watched a mother with a red and green parrot sitting on the handle of the basket she bore on her head. The parrot bobbed about as she weaved this way and that, looking for her son. And then she found him, and with the parrot screeching, they wept openly. I congratulated myself on the vocal and visual imagery we'd captured on film, and felt like an exploiting heel for doing so. Another moment when I too cried, and hoped to avoid the battle-hardened cameraman spotting the tears.

Life next door in El Salvador was absolutely no better. Indeed it was almost certainly worse, not least because it had become a virtual police state. The army had effectively shut the country down to the prying eyes of visiting journalists. Impossible obstacles were put in the way of our attempts even to reach refugee camps, let alone the remaining fighting. El Salvador was already in transition from civil war to a kind of Los Angeles-exported drug-gang warfare. Children who had entered America with their Salvadorean parents had grown up to swell the ranks of American west coast criminal gangs. Once caught they were punished for the crimes they'd committed in California by being deported to El Salvador and set free to commit more crimes in an impoverished, distant land of which they knew nothing and for which they had no care, and where no one cared for them. It was a recipe for national social failure that persists to this day. But at least I could feel as I left El Salvador that Central America's proxy superpower wars, real or imagined, were being wound down.

The wind-chill factor the day Gorbachev landed in Washington outstripped even that in Reykjavik one year earlier. This time, unlike Geneva two years before, Reagan had opted to wear his over-coat. We didn't know then that the timing of the entire Summit was based on the recommend-ations of Nancy Reagan's California-based astrologer Joan Quigley. Reagan's Chief of Staff, Donald T. Regan, told us later that Ms Quigley had read the star charts for both Gorbachev and Reagan and concluded that 2 p.m. on 8 December 1987 would find them in the best possible aspect. Thus it was decided that the two men should sign the Intermediate Range Nuclear Forces (INF) treaty at that very hour. This was to be the moment that would inaugurate the removal of the most dangerous weapons on earth – those facing each other across the Iron Curtain. The timing of the signal that would mark the formal beginning of the end of the Cold War and change the face of national security across the planet was decided by a star-chart gazer sitting in her front room in Los Angeles.

The event itself took place on a very much more elevated plane. Cameras were live, transmitting everything from the handshake on the White House lawn to the choreographed signing of the treaty inside, and in between, the meaningful fireside chats in the West Wing. Gorbymania swept America. Even staid old Washington was falling over itself trying to glimpse him, meet him, shake the hand that had signed for peace. On his second day in town, my small female freelance camerawoman and I were getting coffee on Six-teenth Street when Gorbachev's Zil suddenly stopped in front of us. People gushed out of every building. I lifted the camerawoman, Joan, up onto the traffic-light control box, and suddenly we had a world exclusive. 'Gorby, Gorby, Gorby,' the onlookers chanted; it was beyond Hollywood. That night the US networks were beating at our door for the pictures; we third-worlders, as they regarded us, had just come unexpectedly good.

We all thought Gorbachev a modern miracle, coming as he had from such unpromising political stock from Cold War through detente, *perestroika* and *glasnost*, to active thaw. We were now less than twenty-four months from the collapse of the Berlin Wall itself, but of that not one of us had even the smallest clue.

A stark and snow-swept scene in Vienna early in 1988 conjured up the grim origins which had ultimately led to the building of the Wall. There were perhaps forty television cameras gathered for the fiftieth anniversary of the *Anschluss*, Hitler's annexation of Austria. Barriers surrounded the square in front of the spectacular imperial Hofburg Palace – but there were no crowds to be contained. In contrast to the scenes of jubilant Austrians mobbing the Führer's car in 1938, apart from a few scattered bystanders, the Viennese had stayed away in droves.

Even in 1988 the Austrian Cabinet could not bring itself to bury the country's past. I found myself wandering along streets of shops once owned by Jewish families, still in the hands of the very people to whom Hitler's bureaucracy had illegally transferred them. But Ministers continued to refuse to pay reparations, or to authorise the shops' return to their rightful owners. Then there was Kurt Waldheim, who had returned in triumph from his indifferent stint as UN Secretary General to become Austria's President. On this day at least he was brought low, denied the right to speak as a result of revelations about his activities towards the end of the Second World War. Despite his denials of any personal involvement, he had been an officer in an Austrian army unit that carried out bloody reprisals against partisans in Yugoslavia. He had to lay his wreath, at the ceremony honouring those who had died at Hitler's hand, in silence.

Vienna was also the scene of one of a cascade of European Summits that were now happening almost monthly in an effort to keep pace with the East–West disarmament programme that now, in the wake of the Washington Summit, was proceeding with great speed. The Hofburg was the dusty and chilly setting for Conventional Force Reduction talks. This in turn followed the Brussels NATO meeting which had provided a stage for the start of Ronald Reagan's long international goodbye to his eight extraordinary years as President of the United States.

Replacing Reagan was proving neither an easy nor an interesting exercise. The Democrats toyed with a motley band of no-hopers cowed by the sheer scale of Reagan's achievements. He had for so long been a figure of fun, a guy who hardly knew what was going on, yet he was leaving a legacy of peace unknown since the end of the Second World War. He was also leaving a deftly crafted, if ultimately disastrous, booming US economy. In the event the Democrats settled on the former Governor of Massachusetts Michael Dukakis, one of their weakest presidential challengers ever. Travelling on the byroads of New England with Dukakis was, for me at least, a cosy, uninspiring affair. He was personable and bright, but ultimately boring.

Nevertheless, Reagan's successor for the Republicans was hardly a towering opponent. George Bush had been Vice President throughout the Reagan years. Competent and patrician he may have been, but he was one of the most wooden and unelectable figures I've ever been close to on the road. His speeches verged on the painful. It was little wonder that fewer than 50 per cent of the US electorate turned out to make the awesome choice between Bush and Dukakis. Economic well-being was eventually to deliver for George, and poor old Dukakis was to be humiliated come the November poll, with Bush winning 54 per cent of the vote.

Seven and a half thousand miles away, Afghanistan was providing the best imaginable political backdrop for the Moscow Summit in May 1988 that would bring Reagan and Gorbachev together for the last time. With just two weeks to go to the Summit, the first brigade of Soviet troops had begun to move out of Kabul. By the end of the Summit, a quarter of Russia's 115,000 troops would be home. They would leave twenty thousand of their dead behind after nine years of occupation.

Amid the international celebrations of Russia's courageous but ignominious withdrawal, I wondered about the fate of the Mujahidin I had been with when those first Soviet tanks had rolled in from the north all those years before. So much had changed. They would not have been one of the groups favoured by the Americans with Stinger missiles – they were too closely allied with their Iranian neighbours. Almost certainly they would have suffered badly during the internecine slaughter amongst the competing warlords.

None of us who'd been to the country had any doubts that together Washington and Moscow had combined to leave a powder-keg smouldering in Afghanistan. A desperately poor state in 1979 had become an even more desperately poor and now failed state in 1988. The shoulder-held Stinger missiles had changed the course of the war, bringing down numerous Soviet planes. And now their very existence in militant hands threatened the rest of the world. They were a lurking mini weapon of mass destruction, left in the hands of people radicalised by Muslim militants armed and funded by the United States of America. The object of the war was accomplished: the Russian army in Afghanistan had been defeated and forced out. But the cost to the rest of the world was incalculable, and would not be felt for another thirteen years. In the meantime, Afghans would have to make do and mend with the government the war had spawned – the Taliban. At that moment it was hard to imagine that America would one day supplant the Russians and come here to fight a war herself.

I was in Moscow as the Russians started a propaganda blitz to try to steal the high ground from the Americans in this most critical of Summits. It was intended to slash the vast array of strategic nuclear missiles, intercontinental ballistic and the rest, that each had ranged against the other. Amazingly, the Soviets chose to confront the retreat from Afghanistan head on, with a very senior General being produced to answer questions from an inquisitive press corps. It was a session that turned into a moving confessional, as the man made a neo-Vietnam War analysis of Russian failure. He admitted to thirteen thousand of his men having been killed, and thirty-five thousand injured, which was not far off Western intelligence estimates. He also produced pictures from the Soviet military hospital in Kabul which revealed the human tragedy of the occupation. The Russian people saw them too, alerting the whole population for the first time to the scale of the military failure and the great suffering of Soviet troops.

We learned at one of these sessions that relations between Nancy Reagan and Raisa Gorbachev had become so difficult that when the American First Lady went on her own trip to Leningrad she would be accompanied not by Mrs Gorbachev, but by the elderly wife of Andrei Gromyko. Raisa's formidable intellect had clearly proved too much for the astrologically dependent, if wily, Nancy.

In the few months that I had been away, Moscow had been transformed. The jamming of the BBC and Voice of America had stopped, and the entire place seemed to have been decorated. Georgian restaurants with plentiful good wine and food had sprouted, and any road along which there was the slightest chance the Reagans would travel had been resurfaced, almost certainly for the first time since the Revolution. The old guard grumbled; they hated what was happening, but still no one imagined that what was taking place was anything more profound than a reconfiguration of international relationships.

29 May 1988 dawned bright and cloudless. Moscow, so often grey, was splashed with colour. Even the onion dome next to the Rossia Hotel and the Kremlin clock close by had been re-gilded. There were red flags and stars and stripes all over the city as every available lamp post sported a tribute to the Summit. Bells rang, crowds moved about on Red Square – and suddenly, there they were, in the grounds of the Kremlin. Ronald Reagan was in the very heart of the Evil Empire, fraternising with the enemy, step in step with his erstwhile Communist adversary forging a new architecture for world peace. Yet even Reagan must have imagined, as Gorbachev later told me that he did, that this new world order was built on the premise that a more humane Communist Soviet Union would evolve, interacting and co-operating with the capitalist world. But the Communist state was more atrophied than even Gorbachev had feared. On this day at least, for perhaps the last time in our lifetimes, two superpowers came together as equals. Each appeared to be a restraining and reassuring influence upon the other.

Not everything at the Summit went to plan. The two sides couldn't quite conclude the full arms control agreement, but they did agree it would happen before the year was out. For the rest, we were all caught in a vortex of euphoric optimism, spinning wildly from the recent prospect of mutual nuclear destruction to that of mutual co-operation to make the world a more peaceful and prosperous place. As if to prove it, the crowds in Red Square, into which Gorbachev and Reagan wandered unannounced, sported Wrangler jeans and colourful tops and jackets; grey Moscow itself was already changing before our very eyes. Below the podium upon which Stalin and Brezhnev had variously strutted their stuff, an American President held a Russian baby aloft, and with the General Secretary of the Soviet Communist Party inaugurated a new tomorrow.

From the intensity of the process delivering a new world order, I was dispatched to a remote glimpse of the old. Waking in my bed in the Upland Goose pub, I found myself looking out of the low window at sea birds scudding up the waters off Port Stanley in the dawn sun. Six years on, the British were refighting the Falklands War: it was a purely military exercise that even attracted the criticism of the United Nations.

I had flown the seventeen hours down the Atlantic via volcanic Ascension Island, a barren spot halfway between Britain and the Falklands. I relished the excuse to visit the unseen object of my obsessive time in southern Chile reporting the 1982 war from afar. The southern hemisphere had delivered a rich spring November day for our arrival. Our Tri-Star landed just ahead of the refuelling mother tanker that had enabled a squadron of Phantom jets to fly non-stop all the way from Scotland. Between the remote airfield, upgraded in the aftermath of the war, and Port Stanley itself there was not a single tree to be seen. But the rolling Hebridean landscape was breathtaking. I was thrilled to be staying in the Upland Goose, which before the war had been one of the most obscure hotels in the world. I had worried that British army officers might have taken the few rooms the place boasted, but I found that the army led a life largely separate from the 180 Falklanders still on the islands. Port Stanley had reverted to the sleepy place it had always been. There was a hint of the inbreeding, and many of the tales of domestic, even adulterous, scandal that our old Punta Arenas-based Falklander Monty Short had told us about. The bar downstairs at the Goose was a hub of gossip.

Retracing the footsteps of this distant war, it was no easier to explain than it had been all those years earlier. Somehow a vast military exercise against a now non-existent Argentinian threat seemed deliciously British, as had the original epic. But a thousand people had been killed here, and nearly £5 billion had been spent, and is still being spent, by Britain. I found it hard to place the Falklands War in the context of the emerging East–West detente. It had made Mrs Thatcher, but it marked her as a leader of the old order

431

rather than of the new order, or disorder, to come. What was certain was that the successful execution of the war – albeit with US assistance in both missiles and fuel – so far from home remained a remarkable achievement, as did the skill shown by the Argentine pilots who resisted it. It also brought about the end of the rule of the dictator General Galtieri and his junta in Argentina, thus helping to usher in a more democratic regime.

The Falklands was just one of many seemingly irrelevant factors that, when stacked up, left Britain still emotionally incapable of throwing her entire lot in with the rest of Europe. Few places could have been further from that continent than Port Stanley, yet Port Stanley was far nearer Mrs Thatcher's heart than anything Europe ever did or stood for. Her failure to put Britain at the heart of Europe, compounded much later by Tony Blair, was to become one of the defining features of the new world disorder. For just when the old superpower balances were coming apart, the essentially Britainless Europe was too weak to provide the new counterbalance that America already appeared to need to play a constructive role in the world.

Upon these matters and the sheer stunning, raw beauty of the Falklands I pondered as I lay in bed in the Upland Goose that morning in November 1988.

As if to rub the point home, I returned to London to find that the United States had refused to grant the Palestinian leader Yasser Arafat permission to

432

travel to New York to address the UN General Assembly. With the Cold War not yet quite dead, the soon-to-be lone superpower was already flexing its muscles, riding roughshod over the international protocols that safeguarded the integrity of the UN in New York. The UN held its ground, and the entire General Assembly decamped to the organisation's Geneva head-quarters so that Arafat could address them there. I was dispatched to report the occasion.

On 15 December 1988 Geneva became an armed camp for a day that seemed to sum up so much of past, present and future American entanglements in the Middle East. Arafat was being ordered by Washington to recognise Israel, renounce terrorism and honour UN resolutions safeguarding Israel's security. As ever, Israel was under no such pressure to honour the resolutions visited upon her over the years.

Sweden somehow prevailed upon Arafat to go and address the UN. Ten hours behind schedule, he did just that, and within the hour US Secretary of State George Schultz was agreeing to meet him face to face, at that time the most senior American ever to do so. Schultz himself, never an exciting figure, was mobbed as the session broke up. In its last months, the Reagan administration seemed to have decided to leave the international stage with a bang. On the margins of the UN meeting, I felt the East–West momentum moving too. At this session at least, the Wall between the two Germanys, whose representatives sat in the front row, was a mere two feet of space between two desks.

Things ran so late that I nearly missed my satellite feed to London – at such times we tended to hire transmission facilities from the host country's national television station. I had to drive like the clappers across town to Swiss Television to make it. In so doing I chalked up some serious trouble for myself on a later, even more critical, trip to Geneva.

On the evening of 21 December 1988 I was in the wine bar across the road from my office at ITN in London's Gray's Inn Road having Christmas drinks when news came in that a Pan Am Jumbo had fallen out of the sky upon the Scottish border town of Lockerbie, claiming the lives of all 259 people aboard, together with eleven people on the ground. I was all for heading up the motorway to get to the scene, it being too late to get a flight. Instead I was kept back at base to 'wrap' all the material coming into the building. The BBC, by contrast, invested every effort in getting to Lockerbie and reporting properly from the scene. In media terms, the coverage of Lockerbie was an indication of things to come. Satellite technology was providing us with raw pictures from the scene of the news quicker than we could get there to find out what was happening.

I was in at the very beginning of a new and potentially seriously disinforming period in which I was expected to report events from the studio almost as if I were at the scene. It was to become ever harder for the viewer to tell whether we were actually witnessing what we were reporting, or were holed up in a video editing booth voicing over material fresh off the satellite. That night, and on the succeeding nights, we were not half as good as the BBC.

As to the content of the story, it was to mark the West's further estrangement from two secular states in the Middle East. Libya and Syria would both ultimately be suspected of responsibility for putting a bomb into Flight 103's luggage in Frankfurt, where the New York-bound plane started its journey towards its first stop at Heathrow. The saga would drag on until late 2003. War on Iraq was still to come, but we were already finding ourselves on the wrong side of just about every secular state in the region at the very moment that those states fostering militant Islamic thoughts and actions appeared to be most in the ascendant. It was a grim end to the year.

The beginning of 1989 was no better. American jets shot down two ancient Libyan MIGs off Libya's capital Tripoli, then Washington started thinking aloud about bombing a suspected chemical weapons factory. So in 1989 we had already started talking about 'weapons of mass destruction'. Interestingly, Mrs Thatcher herself, who'd been attending a memorial service for the dead in Lockerbie, was keen to lower the temperature. So volatile was the region, so tender the new opening with Arafat and the Palestinians, that the British at least were wary of further intervention. In any case, British and European relations with Libya were then currently on the up. American relations had never recovered from the unilateral US bombing of Tripoli in 1986, which the Americans said was in response to the

435

bombing of a nightclub in West Berlin. Lockerbie, in turn, was possibly a reprisal for the raids on Tripoli.

Ten days later I was called by Wanda Menke Glukert, our redoubtable Bonn producer. 'Jon, Germany's been shipping nuclear material to Libya and Pakistan,' she told me bluntly. I flew to Hanau in West Germany, to discover that the Nukem reprocessing plant there enjoyed an unbelievably lax regime. Barrels of plutonium had been relabelled as nuclear waste. Bribes had flowed to inspectors, and a couple of suicides had preceded the current furore. But if anything enrichable, that could have been used in a nuclear weapons programme, ever reached Libya, it was never found. A decade and a half later it was concluded by the UN regulatory body based in Vienna that Libya might have come within several years of building a bomb, but had very little enriched plutonium to do so. Not until the rather courageous move by Tony Blair in the spring of 2004 did Gaddafi finally bare all and allow every WMD component that he'd ever had to be shipped out to America for destruction.

1989, the great year of change, seemed to have Mrs Thatcher in the air practically every week. Today it was April Fool's Day, and her official RAFVC10 was bumping about as we crossed the Mediterranean heading for Marrakesh. Morocco was to be the first stop on a swing through Africa amid rising pressure on Mrs Thatcher to agree to significant sanctions against the apartheid regime in South Africa. In fact change was already well under way thanks to the evolving East–West detente in the North.

Space was so limited aboard Mrs Thatcher's plane that ITN and the BBC had had to agree to a shared camera crew. I was twinned with the famous Kate Adie. The crew itself was from the BBC, and I was none too optimistic about the arrangement. My previous experience of Ms Adie had been of someone who liked to get her own way. Even before we hit the Moroccan tarmac she had turned to me from the next seat and said slightly imperiously, 'This doesn't interest me very much, politics isn't my thing. You have the crew, I don't expect I'll have to file.' I was so excited to be on the flight at such a pivotal moment in the battle to liberate southern Africa, and had been so daunted by the prospect of having to battle with Kate Adie to report it, that I could have hugged her with relief; but I didn't. Mrs Thatcher ended up having a banquet with King Hassan's sixteen wives while the old misogynist got on with his own business, whatever that was.

The next day took her nearer the lions' den. Nigeria was technically just a refuelling stop en route to Zimbabwe, but President Babangida came to the airport to give us all a whiff of African anger at Mrs Thatcher's continuing resistance to sanctions against South Africa. She never understood the role US and other countries' sanctions played in finally destroying apartheid, remaining steadfast in her view that her own policy of 'engagement' was what was changing minds in southern Africa.

It's hard to imagine now, but in Harare Zimbabwe's President Robert Mugabe managed a show that to all intents and purposes tipped into a royal visit. He and Mrs Thatcher held hands, and the mobbing crowds were on a wondrous scale. Mugabe was one of the battered league of leaders of front-line states persistently mauled by the South African military. He and Thatcher even discussed his wish to buy British Harrier Jump Jets. Another leader in a similar plight, President Chisano from Mozambique, flew in to talk with the British Prime Minister. His country was prey to the South African-backed Renamo guerrilla group. And Mrs Thatcher would visit Malawi, also a victim of the violence of Renamo, the following day.

As I talked on camera with her in Harare, I wondered what on earth Mrs Thatcher would say if she'd known of my anti-apartheid past. Yet even in front of her government rest house we could see hundreds of Mozambican refugees moving into the city from outlying areas under siege from Renamo. I felt privileged to have been informed by our noisy if naive student action all those years earlier, and particularly proud to have unhorsed one of the erstwhile prime props of white supremacists in the region, Lord Salisbury himself.

Our last stop was pre-independent, South African-controlled Namibia, my first visit there. What a strange place it was, wide and open and unpopulated, with an amazing if unused tarmac road system. The capital, Windhoek, was empty, Germanic and surprisingly white. It all seemed rather genteel, until you remembered that South

Africa had been fighting up on the northern border with and inside Angola for years to keep it that way. Indeed, the very day we'd arrived there had been a clash on the Angolan frontier between six hundred South West African People's Organisation (SWAPO) guerrillas and South African forces. Mrs Thatcher immediately backed South Africa's President P.W. Botha in his claim that the trouble had been started not by the South Africans but by the SWAPO 'insurgents'. The man she should have been seeing was still a banned person in his own homeland. Soon to be President of Namibia, but for now the leader in exile, Sam Nujoma was attending a passing-out parade of his troops in the southern Angolan town of Lubango that day.

It was a decade since I myself had been in Lubango, travelling with SWAPO under the protection of the ruling Angolan MPLA forces. Alan Downes, Don Warren and I had managed to get permission to make a very rare visit to the SWAPO guerrilla camps. We'd had to wait for days in Luanda because the MPLA had decided they could not restrict such a trip to 'Western capitalist running dogs like the British ITN'. East German, Russian and Cuban television crews must go too. The problem was that they did not want to go on so patently dangerous a trip. The civil war with Jonas Savimbi's UNITA forces was at full tilt, and there were fifty thousand Cubans in the country, not to mention the MPLA themselves. But eventually a dignified caravan of Eastern Bloc reporters was rustled up and we set off south.

'Ee all live ma yerrow suvmaree, in a yerrow suvmaree...' The words were sung by Oleg, a very fat Russian correspondent with whom I found myself wedged in the back of a Toyota Land Cruiser. He was armed with large quantities of virtually unobtainable German sausage and Scotch whisky. He spoke no English, but did know practically every Beatles song, including 'Yellow Submarine', or at least his version of it. The further we travelled down the pitch-black Angolan roads the drunker we got, and the more we bastardised the once bearable lyrics and tunes of Lennon and McCartney. Poor Alan, long-suffering and very English, sitting in the middle row, could not take much more. He was never on the longest of fuses, and the blue touchpaper was well gone by dawn. All through the night we had passed convoys of Cuban forces moving in the opposite direction. Daybreak brought us to a forested area; we were clearly nearing SWAPO's main base camp. South-West Africa, as it was, had been colonised by the Germans in the early twentieth century, then handed on as a pro-tectorate to pre-apartheid South Africa, and that was how it still languished, with SWAPO bent on liberation.

Suddenly we were upon the guerrilla camp. Tents were set in amongst the grassy village huts under the trees; beyond, there was a huge circular clearing. Rebel soldiers and their families were everywhere, ten deep around the perimeter. In the middle stood one man: he was SWAPO's leader, Sam Nujoma. An imposing round figure with a full beard, he was every inch the African leader from the bush. It became clear that we were expected to pay obeisance to the great man. We were marshalled with our cameras to one side, and then formed up.

'I'm not going out there to do any of this Viva SWAPO nonsense, Jon,' hissed Alan assertively in my ear. I nodded.

The Cubans were first out, striding towards Nujoma in the centre of the arena. Our cameras turned as, one by one, correspondents and crews shouted 'Viva SWAPO! Viva SWAPO!' Then the megaphone announced 'our friends from the German Democratic Republic', and more Viva SWAPOs followed. The Russians followed suit, and then it was us. I led the way out, Alan sheepishly in my wake. 'Viva SWAPO! Viva SWAPO!' I bellowed with all my strength, and was stunned to hear it echoed by my good friend behind me.

A few weeks later we got a note via the Foreign Office to my editor. 'Was it seemly', it asked, 'for a supposedly independent reporter and his team to be seen shouting for SWAPO?' The British Ambassador in Moscow had seen the incident on Soviet television.

So as I stood with Mrs Thatcher in white, colonial Windhoek, I felt I had indeed seen Namibia from both sides. If Mrs Thatcher had, she might have been better disposed to the South West African People's Organisation, which was then in waiting to take over Namibia peacefully.

The shadow of the swaying Berlin Wall was cast even as far as southern Africa, but Mrs Thatcher seemed not to have noticed the omens. She flew straight back to the House of Commons, where

441

on 4 April she condemned SWAPO's latest incursion into Namibia.

One week later we were in Germany itself. I think it was stuffed pig's stomach, a Palatinate speciality, I was eating in a corner of Bonn's Deidesheimer Hof, close to where Margaret Thatcher and Helmut Kohl were eating similar fare together. The place could not have been more German; for her, that and the presence of her old foe combined to make it a hateful visit, and she did not even pretend that she was enjoying the bilateral with the Chancellor.

Ostensibly she'd come to discuss the gathering pace of nuclear arms reduction and her desire that there should be a new European middle-range nuclear deterrent pointing at the East. Kohl didn't seem to want any lessons from her on the matter, and was anyway under pressure from his Free Democrat coalition colleague and Foreign Minister Hans Dietrich Genscher, who wanted complete nuclear disarmament as soon as possible. In these months I visited Germany often, and came to know Genscher quite well. He was a friend of our Bonn producer Wanda, whose husband Peter wrote speeches for him. Although Genscher was learning English in what was the autumn of his eighteen years as Foreign Minister, Wanda still had to translate at our interview later that day. Genscher told me how Kohl had deliberately brought Mrs Thatcher to his home town, which was not far from the French border. 'Surely now that she's seen me here in my part of Germany, so close to France,' he reported Kohl as saying, 'she will finally understand that I'm not German, I'm European.'

When I asked Mrs Thatcher's foreign affairs guru Charles Powell about it, he said, 'She just got back on the plane, kicked her shoes off and declared, "My God, that man is so German!"' But maybe Kohl really was the new post-Cold War non-nationalist European, and Mrs Thatcher the old-world rigid border-conscious nationalist.

The mock-Tudor panelling in the Soviet embassy in Kensington Gardens provided the backdrop. Here at last was Mikhail Gorbachev, visiting Britain for four days in April 1989, and amazingly, on day two he was talking to me. Our interview lasted nearly an hour; animated, free-ranging, nothing excluded. A great high spot, and I was lucky indeed to get it. By now Gorbachev was at the very epicentre of a developing maelstrom in Eastern Europe. From Poland to Hungary, crowds demanding change were filling the streets, and so far Gorbachev had done nothing to discourage them, nor had he supported anyone else who wanted to stop them.

The success of Gorbachev's visit knew no bounds. An opinion poll showed that in less than a year people, when asked to rank the scale of the Soviet nuclear threat to Britain, had downgraded it from 81 per cent to a mere 29 per cent. Somehow, almost single-handedly, he had transformed the image of the Soviet Union from 'enemy' to 'friend'. His plane took an almost tearful extra turn as it left Heathrow, the collective Cabinet waving below.

A few days later I was summoned to see my editor, Stewart Purvis. The presenter of ITN's Channel Four News, Peter Sissons, had defected overnight to the BBC. I was still diplomatic correspondent on ITN's other outlet, News at Ten, over on the ITV channel, but I had already presented a couple of editions of Channel Four News. I was due to fly to Eastern Europe the next day to look at the gathering forces demanding still-faster reform. 'Jon, could you just do tonight on Channel Four? We think we can get Peter back,' Stewart asked. I was happy to do it, and thought little about the implications. I felt I was a pretty indifferent presenter, and regarded myself very much as a reporter. But they never did get Sissons back, and gradually the days turned into weeks, and the weeks into months. By September 1989 my fifteen years on the road with News at Ten were over, and I had myself defected to Channel Four.

I had been incredibly lucky. Mobile electronic television cameras had come of age in that time. Budgets were still fat, news appetites were still hungry. It was the heyday for reporters going anywhere, anytime, and reporting on the same day. Very soon the 'global village', the feast of digital pictures generated by anyone and everyone, would start streaming across the world so fast that it would render the reporter's presence on the spot well-nigh obsolete. Journalists would be sent to cover only the very biggest stories. The idea of 'one pair of eyes' observing an incident or event on behalf of the viewer who could not get there was dwindling. I accepted the Channel Four job, but with a hint of reluctance. At just over forty, I realised that if I didn't take it someone else would, and by the time I was ready to leave the road, in say five or six years' time, it would be too late.

But here was Eastern Europe in increasing upheaval, populations surging at their borders, and I was often going to have to be lashed to the studio desk, asking questions of those who were there or who were taking decisions, rather than seeing it with my own pair of eyes. It would take years before I felt comfortable in the role. But one plus was that now, with two daughters under seven, I could consolidate my home life and at least aspire to be a more present father.

I still insisted on travelling for some of the time, so I was in and out of Germany and Russia a few more times in the succeeding months, as the streets and squares of the Soviet satellite states filled to bursting. First Hungary opened her border and inaugurated domestic freedoms, then Poland. In October, East Germany's dinosaur President Erich Honecker had pleaded with Gorbachev to use Soviet troops based near East Berlin to intervene and quell the mounting protests; Gorbachev refused.

On 9 November, an hour before we came on air, the East German Politburo opened the Wall. The crowds surged through; people in their hundreds clambered over, pickaxing new openings; men and women in clapped-out Trabants wept at the wheel. It was the most unbelievable night, the

445

upset of the only configuration of Europe I'd ever known. Somehow, caught between old and new television technology, we got a programme on the air with huge reports from both Berlin and Moscow, and we set about taking the entire programme to the Wall.

ITN chartered a Boeing 737 and we took off from Stansted at about midnight. After landing in West Berlin, we made for the Wall and set up camp. My crew and I were on the Unter den Linden in East Berlin in time for the early morning crowds. I turned to my cameraman and said, 'Do you realise that within a decade these two countries could be one?' Within three months it was agreed that they should be, and in less than one short year they were.

That night on Channel Four News we interviewed the smooth, and some thought slightly slimy, Gennadi Gerasimov, Soviet foreign affairs spokesman. I had always liked and got on well with him, but this night even he was ruffled. 'Reunification of the two Germanys?' he said in return to my question. 'Not a chance. They have moved too far from one another.' So I wasn't alone in my misjudgement.

On the second night, as the Wall fell down around us, we tried to anchor a live programme from both sides of it. We deployed ancient microwave technology on the ground, and while most of it worked, our link with our diplomatic correspondent, Nik Gowing, on the other side of the still-closed Brandenburg Gate, behaved oddly. We could hear him, but could only see his apparently headless body coming through in the top half of the screen, and his head in the bottom half. Still, it proved we were human, and it was a hell of an achievement to get on the air at all. And for me, selfishly, it meant I'd got to Berlin and could do some serious reporting, as well as the nocturnal presentation shift.

The next day, with both sides of Berlin awash with people, we drove unhindered through Checkpoint Charlie. Usually East German police stopped you a few hundred yards later, refusing to allow you any further. But this time no one stopped us, and we just drove, mapless, out through the city limits. It was utterly exhilarating, people everywhere smiling, on the move, waving. To our astonishment we eventually arrived in Dresden, the only Western news team in the city. What greeted us was a shattered shell of a place, still grievously wounded from the wartime bombing forty-five years earlier. It seemed to speak volumes about what had happened to the two Germanys in the meantime. The West pumped full of Marshall Aid and Anglo-American ideas and structures; the East pumped full of institutions and ideologies, but little physical aid.

We stopped in the little village of Shöwalder, about 120 miles from Berlin. Here the kerb-stones were etched with the grazes of tank tracks. The Soviet tank corps reportedly came through four times a year on their way to the border. No one here wanted reunification. They just wanted peace, prosperity and freedom. Interestingly, that night most of the people who'd crossed into the West went home again; there was no great permanent exodus to the West.

447

Three years almost to the day from the Reagan–Gorbachev moment in Reykjavik's Hofdi House, it had come to this. We cast forward to the approaching Moscow Summit between the two leaders. I found myself a small, highly graffitied piece of Berlin Wall, which I have on the mantel to this day, and basking in the afterglow of the greatest 'people's revolution' the world has ever known, went home wondering what on earth would happen next.

ELEVEN

Hey, We Never Expected to Win!

'Doors to manual,' the intercom sputtered. 'Welcome to Jan Smuts International Airport.' I had spent a desperate night on a packed British Airways flight from London, speed reading and speed learning Mary Benson's biography of Nelson Mandela. It was 11 February 1990, and the South African government had announced the day before that Mandela was to be freed within twenty-four hours. Now here I was swotting ahead of a live transmission at midday, the appointed hour for his release. I was not even sure that the South Africans would let me in, let alone that the technology of the South African Broadcasting Corporation would stand up to a live transmission to London. The apartheid government had considered television a potentially dangerous force, so its development here had been late, and confined to the state broadcaster SABC. Indeed, our entire endeavour would stand or fall on the co-operation of the apartheid broadcasting regime.

Crossing the tarmac to the terminal building, I mused that it had been twenty years since my anti-apartheid sit-in; twenty years since my arrest at the Springbok rugby match at Old Trafford. Finally, for the first time in my life, I was actually *in* South Africa. South Africa, the nightmare, the dream, the abstract love affair, the passion that had been the unspoken focus of so much of my life. I could not have imagined amid the student mayhem at Liverpool University that one day I would be dispatched to report Nelson Mandela's release after more than twenty-seven years languishing in jail. Almost to my disappointment as a banned person, I had thus far been officially proscribed from getting a South African visa for my entire reporting career – I was waved straight through immigration as if I'd always been welcome.

Although we had brought our own somewhat crude and unreliable satellite dish, live coverage of Mandela's walk to freedom from Victor Verster Prison was to be restricted to SABC. We had not yet escaped the clutches of the very people who'd detained Mandela for all these years. Despite never having worked live with so rudimentary a broadcaster, ITN decided to risk it, and asked me to anchor the live coverage of the event anyway. As midday approached we went live via satellite to London, with no guests to cushion my efforts. SABC had only been able to muster two cameras to cover this historic and seminal moment for the entirety of humankind. Naturally, Mandela did not appear.

Mary Benson's biography began to resurface and weave its way into my commentary as we watched the crowds gathering on one side of the road, and the uniformed representatives of white South African law and order on the other. We craned to try to glimpse movement among the low buildings at the other end of the long drive that led from the prison gates. Still there was none, and still I talked.

At around 12.40 p.m. the SABC camera operative got bored and allowed his camera to tip over crazily on its tripod, transmitting nothing more interesting than the legs and ankles of the waiting crowd. Such was the importance of the event for this particular individual. I talked in all for an hour, the longest utterly unscripted period I have ever spent on television. Normally there are at least occasional formal scripts, or news agency copy, or even a helpful producer whispering facts in your ear. But on this occasion there was none. It was to prove quite a contrast to the death of Diana, or even 9/11, when I was again on air for long periods, but was constantly bombarded with guests, video and endless reports filtered through helping hands.

Finally at two minutes past one, there was movement at the far end of the drive. Cars moved, and then figures – but which one was Mandela? We had seen virtually no images of him for twenty-seven years. Our image of him was still of a strapping, muscular-looking man of forty-five, with a centre parting in his flat black hair.

Suddenly, there he was, somehow taller, slimmer, greyer, but still vital despite his seventy-one years of age. He strode hand in hand with his wife Winnie; now a fist in the air, then a smile, and all the time a presence, an assertive presence. It was spellbinding, and I found it hard to control my own emotions as I reported. I didn't have to speak now, the pictures said it all. Tears were streaming down my cheeks, and down every

451

cheek around me. Mandela was displaying unimaginable dignity, and great restraint, at the moment of his complete victory over those who had wished him and the rights of the black majority dead for two generations.

'I salute the African National Congress.' Mandela's very first words uttered in freedom represented a broadside aimed at his former captors – membership of the banned ANC had been one of the reasons he'd been jailed in the first place. 'I stand before you not as a prophet, but as a humble servant of you the people.' He was making his opening public statement on this, his first night out of prison, to crowds gathered in Cape Town.

My crew and I had returned to Johannesburg and taken up a position on a flatbed truck in the black township of Soweto. Throughout that night's live broadcast the crowds swirled below us in noisy celebration. I remember an improbable moment during a commercial break, having to clamber down and physically haul Mandela's mentor and equally long-serving prisoner, the septuagenarian Walter Sisulu, onto the truck so that I could interview him live on the circuit to London.

Mandela's freedom, wrought with such struggle and pain and crowned with such forgiveness, left many of us confident that a new South Africa could rise without too much more bloodshed. Within four years I would be back to see him wrest the presidency from F.W. de Klerk in the country's first ever democratic election. But for now, I felt privileged to have been allowed to intersect with the two people who were shaping a new and freer world – Mandela in the South; Gorbachev in the North.

So the Wall was down in the North, and the war was done at least in Africa's deepest South. Perhaps peaceful transition in South Africa and along the Iron Curtain allowed us to begin to believe that the Cold War was giving way to the prospect of life beyond conflict. Almost overnight, the countries and the issues that had mattered because of the fragile Cold War superpower balance began to recede.

By the spring of 1990 the Russians were out of Afghanistan. How many of us would be dispatched there to find out what would happen following their departure? In Africa, from Angola to Liberia, from Sudan to Zaire, civil disturbance and war continued without attracting any obvious interest from the outside world. These conflicts did not impinge upon our overall sense of post-Cold War well-being.

Not even the collapse of Yugoslavia and the evolving bloody civil war there managed to dent the optimism that flowed from the downing of the Wall. Although my much lamented friend, Channel Four News foreign correspondent Gaby Rado, who was to die in Iraq much later, committed his reporting life to recording what was happening there, to my eternal shame it would not be until the war in Kosovo a decade later that I would myself report from the region.

We failed to understand what extraordinary restraints Cold War considerations imposed upon even the most domestic and internal struggles in countries around the world. In Eastern Europe and Latin America, the practice and fear of Communism gave way to a genuinely more *laissez-faire* period, but elsewhere liberalisation released pent-up hatred and reprisal. In the emerging 'new world order' few ran to the United Nations asking whether, amid this complete rearrangement of the global political furniture, we should be reforming and restructuring the UN itself so that it might better react to limit bloodshed and the abuse of human rights around the world.

Nowhere was this more obvious than in the Gulf. Iraq's leader, Saddam Hussein, had a continuing dispute with neighbouring Kuwait which centred on overproduction of oil by Kuwait, and Saddam's claims that Kuwait was stealing the stuff from Iraq's Rumaila oilfield near the Iraq–Kuwait border. He was building up his forces on the border, almost certainly to deflect attention from worsening economic conditions at home in the aftermath of his catastrophic war against Iran, that had ended in a ceasefire in August 1988.

The Russians, who wielded no small influence in Baghdad, stayed silent. Worse, April Glaspie, then America's most recent Ambassador to Iraq, in a private audience with Saddam seems to have told him that 'Arab–Arab disputes' were of no interest to America. Many, have seen this as a green light from Washington for an invasion of Kuwait. With no light of any colour coming out of Moscow, the normal constraints that might have prevailed were absent. The differing pace of

Gorbachev's economic and political reforms was such that his hope of retaining power in reformed Communist Party hands was coming apart, which must have been preoccupation enough to explain his failure to sort out policy on Baghdad.

The implosion of Margaret Thatcher's perennial air of impregnability occurred in the same period. On 28 November 1990 I was in Downing Street to see her go, just as I had been there to see her arrive. Stiff-upper-lipped until the car door opened to take her away, and then she began to cry. It was a great fall, and one from which neither she nor her party has ever really recovered. However painfully, she'd created huge change in Britain, particularly in the securing of flexibility in the economy. But like Gorbachev, her understanding of the need for political change – devolution, decentralisation, attacking class, racial and gender prejudice and division – was far behind her economic actions. She rarely if ever thought of applying 'market forces' to social issues, and appeared perfectly happy to live with an honours system and a House of Lords which operated so exactly counter to her economic *diktats*. Dogmatic, divisive and decisive, she may have made remarkable achievements in economic reform, but the words 'Poll Tax' will also forever define her reign.

John Major, who followed her, was nice, personable and collegiate, but he did not give the impression of being a leader who was going to have much impact upon any new world order. I once found myself having to kill twenty minutes with him, waiting for a satellite link to come good. We talked cricket with ease, despite the fact that I'm no sportsman, but not much else. Ten Downing Street in his time was a morgue, no joy to visit. Most times I found it hard to believe that he was Prime Minister. Many people in Britain have already almost forgotten his seven-year stint in office, somehow coming to believe that the Thatcher years slipped effortlessly into the Blair years. As I was to witness, in reality it wasn't quite like that, for within a couple of years of coming into office Major was to suffer a reverse from which the country has never quite recovered.

When Madeleine and I and our two daughters went on holiday to Cape Cod as usual in the summer of 1990, it was to the sound of war drums. Saddam marched into Kuwait on 2 August. Within six days, US Defense Secretary Dick Cheney was in Saudi Arabia arranging for the 'infidel' to base the 82nd Airborne Division and several America fighter squadrons on Saudi soil. That summer the seeds of Osama bin Laden's *casus belli* were sown. Funded by America to fight in Afghanistan, bin Laden would now turn the fruits of those same funds back on the United States in pursuit of his war with the Saudi royal family; but it would take a decade before the West noticed, and then with the most terrible and catastrophic bang.

Halfway through August in Wellfleet, with the Cape Cod skies blacker than I had ever seen them, amid dire warnings to flee the area, we lost contact with the outside world and were struck by the full devastating force of Hurricane Bob. The winds tore at the windows, outside we could barely stand, and the sea had become a boiling grey and spumey cauldron. The town ran out of duct tape, and hundreds of mature trees were ripped down by the winds, taking the phone lines and the power for the water-pumping system with them. We battened down the hatches, retreated to the basement and dug into our emergency supplies. We were joined in our retreat from the winds by Helena Kennedy's family, who rented in the same settlement, and the now widowed Jean Boudin, Leonard having sadly died two summers earlier. So there were at least a dozen of us in that battered and beleaguered place.

The next morning, finding the BBC World Service on my small short-wave radio, I braved it upstairs to the windows overlooking the deck to try to get better reception. The lone oak around which this suntrap had been built was being split asunder by the sheer force of the gale. The radio crackled in my hands as the news came through from Moscow. Gorbachev had been seized at his Crimean dacha in an attempted coup, and there had been neither sight nor sound of him since. My heart sank. Somehow the oak on the deck being wrenched from its roots seemed to symbolise the terrible political storm that was now enveloping Gorbachev. I felt personally wrapped up in his fate. Was he dead? Who was holding him? Could his reforms now be rolled back? Could we be subjected to a new Soviet threat?

There was also frustration: I should be there, in

Moscow. I should catch a flight. But every airport in New England was shut, the roads were blocked. There were no phones to London, no phones anywhere. The age of remote internet access and the mobile had not yet dawned. In every sense I too was now held hostage against my will, and would be for many days to come.

I made it on foot to Main Street to inspect the damage in Wellfleet, and to see who else was about. The owners of the little dress shop on the corner of Holbrook, in common with everyone else, had taped up its windows against the wind. In the top quarter lights above the main glass, someone had used the tape only too poignantly to spell out a message: 'Bye Bye Gorby', it read.

Within four days we heard that he was alive, and coming back to Moscow. All our broken trees and flushless loos became as nothing as we strained to hear every bulletin on the little radio. The President of the reconstituted Russian Federation, Boris Yeltsin, had stood on a tank in front of twenty thousand people near Red Square and called for 'mass resistance'. In periods of bad reception I would switch the radio off and dash outside to dig pit latrines, or push the wheelbarrow, laden with two empty dustbins weighed down with bricks, to collect drinkable water from the firehouse. Then it would be back to Gorbachev's fate, to hear that the incompetent Gennady Yanayev, the leader of the eight-man Communist junta that had staged the coup, was now trying to negotiate his own surrender. A shaken Gorbachev appeared with his family in Moscow, having been bundled aboard an airliner in the Crimea by loyal forces. Yeltsin now held Gorbachev's fate in his hands. His price for restoring him to the presidency of the tottering remnants of the Soviet Union was Gorbachev's signature on an edict suspending the very Communist Party of which he had been General Secretary.

On Christmas Day 1991, Mikhail Gorbachev submitted his resignation: 'Given the current situation, I am ceasing my activities as President of the USSR.' Poor Gorbachev no longer had a country to govern. Soon, in presidential elections for Russia itself, the people would visit a derisory less than half of 1 per cent of the vote upon the man who had, perhaps unwittingly, changed the world. In my study at home in London Sally Soames's remarkable photograph of Gorbachev remains the only one of anybody outside my own family to hang on my walls. When the great love of his life, Raisa, died of leukaemia in 1999, many hearts must have gone out to a man who had lost everything in the course of bringing about such change.

Amid the death of Soviet Communism, the West was heading for the first post-Soviet conflict, with the Muslim if secular forces of Iraq. I was in a deep sleep in my third-floor room at the Intercontinental Hotel in Geneva on 9 January 1991 when three men burst in through the locked door. One of them, who I now saw was armed, told me to get out of bed and made me stand completely naked in front of him. A second ripped a blanket from the bed and wrapped it around me. 'Come with us!' he barked. One of the men worked for the hotel, the other two were Swiss policemen. They frogmarched me out of the hotel and down to the central police station.

I had flown in to report the last-minute talks between US Secretary of State James Baker and his Iraqi opposite number, the ever inscrutable Tariq Aziz. This was an abortive attempt to see whether Saddam Hussein could be persuaded to withdraw peacefully from Kuwait before war broke out. I was due to anchor Channel Four News that night, at no small expense, live from Geneva. It was five in the morning as I was flung, still without clothes, into a solitary cell in the police station. I appeared to have committed an offence, but my erratic French couldn't quite make out what it was. They flashed documents in front of me. I asked to make a phone call, or even for them to make a phone call on my behalf. I was refused. I sat there in my blanket with no further visit from the police until 8 a.m. Soon my crew at the hotel would begin to wonder where I was, and my office in London would be calling me, as arranged, in my room. Once again a policeman came to the cell door flashing a paper he would not let me read, and I demanded a phone call. I began to worry that not only would I lose my hard-fought-for interview with Tariq Aziz and the story itself, but that the naked anchor would neither be clothed nor free by 7 p.m. to present the Channel Four News.

Finally, at eleven in the morning, six hours after my traumatising arrest, my demand for a phone call was granted. Fortunately I knew the British manager of the Intercontinental Hotel, and I called him. I told him I was naked and had no idea what the hell was going on. The French policeman then explained to him why they were holding me. 'You've failed to pay a speeding fine,' my friend told me. 'I'll come down and pay it, and put it on your bill; it's only sixty Swiss francs.'

When he arrived, I told him that I had indeed paid the fine I'd incurred several years earlier when speeding to the office of Swiss television to report the story of Arafat at the UN.

'Ah, but you were fined twice,' said my friend. 'Once for speeding, and once for going through a red light. You were fined sixty Swiss francs for each.'

'I thought the second fine was a duplicate,' I said. 'I had to keep it to claim back the fine on expenses.'

Later I discovered that when James Baker had arrived on his official plane at Geneva airport, the press accompanying him had jumped off the flight first to report, film and photograph his descent from the aircraft steps ahead of this make-or-break meeting that might or might not avert war in the Gulf. The Swiss police had altogether other ideas, and demanded the press get back on board and file through immigration after Baker had left the airport. As Americans tend to, the press continued their work, and the police set about them, beating them and man-handling them mercilessly. Baker's people filed a formal complaint with the Swiss Minister of the Interior. He in turn contacted the police, and they decided to run the name of every journalist

461

accredited to the talks through the police computer.

That's where they found the unsuspecting Mr J. Snow and his 'non-payment of fine' offence. I was the only mug they caught, so they gave it to me with both barrels. I eventually wrung an apology out of the Swiss Ambassador in London, at the second time of asking. The incident gave the bored British tabloid press a story about a naked newscaster, and there was even a Jak cartoon in the London *Evening Standard*. I learned two morals from the story: always work on the basis that Switzerland is a police state; and never sleep in a Swiss hotel in the nude.

The talks failed, and I sat once again in front of Mr Aziz. I'd interviewed him several times in the early 1980s during the Iran–Iraq war, and I would see him again before the war on Iraq in 2003. Somehow he threaded effortlessly through this turbulent period of Gulf history, staying alive, alert, interesting, engaging, and with an ability to survive somewhere near the top of the Iraqi ruling mafia. He was a brilliant front man for Saddam, but did he survive because he was of no consequence, or because he was able constantly to outflank those who would have done away with him? I suspect the latter. The Gulf War was over in four days. I never went to Iraq in that time, and regret to this day that we did not report more exhaustively the terrible carnage the Western allies allowed Saddam to mete out to the southern Shias in general and the Marsh Arabs in particular. We knew then that hundreds of thousands were slaughtered in the

Shia uprising, but so little was said that even Tony Blair was to express shock at the discovery of the mass graves a decade later.

Just as the old world order lost its last great leader in Gorbachev, the United States elected a man who could surely forge a new one. As I chased Bill Clinton round the familiar byways of New Hampshire and the traditional campaign circuit, I found that he displayed a presence, a charisma and an intelligence rarely seen in such a context. He seemed to promise even more than myth has it John F. Kennedy did. To be at a Clinton rally, as I was in New York, was to experience real politics in the raw.

The right wing hated him, and they found his Achilles heel easily, early and often: she was woman. Paula Jones, Gennifer Flowers, Monica Lewinsky. But Bill Clinton's real problem was not women, but that he was out of kilter with the state of party politics in America. Such were his presentational skills, his personal attractions, that he won the 1992 election in his own right, against the grain. The country was still moving rightwards, as was expressed in votes that led to Republican majorities in both the Congress and the Senate, and these proved to be his undoing. Without at least one of the Houses on Capitol Hill, the power of his presidency to deliver was soon crippled.

Even so, Clinton's inauguration was to prove one of the seminal moments of my reporting life. He had asked Maya Angelou, one of America's most celebrated African-American writers, to deliver a keynote inaugural poem. Over the years I'd been lucky enough to become friends with her, for when we had been in Washington she'd come to live in my London home to be near to her mentor, the radical writer Jessica Mitford, who was staying in the next street. Jessica and Maya went back three decades or more: they had met and travelled together in the then segregated American South. Jessica, who was only twelve years older than Maya, told me that she had stipulated that if anyone asked the nature of the relationship between this striking white British aristocrat and this black daughter of Arkansas, they were to be told that they were mother and daughter. If they still probed, they were to be told that 'In those days, terrible things happened...' Then the voice was to tail away, and the head droop. Many were the times that the three of us, and other friends, would break into renditions of such banal songs as 'My Old Man's a Dustman' or 'Right, Said Fred'. I remember Salman Rushdie, seriously on the run from the *fatwa* that Tehran had issued against him, singing particularly lustily with them in our curtained front room.

For a time after we came back from Washington in 1986, we lived at Madeleine's house in Tufnell Park. Washington had been the very first time we'd actually cohabited in the same home. Mine, to which Madeleine would soon move, was nearby in Kentish Town. Maya was still there, and I would often go round to breakfast with her. She's an early bird and would read me what she'd just written; or right there, standing in the hall, she'd perform some story she'd just remembered, or sing yet another song with all her voice. Heaven knows what the neighbours made of it; they lived awfully close by.

On the eve of Clinton's inauguration in January 1993, I flew down to Winston Salem in North Carolina to interview Maya for Channel Four News. There, across her kitchen table, she declaimed her inaugural poem. She described the themes enshrined in 'On the Pulse of Morning'. Centred around 'a rock, a river, a tree', the poem appealed to the great American themes of the embrace of the immigrant, and learning the lessons of history.

Two days later I was with my camera crew atop the farmworkers' union building four or five hundred yards from the Capitol rotunda. There on the dais below, flanked by the Chief Justice, the President, the Senate and the Congress, was the six-foot Maya Angelou, adorned from head to toe in red. In the viewfinder of my camera she was an inch-high figure, but her huge voice filled the skies and made it an inauguration unlike any other.

...You, the Turk, the Arab, the Swede,
  the German, the Eskimo, the Scot,
You, the Ashanti, the Yoruba, the Kru, bought,
Sold, stolen, arriving on the nightmare
Praying for a dream.
Here, root yourselves beside me.
I am that Tree planted by the River,
Which will not be moved.
I, the Rock, I the River, I the Tree

465

I am yours – your passages have been paid.
Lift up your faces, you have a piercing need
For this bright morning dawning for you.
History, despite its wrenching pain
Cannot be unlived, but if faced
With courage, need not be lived again.

Back in Britain I had been briefly detached from
Channel Four and lent to ITV. I'd been warned
that I would not be able to pee for ten hours, and
told that I should eat bananas for energy. It was
the night of 9 April 1992, and ITN had given me
the chance of a lifetime, to anchor the ITV
general election results programme. In many
ways this is the very summit of every aspiring TV
presenter's ambition. I suspect I may have been
chosen because after thirteen years of Conservative hegemony I was one of the few ITN journalists, let alone anchors, who had any
relationship at all with Labour. While I wasn't a
member of the party, I had good friendships with
the Kinnocks and Foots, and I knew some of
Labour's leading figures like Jack Straw, Patricia
Hewitt and John Reid.

It was an amazing, rollercoaster experience –
vast resources, cameras at a hundred counts the
length and breadth of the country, and yet organ-
isationally it was sometimes well up the Khyber.
At times I was almost having to direct from the
presenter's chair. We missed the critical signifi-
cance of Basildon, a key Essex swing seat that
Labour had to win to have a chance of gaining
power. In the end the improbable John Major
won, and poor Neil Kinnock, who'd devoted a

decade to making Labour electable, resigned. He had to leave the stage to the Scottish lawyer and Shadow Chancellor John Smith, who would potentially taste the fruits of his labours. Smith was to be robbed of the chance by a devastating heart attack within just two years of becoming leader. He was a good man, great company, and I must admit we were together supping white wine at the South African High Commission in Nelson Mandela's honour the very day before his premature death.

For the time being, Major survived another day. But within eleven weeks of getting back into Downing Street he was fatally winged and rendered the lamest of ducks for the remainder of his five years in office.

He had inherited from Mrs Thatcher the extraordinarily unThatcherite decision for Britain to enter the disciplined European Exchange Rate Mechanism (ERM), which lashed the pound to a basket of other European currencies. The pound was allowed only very limited fluctuations in value, and the main tool of control was the lowering or increasing of interest rates. It all came adrift during a massive speculative move against the pound on 'Black Wednesday', 16 September 1992. The luckless Major, divested of his residence at Number Ten owing to building works, was stuck virtually incommunicado in a temporary office in Whitehall, having to listen to the evolving disaster on the radio.

We went to air on Channel Four News at seven o'clock, with the UK interest rate at 12 per cent after one panicked rise, and another one planned which would have taken it up to 15 per cent. The balloon was clearly going to burst, and in case it did while we were broadcasting we lined up the man who had laid down his political life to get rid of Thatcher, my old friend the former Foreign Secretary and Chancellor of the Exchequer Sir Geoffrey Howe. I also got hold of Gavyn Davies, then Chief Economist at Goldman Sachs, who was close to the Labour Party.

At exactly 7.40 p.m., with twenty minutes of our programme to go, Britain fell ignominiously out of the ERM. But that was not what it sounded like. Norman Lamont, the Chancellor, had stood outside the Treasury to declare, 'Tonight we have suspended the pound within the ERM.'

'So,' I asked, 'you're a former Chancellor, Sir Geoffrey, what does that mean?'

Candid as ever, Howe replied, 'I haven't got a clue. Ask Gavyn.'

So I did. 'The United Kingdom has just devalued the pound by 14 per cent,' he declared.

Britain's catastrophic withdrawal from the ERM has marred every attempt since to persuade the body politic to get any nearer to joining the euro zone. Yet without such a move, Britain's membership of and commitment to Europe will never be complete. And without Britain, Europe, as counterweight to the lone American super-power, will continue to fail to make the grade.

In October 1992, three years after the Berlin Wall came down, I found myself reporting news of the deaths of eighteen US Rangers in Somalia. It was the climax of a disaster that could be tracked back to the fall of the Wall and the ending of the Cold War four years earlier. In that time I had never gone back to Mogadishu, despite scenes of human suffering that outstripped anything I'd seen when I was there in the seventies and eighties. In fact journalists spent the absolute minimum of time there, so dangerous had it become.

Back in 1990, within weeks of the ending of the Cold War America had summarily pulled the plug on its multi-million-dollar military supply line into Somalia. With the Cold War over, it had no further strategic interest in the place. Russia had dominated Somalia in the seventies; the US had managed to take it over in the eighties; and with the overthrow of the old strongman Siad Barre in 1991 – with all superpower interest now departed – open civil war between rival warlords was to tear the country to pieces in the nineties.

The US Rangers had gone in under cover of UN resolutions in response to the famine that had swept the country, but by the time they got there the famine was effectively over. So they tried to deal with a key factor at the centre of the country's instability by capturing or killing one of the principal clan leaders, General Mohamed Aideed.

The abortive international adventure in Somalia can be seen as a sincere but ultimately unsuccessful attempt to invent a template for the imposition of some kind of new post-Cold War world order. In common with the US television networks, we were transmitting nightly scenes of starvation and violence in Somalia. George Bush Senior had already inaugurated a policy in which US troops would support the UN force for the first time in history in 'peace enforcement' rather than 'peace-keeping'. In other words American forces would intervene under UN auspices but would remain American, not wearing blue UN berets or coming under UN command.

'Operation Restore Hope' in Somalia represented many 'firsts' for both the UN and the US. The former Egyptian Deputy Prime Minister for Foreign Affairs, Boutros Boutros-Ghali, became UN Secretary General in January 1992. Clinton took over in the White House one year later. Boutros accused Western leaders of fostering a 'European tilt' to the UN's priorities, and of being 'racist', which caused quite a stir. It may have contributed to his becoming one of the few Secretary Generals not to have his term extended. The Americans disliked his independence.

America grotesquely underestimated the scale of the challenge in Somalia, and eventually in 1993 Clinton had to follow Bush and send in still more troops, bringing the US presence there to eight thousand servicemen. Pakistan, with five thousand troops, also had a major presence in the UN effort, alongside troops from twenty-nine other nations. All this at a time when Western leaders were under pressure for not doing more in Yugoslavia. A source in Clinton's National Security Council told me, 'We did Somalia because we found Bosnia too hard to grapple with.' Some of us were to wonder much later whether we also 'did' Iraq because Saudi Arabia, where the 9/11 hijackers came from, was also 'too hard to grapple with'.

One Blackhawk helicopter down and eighteen dead Rangers was enough to panic Clinton into abandoning Somalia altogether. With America gone, the UN could do little. Somalia slipped off into the wastes of the 'unreported'. It would not be until after the events of 9/11, a decade later, that people spoke of Somalia as a 'failed state', and a 'breeding ground for terrorism'. But Somalia was above all a state that the world community failed, before it failed of its own accord.

The failings of the UN as a post-Cold War peace enforcement agency remained unaddressed. But none of us was particularly concerned. We were fixated by Bosnia; Rwanda was still to come. The sunny uplands of the post-Cold War period freed of 'nation on nation conflict' were already becoming gravely cratered by civil strife within borders. Technically these were conflicts over which the United Nations had little remit to act.

The great shaft of light in the mid-1990s remained South Africa, despite the most daunting odds. In the course of covering the country's first ever democratic elections in April 1994, I found myself boarding a bus in the Northern Transvaal at 3.30 in the morning. The bus itself was a Spartan tin, with stark, upright seats, a metal floor and condensation dribbling down its dirty windows. The street lights outside accentuated the gloom as the bus made regular stops to pick up black workers. This was apartheid in action; the huddled figures who once aboard tried to resume their sleep were being carted two and a

471

half hours from their homes to their place of work. They were the living consequences of the policy of racial segregation, and the wholesale and enforced decamping of hundreds of thousands of black people from swathes of South Africa that occurred in the 1950s. Yet the people I was travelling with were effectively the economic elite: they had jobs. Most of them worked in a cosmetics packaging plant in the distant suburbs of Johannesburg.

The factory hooter was sounding as we swung in through the gates at 6 a.m. White managers, fresh from their five-minute journeys from home, swept past as the workers got down from their two-and-a-half-hour ordeal. Inside the factory, the black workers mingled with white working-class Afrikaners. I spoke to one of these, Pik, a twenty-three-year-old who lived in a poor district in Jo'burg. He was playing draughts with a black colleague during a fifteen-minute tea break. 'At home, I'm a member of the AWB [the extreme white supremacist political party], but it doesn't affect me in the workplace. I like these guys, but I don't like the idea of being ruled by them. I'll be voting AWB.'

Maurice, the black man across the table from him, told me, 'I'll be voting for Mandela and the ANC.'

At 6 p.m. the factory siren sounded again. The twelve-hour shift was over. The black workers boarded the bus for their two-and-a-half-hour journey home. Five hours on the road, twelve hours in the workplace, six days and six nights a week. Yet there was little tension, little evident resentment, simply a sense of resignation, patience and hope that one day there would be change.

Across the country, from rally to rally, from urban township to rural sprawl, the impending poll stirred a surge of euphoria that was in stark contrast to the atmosphere on the factory floor I'd just visited. At 3.30 on the morning before the vote on 27 April 1994, I found myself dispensing whisky to Essop Pahad and Thabo Mbeki in my room in the Carlton Hotel in central Johannesburg. We talked the night away. Mbeki was beyond question one of the brightest and most committed leaders I'd met. When Tony Blair was still asking what the internet was, Thabo was already on it nightly. Sometimes I suspect his endless surfing in search of still more information may have been one reason why he came under the spell of the disregarded minority of scientists who questioned the link between AIDS and HIV, which was to do South African sufferers of AIDS and Mbeki's own reputation incalculable harm. At times I have seen him as many saw Jimmy Carter, as so voracious a reader and searcher after truth that it made the process of daily decision-making all the harder.

It was extraordinary to see Mbeki, with whom not so long before I had eaten pasta at Bertorelli's in Soho, as Mandela's chief lieutenant. Thanks to him I got an exclusive interview the next day with Mandela, his first as President of South Africa. The magical moment was slightly marred by the consequences of my late-night consumption. Looking at the interview recently, the interviewer looks puffier than usual around the eye. I wrote a diary piece at the time for *Index on Censorship*:

The President-to-be comes in at 8 a.m., smiling from ear to ear. He recognises Judy Aslett, our correspondent, and Themba our Sowetan sound man, whom he treats like a son. I have only met him across the satellite links from London. Charming, charismatic and never seventy-five – maybe fifty-eightish? He has unexpectedly muscular hands. Walter Sisulu told me it was a direct consequence of their early life in jail – breaking rocks with a heavy hammer. Like Gorbachev, Mandela made absolute eye contact, and perhaps because like the Russian he had been spared media exposure until his maturer years, he responded with a candour and openness you hardly if ever see in a seasoned Western politician. At this point this dispassionate media operative felt in both Mandela and Gorbachev he'd met two people fully capable of walking on water!

We start, and Mandela unleashes an uncharacteristic fusillade of anger: there has been 'massive electoral fraud', he says. That off his chest, he returns to the theme he had stressed throughout the week: 'Let bygones be bygones, we must forgive, but cannot forget.' Half an hour later, that handshake again, and being in the presence of one of the great figures of the twentieth century had gone. Forget the dispassionate journalist; the prisoner had become a President, and I had been allowed to talk with him.

To Adelaide Tambo for lunch ... a wonderful

gathering of the great campaigners. Walter and Albertina Sisulu, Mary Benson, Nadine Gordimer, Anthony Sampson and many, many more. A marquee in the garden, a band in the porch – and even the most seasoned amongst us can't quite believe that it really has happened. South Africa is free!

On 26 April 1994 I stood on the balcony with F.W. de Klerk, outside the office he was about to vacate. He was granting me his last ever interview as President. A confident, bullish Boer, he had been the more stolidly right-wing of the two candidates to replace the dreaded P.W. Botha five years previously. But he it was who, despite a ministerial record in pursuit of the most absolute imposition of apartheid, had released Nelson Mandela. It was his action, however pragmatic, that kindled the possibility of a peaceful transition to democracy.

With just a few hours to go, de Klerk still claimed to me that it was he and not the rest of the world who was responsible for the 'great change'. 'We were coping with the external pressures, surviving sanctions, winning the wars around us – no, what happened here is that I and others decided what was best for South Africa.' I asked him if he called Mandela 'Nelson'. 'No, I call him Mr Mandela,' he said, 'and he calls me Mr State President.' Did he like him? 'We worked together, it was not a question of liking him.' I felt he was jealous of Mandela, and that he was arrogant and resentful. I came away from the interview feeling I'd spoken to a truculent pragmatist who'd done a great thing, but was not himself a great man.

Would that other world hotspots had been fortunate enough to breed a Mandela. Within a couple of months of the South African elections I was with Yasser Arafat in Gaza. The Chairman of the Palestine Liberation Organisation had just returned home from thirty years in exile, and I had gone there to witness the moment. Alas, he was no Mandela. I shuttled to Gaza City from Jerusalem, criss-crossing the grim Israeli checkpoint three or four times a day for four days in pursuit of an audience with the old man. His office was chaos, in keeping with the overall condition of Gaza itself.

For hours at a time I sat on an old tubular-framed chair with a raffia seat with a hole in it, in a corridor outside Arafat's door. The interview was always going to be 'this afternoon', 'tonight', 'later', 'in a few hours'. When eventually it came, we spoke in English, though the language made little difference; Arafat could not be anything other than his usual suspicious, wary self. The stubble said more than the man, the eyes darted about, the voice was occasionally high.

His return to Gaza, with Israel's Prime Minister Yitzhak Rabin still in charge in Tel Aviv, was one of many moments of hope. Yet it was part of a rollercoaster pattern that veered from hope to despair, a pattern that made keeping viewers' interest very difficult. The story never changed – killings, outrages on both sides, and foreign interference. The ending of the Cold War offered a chance here too, a chance that was never fully pursued. And eventually the downing of the Berlin Wall would produce another wall here to replace it.

I was to go back to Israel many times, most horrifically and memorably in April 2002, when Bethlehem, of all places, was under siege. The Church of the Nativity had become a sanctuary for armed Palestinians whom the Israeli army wanted. There were thirty-five friars holed up with 240 'others'. Smoke billowed from somewhere near the belfry. Israeli tanks and armoured personnel carriers also belched smoke as they pounded round the town. The streets were otherwise utterly deserted. Thirty-five thousand souls hid behind their steel shutters. The Israelis had finally managed to alienate even the predominantly Christian community who live in Bethlehem's core. We were shot at by an Israeli soldier as we neared Manger Square with volunteers trying to take food to beleaguered families.

We took cover in an upstairs room with the Halaman family, seventeen of them sitting on sofas and armchairs well back from the window, listening to the crack of gunfire. Sadeq, the father of the house, is a Christian and a successful middle-class trader. 'I tell you frankly, I support the suicide bombers,' he told me. 'What do we have left? How can we defend ourselves and our lives? I was educated by the British, taught English by them. Why do you people let this happen to us?'

On the roof of the Star Hotel, overlooking the centre of Bethlehem, high-idealed if naive international human shields retreated from their attempts to put themselves between the tanks and the Palestinians. As we drove out of town, I noticed that the police station and every Palestinian administrative office had been flattened by aerial bombing. Part of the European-funded Oslo Peace Accords had been the establishment of these elements of a 'civil society'. This proved to be part of a pattern of deliberate Israeli destruction of every element of administrative infrastructure so recently installed. In every Palestinian town I visited there was clear evidence of an Israeli determination to render Gaza and the West Bank ungovernable. The Palestinian Authority was deprived of every mechanism for running a country.

Suddenly a military escort flashed past, accompanying a Jeep sporting an Italian flag. Amazingly, an Italian diplomat called Claudio Ginbergia had contrived to get ten tons of food and drugs right into the heart of Bethlehem, the first such supplies in three weeks. He'd used every diplomatic twist to do it. In our undefended, far from bombproof Palestinian taxi, we tagged dangerously along behind his convoy. We were led beyond the Church of the Nativity, past great ranks of tanks. The convoy stopped suddenly; people began to emerge from nowhere, and soon the street was heaving with boxes, bags, fruit, bread and cans. Chaos enveloped the Italian and his tons of provisions, and soon the lot was gone. As we drove away through streets that were once again deserted I thought, 'So this is diplomatic siege-breaking.'

That afternoon I took tea with the Rabinowitz family in a sharp-shadowed stone suburban street on the far side of Jerusalem. Alan is a tour guide, but there are no longer any tourists. 'It has to be done,' this once-moderate Israeli said of the army actions on the West Bank. 'Sadly, it will have to be seen through this time.'

The next day, America's Secretary of State Colin Powell hit town for talks with Prime Minister Ariel Sharon. I never saw a man look more as if he wanted to be somewhere else. Powell had no feel for this; he simply sustained the pretence of even-handedness that has so exacerbated the crisis here. A suicide bomber greeted the moment with a terrible detonation at a bus stop five hundred yards from our office. She was a nineteen-year-old from devastated Jenin, whose brother had been shot dead by Israeli troops. Six Israelis died instantly, among them three Arab beggars hoping for loose fruit from the market nearby. 'Get out, you bastards!' a black-clad Hassidic Jew shouted as he pounded his fists on my chest. 'Get out! You brought this, it's you!'

The next day we struggled into the West Bank, to Ramallah with Powell, to see Arafat. The old man's compound had been blown to pieces. The Israelis had carted away the devastated trucks and cars and some of the rubble from their attacks, but the gaping shellhole in his office complex could not be disguised. Powell came out grim-faced and said nothing. Poor man, he's presided over a period that has seen more Israelis and more Palestinians die than at any time since the birth of the Jewish state. He will not go down in history as America's finest Secretary of State.

But I have run ahead of myself. The nineties were turning sour. To the Middle East, add the former Yugoslavia. Every night I was reading out the news of more terrible atrocities. But as with the Middle East, viewers felt a helpless lack of interest: human rights violation fatigue, ethnic cleansing fatigue set in. Even in my newsroom they were asking, 'Must we lead on that again?'

Then, in the summer of 1995, Srebrenica shattered the capacity to switch off, when appalling carnage was inflicted on Muslim men, witnessed and unprevented by the UN. Even attempting to report it from the clinical confines of a studio brought a lump to the throat.

In December 1995 the Yugoslav President Slobodan Milosevic and the other Serb, Croat and Bosnian leaders made it to Paris to sign up to the Dayton peace process. We decided to anchor the news from the French capital, and by 7 a.m. I was standing in the foyer of Milosevic's hotel. All day there were comings and goings, but he never came and never went. This is journalism. We knew he was up there on the top floor; we were well in with his odious crew.

Halfway through the day my cousin Peter Snow turned up with a team from our BBC rival, *Newsnight*. They had invested less in getting Milosevic. Peter was starting from cold. It was awkward; we'd never been against each other since Denis Hills all those years ago outside Idi Amin's Ugandan Command Post. I behaved like a journalist shit, and told him less than nothing about what I knew. An hour later, with two hours to go to our transmission deadline, Milosevic allowed me, one cameraman and no tripod up to his quarters.

He cut a ludicrous, Napoleonic figure, framed by the dormer window of his top-floor suite. One arm was actually inside his jacket as he swung round to assess my entrance. There seemed to be no one else in the pink room; in reality there was just one security man at my cameraman's elbow. Normally there is so much setting up before a keynote interview, but now here there was none, just shoot from the hip. Which Milosevic did, in excellent, seductive English. So reasonable and calm, and patently villainous. The camera, even without a tripod, never lies. We had a scoop, but I felt bad about it, and about him. Once again I had been within killing distance of a mass murderer; in my mind I glimpsed Idi Amin across the gangway.

'Why can't you do more, Jon?' Jill Craigie had accosted me near the Corn Flakes in the Camden branch of Sainsbury's in north London. I was in the frame for failing adequately to expose Serb atrocities on the nightly news. Jill always spoke her mind, and she and her husband Michael Foot were passionate about Croatia; they went there regularly, collected art there, and grieved together over the dismemberment of Dubrovnik and the atrocities inflicted on the population there. They talked less about one of the other bad men of the Balkans, Franjo Tudjman, by now the Croatian President, and Milosevic's equally blood-spat-

481

tered counterpart. 'Come to supper on Sunday,' Jill urged, 'and we can talk more.' But before she turned away, I had a sudden thought. She herself was one of the finest documentary film-makers of her age. Why didn't *she* go and report the Balkan War? The idea was born, and that Sunday night as I sat with the beleaguered Salman Rushdie and a few others, the plot was hatched. Jill would direct the film, and Michael would report it. It was a project of complete madness. Jill was over seventy, Michael over eighty, but they were determined to go themselves. They would sink their savings into it, it was horribly risky – and it had been my idea.

Six months later, the call came. 'I want you to come and see our film, and you must bring Michael Grade too,' said Jill. 'I want Channel Four to show it.' Grade was then my boss, the chief executive at Channel Four. I was petrified by the time I sat on the sofa in Jill and Michael's front room to view it. What if it was untransmittable? But it wasn't: it was the most amazing and vigorous polemic. *Two Hours from London* was great and opinionated television, and BBC2 eventually broadcast it in 1994. As I had feared, though, Tudjman escaped serious criticism in it.

While the world was coming apart around us, John Major's Conservative Party was coming apart around him. Just before 6 p.m. on 22 June 1995, Major suddenly resigned. It took a few minutes to realise that although he was still Prime Minister, he'd resigned the office that had enabled him to become so – leader of the Conservative Party. There was complete chaos in Whitehall and in Downing Street; we had an hour to go before our news transmission, and no civil servant would accept a request for an interview with Major because they said this was a 'party matter'. I hared out of the office and jumped on my bike. Pedalling as if there was no tomorrow, I reached Downing Street in eleven minutes from our studios in Gray's Inn Road. I banged on the great black door, and a startled attendant let me in. Major's excellent political secretary Howell James was coming down the stairs at that instant. 'Howell,' I panted, 'gotta have an interview with him ... now ... it's half past six, it'll take me nine minutes to get back... I must leave here at 6.45 to make the air ... otherwise there'll be a terrible hole.'

'Go on then, get into the garden, set up and I'll get him,' said Howell.

But I had no crew, they were carbound, stuck in traffic. I panted out of the door, grabbed a Reuters crew, promising the earth, and a cameraman I recognised from GMTV. We belted down into the garden, and there was Major. 'I'm flushing them out, they've got to put up or shut up, this is their chance,' he told me, referring to the men he'd once called 'bastards'. 'We shall have a leadership election, I shall win, and this will be an end to all this backbiting.'

But it wasn't; it proved to be the start of a long, dark sojourn for the once-dominant party in British politics.

I sprinted out of the black door, feeling almost half in possession of Downing Street – certainly no one else seemed to be in charge in that moment. I hurtled up Whitehall on the bike, past Nelson's Column, along the Strand, up Kingsway and into Gray's Inn Road. Nine minutes it was, but I was now in a disgusting and untransmittable condition, albeit with an exclusive interview with the ex-leader of the Tory Party, and Prime Minister, John Major. Joan Watson, the best make-up artist in television, dashed to the fridge and produced some ice cubes, which she stuffed behind my ears. At four minutes to seven, the sweat began to recede. Spot on seven, hair brushed, freshly Max Factored, 'Good evening...' My worst nightmare, of hearing the signature tune for the news and not being in my chair, had been avoided.

From the ashes of all this came Tony Blair. That blue red dawn over the Thames on 2 May 1997 heralded an outpouring of relief, hope and expectation in competing measures. Engine drivers stood on the roofs of their cabs on the Charing Cross railway bridge, taxi drivers strained over the parapet of Waterloo Bridge to glimpse Blair in his hour of victory on the river walk below. It was intoxicating stuff; the past seemed finally to be over, and the future seemed to be there for the taking. Covering it as a journalist was frenetic and difficult. 'Steer clear of the euphoria, mate,' I said to myself. It had not yet struck me that with so vast a Labour majority, the media would inevitably be cast in the role of some kind of questioning opposition. I trundled home to Kentish Town at 6 a.m., driven by my near neighbour the Labour MP Tessa Jowell. She was soon to be granted a ministerial driver; I must have been one of the last people she would drive during working hours for a long time to come.

We thought we had seen a domestic election, about domestic change; we little thought the new world disorder would inflict half a dozen wars upon Tony Blair which demanded British participation. We had failed over Rwanda, as had everyone, we had failed in Bosnia; Blair was under pressure almost from the outset to become an international operator.

Hong Kong at least was straightforward, simply a pageant-packed goodbye to an imperial cypher. On the night of the handover, 30 June 1997, the pouring rain matched the tears of the departing gubernatorial family. Chris Patten was not in an ostrich-plumed hat, but the colony lit up the night sky with the most spectacular fireworks. For this, regrettably my single brush with China, the People's Republic came to me in the audible form of footsteps drumming across the border as the Red Army replaced the Royal Marines. From the hills of Hong Kong's 'New Territories' I had a clear view of China's soulless concrete tower-blocks and fluorescent filth. It did not look inviting, yet I knew I was gazing at the landscape of one huge gap in my reporting experience.

I should have gone to China for the Tiananmen Square massacre nine years before, but did not, in part because I was in mid-transition from 'the road' to the studio. In truth I had also allowed my America-centric, Africa, Middle-East bias to get the better of me. Although I am the presenter of

485

Channel Four News, I also have a strong if informal input into the editorial process. I can push to be sent somewhere, or push to have a story covered, or alternatively indicate a lack of interest which can at times lead to a story not being covered.

On 1 July 1997 a Britain I hardly identified with sailed graciously out of Hong Kong harbour bearing neither hope nor fear. But chiming the midnight hour as it did in such close proximity to victorious 'New Labour, New Britain', the handback of Hong Kong to China that summer's night in 1997 seemed to add to the sense of 'all change'.

On 30 August 1997 I had gone to bed in the green, pheasant-strutting Berkshire countryside. We rented a cottage there, and many weekends we retreated there to recharge. At 12.30 a.m. the phone rang. 'Jon, Princess Di's been in a car crash in Paris,' said the voice from my newsdesk. 'She's still alive, but it's looking bad. We think you'd better come in.' I started to get dressed, realising I only had my jeans and a T-shirt. The phone went again. It was 1 a.m. 'You might as well stay there, Jon. There's reports she's been pulled from the wreckage.' I cancelled the taxi from Newbury, and went back to bed. At 3 a.m. the phone rang again. 'She's dead, Jon,' intoned the newsdesk voice. 'Get here quick.' Madeleine drove me to the level crossing at Kintbury near the A4, and we met the reactivated taxi. The driver went over a hundred miles per hour all the way. I got to the studios in an hour and ten minutes, far faster than I'd imagined possible.

Barely four months from Britain's great moment of electoral upheaval, in the morning sun, here was Tony Blair declaring, 'She was the people's Princess.' She was also definitely dead, and the nation now launched upon an unprecedented period of introspection-free mass hysteria on a scale I had never known. It felt like being in a vortex, caught up with, and spinning with, an emotion-charged outpouring of such power that I felt virtually anything could happen. Almost overnight the royal family, from which Diana had been de-royalled, had moved from farce to an object of hatred. Crowds surged up and down the Mall demanding that the Queen come back from her holiday castle in Scotland, and that she lower the flag on Buckingham Palace to half mast.

Blair could probably have heaved the royals out, or at least reduced them to a 'bicycling monarchy' had he chosen, but not for the last time he conformed to what is expected of a British Prime Minister: he went into overdrive to rescue them.

'Is that you, Mr Snow?' a slightly querulous aristocratic voice on the phone asked.

'Yes, it's me,' I said helpfully.

'Well, look,' he said imperiously, 'you don't know me, but I was taught at Eton by your father, and there's something I think you ought to know.'

'Crumbs,' I thought, that makes him old.

'I think you ought to know that there is a Dickens of a fight going on up here between the two palaces.'

'Sorry, sir,' I interjected, 'up where, and what palaces?'

'I'm talking to you from Scotland, and I'm talking about Charles and Balmoral.'

'Ah.' I looked at the read-out on my phone. 'Number withheld', it said.

Over the next ten minutes the aristocratic voice, which soon identified itself, recounted what had been going on 'up there' since Diana had died two or three days earlier. It seemed the Queen wanted the royal family to have nothing whatever to do with 'the return of the body'. Indeed, Diana was to be treated as 'no royal at all'. I was told that Prince Charles, wishing 'to do the best by his boys', wanted to bring 'the mother of the future King back with appropriate honours'. Such protocols could only apparently be triggered by the Queen herself. According to the voice, which was clearly operating on the Prince of Wales's behalf, Charles had terminated an angry telephone argument with the Queen's Private Secretary with the words, 'Why don't you just go and impale yourself on your own flagstaff!'

In the past we had had a policy on Channel Four News of not covering royal stories, but this one clearly transcended that policy. I had the good fortune that evening to encounter a minister who was in a position to confirm the whole 'return of the body' saga. On being blocked by his mother, Charles had ordered up his own plane from the Queen's Flight and headed for Paris. But there was no one there even to get flowers or provide a royal standard to drape over the returning coffin, no guard of honour, nothing. So Charles had got on the phone inside the plane, called Tony Blair and asked the government to help. The

Queen had ordained that the body should go to an undertaker in Fulham, saying that she did not want it in any of the royal chapels, or indeed chapels royal. Charles had the body taken to his own chapel at St James's Palace, which was the only bit of royal *terra firma* he had any power over. And so the deed was done.

We had this bizarre and hate-filled tale to ourselves, and went to air with it. It exposed us to a torrent of abuse, not from any of the royal palaces, but from the tabloid press, for this was a most tabloid story. They had got nothing, and were enraged that so improper a royal reporting quarter as Channel Four News should have it all. The next morning's *Daily Mirror* really went for me: the front page was dominated by a lurid headline – 'QUEEN BLASTS DIANA TV LIES' – and oval-framed photos of the Queen and me in rival corners. The opening paragraph started: 'The Queen angrily denounced TV newsman Jon Snow...' Seven paragraphs down it went on: 'Her statement did not mention forty-nine-year-old Snow by name...' I never heard directly from the Palace, nor did I read the Queen's statement, nor in the end did I ever hear from 'the voice' again. But my relationship with Charles's team suffered not at all.

The tonnages of flowers outside Diana's home in Kensington Palace, the funeral, the crowds lining the roadside for her cortège, all served to sustain the air of bewildered frenzy. And we in the media played our dangerous part in milking it to the full. Not since the papal voyages had I seen such mass hysteria, and this in some sense was less explicable. But the power of the glossy magazines, the absurdity of medieval royal protocols embraced and then discarded, all did their stuff.

Five years later, in 2002, I had the chance to make a documentary called *Secrets of the Honours System* for Channel Four. It was a bizarre voyage through the absurd and class-ridden process for giving honours; the hierarchy of awards, the anachronistic embrace of empire and the need to sustain the fiction of royal patronage all figured. During Tony Blair's premiership no serious reform of the honours system had been attempted, and the House of Lords had become even more of an unelected farce. Camden Borough Council proposed me for an OBE in the New Year list in 2000 for my work at New Horizon – at least my enquiries suggested that it might have been Camden. I had little option but to reject it, on the grounds that working journalists should take no honours from anyone, and that the entire system centred on the word 'Empire' was a complete anachronism. It's a pity, because any decent society needs ways of enabling its citizenry to celebrate achievement.

We in the media spent very little time analysing our role in the Diana business, and moved on. I suspect it was guilt that blew the event all out of proportion: people felt guilty about gossiping like mad about her when she was alive, and now she was dead. What her death did at least contribute was another element in a moment of transition. The change from cap-doffing deference to serious questioning, combined with the glitzy loss of

Empire in the East and Tony Blair's protestations of the advent of a New Britain, all made us feel that domestically we were at last 'coming of age', even if our response to Diana hysteria had proved less than entirely adult.

Bill Clinton's re-election in 1996 in the face of a prolonged right-wing assault on his presidency had only served to add to the sense of renewal – not least because he and Tony Blair forged an immediate transatlantic bond.

Monica Lewinsky first entered my life in January 1998. I was changing planes in Los Angeles after a flight from London on my way to San Diego to attend the American football Superbowl. The new boss of Channel Four, Michael Jackson, had invited me to join his group as the channel owned the UK rights. I had gone more for the anthropology than for the sport. But I also wanted to get to know Michael and try to convince him to back a major millennium project I'd hatched.

My journey was interrupted in the Los Angeles terminal by a flight attendant who called out my name and grabbed me by the sleeve: 'They told me to give you these, and tell you to get on the next flight to Washington.' With that she handed me a ticket and a copy of the *New York Times*. Within ten minutes I had left Jackson's freebie and boarded the five-hour flight back across America, and was reading about the President and the intern. Suddenly that name, Monica, would never be the same. The *New York Times* believed the President was finally done for, and was on the verge of resignation. The girl was portrayed as an opportunist, cheap, available, of easy virtue – all but a whore. In those early days of the scandal breaking her disapproval ratings would have rivalled those of Pol Pot.

That night, when I was standing on the White House lawn telling the tale across the Atlantic, and later calling out to her as she dashed into her Watergate apartment, Monica Lewinsky had been reduced to an object. She never spoke. All that existed of her were grainy shots of big black hair, lips and teeth, and talk in front of endless committees of men of intimate activities that had never been discussed so openly in news reports before. And the story roller-coastered from Clinton's 'I did not have sexual relations with that woman' to the most prurient of Oval Office detail.

Some months later I had a small hand in securing the first international interview with Lewinsky. She had decided to give one American and one 'worldwide' interview. Barbara Walters of ABC got the American one, and Channel Four reportedly paid Monica $400,000 for the worldwide rights. It was to play in forty-six countries, to an audience in excess of half a billion viewers. Amazingly, of all the lawyers in New York, the one handling the deal happened to be one of only two or three I knew in the city. Marty Garbus had worked with my old mentor Leonard Boudin, and recognised my name on the Channel Four bid.

It was as I was checking in for the flight to New York ahead of the interview that I bumped into Lord Owen, the former Labour Foreign Secretary, recently retired from his efforts to broker peace in Bosnia.

'Where are you going?' he asked.

'I'm flying to JFK,' I said. 'More Clinton trouble.'

'Think Kosovo,' he urged. 'You haven't seen anything yet – it could make Bosnia look very small beer.'

But I wasn't thinking Kosovo, I was thinking Monica, and so were too many of the rest of us. Clinton's dalliances were welcome relief. The repetitious incidents of inhumanity in the Balkans had dulled the media's appetite for more. Worse, when the American legislative classes should have been urging intervention in Bosnia and Rwanda, their minds were taken up with impeaching the President over an apparently unconsummated affair with a White House intern. I had just been involved in hosting a debate about our failure to do more on Channel Four, provocatively entitled *Bugger Bosnia*. But that did not reduce my sense of guilt as I boarded the plane for America.

The door to the apartment thirty-four floors above West Fifty-Seventh Street was opened not by Monica but by her mother Marcia – hair again, and teeth, hair that had been burnished by both the salon and the sun. Marcia until now had been 'the mother from hell'. She too had never spoken publicly, but we had been told by the American tabloids that she had 'thrilled to her daughter's conjunction with the President', 'urged Monica to keep the semen-stained dress', and 'was herself a scalp hunter, having hinted that the opera star Placido Domingo had succumbed to her charms'. But here at the door was the reality – formidable, charming, direct, a classic West Coast American grande dame. She seemed pleased to see me, and swept me into her home. A stream of statements enveloped me: 'I love England – you know we lived there. Monica's Californian father, Bernard, was a cancer specialist at the Royal Marsden Hospital in Surrey. We really should have stayed there. I do love the English.' And then, as an afterthought, she added, 'You know, I never even knew about the dress with that stain – first I heard was when I saw something about it on television. But Monica's been through hell.'

Marcia was a very angry woman – angry about what 'they' had done to her daughter, and angry about what the media had done to her. She was bursting to tell all, but she was also mindful that this was Monica's moment, not hers. In the many hours that I was to spend in their apartment there was a permanent tension between mother and daughter, as if each was battling the other to be the first to release their year's pent-up distress upon an unsuspecting world.

After several minutes in the flat, there was still no Monica – instead her stepfather Peter Strauss appeared in a maroon smoking jacket. Peter was the perfect gent – seventy-four years old, trim, dapper, he'd served as John F. Kennedy's Assistant Secretary of State for Africa. Into this taut atmosphere he brought charm, humour and fresh recollections of skiing in Klosters. It was clear that in all their tribulations Peter had been the rock, the adviser, the wise old head who knew how the law and government should work. But he too was angry, angry with Judge Kenneth Starr, the

Special Prosecutor who had gone so many extra miles to try to nail Clinton. 'He should be disbarred,' he said. 'In fact I'm going to see to it that he is, that he never practises law again.' I'm afraid he failed.

Finally Monica came into the room like a dervish, unmistakably the young woman whose image in a beret, with one hand clasping the President's shoulder, had dominated so many newspapers across the world. Initially it was only the face that I noticed – pre-Raphaelite, clear-eyed, rose-lipped – you wouldn't miss Monica in a crowd even if you *were* the President. She was in big jeans and a loose-fitting sweater. I was suddenly conscious that I was the same age as the President. And so very far from Rwanda or Bosnia; here I was in the very epicentre of a ridiculous scandal that had taken the most powerful man in the world to the brink of political extinction.

Monica, from the outset, exuded relief that she was finally able to talk to someone who wasn't waving a writ or a subpoena at her, someone who appeared to be on her side rather than 'theirs'. I became worried that she would tell me all before we'd even got a camera set up, so we talked about other things as much as possible. We examined the leather-bound editions of Thackeray and Dickens on the bookshelves, the prints of a coach and four dashing through Hyde Park. But she kept coming back to the President, to Kenneth Starr and the investigation that so nearly drove her to suicide.

Once the camera rolled, Monica was candid

about what she had thought of Bill Clinton before she ever met him: 'An older man with wiry grey hair and a big red nose. I did not find him remotely attractive before I came to Washington. But when I got to the White House there was a lot of talk about him. A lot of the female interns would gossip about him like he was almost the star of the football team.'

'So what was he like in the flesh?' I asked.

'Oh, it was a humungous contrast – the first time I saw him it sort of took my breath away. He has a very magnetic sense about him, and he's very sensual and attractive and draws you in to his energy, really!' In conversation she seemed straight out of the upper sixth, much younger than her twenty-five years. I tried to imagine the impact this vivacious, bright-eyed kid must have had on the buttoned-down, strait-laced Washington types who made up the usual fare of politically driven students entering White House service.

Monica described public events at the White House, at which other staff and interns like herself would be present. At such events she said that the President would give many of them 'the full Bill Clinton': 'He just sort of looks at you, and he locks eyes with you and sort of peels away the layers of your being with his eyes and with his spirit, and it's very intense.'

But at that stage did she really want it to go further? Was she already perhaps 'stalking' him? No, she denied stalking, preferring the idea that she became open to the possibility of 'something happening'. I suggested that it was not love but lust that might have been spurring her on. 'Lust,' she admitted. At one moment she stopped the interview and, stuffing flesh back into the ample waistband of her jeans, declared she was on a 'roll watch'.

Looking back on it all, could we have afforded such a media indulgence in the Cold War? Kennedy himself was never so intensely scrutinised, although we now know that he too 'had' interns. Probably other Presidents did too – who knows? The Wall comes down and the President of the winning superpower is nearly unhorsed for lying about a sexually charged liaison; whatever next?

TWELVE

Shooting at the Messenger and Coming Full Circle

I first caught sight of him as I was queuing to enter Macedonia. Tall, dark, good looking, he was urgently trying to push towards me in the immigration line.

'Jon Snow!' he exclaimed. 'What you doin' here?' I explained that I'd come to see the military build-up for the impending war in Kosovo. It was May 1999, and at last I had escaped Monica Lewinsky in favour of the real issue of the day: the flood of Kosovan refugees pouring in their thousands out of the former Yugoslavia.

'My name is Menendes,' the man said. 'I know you. I watch Channel Four News every night.' He told me that in common with most of the others in the queue, he had come from Britain to try to find out what had happened to the family he had left behind in Pristina, the capital of Kosovo, when he himself had had to flee seven years earlier. 'Why don't you come with me?' he asked.

He seemed just a bit too good to be true. I had initially persuaded my editor, Jim Gray, to let me come for the weekend to the Macedonian capital Skopje to do a refugee report, but as so often before, I had little idea what we were going to do

498

when we got there, and how we were going to do it. Now, before I'd even entered the country, here was a fluent English-speaking Kosovan offering to let me and my crew accompany him while he tried to find up to eighty-four of his family members. It felt almost like a set-up, yet it was also clear that he saw in us a passport to the UN authorities which might make his own task a lot easier.

Within an hour I, my cameraman, my producer and Menendes were squashed into an elderly Macedonian taxi making for the first of a series of UN refugee camps. My first glimpse of our destination was of what appeared to be great white scars etched on the lower slopes of the hills across the valley. It was only as we got much closer that they became more clearly defined as row upon row of white canvas tents.

As Menendes told us more of his story I felt increasingly guilty for ever having imagined that he could be anything but the real thing. All the young ethnic Albanians in his suburb of the Kosovan capital had been subjected to systematic persecution, arrest and beatings by the Serb security forces. Eventually he had fled, leaving his family behind. After a harrowing journey across Albania and Italy he had eventually made it to England. In seven years he had never dared come back. Now we were looking for grandmothers, grandfathers, aunts, uncles, cousins, sisters and brothers.

There were thirty-eight thousand souls in the camp we'd seen from across the valley; it was about four miles from the border, near the crossing point at Blace. There was no reception office, no one on the gate to question, but I noticed that the tents in the first row sported makeshift family name-plates. My heart sank as I wondered how on earth we would ever be able to check each of several thousand tents.

'Blairee, Blairee, Blairee!' A ragtag band of ten-year-old boys suddenly dashed amongst us, celebrating the British Prime Minister for bombing Serbia, which American and British jets had been doing now for several weeks. Menendes slipped a few coins into one or two of the boys' hands and told them to spread the word that he'd come back and was looking for his family. They scattered as fast as they had appeared. Within minutes they were back. Coming along behind two women were running, their skirts flying, their faces full of expectation. They proved to be Menendes' sister and aunt. With a shriek, brother and sister buried their heads in each other's shoulder, soon to be joined by the aunt.

'You've become like a German, Menendes,' she exclaimed through her tears. It was her way of referring to his now sturdy build, that contrasted so starkly with the emaciated forms around the camp.

We had struck gold, and were soon to find more than half the surviving family members. But each told us of losses and disappearances – of two brothers who'd been taken away in the night, an uncle who'd been arrested, and cousins who'd been killed. The tears streamed in the hot afternoon sun as the small boys shifted awkwardly amid the adult grief. We learned from Menendes' sister that their mother was stranded in another camp half an hour away. We set off in the late afternoon sun, the rows of white tents casting ever longer purple shadows between them.

A high wire fence delineated the next camp. Here the tents were khaki, patched and well used. The refugees had clearly been here much longer. Once again it took no time to locate the tent. Menendes' mother howled with the sudden release of the pain and suffering when she saw her son for the first time in seven years. They remained convulsed in each other's arms while we filmed discreetly, but even so intrusively, from a few feet away. The agony of Kosovo was being laid bare for us in one Macedonian afternoon. Soon the mother wanted to take me, and my producer Tristana Moore, and my cameraman Mike Borer, in her arms in gratitude for bringing her son home. For a long time she laid her head on my chest and just cried. Menendes cried, his sister cried, we all cried. We had no immediate answers; we could not tell her when she would go home, or if she would ever go home, or when she'd be reunited with her surviving family. The UN had rules about who was to be located where, and in any case the reunification of families came second to the mere location of them at all.

I walked down the rows of tents with Ron Redmond, a senior American official from the UNHCR, the UN agency for refugees. Ron was taller than any tent he surveyed, and more experienced than anyone else on the refugee team. Although it was still only spring, he talked of his fear of the next winter, when temperatures

501

would plunge far below zero, and said that to get winter tents would require a huge and immediate order. With a million refugees already outside Kosovo and more coming, the pressure was on Blair, Clinton and the other Western leaders to move quickly.

The point was emphasised when we reached the border the next morning. Straggling along the single-track railway line were unbroken lines of refugees stretching as far as the eye could see. It was like a scene out of *Schindler's List*. Along the main road they walked ten abreast, while others clung to great piles of possessions heaped on tractors and trailers. Humanity was on the move wherever I looked.

I was witnessing just one small part of the Balkan inferno, and was yet again filled with guilt at my own failure to do more about what had gone before in Bosnia, Croatia and Serbia itself. I never visited or reported from the Balkans during the Bosnian war. While I'd been anchoring Channel Four News, my colleagues Gaby Rado, Lindsey Hilsum and Alex Thomson had been in the field; but I had not. So although I had done endless interviews and introduced endless reports, I had invested no personal capital in actually being there myself, breathing what was going on; hence my sense of guilt.

With the spring sun turning to summer heat, the greens fading to browns, the forward camp of NATO's force in Kosovo, KFOR, was by now well established just outside Skopje. General Sir Mike Jackson was the KFOR commander. I took an instant liking to him. He was bright, engaging, down to earth and accessible. Our interview went out uncut, no spin, just straight talk. And the talk was worrisome: there was a very small window of opportunity if the refugees were to be got back home before winter. The trouble was that Jackson was charged with peacekeeping, not pacifying, and the situation inside Kosovo was still active and far from pacified. There was a huge presence of Serb armour, and Serb forces were swirling around the towns and outlying villages meting out vengeance, provoking more Kosovans to flee.

Young British squaddies beavered away in the hot sun, stripped to the waist and displaying their crude tattoos. I have never more wanted a force to go to war. This time I had none of the misgivings that were to dog the Iraq adventure four years later. The sheer mass of humanity in peril had convinced me. Michael Jackson did nothing to dissuade me either. An amazing man with a craggy, Audenesque face, he made me wonder where so able a man had been all these years. Somehow the military in Britain is a breed apart; we only notice them when we need them.

With the UN incapacitated by arguments about intervention in 'internal' disputes, NATO had unprecedentedly decided to act 'out of theatre'. The UK had the lead role. Finally we were on the road, with British tanks hurling dust into the Balkan skies. We were heading towards Kosovo across the Macedonian border. The tanks kept rather politely to one side of the road as we sped past filming them. The convoy stretched uninterruptedly for three or four miles, and met with no resistance. It was utterly exhilarating sweeping

503

across the frontier grasslands to provide remedy for a place where so much suffering had been inflicted. It must seem simplistic now, but at the time we felt like a small part of a high aspiration to bring humanitarian succour to a people who had been deprived of so much for so long.

That night we were able to transmit live from Kosovo's capital Pristina itself. Mike Jackson granted us an exclusive live interview, his first on Kosovan soil. He revealed the diplomatic mine-field through which he was moving. His confidence in the military aspect of what he was doing was absolute. Afterwards he growled, 'You haven't any whisky, have you?' Though I rarely drink the stuff, I'd brought some awful plastic bottles of Bell's off the plane to use as bribes at roadblocks. I had two half-litre bottles left. Later that night I had none.

Within a few days the Serbs launched a full-scale retreat from the country. They were granted safe passage out of the NATO zone that extended for fifteen miles around Pristina, and we set out to film the retreat. A bedraggled, pathetic and broken thing it was. Many vehicles had to tow others for lack of fuel, and there were men slumped in open trucks. I was surprised we were getting away with filming it.

By now, right was not entirely with the Koso-vans. Vengeance attacks had been launched in the Serb enclaves upon Serbs who had lived in the region for as long as any Kosovan. A new dimension of ethnic cleansing was now accompanying the retreating forces on the road to Belgrade. Serb tractors now carried the bundles of human beings

504

and their possessions that had formerly characterised the flight of Kosovan refugees.

We paused on the limits of the NATO zone to film more. But without my noticing, the few camera crews that had come with us had turned and gone back to Pristina. We were very suddenly alarmingly alone. The old pro that I thought myself to be had failed the ultimate test. I had neglected to keep track of the herd, and now the herd was gone, and we were left exposed on the side of the road watching the retreating Serbs.

It was at that very moment that I saw them looming into view; three vast, Russian-built Serb tanks festooned with swarthy, black-uniformed men armed to the teeth. They seemed to be piled like a militarised human pyramid from the gun-barrel to the driver's turret. Ahead of the tanks coming towards us from the direction of Belgrade was a senior officer in a command vehicle. He stopped a few yards away, jumped out and came straight over to us. He grabbed Mike's camera and tried, unsuccessfully, to extract the tape from it, then threw it onto the ground, grabbed Tristana by the arm, propelled her into our waiting car and ordered the driver to go. Mike and I were now alone, with the convoy moving one way, and the guns of the men on the tanks pointing the other, which happened to be our way. This was not looking good. The commander ordered Mike to pick up the camera. The men on the tanks were watching his every move. I could see no reason why he, or they, or both, should not simply shoot the two of us dead. Who would notice? So many other lives had been lost; what would a couple of

Brits matter? Suddenly he ordered us to walk ahead of the tanks, in the direction of Pristina. Shots rang out, and I waited for the sting in my back, thinking, 'You stupid fucking idiot, how could you get into such a crazy situation?' We continued to walk, they continued to shoot from behind, the bullets whistling above our heads.

We did not die. Around a bend in the road I could see our car waiting in the distance. I said to Mike that we should not change our pace, and just keep walking until we reached the car. When we reached it we got in and sped like the clappers for Pristina. It had been a narrow and entirely unnecessary squeak, and we were badly shaken. Mike and I were experienced, and we had subjected Tristana and our driver to unacceptable risk. Had I been sitting in the comfort of the presenter's chair just a little too long? I decided that when I got home I would go on one of the 'battlefield survival' courses that I had previously so looked down my nose at. A few months later I did, and suffered being kidnapped, hooded and roughed up somewhere in the Surrey country-side. I also mastered the zips on a chemical-weapons-resistant survival suit.

Although Kosovo was not resolved entirely through the United Nations, Clinton and Blair had somehow managed to involve international institutions enough to give the impression of a multilateral effort. It did not have the feel that the Iraqi war was to suffer from; that of a unilateral American endeavour with a British force hanging onto its coat-tails. The events of 1999 encouraged a slight hope that perhaps the new world disorder was more containable than we had feared. War crimes tribunals were being set up for both the Balkans and Rwanda, and the bloodletting was easing.

It was in this period that Africa re-entered my soul, with an unexpected return to Uganda and Namasagali. The *Sunday Telegraph* had the idea of sending me and a photographer, Neil Drabble, back to my old VSO school three decades on.

When I arrived in Namasagali in 1999, my old houseboy, John, was dead. His wife Elizabeth was also dead. The strong young man who washed my shirts, swept the ants from the front step and cooked indifferent dishes of Nile perch and sweet potato thirty-odd years before had died of AIDS. For years the terrible statistics of death in Uganda had dribbled out in the unread sections of the broadsheet papers, but still it was a shock to learn of the death of the man who lived in the lean-to at the back of what had been my home for a whole year. Alas, poor John Luwangula, I knew him – sent him money for his wedding, wrote with joy at the birth of his first child, and then gradually lost contact. Returning to Uganda was to prove both nostalgic and desperate.

Entebbe Airport in 1999 was less traumatic than it had been in 1967. There was no Father Grimes to meet me; there were no tin huts at the end of the runway either. Amazingly, Grimes still ran the school thirty years on, and he was far too busy to come and collect me. This day at Entebbe Airport there was ordered immigration, polished floors, and glass in the windows of a terminal building I had last seen shattered by Amin's grenades twenty years ago. A very small blonde girl ran forward with a garland of flowers. Her father was the VSO field officer, come to introduce me to his Ugandan deputy Proscovia, who was to be our guide. When I had first come as one of the organisation's last 'cadets' there had been no field officer, just a rather ineffectual figure from the British Council who never visited me from the moment I arrived to the day I left.

Uganda appeared to be what it had been before, lush, green, with vast birds – crested cranes, vultures, and hawks – swooping across the red-brown tarmac and murum roads. What was different this time were the people; much larger numbers of them moved in dense throngs either side of the road. New villages, new houses, built now with bricks. There were motorbikes and bicycles, and still all manner of cargo being borne along on heads, on backs, and slung on overloaded transports. Thirty years ago Uganda's population was eleven million – now it had hit twenty-two million, despite the war and pestilence in the intervening years.

In Kampala, ten hours from England, the first uncertainty about returning began to dawn. What was it about Uganda that had made me once want to stay, and having left, made me want to come back so much? In part I had only ever become a journalist in order to get back here.

As Proscovia drove me to Kamuli College, she recounted her own escape from Uganda along this same road in the very year of Jim Callaghan's visit when we had rescued Denis Hills, cooped in the ceiling of a Kenyan petrol tanker with her teenaged sister and a baby they prayed would not cry. Her father had been a prominent economist and playwright. Like so many Ugandans she had lived fifteen years in exile, and was now back, her father dead, her mother still in London – a care worker for Lambeth Council.

Fifteen miles out of Kampala where the forest thickens we passed the spot where twenty years before I had seen corpses scattered at the roadside – Amin's men cut down as they fled the invading Tanzanian forces. Finally the tarmac ended and the damp murum track began. The vegetation had encroached since thirty years earlier. The Toyota Land Cruiser slithered from the crown of the road, sliding along at forty-five degrees from the straight. Here at last were the familiar tree-trunks I had cycled past in my weekly fifteen-mile runs for the mail.

When it came, the school was both familiar and unfamiliar. The priests had put up a new church. The disused old railway buildings that principally housed the school beside the Nile seemed to have slipped slightly further into the undergrowth. They were browner, their whitewash more smeared, their corrugated roofs darker. The trees were thicker, more disorganised. There were no blue flowers on the jacaranda; only the indefatig-able bougainvillea lent any colour. Dank despair overwhelmed me. Was this the place that had changed my life so profoundly?

The geography of the school was still the same as we made our way to the headmaster's house. I

509

could hear Grimes long before I could see him, intoning the mass on his battered veranda. The place had decayed. Dead flies clung to the torn mosquito netting, and still more of the pale green paint had flaked off. The lawn was no longer trim, the borders no longer kempt. The school tractor and lorry were parked against the bedroom window in a bid to deter thieves. When I had been nineteen I had supposed that Grimes might be fifty. So now I presumed he must be eighty.

The voice was coming closer, that unmistakable Ugandanised, high-pitched Leeds accent talking in staccato sentences to his house-boy: 'You'll have lunch ready in an hour.' The door swung open and there was Grimes, miraculously unchanged, the Mill Hill father adorned as ever in dog collar, black shirt and black slacks – perhaps a little more of a stoop, but the wispy thinning pale hair had thinned only a little more, the teeth were no worse, and he was emphatically not eighty. In a matter of moments we were where we had left off thirty years before. He, the seasoned white man in the bush, who knew how to handle Africans; me, the naive, enthusiastic student who knew nothing. He still ran the school, and I gave no evidence of having acquired a partner, children, wealth, employment or home. My white shirt was no better ironed than thirty years ago. For two days the relationship of old was to resume as if absolutely nothing had happened in the intervening three decades. Yet Father Grimes had survived in a country that had been to hell and back. In reality he was now

510

sixty-seven; he had been only thirty-seven when I had last seen him.

He showed us through the dusty entrance into his home. All was just as it had been – the same bare bulb in the ceiling always on; the view to the Nile that anyone else would have died for all but obscured by the same debris on the veranda. As we entered the living room, a cat flashed from under the sofa. *'Bashi bazuk!'* shouted Grimes. 'Out of here!' There was a knock on the outer door, and in just the same tone he called, 'Come!' A graceful girl came in and asked about orders for school. Grimes was blunt and short with her in a way I had forgotten. My memory had caught his authority, but not his occasional menace. 'And your socks,' he said to her – a girl of fully seventeen or more – 'how many times do I have to talk to you about your socks? I do not want to see them round your ankles – pull them up!' The girl bowed out of the room, embarrassed.

Grimes ushered us to the sofa – a maroon affair with a wooden board beneath threadbare cushions and a Ffestiniog Railway tea-towel draped across the back. We began to fill in the years since our last encounter so long ago. The priest and the dictator had shared the same passion – boxing. Ostensibly playing the role of referee, what Amin had really wanted was not a result, Grimes told me, but a medal. He recounted how he'd handpainted an old bronze thing gold, and ingratiated himself with Amin by awarding it to him at the end of a match. It was to prove a wise investment, for in the worst of years when so many others suffered, Grimes and the school were to survive. Amin's henchmen

511

did of course come for Mr Karrier and Mr Patel, the two Asian members of staff, and there were Ugandan staff who never returned from leave, but in large measure the school was left alone. Amin was terrified of intellect, and had tried to exterminate it, not least by expelling the Asians.

Grimes told me of the bodies floating in the Nile, the occasional chase that ended in a firing squad at the water's edge, which ensured that he and the school knew of the much wider reign of terror elsewhere in Uganda. Once when he had been unwise enough to expel the son of a military commander, the officer had come to the school fully armed to remonstrate. The priest's clipped and purposeful verbal assault drove the officer and his men out of the place, and the boy did not return. The school's remoteness ensured not only that the terror rarely reached it, but that the register was forever under siege from families anxious to get their children as far away from the capital as possible. But today, in a time of safety, the student numbers were dwindling as economic boom encouraged new scholastic foundations.

I asked about AIDS. 'Hardly a problem here compared with elsewhere in Uganda,' Grimes said. Yet besides my former houseboy, other members of staff had died as well – a European or two and many Ugandans. Grimes dealt with their passing as if they had been struck down by a truck in one of the myriad road accidents here. AIDS seemed to him simply one of many ways of dying.

During my stay at Kamuli it gradually emerged that the disease had a permanent but unstated presence in the school's life. Grimes confessed that never a week went by without a child leaving to go and bury a loved one – all too often a mother or a father. This in a country where a crusading President, Yoweri Museveni, had actually managed to turn the disease round, halving the number of new HIV positive cases in adults.

Grimes banged a bell on the table, and a discreet cook came in bearing soup. A Chatsworth House teatowel, an array of fading photographs of beautiful young women prefects and an award for thirty-five years in the priesthood took the edge off the bare and unloved walls around us. We began to talk of his retirement, and what would happen to the school. The neighbourhood's other white priest joined us, and the only other *muzungu* (white man) on the staff sat silently at the end of the table. I saw in him the morose man I might have been had I stayed. The problem was that the best and the worst of the school depended entirely upon Grimes himself. Thirty-five years had rendered him simply irreplaceable.

The worst was enshrined in his 'bark', and the dark dormitories, glimpsed through barred windows – they had the feel of dungeons. The best lived on in the classrooms. I sat at the back of my old class, 2b, while the Ugandan biology teacher talked of bean species. 'There is a very black bean grown in Tanzania – they call it the Obote bean. And why?' he asked. 'Because Mr Obote is a very black man.'

Every other night at Namasagali, the settlement in which Kamuli College sat, there was a power cut from around 7.30 until 10.30 p.m. For our

513

second evening Father Grimes had laid on some supper and dancing. His enthusiasm for modern dance had earned him a bit of a reputation beyond the confines of the school. With the food hot on the table, the lights failed at 7.20. Almost immediately about twenty girls and boys arrived in body-clinging leotards. But with no power, the music system was dead. Batteries were sought – every gadget in the house was stripped for the one more A4 battery that would make the difference, and members of staff were dispatched to trawl for more. Eventually there was sound, and torches, and candles, and Grimes giving orders. And did they dance – they were superb, energised, erotic, co-ordinated and imaginative. But I could not help wondering what the Holy Father would have made of the scene in the priest's house that night should he have chanced upon it – pop music in the pitch blackness of the African bush, with priest-held torchlight pencils of light playing on writhing bodies.

At seven o'clock the next morning, there was Grimes as I'd seen him every morning that I had lived there – pacing up and down outside the main school buildings, head bowed, Bible open at today's gospel. Assembly an hour later found all 690 secondary children present. The community life of the school had a whiff of the colonies, and a dash of the Spice Girls. Grimes certainly appreciated both. The girls' skirts were high, but so was the level of discipline. The cane was still administered liberally to children of all ages. And despite the dormitories, the decay and the cruelty, there was intense kindness and extraordinary achievement. Somehow the school still worked.

After assembly I wandered down to the water's edge, now lost in the rampant tangle of wild hyacinth that has gummed up Uganda's waters. The Nile was perhaps a mile wide here. Someone had snapped the rusty cable that once sustained the dockside crane in the vertical; now it lay flopped forward. In amongst the hyacinth I spotted the old boat on which as teachers we spent so many Sunday afternoons. It was under the shade of its battered tin roof that I had once kissed Praxedes Namaganda, the gorgeous student teacher from Makerere University, an intoxicating, virginal experience. But alas, this tender culmination of a wondrously innocent and lengthy courtship occurred on her very last day in the school, and although we wrote, I never set eyes on her again. The old boat was reputed to have seen far more romance even than this. It was said to have been a support vessel for the shooting of *The African Queen*. Grimes said that the former owners of the school's buildings had told him that Humphrey Bogart and Katharine Hepburn stayed a day or two here in Namasagali during the filming, at some shock to their Hollywood systems. All that now remained of Praxedes, Bogart and Hepburn was this rusting old hulk amid purple flowers in the shallows.

At our goodbye lunch, Grimes was picking away at some needlepoint embroidery he was doing for a friend. I returned to the issue of AIDS, asking him about his Church's attitude to condoms. 'Well,' he said, 'if you are going to commit the sin of fornication, for God's sake wear a condom. The

515

sin is bad enough, and certainly made no worse by a condom,' he added. 'Come!' Another student was at the door. After he'd gone, Grimes said, 'That's Jimmy Katumba. I taught his father at "A" level – he died of AIDS.' I asked him why the school worked. 'Being a priest helps,' he said. 'Being a *muzungu* dressed in black gives you an authority – you get along with staff in a way no local could.'

A teacher like Grimes could not possibly have survived in Britain. Even in Africa the likes of this pale, untanned man who shouted at the children, and used that same shout to scare off Amin's thugs, would not easily be found again. The school was in debt. The staff had not been paid properly since May. I thought to myself, 'If I come again in another thirty years, the vegetation will have taken over altogether.'

Heading out along the mud road again, I felt relief to be on my way home from Namasagali – as much relief as the regret I felt when I last left, thirty years ago. Voluntary Service Overseas did indeed change my life. These days, an unqualified school or university leaver would never have been sent here. These days too the internet, the mobile phone and more would have connected and transmitted my initial agony at being here to my loved ones in the world beyond. Would that have curtailed my odyssey here, or eased it? Today too, VSO has an in-country infrastructure wherever volunteers are posted. Looking back, I fear I may not have contributed as much to Namasagali as I gained from it. Yet perhaps there is a place for the many 'gap year' students who want to go somewhere to broaden their horizons and give a little in return. Maybe in an age when VSO finds it hard to recruit enough skilled volunteers, they should think again and add to their number with the likes of the young man I had been at eighteen.

If I had had my way then, I would still be in Uganda now, in a country and amongst a people I loved. But time had proved the great betrayer. Accustomed now to the comfort of the 'North', I found myself grateful that I had managed finally to put behind me what I had spent thirty years looking back upon as a small slice of Utopia.

One year later I was once again in Africa, but this time on the other side of the continent. I was staring at a rock, a little too far offshore to swim to. The waves lapped about its base as it stood black against the grey sea which stretched un-interrupted from the coast of West Africa all the way to Antarctica. I was standing outside Tema dockyard in Ghana, looking at the Meridian Rock, the curious outcrop that marks the point at which the Greenwich meridian hits the African continent from the south.

It was the Dome that did it, Britain's osten-tatious, corporate, 'me first' millennial tent sited off Greenwich itself on the River Thames in London. Walking in a cornfield with a friend from Oxfam two years earlier, in 1997, we had been wondering aloud how we could use the millennium for a more altruistic purpose. We fell to wondering where the Greenwich meridian actually went. A look at the atlas revealed that it passed through three rich post-imperial countries in the North – Britain, France and Spain – and five developing countries in the South – Algeria, Mali, Burkina Faso, Togo and Ghana. What better could we do than to try to forge millennial links down the line between North and South? We called the project 'On the Line'.

Oxfam came on board very quickly, and Channel Four followed. Eventually the World Wide Fund for Nature, Action Aid and VSO also joined. Events ranged from football matches to a tour by Damon Albarn of Blur through Burkina and Mali. Some of the links between schools and communities still exist to this day. Channel Four's commitment centred on a huge ninety-minute documentary in which I would travel the meridian from Ghana northwards, and the Guyana-born British writer Ekow Eshun would travel south down it from Spurn Head, where it strikes the coast of Britain. The climax would be our meeting in Timbuktu, in Mali.

Hence the focus of my gaze upon the Meridian Rock off Tema that day. Behind me, a half-hearted start had been made on planting lines of palms intended in theory to run all the way up to the Sahara. In reality they stretched perhaps three hundred yards. My own journey with my director, John Bridcut, and film crew was to last a month, and was guided by a ludicrous hand-held, satellite-linked Global Positioning System (GPS) device which beeped noisily whenever we hit the meridian. We were all crammed into Land Rovers, and four days into our voyage up West Africa we found ourselves in Yendi, in northern Ghana. Here the prosperity and tarmac of southern and central Ghana had given way to pampas grasses spilling out across the mud roads. There were no telegraph or electricity poles along the roads. Rivers were swollen, and bridges were either down or submerged. In Yendi itself, the palace of the Yana, the traditional king of the Dagomba tribe, actually straddled the meridian. The palace was of mud-and-wattle construction. Talking drums announced our arrival, and people swarmed across the town square to greet us. Under trees around the fringes women sat stirring stiff brown bowls of shea-nut butter that would one day end up in cosmetics smeared on pale European faces.

We were not allowed to look at the Yana. I had to back into his court and take my seat on the steps below the dais, facing away from where he presided. Only his secretary Mohamed was allowed to speak directly to him. I took my place between elders who appeared to be jockeying for audiences. CNN played in the corner on Yendi's lone television set, driven by the lone generator and supplied by the community's lone satellite dish. Mohamed was translating our conversation into the vernacular. But then I began to detect the Yana sniggering at some of my untranslated jokes, and when I got on to Manchester United and David Beckham, he could contain himself no longer. Soon we were facing each other and discussing everything from Noah's ark to the internet.

The next day the Yana ordered a festival outside his palace. Fifty horsemen in flowing robes hurtled into the town square. Everyone was adorned in rich printed smocks, and I too was equipped with one. Very soon we began to dance, the whole community linking hands across the square. Everyone was included as the Yana progressed across the square in kingly robes and Chelsea Cobbler boots, a vast red umbrella held above his head by several flunkies. Despite the footwear and the sunglasses, it made for both a fabulous spectacle and a direct cultural link with generations of Ghanaian tribal rulers. (Sadly, two years later the Yana and twenty-two of his closest cohorts were to be cut down in some dastardly tribal dispute which left only his scholarly old secretary Mohamed alive to report the tragedy.)

North from Yendi we came to the triple border town of Cinquasi, where the frontiers of Ghana, Togo and Burkina intersected in one slum-stricken border sump. There was more petrol than drinking water, and the entire concept of sanitation seemed to have evaded discovery. Yet even here they danced, this time in the forecourt of the Shell service station.

In all our journeying, however, we never saw a distended belly, never spotted a gun or a bullet, and never witnessed violence, despite what was to happen later to the Yana. Every night we slept unmolested under open African skies. To our south-west and west, though, coastal Africa was in turmoil. Ivory Coast was smouldering, Liberia had erupted into long-term civil war, and British troops were trying to contain the bloodbath in Sierra Leone.

Thirty miles inside Burkina Faso, the GPS beeped into life along a muddy track far from the muddy main road to the east of Tenkodogo. Here we found a grass-roofed, mud-hutted village presided over by a wondrously toothy chief. Toothy perhaps is a misnomer, for in truth he appeared to have only one upper tooth, in the middle, and a couple of lower ones. He was an absolute star, and knew full well he was 'on the line': 'I see those aeroplanes every night flying up and down it,' he declared. Yet on the ground he had no mechanised vehicles; indeed there was no evidence even of a wheel. And when we produced our standard 'gift', a cheap inflatable globe, he was flabbergasted to be told the earth was round. Even without that knowledge he appeared to me to be one of the wisest of men, and lived a calm, peaceful, if impecunious existence. His small village compound was meticulously laid out, with the 'master bedroom' in the centre of a cleanly swept surround, onto which assorted one-roomed dwellings spilled, with wives sitting in their shaded doorways. When we left he insisted upon presenting us with a sequence of gifts, including a hat and slipper-like shoes that were all made out of calfskin. I felt guilty taking them, yet not to have done so would never have been understood. They sit even now, looking down upon me in my study, a round world away from their giver.

Gradually the greens gave way to pinks and browns and greys and yellows, as the grasslands petered out in the face of the encroaching Sahara. By the time we reached Gao in Mali we were in a walled town laid out on a kind of a grid. Further north still the desert began to undulate, and we came upon an oasis where nomadic

Tuaregs had set up camp. In the searing midday sun we crawled into their carpeted, tented shade and sat with them as they smoked languid pipes and thought about the world. Casting around the tent, there appeared to be a bedroll apiece, one old trunk, a teapot and glasses, the Koran and little else. I asked the Sheikh, our host, what he thought the world's greatest invention was. 'The Toyota Land Cruiser,' he opined immediately. 'It's worth at least twenty camels.' The logic of his answer centred on his true tribal role, that of cigarette smuggler. You could load far more fags, and move them far faster, on a Land Cruiser than anything known to man, and that was how he judged the world.

Even so, we had brought with us more kit to survive six days in the desert than they had had to survive six centuries. This sense of a contrasting sophistication to our own really came home when we entered Timbuktu. Here the river Niger had diverted itself spontaneously twenty years before, but the gritty town still straddled the waterless riverbanks. Salt trains, camel caravans, trade, romance – I knew all that of Timbuktu, the place that was further away than anywhere in the world. What I did not know about were the books – great Arabic works of literature and spiritual guidance, masses of them, tumbling out of dusty cupboards, piled in the doorways of impenetrable rooms. Nor did I know that the still surviving, if battered, University of Timbuktu had twenty-five thousand students in the twelfth century – many more than Oxford University could boast at the time. Books were the main

traded commodity of the day. Somehow the realisation turned my whole sense of North Africa
on its head.

On our final day I clambered onto the roof of
Timbuktu's central mosque, which had the
appearance of a crouching hedgehog. This was the
spot where I was to meet Ekow Eshun and his
team, fresh from Algeria. I had never met him
before. At the appointed hour of midday we strode
towards each other from opposite corners of the
roof. Our contrasting experiences of the 'line' were
the essence of the documentary. It made improbable but intriguing television. Even now I wonder
whether such a documentary adventure will be
funded again – let alone so holistic an attempt to
set it in the context of North–South development
and interdependence. I am amazed that we
managed it even once; it was, after all, a crazy idea.

Nine months later, in the autumn of 2000, I was
half a world away.

The blade caught the morning sun. Despite the
gloom beneath the bridge, I'd seen enough to
know that it was at least the size of a carving knife.
This man meant business. Even though we were
on the other side of the river, talking with other
homeless men, he'd clearly decided he was going
to see to us. With a roar he grabbed his old
bicycle, charged up the embankment onto the
bridge, and headed straight for us. This was not
Africa, this was Japan. I was concluding the millennial year with another documentary journey,
this time to try to understand the economic
malaise and consequent suffering in the land of

the world's second biggest economy. Recognising the threat from the man, we headed for a block of flats a few hundred yards away. Our film crew of four split up and headed for different stairwells. Four floors up, Mayu Kamide, my Japanese producer, was hammering on doors begging to be let in. The crazed knife-wielder was closing in.

And then, as suddenly as he'd come after us, he disappeared. We sneaked down the hallways and out onto the street again. In seconds he was back. But this time he had the police with him. It was an amazing sight, a dishevelled vagrant ordering first two, then three, then five, and finally eight policemen to arrest us. And arrest us they did, two squad cars and the superintendent's limo attending the scene.

Our first night in Kyoto was spent mainly in the cells. In the chaos of our arrest Mayu had become separated from us, so that only the three Europeans of our team found ourselves behind bars. The complainant arrived, still on his bicycle but with no knife, about ten minutes after our arrest. Our linguistically challenged confinement and eventual release lasted three and a half hours, and preoccupied the attention of all eight of the arresting officers. There is little crime in Kyoto, but there is much homelessness. Yet even the homeless have powers when foreigners come to call. They may have no social security, but they can still make a citizen's arrest.

Somehow you don't expect this rich, successful, managed country to have rows of cardboard-box homes with desolate hungry men beneath every bridge in town. There are ten bridges in Kyoto, and I suppose we saw at least two hundred homeless people, although there were clearly many more than that. It was a new phenomenon that had hit a society that has almost no provision for coping. Pride is the Japanese watchword, and nothing assaults pride so much as the loss of everything else, hence the fury that had accompanied the threatening blade beneath the city's most westerly road bridge over the Kamogawa River. It was never entirely clear what we were suspected of, nor did the police seem to feel any need to apologise.

Many of those men had never confessed to their wives that they had lost their jobs. They left home as if for work each morning, and upon reaching the bridge would change out of their business suits and leave them hanging in the wind.

Hajime Tanaka slurped tea. He'd run a small business, lost it, lost his wife and lost his three children, and now he'd lost his home. His pride, like his dirty white gloves, was still just about intact as he scoured the riverbanks for discarded tin cans. He could make £7 a day selling them in a country where the average wage was £500 a week. Japan was in largely unreported trouble. Sure, the statistics revealed little more than zero per cent growth for the previous ten years, but they told little of the precipice the country was facing.

Mayu, our locally hired crew and I were travelling the Tokaido Way – the old four-hundred-mile imperial route that leads from the former capital to Tokyo – passing through a G7 economic powerhouse, an industrial miracle-maker: the home of my hi-fi, my microwave, my television, even the Walkman on my belt. We travelled on foot, on bicycles, and occasionally by car.

The dense, elongated concrete coastal sprawl spawned by Japan's success still felt prosperous, the trains ran, the neon flashed and the cranes sprouted above the skyline. But like the white gloves of the homeless scavenger, appearances in Japan were deceptive. Beyond the convenience stores, the gambling halls and the noodle bars, there was an economic upheaval under way that left any postwar recession Britain had experienced sitting at the starting gates. I was captivated by the strangeness of Japan and yet its familiarity too; like Britain, it was an island state ambivalent about those who dwelt on the continental landmass across the sea. It was part of the totality of our world order and disorder, and yet had no strategic part in shaping it.

No single moment in my reporting life so traumatised the world as the assault on New York's Twin Towers. 9/11 was to throw into the very sharpest relief the true scale of our disordered world.

The heat was coming up through the soles of my Timberland boots. There was smoke and steam still billowing from the ground, occasionally the debris still glowed red. I was standing in the tangled epicentre of Ground Zero eight weeks on from the devastating attack on the World Trade Center of 11 September 2001. Fire crews still sprayed vast jets of water over the wreckage, and the clouds of spray and steam enveloped most of the skyline about. Small groups of firemen continued to hack away at piles of concrete, twisted girders and rubble in a hopeless search for human remains.

Joel Meyerowitz, one of America's foremost landscape photographers, had taken it upon himself to ensure that an evolving record was kept of the site. He had become a fixture of Ground Zero, securing from the police the only photographic pass that allowed him to come and go freely at any time of the day or night. Joel and his wife Maggie were friends we had made at Cape Cod. A month after 9/11 he had called me in London and said, 'Jon, I think I can get you and a cameraman into Ground Zero. You must come, it's an unbelievable experience.' After a few false starts, on 13 November 2001 we got in as Joel's assistant and deputy assistant.

It was strangely difficult to relate where I was to what had happened. On that fateful September day I had been lunching with some telecoms people who were talking tedious broadband in a restaurant in London's Soho. I would not normally have bothered to answer it, but somehow the ring of my mobile seemed more insistent than usual.

'A plane's gone into the World Trade Center in New York, Jon,' said the voice from my newsdesk. 'Come back, we need you right now.' It was 2 p.m. on 11 September 2001.

I had no sense then that this was an event that would change the world. As I pedalled furiously towards the studio, I imagined that a little ten-seater plane might have hit the building by

527

accident. Seven minutes later, in the aftermath of the second plane hitting, I sat down in the studio. By now the awesome physical evidence that the planes were fully-fledged airliners packed with passengers dominated every television screen in the world. Half an hour later, while we were live on air, a third plane hit the Pentagon, and a fourth went down in Pennsylvania. We knew by then most assuredly that this was some kind of full-scale militant assault. Even in the course of that day I was convinced that, though these events were appallingly traumatic, America was capable of taking them in its stride. I did not bargain for the searing power of the Hollywood imagery of the Saudi assailants' attack on the United States. Worse, I did not factor in the neo-conservative American hunger to go after Islamic fundamental-ism in general, and secular Iraq in particular.

The Afghan capital of Kabul fell to the coalition forces the day I stood in Ground Zero. Everywhere I looked was busy and desolate; busy with grappling gear, vast cranes, dumper trucks, fire tenders, and still those firemen picking at the rubble. I thought of the dustier, sandier rubble in Kabul, of a new wave of grief from new families stricken. I found no one at Ground Zero who even knew where Afghanistan was, let alone that its capital had fallen. The war on the noun had started, the ill-defined 'war on terror' was under way. Saudi bombers who'd helped to bring about this wasteland were being hunted in Afghanistan. Osama bin Laden had become as well known as Elvis Presley.

Night fell in Lower Manhattan; the arc lights

glared through the firemen's spray, billowing steam caught orange, blue and green from the assorted emergency lights that burned across the site. It didn't feel like war, the sense was more of Dante's Inferno. Just past midnight my cameraman Malcolm Hicks, Joel and I paused near the stump of the lift shaft of the first tower. I thought again of Afghanistan, of America now at war against the very forces she had recruited, trained and armed. I had witnessed in Herat and Kandahar the dangerous tactics deployed to drive the Soviets out of Afghanistan at any cost. Now I stood in the epicentre of that 'any cost'.

Our film from Ground Zero was grim, exclusive, and ultimately rewarding, in that it won recognition when it came to the season of TV awards at home. But venturing into that place had proved very close to hell. I was on site for little more than thirty-six hours, but the smell lingered about me for what seemed days; my hair and boots stank. And with the smell lingered the remembrance of the faces of the rescue crews and their elation at finding a human bone or a strand of fabric. They were faces too that had shock and incomprehension etched in the grime that daily enveloped their features.

I was wrong to imagine that America could take this direct hit in her stride, this first violation of her mainland virginity. War in Afghanistan was to prove a mere overture. So questioning were we on Channel Four News of that war that the *Sun* newspaper in London had a front-page shot of me pasted upon a green jelly: 'Channel Four Jellyvision', it exclaimed, referring to our panel of

529

'wobblers' – viewers uncertain about the war on Afghanistan.

The Union Carbide plant at Bhopal in the centre of India stank too. One year after Ground Zero I was standing in the wretched, weed-entangled wreckage of the chemical factory where in 1984 eight thousand Indian workers and people living nearby had died in the three hours following a devastating gas explosion.

In the course of a season of reports from India, I had returned to the Bhopal plant eighteen years after the blast to see what had been done. What I found was a shocking, still-pungent pile that continued to pollute the local water and to exude a continuous and nauseating stench. The place was wired off from public access, but people lived right up against the fence, and children played in puddles of dark brown contaminated water. The contrast with New York was stark: those rescue crews achieved more in clearing Ground Zero in eighteen weeks than an American multinational had achieved here in Bhopal in eighteen years. Here sat the central injustice. The lone superpower, contorted in grief for its own loss, was either oblivious or worse when it came to American-inflicted suffering in the developing world.

I had gone to India in the summer of 2002 for no better reason than that Channel Four, having secured the broadcasting rights to England's cricket Test series against India, had decided to go the whole hog and declare an 'Indian Summer'. In amongst the Bollywood film seasons, Indian soap operas and documentaries, I had suggested that we should do the news from India. The idea was to try to look at the world from an Indian perspective. How did they see the Middle East, or domestic events in Britain and America?

For two weeks my team and I criss-crossed India, from Gujarat and recent communal violence, to Bhopal, still stranded in the distant chemical explosion. Each night, against spectacular backdrops, we transmitted the bulk of an hour of Channel Four News from Delhi. We were fortunate that no news of great import happened anywhere else during that time. We were also in the midst of yet another nuclear stand-off between India and Pakistan. US Secretary of State Colin Powell came for talks to try to defuse the tension, and, as when I had seen him before in Israel, he looked like a man who wanted to be anywhere else. India saw the Israelis as their most natural allies in the 'war on terror', and defence pacts and discreet joint committees between the two countries were burgeoning. The radical Hindu BJP (Bharatiya Janata Party)-dominated Indian government seemed to find a natural affinity with Sharon's Likud hawks. It was one of many revelations.

Another was the superb George Fernandes, still Defence Minister despite having been caught in a TV sting shovelling suspect cash into his bottom ministerial drawer. He was a real card, in his late sixties, with a full head of white hair and a splendid white handlebar moustache. He was beautifully turned out in a white, high-necked Indian waistcoat and baggy cream trousers. We got talking, and he immediately probed me to find out which of his left-wing British friends I knew. We found that we had Michael Foot in common, and got on like a house on fire. Halfway through a sensitive interview about nuclear war, sitting in his vast, Lutyens-designed imperial office, we were suddenly interrupted by a ferocious knocking from under the floor, right beneath us. Fernandes got up and stamped on the floor. 'Monkeys!' he cried, and sat down, having stilled the noise. Apparently they had been introduced to chase the rats out of the concrete ducts between the floors. Was there some wider political lesson in the fact that the monkeys themselves had now become the vermin?

That Indian odyssey was an absolute first, a mainstream Western news programme devoting itself to another country's perspective on events for a whole week. I would count it as the assignment that got nearest to my ambition to expand horizons and understanding. Incidentally, our viewing figures went up significantly that week.

Visiting India in recent years, I've been more and more charged with optimism. This is a country that is arriving fast. The hatchet with colonial Britain is buried, but the best of the Raj's legacy has been seized and built upon. The intellectual and creative power of the place does not yet offset the abject poverty of the states of Behar or Uttar Pradesh or the slums of Kolcata (formerly Calcutta) or Mumbai (Bombay), but the potential is realisable. Our response matters too; we cannot go on postponing our embrace of India at the UN's high table in the shape of a permanent seat on the Security Council; world trade regulations cannot continue to be loaded against aspirants like India.

An attack on New York; trade injustices in India; pigheaded oil dealing in Saudi; pre-emptive action on Iraq based on ill-founded intelligence – they all combine to create a dangerous puzzle of self-interest and deliberate blind-eye-turning. The 'war on terror' declared by President Bush in the aftermath of 11 September 2001 has proved a myopic approach to a cancer whose spread is aided by poverty and ignorance. Clamping down on 'terrorist networks'; starting a war with a largely disengaged, secular, oil-rich Arab state because it is winnable – these moves will make little if any difference.

For me, travels in and out of Iraq, to the Middle East, back to Africa and even to Japan since 9/11 have only served to underline what a rich, white, Euro-American response to a deepening global crisis the 'war on terror' has proved to be. Nowhere did I observe this more blatantly than in Iraq. In November 2003 I found myself sitting down to breakfast in the very heart of Saddam's grandiose former Baghdad palace, now the headquarters of the Coalition Provisional Authority (CPA). This vast ballroom could now seat 2500 people at a single meal, yet as I moved amongst them I realised they were all Americans. The only Iraqis present were mopping the floor or serving the food. The division between the Americans and the able, PhD-rich Iraqi popu- lation was all too clear-cut. Alone, the Americans did a fine job of inaugurating the rebooting of

533

Iraq's mangled infrastructure, but in their exclusivity they won no hearts or minds, and made few friends and plenty of new enemies.

The reluctant, frequently part-time US troops along the roadways were positively hostile; rarely equipped with translators, they simply shouted at the populace. 'Get the fuck outahere!' was the oft-heard cry. It was one of the most alienating and heavy-handed occupations I have witnessed, and supposedly I speak the same language, and understand the culture, of the occupiers. Iraqis were at first bemused, then frightened, and finally deeply angered and resentful.

Saddam's translator, the Birmingham-educated Dr Zubaydi, did not die. Contrary to my expectation, he was never even on the list of Saddamites to be lifted. When I met him for lunch in an old Ba'athist restaurant after the war, he told me of his efforts to ingratiate himself with the Foreign Ministry in the hope of being employed once again as a translator. The shine had gone off the old Shakespeare scholar. He had been reduced by the conflict, stripped of his romance. Now he was revealed as a rather jaded old Ba'athist, but still intriguing for the fact that he'd sat for so long at Saddam's left hand.

The war on Iraq, risking the triggering of a theocratic uprising, had nothing whatever to do with 9/11. It came from inside the White House, an agenda item that might well have been listed simply as 'Daddy's unfinished business'. If any of us had grown up a Texan, lived a narrow golfing, oil life that rarely took us abroad, we might have seen an assault on Iraq as a clever opportunist

534

move, even good business.

But attacking Iraq only served to exacerbate what we in the West never adequately confronted – the sense of barely suppressed, at times blatant, joy in many parts of the world at the events of 9/11, and the grievous resentment at our response. It seemed that in our grief we could not bear such a truth. Widespread text messaging was reported in Saudi Arabia, in Indonesia, even in Mexico, eulogising the achievements of the hijackers in diving the airliners so accurately into the apple of the Big Apple's eye.

We can constantly blame politicians, but in the end the media are complicit in the ignorance that fuels such responses to the global threat from terrorism. The media's capacity to reach and transmit from the farthest corners of the world is greater than ever before. Indeed, it is through the medium of television that the world's dispossessed now know more than they have ever known about the full extent of the material wealth *we* enjoy, and *they* do not.

But as Al Jazeera and the other Arab satellite channels expand; as CNN and the BBC feed more and more Northern concepts and imagery to the South, we in the North are presented with less and less of the reality of the world in which the South lives. It was in some senses the South that struck the North so forcibly on 9/11. At our peril do we limit our explanation of the inexplicable to just a band of disaffected educated Saudis. These people are emotionally succoured and backed by great numbers in the world who see no hope, who have nothing to lose, and who think 'America had it coming to them'

Who is seriously tackling the North's defoliation of the South? Who is seriously considering our emissions? Certainly not the SUV drivers on the Los Angeles freeway, or the Mercedes drivers on the autobahns and motorways of Europe. The North's media are providing a deft counterpoint to the terrorist endeavour by keeping our 'developed' populations in ignorance of the world beyond *Pop Idol*, *ER* and *EastEnders*.

As our technological capacity to reach and inform grows, so our horizons shrink to the stuff of soaps, sport and scandal. Our world is narrowing just as theirs is expanding. The cocktail is truly explosive. Where once we could have looked to the repressive forces of Communism to keep much of the despair of the dispossessed in check, today we cannot. Left with the most powerful superpower in the history of humankind, some of us, like Tony Blair, try to hang onto a trailing bootstrap in the hope of dissuading America from more pre-emptive unilateral action.

This is a time for nations and peoples to come together, a time to rekindle the United Nations dream and let it reflect more honestly a fairer new world order. But the national politicians don't want to talk about it, and the media is relieved – for it is the stuff of boredom. If the fashion for war against a noun is with us, why not a 'war against ignorance'? We have an obligation to our children and our children's children to break out of our self-centred lethargy and to engage – not as we did before, extracting whatever we felt was worth taking – but in enabling everyone to share in

536

whatever is productive and enriching for all of us. If we do not, assuredly the resentful and dispossessed will come for us with greater and greater ferocity. They will not come in an overwhelming Second World War kind of a way, but in never-ending stabs that render our developed daily lives more and more insecure.

Forget the rationing of my childhood – this will be the age of the magnetometer, the explosive-sniffing processor, the fingerprinting of you and me, just so that we may go about our civil business. We are threatened by a war like no other, from within and without. We are doing all we can to alienate and radicalise every Muslim in our midst; we appear to be doing all we can to exclude the poor from our lives.

Standing once again on the bridge in Kirkuk in Iraq in November 2003, I remembered Saddam's young, fresh-faced Revolutionary Guards, who'd posed for photographs with me amongst the buzz of the Kurdish market traders before the war. This time, though the buzz was still there, the guards had gone; the ethnic mix of Arab and Turkman had receded too. There was a new tension in the air, but it was as nothing when compared with Kerbala to the south of Baghdad. There that tension had already turned to violence and resistance to the US-led occupation. By April 2004 the Americans had been forced to retreat from nearby Fallujah, leaving one of Saddam's old generals in charge. Days later the brutal, pornographic abuse of Iraqi prisoners by their American captors was graphically exposed in the world's media.

Iraq is no model for confronting the challenges we face. In so many ways, in invading Iraq we were shooting history in the foot. A friend who is a Law Lord in London told me that he knew of no senior colleague who regarded the war as legal. Pre-emptive military action orchestrated by the lone superpower on the basis of unreliable intelligence has proved a devastating cocktail. We might now have been celebrating the success of British and American pilots in the pre-war UN no-fly zones in north and south Iraq in containing Saddam and preventing a new weapons programme. Instead we went to war.

The invasion of Iraq has brought fifteen years of post-Wall history to a head. It has exposed the drivers of the adventure, America's neo-conservatives, as never before. They got away with overthrowing Mossadegh in 1953, Arbenz in 1954, and Allende in 1973. They escaped the consequence of carpet bombing Cambodia. But I'm optimistic enough to believe that their mere exposure in the open war for oil in Iraq, in which they talked of the high moral imperative of removing a brutal dictator, has perhaps rendered a new war on Iran, or another on Syria, less likely. The war on Iraq has also exposed Britain's 'special relationship' with America for what it is, a one-way affair. Britain's role in the 'coalition of the willing' left her with responsibility for being in Iraq but no authority. It is hard to see any future British leader going to war on such terms.

I'd like to think that my next period as a working journalist will be challenged less by the need to survive on a battlefield than by the search for the new international order that has eluded us since the Wall came down. I would like to see it challenged too by trying to get the benefits of technology into perspective – a time to determine whether the world really is a more dangerous place, or whether we simply know more now about what is 'out there' than ever before.

Anyone for Mogadishu?

The publishers hope that this book has given you enjoyable reading. Large Print Books are especially designed to be as easy to see and hold as possible. If you wish a complete list of our books please ask at your local library or write directly to:

Magna Large Print Books
Magna House, Long Preston,
Skipton, North Yorkshire.
BD23 4ND

This Large Print Book for the partially sighted, who cannot read normal print, is published under the auspices of

THE ULVERSCROFT FOUNDATION